Creative Therapies

Creative Therapies

A Psychodynamic Approach within Occupational Therapy

Kim Atkinson
Lecturer in Occupational Therapy and Physiotherapy,
University of East Anglia

Catherine Wells
Lecturer in Occupational Therapy and Physiotherapy,
University of East Anglia

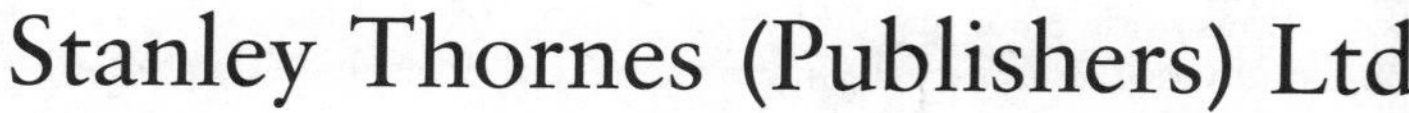

First published 2000 by
Stanley Thornes Publishers Ltd
Ellenborough House
Wellington Street
Cheltenham
GL50 1YW
UK

ISBN 0 7487 3310 8

00 01 02 03 04/ 10 9 8 7 6 5 4 3 2 1

Typeset by Acorn Bookwork, Salisbury, Wiltshire
Printed and bound in Great Britain by TJ International Ltd, Padstow, Cornwall

Contents

PREFACE

This is a textbook on creative therapies, an area of practice which is of personal interest to both of us. We have found that there is little specific literature devoted to the ways in which occupational therapists use creative therapy as a therapeutic intervention. This textbook acknowledges and addresses this situation by providing an explanation of creative therapies, the underpinning theory, the use of the media, and the way this treatment strategy fits within health care today. Creative therapies are not an easy area to define; many of our colleagues and associated professionals are unsure of the parameters of this aspect of our work. We have the additional need to address this in our teaching of undergraduate occupational therapy students. The material for the textbook has been drawn together through our experience of using this approach within mental health, and through our teaching. We have used examples from both aspects of our backgrounds in an attempt to make the strategy specific, one which can be clearly grasped and understood, and which will then fit within the health care arena of current practice.

We consider that creative therapies are an application of a psychodynamic approach within occupational therapy. They are firmly grounded in the philosophical base of the profession as their core elements focus on occupational performance, client centredness and activity. It seems appropriate, at a time when occupational therapy is reclaiming its roots in activity and occupation, that we should develop this area of practice.

The use of creative therapies obviously relies heavily on exploring both the media we use as our tools within the approach and the creativity which becomes a central key to the process. Creativity is the consistent theme throughout this text. We have suggested that it is apparent in four ways: within the activities we use, in the style of the therapist, in the individuals involved and in the therapeutic process of change. It is the relationship between these aspects of creativity and the media that facilitates the process of change.

Our textbook breaks new ground in creative therapies. It is the first to provide a coherent definition of this approach, one which is supported by occupational therapy and psychological theory as well as practical application. This is achieved within the context of modern-day health care practice, recognising the challenges that this brings for such an approach.

The book is divided into three parts: Creative Theories, Creative Media and Creative Progress. Each chapter within these sections has a very different essence, but they build upon one another so that the whole becomes much greater than the sum of its parts. We start with a solid theoretical base, moving on to the practical experience of using the media and conclude with issues that surround progress. We felt that these key issues had to be clearly identified to enable the approach to become explicit.

The initial section, 'Creative Theories', sets the scene and provides the theoretical underpinning of the creative therapy approach. In the first chapter we offer a sound outline of this area of practice, providing a definition which serves as an anchor for the rest of the text. This explores and confirms the relationship with occupational therapy theory, enabling the reader to understand why we use this approach as occupational therapists. Chapter 1 also addresses the interface between creative arts therapists and occupational therapists, as clarifying these two professional approaches is an important issue. Chapter 2 offers a starting point for psychological theory, as we believe that it is important to be able to justify the theories that underpin our work. We have defined the ways in which these theories relate to creative therapies through specific summaries, in order to clarify their application. The third chapter addresses the process and context of the therapeutic experience. It suggests that this creative approach occurs on a number of dimensions which unfold to offer a view of a complex, multifaceted and interrelated process. This is the part which really addresses the 'how' of using creative therapies, all the aspects that have to be taken into account and considered to ensure effective practice. Only by acknowledging the role each of these takes will the process of using creative therapies become explicit. We have supported this by a clinical example.

Part 2 consists of just one chapter: The Creative Media, divided into six parts which address the use of a range of creative media in this approach. We have deliberately chosen broad titles to encourage a creative use of the media, one that is not bound by technical expertise or a focus on the skills of achieving an end product. So we address paper and paint, body and movement, clay and sculpture, sound and rhythm, text and verse. These titles are more liberating as they develop the range of activities in a truly creative manner. The final section considers the use of the environment and new ideas, which again fits within our creative approach. We have deliberately not given recipes for using activities, but have chosen to illustrate the sections with examples from clinical practice and from our experience of teaching students.

Part 3 moves us on with the theme of Creative Progress. Occupational therapy cannot stand still and managing change is a feature of professional work. Chapter 6 relates this to the changes in the ethos of care, the drive for quality and evidence-based practice and the focus on continuing professional development. In this chapter we accept these forces as positive pressures and ones in which we can be proactive, influencing the direction of change and taking responsibility for developing our own practice. Our text concludes with a chapter on endings, where we address the process of ending therapy from the perspective of the group, the individual and the therapist. We also relate the ending of our journey, the journey of writing this text. This in itself has been a creative process for us, one which mirrors very closely the process of change our clients undergo through creative therapy.

Our intention throughout has been to make the area of creative therapies explicit and understandable. We both feel that this is a very important aspect of our practice, uses our core skills and fits comfortably into the new arena of health care. We hope that you enjoy the product of our journey as much as we have enjoyed the process of preparing it.

Kim Atkinson and Catherine Wells
Norwich, 1999

Acknowledgements

We would like to acknowledge the ideas and interest offered by our students, the support we have received from our friends and colleagues and the practical assistance with our teaching given by David Friend.

The authors and publishers would also like to thank the following individuals and organisations for permission to reproduce material:
AP Watt Ltd for the extract from *The Trick is to Keep Breathing* by Janice Galloway on page 226; Moya Willson for *Flubbadub* on pages 244–5; Moritz Egetmeyer of OH Publishing for the OH cards on page 248 and Jean Clark for the poem 'Change is Boundaries Dissolved' on page 277.

Every effort has been made to contact copyright holders and we apologise if any have been overlooked.

Part One

Creative Theories

1 BEGINNINGS

INTRODUCTION

We have to begin ... we have embarked upon a journey of discovery about creative therapies which was inspired by our teaching and clinical experience. In both areas we found creative therapies a difficult approach to define, yet the potential and quality of this way of working encouraged us to explore it more fully. Through this process we have come to realise that the issue goes beyond simple definition into theory building and we hope this text will raise the understanding and credibility of working in this way, offering theory to support the use of creative therapy as a truly rich and versatile intervention.

When we set out we thought long and hard about why creative therapies was such a difficult approach to define within occupational therapy, perhaps because it is not tangible, has no boundaries and involves a commitment from the therapist that is so different from that required by other areas of specialism. These difficulties may suggest why the subject has been minimally (and rarely) addressed in our literature or evaluated in our practice. How can we explain to others what creative therapy is really about when we may have no end product, when every scenario creates a different outcome? Where is the evidence for this approach to therapy, that it is not the **product** of the work we seek but the experience of a **process** of working that never happens in the same way twice? Among our colleagues this work has been seen as 'having fun', 'playing around with paint'; an easy session to be slotted into a formal timetable. The art of the therapist, or in our case of the teacher, is not apparent as it is the personal commitment, the investment of one's personality, the risk, the exposure, the 'take a deep breath and go for it' feeling when we begin a session with no indication of what may happen for the people with whom we are working. It is the ability to personally invest and yet survive the experience, to facilitate growth and movement in others and to attend to the evidence of this growth along the way which is the true creativity of creative therapies.

Writing this text has required us to examine our thinking and understanding repeatedly, and we find this an ongoing process. This has been a happy state for us, one which has reflected the process of creative therapies – where ideas are tested, where discussion and sharing take place, where we risk new thinking and enjoy the excitement of revelation – as the threads become clear. We hope that this book fills some of the gaps in the underpinning of this area of practice. It offers some boundaries to creative therapies, draws together and develops the theoretical base and discusses the richness of what is involved in experiencing this way of working. We do not intend to offer a manual of activities or exercises that might be applied in creative therapies: such books are widely available and only serve to provide some tools for this approach. Using creative activities effectively in therapy requires theoretical knowledge, an understanding of the process, awareness of the potential media and artistry on the part of the therapist. These are the qualities that we set out to address.

Although it is written principally for occupational therapists and students, we hope that other health care professionals using the psychodynamic approach in their work will also find the book of value.

So, to the real beginning. This chapter provides a baseline introduction to the area of occupational therapy practice called **creative therapies**. It outlines a definition, which is something we have found students always value as a starting point and which has a place in 'marketing' this approach. In this rich and complex area of practice such a definition provides a useful anchor to refer to when considering some of the more complex issues and when applying the approach in practice. We then go on to introduce the theoretical and philosophical underpinnings, explore the inherent creativity of the approach and provide an overview of the existing knowledge base. The chapter closes by considering the interface between the creative therapy approach in occupational therapy and the approach used by creative arts therapists.

CREATIVE THERAPIES WITHIN OCCUPATIONAL THERAPY PRACTICE

We offer this definition as a starting point:

> *Creative therapies are one area of psychosocial occupational therapy practice. They are an approach which helps the individual to explore and express conscious and unconscious feelings. Through this the individual works towards resolution of interpersonal and intrapersonal conflict, thus effecting change. The process involves self-exploration, self-discovery, self-determination and self-help. Creativity is the core element and exists on four levels:*
>
> - *the activities used all offer the potential for creativity;*
> - *creativity is fundamental within the style of the therapist;*
> - *creativity exists within each individual involved in the creative therapy process;*
> - *creativity is inherent within the therapeutic process of dynamic change.*
>
> *We suggest the following key principles of the creative therapy approach:*
>
> - *that the individual operates within a unique personal, physical, social and cultural environment;*
> - *that the unconscious has an important role to play in present conflicts;*
> - *that individuals are capable of choice, are responsible for themselves and have the potential for their own development;*
> - *that both therapist and client are active within the creative therapy process.*

These principles are grounded within psychodynamic theory and the humanistic philosophy which lies at the core of occupational therapy. By combining the unique philosophy and practice of occupational therapy with the application of psychodynamic theory we have the area of occupational therapy practice termed creative therapies.

The above presents a very succinct outline for a truly rich and expansive area of practice and it is necessary to explore this in much more detail. Through the text we endeavour to offer sufficient breadth and depth of information for the reader to gain a good understanding of what the theory and practice of creative therapies might be. In this chapter we offer just the beginning – an *overview* of creative therapies. Each subsequent chapter will explore the various elements that link together to constitute this approach in all its richness.

Figure 1.1 summarises creative therapy. We will begin to explore this summary by introducing the key principles of psychodynamic theory and occupational therapy philosophy as they relate to creative therapies. Chapter 2 supports this through detailed information on the relevant psychological theory bases.

Psychodynamic theory + Occupational therapy ⇨ **Creative therapies**

Figure 1.1 The constitution of creative therapies

THE PSYCHODYNAMIC APPROACH

As creative therapies are a psychodynamic approach to occupational therapy practice we should discuss what this term means. Like all forms of psychotherapy the psychodynamic approach stems from the work of Freud, who developed psychoanalysis (Brown and Pedder, 1991). However, Freud's work has received criticism, and subsequent theorists who still sit within the psychodynamic school have built upon his ideas. Some of these theorists offer refinement while others (the neo-Freudians) suggest significant restructuring of key aspects (Jacobs, 1988). An important development of Freud's work which informs creative therapy practice is the acknowledgement by the neo-Freudians of the influence of people, society and culture on the development of personality (Morgan, 1996). This shift of theory offers a more optimistic view, implying a greater potential for change than Freud's focus on biological impulses and unconscious drives.

The term 'psychodynamic' suggests an active process, which is evident in the way the psyche, consisting of the mind, emotions, spirit and sense of Self constantly interacts in a dynamic way (Jacobs, 1988). Interaction occurs on two levels:

- interpersonally, in relating to people and objects outside the Self;
- intrapersonally, within the Self, involving concepts such as ego integrity, the unconscious and defence mechanisms.

The two levels are connected, with intrapersonal processes impacting on interpersonal relationships and vice versa. The role of the dynamic psychotherapist is to connect with the patient's internal experiences, helping them to identify and understand what is happening (Brown and Pedder, 1991). Through this, and subsequent resolution of conflict, the individual can be helped to achieve more satisfying interpersonal relationships.

An important quality of the psychodynamic approach when applied through creative therapies is that individuals are encouraged to outline their own agenda, define their own problems and set their own objectives. To facilitate this the therapist needs to allow clients space to express themselves, which in practice often means tolerating silence and uncertainty. This quality of the psychodynamic approach arises from Freud's work on free association (McMahon, 1993). Another important element of the psychodynamic approach is that *all* behaviour has meaning. The term 'behaviour' is used broadly to include interpersonal style, symptoms, dreams, fantasies and creative expression. The premise behind this is that behaviour is an outward expression of the individual's inner world which in turn is shaped by past experiences (McMahon, 1993). In its application to creative therapies, the psychodynamic approach is concerned with the past only in as much as it shapes the inner world and thus impacts on the present.

To summarise, the psychodynamic approach as applied through creative therapies is principally concerned with intrapersonal processes and how they affect interpersonal relationships. Within this the individual is encouraged to take an active part in the process which is present oriented.

OCCUPATIONAL THERAPY PHILOSOPHY

In Figure 1.1 we suggest that creative therapies are informed by psychodynamic theory and aspects of occupational therapy philosophy. We now need to consider those aspects of occupational therapy philosophy which are most relevant to the theory and practice of creative therapies. We believe that the key areas of occupational therapy philosophy which should be considered are those of occupational performance, client centredness (which is a central concept of humanistic psychology) and activity. For a comprehensive overview of where creative therapies fit within the scheme of occupational therapy philosophy we will consider them within the philosophical and theoretical framework proposed by Hagedorn (1997).

Occupational performance

Occupational performance is the selection and performance of culturally defined meaningful occupations (Canadian Association of Occupational Therapists, 1997; Nelson, 1997). In the practice of occupational therapy, occupational performance is significant in two ways:

1. We strive to promote occupational performance in the individual. We aim for them to achieve a balance of occupational roles and to experience fulfilment in those roles.

2. Occupational therapists use occupational performance as a tool to promote change. Occupations provide the treatment media to achieve the specific aims of intervention.

As an area of occupational therapy practice, occupational performance is equally significant in the practice of creative therapies. Thinking psychodynamically, occupational performance can be affected by conscious and unconscious feelings and intrapersonal and interpersonal conflict. We use creative therapies to promote satisfactory occupational performance in the individual through exploring conscious and unconscious feelings and working towards the resolution of intrapersonal and interpersonal conflicts. Creative therapies also use occupational performance to promote change. Here creative activities and occupations are selected, adapted and used to help the individual work towards the achievement of specific aims.

Client centredness

Client centredness is an integral part of occupational therapy philosophy. It originates from humanistic psychology – and in particular the work of Carl Rogers, which is discussed in Chapter 2. Client centredness involves a collaborative approach to working with clients, keeping their perspective central to the treatment process. Inherent within this is respect for the individual and acknowledgement that he or she is an autonomous being with their own strengths (Canadian Association of Occupational Therapists, 1997). In practice, a client-centred approach means that individuals should be involved in identifying and prioritising their problems, setting goals for intervention and deciding on what form that intervention should take.

Client centredness is central to the practice of creative therapies. In this approach to practice it is essential to work with the client's perspective, involving them actively in the whole process; it is through this focus and level of involvement that the individual will develop a sense of personal ownership and responsibility within the treatment process. Such a high level of participation requires the client to be educationally, socially and developmentally capable (Hagedorn, 1995), and this should be considered when reviewing a client for intervention through creative therapies (this issue is discussed more fully in Chapter 3). Problems with client-centred practice can emerge when the therapist and the client hold different opinions about what the problem is and what the priorities should be. In creative therapies it would be appropriate to explore this difference of opinion but it is important to start with the problems that the client sees as priorities (Hagedorn, 1995).

On the surface, the combined influence of humanistic psychology and psychodynamic theory in creative therapies could be seen as a possible source of tension. Humanistic theory takes a positive view of the individual, viewing each person as capable of choice and responsible for his or her own development with a natural drive towards growth: psychodynamic theory takes a more deterministic view, suggesting that instinctive impulses and unconscious processes drive the individual. In reality a tension between these theoretical stances does not exist in creative therapy practice. Because of their professional background occupational therapists always take a positive and enabling view of the individual, and this provides the starting point for any intervention from which the occupational therapist using creative therapies will apply aspects of psychodynamic theory. These will contribute to an understanding of the individual within an interpersonal and an intrapersonal framework. Psychodynamic theory will also guide the therapist in selecting appropriate activities to access and exploit psychodynamic processes through the intervention of creative therapies.

Activity

Activity features highly in the philosophy of occupational therapy, and it is the focus on activity and the use of it which contributes to the uniqueness of the occupational therapy approach. There has been much debate in the professional literature about the term 'activity' against the terms 'occupation' and 'task' (Ilott, 1995), but it is not the purpose of this text to contribute to the debate. No doubt the debate will continue and we have an open mind on the issue and its usefulness to occupational therapy; however, it is necessary to define our use of terms as far as possible within the current thinking. Like Hagedorn (1995), we view activities as the building blocks of occupational performance. The individual engages in a range of activities to achieve specific purposes at specific occasions and thus these activities contribute to the wider and more encompassing domain of occupational performance. So, while occupational performance is both our goal and our medium of occupational therapy as outlined, activities are a vital part of this process.

Leaving the issue of terminology aside, it is worth exploring the activity base of the profession. Our own opinions have shifted and developed as a result of our work with students and our thinking in preparing this text. We have found a continuum concept a useful framework for viewing the use of activity within the profession (see Figure 1.2).

The purpose or aims of the activity form the continuum. At the lower end of the continuum is what might be called the 'general' or 'non-specific' use of activity. Here there are no specific aims and the activity might be used as a diversion or time-occupying entity. This use of activity might achieve certain

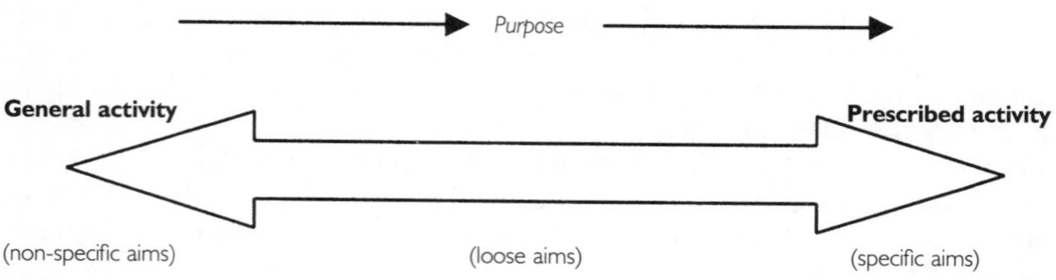

Figure 1.2 The activity continuum

functions, such as reducing boredom and thus improving mental state, but there is no *specific* aim to its use. Activity at the level of this end of the continuum is rarely used as part of an occupational therapy programme.

At the higher end of the continuum is the 'prescribed' or 'specific' use of activity. Here activity is used to achieve very specific aims, such as using woodwork to increase muscle power and work tolerance following a nerve injury to the hand. At this end of the continuum we would place the use of activity within creative therapies. For example, an activity like pottery might be used to work on an individual's concept of themselves within the dynamics of their family.

Between these two extremes is a range of gradations relating to the use of activity, with the purpose and aims underlying this becoming increasingly defined as one progresses along the continuum. Within occupational therapy activities are selected for their potential for grading, so many of the activities we use could be applied anywhere along the continuum with some adaptation.

Inevitably in practice the boundaries are not so clear. Creative therapies, at their most pure, sit at the higher end of the continuum. However, in using creative therapies we often slip backwards and forwards along the continuum with good reason; we may use activities at a level lower down the continuum to build the foundations for higher-level practice. For example, we may use activities at a lower level to develop group cohesion and trust before group members feel secure enough to work on specific aims. Throughout any series of sessions of creative therapies, and often within individual sessions, we will move between higher and lower levels of the continuum in our use of activity. The ability to achieve this movement when it is appropriate enhances the effectiveness of intervention through creative therapies, and this ability is part of the skill or artistry of the therapist.

To help clarify this, consider the example of creative therapies focusing on the media of sound and rhythm and how sound and rhythm activities can be used in creative therapies at various points along the continuum (Figure 1.3). As Levens (1986) states, 'It is partly how the occupational therapist develops the

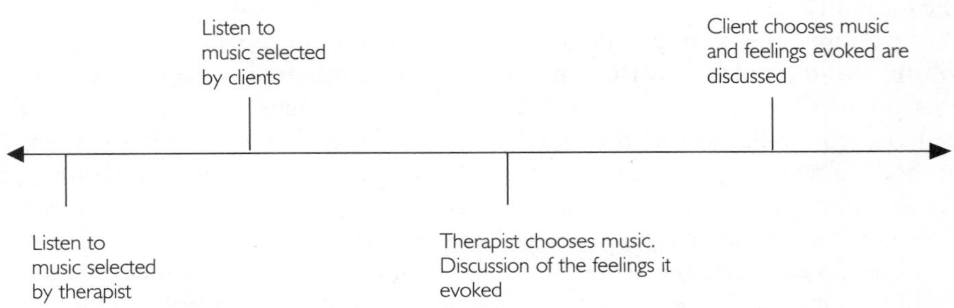

Figure 1.3 Example of the development of creative therapy activities along the continuum

use of any particular activity which leads to it being utilised in a more psychodynamic way.'

At stages in the history of the profession the activity base has not always seemed secure. Practitioners, uncomfortable with this base, have turned towards other techniques. For those occupational therapists working with clients with psychosocial problems this has frequently involved a move towards counselling techniques, with many clinicians achieving counselling qualifications and for all intents and purposes working as counsellors. Counselling skills are invaluable in all areas of occupational therapy practice and a counselling qualification is an excellent addition to the repertoire of skills of an occupational therapist. However, the activity base is a unique and central aspect of occupational therapy and should be our primary treatment medium. Creative therapies offer occupational therapists working with clients with psychosocial problems an approach to treatment which is firmly grounded in the activity base of the profession.

Philosophical and theoretical framework

Occupational therapy, like many other professions, has a complex philosophical and theoretical foundation. It is not our intention to enter into a lengthy discussion of this but it is useful to consider where creative therapies fit within these philosophical and theoretical foundations. We have used a framework offered by Hagedorn (1997) for this task as she is one of the key authors on this aspect of our profession. It is useful to view this framework as a hierarchical structure, discussing the most deep-rooted parts of the philosophy and theory first and those parts which are more visible and evident in practice later.

In her framework Hagedorn (1997) outlines six concepts:

1. The Grand Design
2. Borrowed Knowledge
3. The Occupational Therapy Version
4. Pure Occupational Therapy
5. Making it Work
6. Processes of Change

The Grand Design

This explores the two paradigms which underpin occupational therapy: the holistic and the reductionist (a paradigm can be considered to be an overview of what the profession is concerned with in the broadest sense). In very brief terms, the holistic paradigm views the individual as a whole, with the various systems of the body interacting with one another. Thoughts, feelings and perceptions are seen as important because they affect behaviour. The individual is considered to be in control and is attributed with the ability to make conscious and rational decisions. In contrast, the reductionist paradigm views the individual as a set of distinct systems which are closed and fixed. It suggests that control is external to the individual with choice determined by factors such as environmental conditions and the effects of past experiences.

The foundation of knowledge in occupational therapy is drawn from both of these paradigms, which can be an uncomfortable position as they are fundamentally opposed. Creative therapies draw on occupational therapy philosophy, which sits within the holistic paradigm, but they are also informed by psychodynamic theory, which is reductionist in basis. However, this discomfort is reduced because the humanistic stance at the core of our professional philosophy provides the starting point. From this, aspects of psychodynamic theory can be applied in a manner congruent with this professional philosophy.

Borrowed Knowledge

Borrowed Knowledge is divided into borrowed science and borrowed skills. Using this framework, borrowed science refers to the theories which underpin creative therapies – such as psychodynamic and humanistic theory – as well as knowledge of pathology. Borrowed skills refers to the skills of group work and the therapeutic use of self.

The Occupational Therapy Version

This refers to the application and adaptation of theory and skills in the context of occupational therapy for specific settings. In relation to creative therapies this is one step on from borrowed knowledge. We are still drawing on the knowledge base of psychodynamics, humanistic psychology, group work and the therapeutic use of self but we apply and adapt them in a way specific to occupational therapy within a defined clinical setting. Other professional groups might also 'borrow' this knowledge and work psychodynamically but their approach would not be the same as the one used by occupational therapists: their application and adaptation of this 'borrowed knowledge' would be different because each professional group undergoes a unique professional socialisation.

Pure Occupational Therapy

This applies to the construction of a theory and practice base which is specific to occupational therapy. Creative therapies, as presented in this text, are an example of such a theory and practice base; it is unique to occupational therapy, grounded in occupational therapy and has arisen from occupational therapy.

Making it Work

Making it Work is concerned with putting the creative therapy theory base into practice; it is the stage where theory and practice meet in the techniques and methods used. For creative therapies this refers to the various media, activities and techniques used to facilitate the therapeutic process of change.

Processes of Change

The final part of the framework is where change is effected through the therapeutic process. Hagedorn (1997) suggests four processes of change: development, education, rehabilitation and adaptation. In creative therapy change might occur through any one of these processes, as appropriate to the individual's unique

Table 1.1 Key points of psychodynamic theory and occupational therapy philosophy in relation to creative therapies

Psychodynamic theory	Occupational therapy philosophy
• An acknowledgement of the influence of others, society and culture on the development of individual personality. • All behaviour has meaning as it is an outward expression of the individual's inner world. • 'Psychodynamic' refers to interactions occurring interpersonally and intrapersonally. • The individual is active within the psychodynamic approach. • The past is important only in how it impacts on the present.	• The client's perspective is central, they are respected as an individual, autonomous being and are actively involved throughout the creative therapy process. • The main areas of relevance to the practice of creative therapies are occupational performance, client centredness and activity. • Creative therapies constitute a specific use of activity in occupational therapy where clear aims are identified and worked towards. • Through creative therapies we can promote satisfactory occupational performance as well as use occupational performance to promote change.

circumstances – for some it might be a developmental change through maturation of the personality, for others it might involve adaptation to changed circumstances such as loss or bereavement.

To return to Figure 1.1, as creative therapies are informed by a combination of psychodynamic theory and occupational therapy philosophy it would be useful at this juncture to summarise the key points of these two bases – and this is provided in Table 1.1.

CREATIVITY

In our definition of creative therapies we have suggested that creativity is a central force and exists on four levels:

- within the activities we use;
- within the style of the therapist;
- within the individuals involved;
- within the therapeutic process of change.

As such a key element, creativity requires some further exploration. Creativity is explored throughout the book, and it is this gradual development of the essence of creativity which conveys its richness within this approach to working. It is almost too rich and intertwined to explore as a separate entity but we need to provide a starting point on which the other chapters will build.

At this first stage we need to consider what creativity actually is. Creativity is variously defined as:

- a uniquely human characteristic which everyone possesses to some extent (Jones, 1972);
- bringing something new into being (May, 1975);

- a combination of psychomotor and intellectual skills which enable the individual to work with materials around or within them to express feelings and ideas using the tools of critical thinking and problem solving to reflect on the process (Marksberry, 1963).

This last view links most closely to the concept of creativity applied in the creative therapy approach.

Creativity within the activities we use

All the activities we use in creative therapies must offer the potential for creativity at the level outlined by Marksberry (1963). They must allow freedom from conformity, provide opportunities for uncrystallised ideas to emerge and allow individual thinking and exploration. There should be no right or wrong to the activity and no pressure to produce an end product: the value of the activity for creative therapies is within the process of using it. Activities which demand specific technical skill, use complex machinery or are particularly slow would therefore not be considered suitable (Steward, 1996). For these reasons there is no definitive list of activities which can be used in creative therapies. In Chapter 5 we explore the use of some of the more usual media (such as paint, clay and sound) but we also explore less obvious activities. We have become convinced that if the therapist is mindful of the above issues almost any activity can be presented and adapted appropriately to allow creativity to emerge.

Creativity within the style of the therapist

Creative therapies focus on using activity to achieve change. To enable this the therapist needs to be able to explore, present and use the whole approach in a creative way. One feature of this relates to the way we construct and present activities, and you will find examples throughout the text of our thinking in relation to this. The creative process defines the aim for the intervention, and then selects the appropriate route for achieving it. It is at this stage that the creativity becomes explicit, as it is our tool for making the activity work.

There has to be a conceptual leap which allows the therapist's thinking to change a collection of old boxes into a boat, and to understand and justify the purpose of doing so. This is another skill of the therapist which involves creative artistry. The therapist is gathering threads of evidence to inform their thinking. These threads are the theory bases, the clinical knowledge, the group work skills and the client-centred focus which underpin the intervention. Creativity arises through selecting the information required and discarding that which detracts, thus making sense of the threads used. Reflecting on an activity at the planning stage enables this process to become explicit. It provides the justification for the approach used and ensures that we can be explicit over why a particular activity fulfilled its intentions.

Creativity exists within ourselves in managing this type of intervention, and enjoying it. This is important as there is an element of risk taking and investment of the self. To work effectively we need to recognise our creativity at each stage, using it to fulfil the intentions of the approach.

Creativity within the individuals involved

The approach of creative therapies acknowledges the creativity within the individuals involved in two ways: it utilises the creativity present within every individual as a component of the therapeutic process and facilitates the development of this creativity (Stein and Cutler, 1998).

Creativity exists within all the individuals involved in creative therapy, but for some this creativity will be easier to access than for others. Often creativity is confused with talent and this association can suppress creativity in those who are not viewed, or who do not view themselves, as having talent. For many of us our formative experiences through school have not involved being allowed the freedom to create; rather we were expected to develop talent by becoming competent in the technical aspects of using a medium. Our purpose in using creative therapies is not to develop talent or the perfection of skills and there is no expectation of competence; our purpose is to allow creative experiences to occur through exploring activities in different media. In this way the creativity, in the freest sense of the word, present within us all is allowed expression; there is an air of permission and spontaneity. This process accesses the right side of the brain, where spontaneity, creativity and intuition live, and where free thoughts and images arise from the subconscious (Silverstone, 1997).

Creativity can also be developed. Natalie Rogers (1993), daughter of Carl Rogers, draws a profile of what she terms a conscious creative person. This profile reflects the intrapersonal qualities which we seek to develop through creative therapies. To be creatively conscious requires self-awareness and self-esteem, a growing understanding of oneself as an individual and a belief in oneself as a valued person. The conscious creative person is in touch not only with themselves but also with those around them. Thus, in group work communication becomes an important feature with exploration and discussion around differing views, listening to others and engaging them whilst clarifying a personal value system. Through creative therapies we seek to facilitate this state and use interpersonal dynamics in conjunction with the creative media as the tools for developing this sense of self.

Creativity within the therapeutic process of change

The aim of creative therapies is to effect change. A model of that process in creative therapies is not a straightforward linear representation, as this would be too constrained and limited. We seek change which is multidimensional and multifaceted reflecting the complexity of achieving change. Creativity is at the core of this approach and is present at every level of the process – in the activities and media chosen, in the interpersonal dynamics, within the self and within the therapist's way of working. Working creatively involves freedom, opportunity and lack of constraint, it is not a structured or organised approach to work and there is no clear route to follow. However, risk taking is also at the core and present at every level of this therapeutic process of change. The therapeutic process of change is exciting and invigorating for all those involved but it is also scary, unrehearsed and unpredictable. The spontaneity of this approach is a key feature of creative therapies – and you will find that this aspect recurs throughout our text.

THE EXISTING VIEW

Part of our motivation to write this book was that in teaching our undergraduate students we became aware that there was no comprehensive key text on which they could draw. Information on the theory and practice base for the creative therapy approach in our work was fragmented and limited. The starting point for creative therapies in occupational therapy is with the work of Gail and Jay Fidler (1963). Because of its age this text is not widely available, and practice and working contexts have moved on since its publication, but nevertheless it offers a very sound starting point.

The Fidlers identified that increased emphasis on the use of the self and interpersonal relationships in therapy led to a decreased investment in the use of activities. They strongly support the activity base of the profession and present activity as the single factor which constitutes the uniqueness of occupational therapy. They suggest that our emphasis on action rather than verbal therapy has many advantages.

The Fidlers suggest that as a basis for using the psychodynamic approach the therapist requires knowledge of the phenomenon of the unconscious, of symbolic meaning and of individual psychodynamics. The therapist needs to be sensitive to the reciprocal relationship of these factors and to be able to integrate this awareness into a therapeutic experience for the patient. They draw out three concepts as central to the psychodynamic approach in occupational therapy: activity, communication and object relations. These concepts are not distinct from one another but are interrelated, with communication being the thread expressed through and within activity and object relations. They see occupational therapy as primarily a communication process. Activity is pivotal in this as it has meaning and can be used in the expression of feelings and thoughts; it is a way of transforming inner thoughts into external, public, ones. Object relations involve the attachment of meaning to objects outside the self – a human, a 'thing' or an abstract concept. Thus, activities presented to the individual through occupational therapy will have meaning, making the freedom to create through activity important. The objects used in the action process, as well as those that result from it, are key in this approach to occupational therapy.

Another part of object relations theory, which the Fidlers emphasise, is the significance of relationships: within the self, with the therapist and, when appropriate, with other group members. Within the self there are the aspects of 'how I see myself', 'how others see me' and 'how I would like to be seen'. Any distortions in these three aspects need to be reconciled through the therapy process which, as well as the individual concerned, includes the therapist and other group members. In the psychodynamic approach the dyadic relationship between therapist and patient is vital. The therapist needs to really try to understand the patient and how they perceive themselves. To achieve this the therapist must fulfil their role convincingly and effectively, perceiving what action on their part will be most useful to the individual patient. If the patient has confidence in their therapist it is more likely that the intervention will be effective.

To summarise, the Fidlers emphasise the importance of the activity base in occupational therapy. They suggest that in order to work from a psychodynamic stance the therapist needs an understanding of psychodynamic theory and, associated with this, a working knowledge of activity, communication and object relations to be able to integrate these therapeutically.

We will now review the more current literature on creative therapies in key British occupational therapy texts. We found detail on this approach under a range of titles, which to some extent reflects the unresolved issue of the use of terminology in our profession:

- Creek (1997) – The psychodynamic frame of reference
- Finlay (1997) – The psychodynamic approach
- Hagedorn (1997) – The analytical humanistic and groupwork applied frames of reference
- Steward (1996) – Creative therapies

The reader is strongly advised to refer to these texts.

Creek (1997) – The psychodynamic frame of reference

Creek suggests that Freud and the work of the Fidlers primarily influence the psychodynamic frame of reference in occupational therapy: Freud contributes an understanding of the role of the unconscious and its influence on behaviour and the Fidlers propose the innate drive within humans to be active, the value of activity and the significance of object relations theory. Creek states that occupational therapists using the psychodynamic frame of reference need knowledge of psychiatry, psychoanalytic theory, psychopathology, group dynamics, the symbolic potential of activities and object relations theory.

Creek suggests that in the psychodynamic frame of reference the therapeutic process of change occurs through two routes: first, bringing unresolved conflicts from the unconscious into the conscious to be worked on and secondly through supporting existing coping mechanisms and finding new ways of gratifying needs. She suggests that the general goals of psychodynamic therapy are to:

- assist in finding ways to satisfy frustrated needs;
- reverse psychopathology;
- provide conditions for normal psychosexual and psychosocial development;
- facilitate development of a realistic view of the self;
- help build a healthy and integrated ego.

For occupational therapists using this frame of reference Creek emphasises the importance of activity throughout these processes.

Creek's work, although limited, offers some useful information. It highlights the significance of the Fidlers' foundational work and it provides an outline of the process and purpose of the psychodynamic frame of reference.

Finlay (1997) – The psychodynamic approach

Finlay states that the psychodynamic approach is based on the work of Freud and subsequent theorists; she details the influence of Bowlby, Erikson and Bion. Like Creek, Finlay emphasises the significance of the unconscious in this approach, and she outlines the importance of childhood experiences on development. Finlay also acknowledges the contribution of the Fidlers to the application of the psychodynamic approach in occupational therapy practice. Finlay makes the distinction between the terms 'psychoanalysis' and 'psychodynamic' suggesting that 'psychodynamic' refers to the theory base which has been developed from Freud's work. She states that occupational therapists do not practice psychoanalysis but draw on psychodynamic ideas, which is a useful distinction.

Finlay states that in the psychodynamic approach the therapeutic process of change has two stages: expression of unconscious feelings and working through conflicts. She suggests that occupational therapists using this approach should:

- focus on the importance of interpersonal relationships;
- recognise the power of the unconscious;
- recognise the importance of ego boundaries;
- use the projective potential of activities to encourage the expression and exploration of feelings.

Finlay usefully develops the information provided by Creek. She acknowledges the work of the Fidlers but goes on to detail the influence on the psychodynamic approach of theorists subsequent to Freud. She also addresses the distinction between the terms 'psychoanalysis' and 'psychodynamic' before going on to provide a brief outline of the process of the psychodynamic approach as used in occupational therapy.

Hagedorn (1997) – The analytical, humanistic and groupwork applied frames of reference

Hagedorn does not write of this approach in occupational therapy as a distinct entity: she separately discusses the influence of the analytical and humanistic schools of thought and groupwork theory on occupational therapy within the context of what she calls 'applied frames of reference' (theory bases relevant to occupational therapy drawn from other disciplines and applied and adapted to occupational therapy practice). From all of the applied frames of reference she outlines, we have selected these three as expressions of this area of practice because each details some of the flavour of what we understand to be creative therapies.

When outlining the **analytical** applied frame of reference Hagedorn makes a clear distinction between psychoanalysis and the application of this theory base in occupational therapy. She categorically states that the 'occupational therapist is not, and should not try to be, a psychoanalyst or psychotherapist' (p. 86). She emphasises the importance of Freud and object relations theory as significant within the theory base. For the application of this frame of reference in occupational therapy, she identifies that we use creative and projective techniques, that the individual's reaction to their creativity can help uncover hidden symbolisms or emotions and that subsequent discussion provides insight into defence mechanisms. Within the process of this application she acknowledges the importance of creating a sense of trust and safety. As examples of occupational therapy techniques in this frame of reference she offers psychodrama, music therapy, guided fantasy, projective art, creative writing and creative activities.

Within the **humanistic** applied frame of reference, Hagedorn focuses on the client-centred approach, where clients take responsibility for and direct their own therapy. As an example of occupational therapy techniques in this applied frame of reference Hagedorn offers creative therapies, but does not expand on this.

The **groupwork** applied frame of reference draws on the theory of group dynamics. Hagedorn suggests that in occupational therapy the group uses activity to facilitate the group process. She outlines the psychotherapeutic group approach in which, she says, we borrow or adapt techniques from psychotherapy practice. Here the process of the group work is more important than any product; it provides insights and learning experiences and gives the therapist opportunities to explore both individual issues and group dynamics. Projective techniques are offered as an example of an occupational therapy technique in this applied frame of reference.

Hagedorn offers some richly detailed information but it is fragmented between the analytical, humanistic and groupwork applied frames of reference – and it takes awareness on the part of the reader to synthesise this information as background theory to the psychodynamic approach in occupational therapy. Hagedorn used the term 'creative therapy' as an example of an occupational therapy technique in the humanistic applied frame of reference. However, she fails to develop this, or to make the links between this frame of reference and the analytical and group work applied frames of reference, which also contribute to creative therapies.

Steward (1996) – Creative therapies

This source is qualitatively different from the others we have summarised and reviewed. It outlines creative therapies as a distinct area of practice rather than as a frame of reference or as an application of a psychological approach. It is the most comprehensive and explicit for our purposes, offering a historical perspective, a discussion of the distinction between the work of occupational therapists and creative arts therapists, an outline of the therapeutic process, a discussion of problems and some thoughts on the future of creative therapies. Steward suggests that the humanistic and psychoanalytic models inform this area of practice but that it also contains eclectic philosophies from the Gestalt and behavioural schools and from rehabilitation and occupational therapy models.

Steward identifies the common goals, approaches and philosophies of creative therapies, suggesting:

- that no artistic skill is required;
- there is emphasis on the process rather than the product;
- that co-operation is fostered, rather than competition;
- that the process of creativity allows participants to experience emotions and new understandings about themselves;
- that the product can be used as a medium for communication;
- a recognition of the importance of the physical, psychological and social environment for the session.

Steward's work constitutes a chapter of a book and thus can only provide the briefest overview of this rich area of practice. She succeeds in this but her work also serves to highlight the gaps in the theory and practice base and raises a number of questions.

Summary of the existing view

From the texts reviewed above we can see that after the starting point offered by the Fidlers the view to date, whilst generally complementary and avoiding contradiction, is superficial and fragmented. The creative therapy approach to occupational therapy practice has a limited literature base that outlines it as a distinct area of practice. Here we have only reviewed British occupational therapy texts offering an overview of the approach. There are also texts from other countries (most notably North America), literature from the creative arts therapies and materials which provide ideas of techniques and activities to use in applying this approach to particular client groups. Although their purpose is different, all of these sources have something to contribute and many are used elsewhere in this book. However, a comprehensive and fulsome presentation of this approach to our work is lacking and it is an acknowledgement of this which we set out to address.

CREATIVE ARTS THERAPISTS

Having discussed the existing view of the approach of creative therapies within occupational therapy we now need to consider the interface between it and the closely linked area of the work of creative arts therapists. As with many areas of professional boundary the distinction is often unclear and many of the differences very subtle. This lack of clarity is often compounded by the varied way in which individual occupational therapists and creative arts therapists work, making the distinction between some individuals less clear than between others. What we present here are our personal opinions, reached through our experience of working with creative arts therapists in both clinical and academic settings and through extended discussion with creative arts therapy colleagues.

Whilst acknowledging the qualitative and subtle differences there seem to be four broad areas where these are most evident. These relate to education, the focus on one creative medium, the importance placed on the product and the level of direction used within the approach.

Education

Creative arts therapists enter their profession at postgraduate level, already holding an undergraduate degree in a related subject (often in a creative discipline such as art or music but also in other related areas such as social science). At postgraduate level therapists complete a diploma through which they learn the theory base and practical skills of using the specific creative media therapeutically. Psychodynamic theorists such as Freud, Jung, Winnicott, Klein and Bowlby heavily influence the psychological theory base studied at this level. Humanistic theory is studied, but it does not take such a central focus as it does in the theory underpinning occupational therapy practice.

The focus on one medium

Creative arts therapists tend to focus on one medium – art, music or drama – and practice within that medium. Their focus is specifically on using that medium, and while, for example, an art therapist would acknowledge the role of words or movement in their work this would be very much a secondary focus. An occupational therapist using creative therapies would use a whole range of media: paper and paint, sound and rhythm, body and movement, clay and sculpture as well as the environment. The approach in occupational therapy is much broader, as reflected in the use of the wide range of media.

The focus on one medium in the creative arts therapies is also evident in the technical skill that members of the profession hold in their creative discipline. They all practise and use their creative discipline in their wider lives as artists, performers or musicians – but it is certainly not the case for many occupational therapists who use creative therapies in their work. In fact, technical skill on the part of the therapist in using a medium is neither necessary nor often desirable.

The importance placed on the product

For creative arts therapists the creation of the product – the picture, the musical pieces, the dramatic sketch – would always be seen as an integral part of the process. In our work with creative therapies the product may be viewed as much more peripheral to the process, sometimes serving only as a vehicle for the dynamic forces of change. The integral role of the product in creative arts therapies is reflected in the issues surrounding what happens to it. In art therapy the client would always be given a choice regarding the product – whether they or the therapist keeps it or whether (and how) it is disposed of.

Level of direction within the approach

Creative arts therapists tend to be less directive than occupational therapists using creative therapies despite the client-centred focus. This decreased level of direction is evident in a number of ways.

In many instances a creative arts therapist would not plan a session, preferring to wait for the client or group members to arrive and to work with what they bring on the day. We tend to have some activities in our mind, often based on the experiences of the previous session with the individual or group but are flexible in our choice and always ready to change or adapt activities in response to the mood or preference of the client.

The occupational therapist using creative therapies would place a great deal of emphasis on setting up the environment for a group or intervention. A number of factors would influence the decisions but the choice of activities would be quite important. So we might move tables, alter lighting and bring in floor mats as appropriate. The creative arts therapist would tend to see the room as a container that should remain as constant as possible, the clients being free to use it as they wish and making their own choices. Thought goes into the creation of the room in the first instance but from that point the environment should be as constant as possible. If the creative arts therapist has to access other facilities on a sessional basis, efforts should be made to set these up in a similar way for each session so that the quality of constancy is maintained.

Another issue in the level of direction is in what happens to the created product. The creative arts therapist would generally offer clients a choice, whereas the occupational therapist may be more directive in their approach, giving a clear instruction that the product will be destroyed at the end of the activity or session. Qualitatively the two approaches – that of the occupational therapist practising creative therapies and that of the creative arts therapist – are quite different in this issue of directive practice. However, this difference may be very subtle in the reality of clinical work. The creative arts therapist tends to allow clients to direct the approach themselves; an example of this might be in allowing the client to opt out of the intensity of the experience by taking time to withdraw to the technical task of glazing a clay sculpture. The occupational therapist, while client centred, would direct this process much more, selecting and adapting activities to facilitate withdrawal.

An occupational therapist using creative therapies would slide backwards and forwards along the activity continuum (Figure 1.2) in their psychodynamic use of activity. At times, when using creative therapies in their purest form, practice would be right at the highest end of the continuum. However, very often, and with good reason, we move up and down the continuum in creative therapies. In contrast to this the approach of the creative arts therapist would tend to sit much more consistently at the higher end of the continuum, applying what might be considered a deeper approach to practice. For example, they would be unlikely to suggest making pizzas with a group in order to shift the dynamics whereas this might be perfectly appropriate in our practice – as we describe in Chapter 3.

The philosophical bases of creative arts therapies and occupational therapy are well suited and it is very common for these professions to work closely together, often running groups together and sharing departmental space. Some occupational therapists further their education by gaining additional qualifications as a creative arts therapist. It can be difficult to make distinctions between the approach of these two professional groups: the philosophical bases and areas of practice are closely linked and individual therapists bring their own style and their own post-registration experience, so boundaries can become very blurred. However, we are convinced that, while the two approaches are complementary, there is a qualitative difference in the approach of occupational therapists using creative therapies and that of creative arts therapists. We would encourage you to explore the work of creative arts therapists and to take opportunities to work alongside them.

CONCLUSION

This chapter offers a starting point for the therapist or student who wants to find out more about creative therapies or consolidate their existing knowledge. We hope that the definition of creative therapies provided will be used by the reader as an anchor when referring to other parts of the book and when considering the application of this approach in practice. This chapter gives introductory detail on the components and theoretical and philosophical base of creative therapies. It also provides a review of the existing knowledge base of this approach to occupational therapy in key British texts and considers the interface between the occupational therapy approach and that used by creative arts therapists. The concepts introduced here will be revisited and developed throughout the book as we gradually present the various aspects involved in this rich and stimulating area of our work.

REFERENCES

Brown, D. and Pedder, J. (1991) *Introduction to Psychotherapy. An outline of psychodynamic principles and practice,* 2nd edn, Routledge, London.

Canadian Association of Occupational Therapists (1997) *Enabling Occupation: An Occupational Therapy Perspective*, CAOT Publications ACE, Ontario.

Creek, J. (1997) Creative Activities. In: *Occupational Therapy and Mental Health,* 2nd edn (ed. Creek, J.), Churchill Livingstone, Edinburgh.

Fidler, G.S. and Fidler, J.W. (1963) *Occupational Therapy*, Macmillan, New York.

Finlay, L. (1997) *The Practice of Psychosocial Occupational Therapy*, 2nd edn, Stanley Thornes, Cheltenham.

Hagedorn, R. (1995) *Occupational Therapy Perspectives and Processes*, Churchill Livingstone, Edinburgh.

Hagedorn, R. (1997) *Foundations for Practice in Occupational Therapy*, 2nd edn, Churchill Livingstone, Edinburgh.

Ilott, I. (1995) Let's Have a Moratorium on Activities (The Word Not The Deed), *British Journal of Occupational Therapy*, **58**(7), 297–298.

Jacobs, M. (1988) *Psychodynamic Counselling in Action,* Sage Publications, London.

Jones, T.P. (1972) *Creative Learning in Perspective*, University of London Press, London.

Levens, M. (1986) The Psychodynamics of Activity, *British Journal of Occupational Therapy*, **49**(3), 87–89.

Marksberry, M. (1963) *Foundation of Creativity,* Harper & Row, London.

May, R. (1975) The *Courage to Create*, W.W. Norton and Co., London.

McMahon, B. (1993) Psychodynamic Approaches. In: *Mental Health Nursing. From First Principles to Professional Practice* (eds Wright, H. and Giddey, M.), Chapman & Hall, London.

Morgan, S. (1996) *Helping Relationships in Mental Health*, Chapman & Hall, London.

Nelson, D. (1997) Why the Profession of Occupational Therapy will Flourish in the 21st Century. The 1996 Eleanor Clark Slagle Lecture, *American Journal of Occupational Therapy*, **51**(1), 11–24.

Rogers, N. (1993) *The Creative Connection. Expressive Arts as Healing*, Science and Behaviour Books Inc., California.

Silverstone, L. (1997) *Art Therapy The Person-Centred Way*, 2nd edn, Jessica Kingsley, London.

Stein, F. and Cutler, S.K. (1998) *Psychosocial Occupational Therapy. A Holistic Approach*, Singular Publishing Group Inc., California.

Steward, B. (1996) Creative therapies. In: *Occupational Therapy in Short-term Psychiatry*, 2nd edn (ed. Willson, M.), Churchill Livingstone, London.

2 Theoretical foundations

Introduction

In Chapter 1 we stated that creative therapies are a psychodynamic approach to practice and that, because we are occupational therapists, they are also strongly influenced by humanistic theory. The theoretical foundations of an approach to practice like creative therapies are very important as they influence our work in three ways:

- how we view our clients and their problems;
- the process of therapy – what it is that we actually *do*;
- the outcomes of therapy – what it is that we try to *achieve*.

This chapter provides background information on psychodynamic and humanistic theory. Rather than provide a broad overview, we have chosen to include detail on the work of some specific theorists under the broad headings of psychodynamic and humanistic theory as we feel that such depth of knowledge offers valuable insights to our work. We have included information on the work of Freud, Jung, Erikson, Berne, Maslow, Rogers and Perls. By no means do we suggest that this offers comprehensive coverage – we could have also discussed the work of Horney, Fromm, Anna Freud, Adler, Klein, Hartman, Winnicott, Guntrip and Bowlby to name but a few as they all have something to contribute to our work in creative therapies – but a compromise is essential and we hope that the information offered here will give you a sound flavour of these theory bases and their implications for creative therapy practice. For the very interested reader this will provide a good starting point for exploring further.

Each of these theoretical foundations provides us with a different perspective on the client or the process of therapy. No one perspective is 'right' and one might feel more 'right' than another at a particular time (Westen, 1999). This is the issue when deciding on the balance between a psychodynamic and a humanistic stance in our practice of creative therapies and when drawing on the view of one particular theorist over another. There is no recipe for this balance: knowledge of the theoretical foundations of creative therapies will inform the practitioner and allow them to develop their own perspective. One joy of occupational therapy is that a wide range of perspectives informs its practice, and even when working within a psychodynamic framework we consider it appropriate to draw on other perspectives. Occasionally we use the cognitive and behavioural approaches, as aspects of these may accompany a psychodynamic approach with certain clients. For this reason we have provided some very brief information on these theory bases, and some suggestions of the ways in which they contribute to creative therapy practice.

In the discussion of each theorist or approach key terms are set in bold type and applications of the theory to creative therapy practice are detailed in a series of text boxes. A summary is given in Table 2.1, which can be found at the end of the chapter.

PSYCHODYNAMIC THEORY

In essence, psychodynamic theory focuses on the private personality and as such it offers a great deal to the processes involved in creative therapies of self-exploration and self-discovery. In this section we will explore in detail the work of Freud and Jung, as they were very influential in the founding of psychodynamic theory. We also explore the work of Erikson and Berne, both of whom offer useful concepts to our work in creative therapies. We reiterate, the information presented here is not exhaustive: we could have included the work of other theorists and gone into greater depth. For this we make no apology but urge you to use the information we do give as your basis for further study.

Freud

Sigmund Freud is considered the founder of the psychoanalytic movement. Although much of his theory has been discounted or developed, his ideas are still very important because of the extent to which they underpin modern psychoanalytic theory. Freud wrote extensively and there are a number of very accessible summaries of his work, from some of which we have drawn to support the information given here. Because of the extent of Freud's work, it would be inappropriate for us to provide detail on every aspect: for this reason we have focused on those aspects which contribute most to the practice of creative therapies.

The instincts and the unconscious

There are two fundamental aspects to Freud's theory:

- the role of instincts;
- the role of the unconscious.

The role of instincts

Psychoanalytic theory has a deterministic view of individuals seeing them as under the control of instincts which it groups into two broad categories: the **life instinct (Eros)** and the **death instinct (Thanatos)**.

Relevance to creative therapies

The deterministic view of individuals is an aspect of psychoanalytic theory that the creative therapy approach rejects in favour of the more optimistic view of the humanists, which suggests that individuals are capable of choice and have the potential for their own development.

Since the 1950s psychoanalysts have been moving away from Freud's instinct theories towards **object relations theory**. All psychoanalysts believe that fulfilling sexual relationships are important for health and happiness. However, since Freud many, led principally by Klein and Winnicott, have assumed that the ability to achieve these fulfilling relationships depends on the prior establishment of loving ties with parents and significant other people rather than on instinctual development (Storr, 1989). Object relations theorists have suggested that the primary motivational drive in humans is to seek relationships with others or objects at different stages of their development – beginning with the mother – rather than to seek to satisfy instinctual drives at different stages (Brown and Peddar, 1991). The 'objects' may be non-human but they still have the potential to satisfy needs, so a child's teddy bear provides a good example. Neurotic problems are attributed to early difficulties in interpersonal relationships rather than to blocked instinctual development.

Relevance to creative therapies

The client will attach meaning to the activities and media used through creative therapies as well as the relationships that form an inherent part of the process. These are important for their potential to satisfy needs. As well as this, creative therapies help an individual to work towards the resolution of interpersonal conflict; for this an understanding of **object relations theory** is useful. Problems with establishing interpersonal relationships at various stages in the development of an individual are likely to be significant to the present situation and therefore worthy of exploration.

The role of the unconscious

Freud suggested that there are two types of unconscious: the **unconscious** and the **preconscious**. The unconscious contains material which has been made inadmissible to the conscious through the process of repression. The aim of psychoanalysis is to help bring some of this material into awareness. The preconscious consists of everything which can easily move from the unconscious to the conscious. It may remain in the unconscious but often finds its way into the conscious without the help of psychoanalysis (Nelson-Jones, 1982). Freud believed that past emotions are the cause of present problems, with repressed sexual emotions particularly being the cause of neurotic symptoms (Storr, 1989).

Relevance to creative therapies

A key principle of creative therapies is that the **unconscious** and the **preconscious** have an important role to play in present conflicts. In creative therapies we help the client to bring unconscious and preconscious material to a conscious level, to explore it and to work towards resolving conflict. We select and adapt activities with this specific purpose in mind; they provide a route for transferring inner thoughts into external ones.

Theory of personality

Freud suggested that individual behaviour results from interaction between three subsystems within the personality: the **id**, the **ego** and the **superego.** Psychological well-being depends on the effective interaction of these three subsystems (Nelson-Jones, 1982).

The id consists of everything which is inherited and constitutional, including drives which provide the energy for the other two subsystems. The id strives for immediate satisfaction of instincts.

The ego is a portion of the id which has been modified by the influence of the external world. The ego seeks pleasure and avoids displeasure but, unlike the id, is under the influence of the reality principle; it delays gratification in recognition of social requirements. The ego acts as a mediator between the demands of the id, the superego and the external world (Patterson, 1986). During a child's early years the ego is weak, yet has to deal with strong instinctual impulses. In order to cope with the anxiety caused the ego uses **defence mechanisms**. These include:

- repression – material is denied access to the conscious;
- denial – the ego denies perceptions from the external world which would involve acknowledging the reality of the situation;
- fixation – the individual finds it very difficult to move onto the next stage of their sexual development;
- regression – an individual returns to an earlier stage of sexual development;
- projection – an individual attributes their unacceptable instinctual impulses to others rather than seeing them in themselves (Nelson-Jones, 1982).

For much of the time the ego is unconscious but it can easily be brought into the conscious.

The superego is the socialised portion of the ego. It has incorporated society's standards in early childhood, mainly through the influence of parents but later on through significant others and the individual's own ideals. The superego works to inhibit the impulses of the id and strives for perfection. Much of the superego is unconscious (Patterson, 1986).

Relevance to creative therapies

Knowledge of this theory of personality can be useful in helping a client to understand their behaviour and perception of the world. It might be that one of these systems is particularly strong.

You are likely to see **defence mechanisms** at work in creative therapy sessions and the therapist's role is to recognise them. Sometimes defence mechanisms serve a very useful purpose such as when an individual is going through an acute crisis. However, they can often be a barrier to progression and the therapist must work towards drawing them to the client's attention and encouraging their resolution.

Freud suggested that personality develops through the stages of sexual development and that the individual could become fixated at any of these stages resulting in certain personality types. The first of these stages is the **oral stage**; fixation results in traits such as passivity and optimism. The later part of this stage is the biting phase, and fixation here results in traits such as aggressiveness and exploitative behaviour.

The second stage of sexual development is the **anal stage**, which occurs around the time of toilet training. This stage is the child's first experience of external control of an instinctual impulse, postponing the pleasure of the relief of anal tension. Fixation at this stage might lead to traits such as obstinacy and destructiveness.

The third stage is the **phallic stage**, and it is at this stage that male and female development becomes differentiated. The **oedipus and electra complex** develops, in which the male develops possessiveness of his mother and jealousy of his father (vice versa for the female). The male develops a fear of castration by his father and the female thinks she has been castrated and blames her mother. After the phallic stage, around the age of five or six years, there is a **latency period**, in which sexual impulses are repressed and inhibitions develop.

The final stage is the **genital stage**, when puberty reactivates the pregenital impulses. If these are successfully sublimated by the ego the person passes into the mature genital phase. It is at the genital stage that the individual passes from being a pleasure-seeking child to a reality-oriented socialised adult (Patterson, 1986).

Relevance to creative therapies

In working with clients in creative therapy sessions it may become evident that they have personality traits which relate to a particular **stage of psychosexual development**. Through using the media we may help the client to become aware of this and explore how it impacts on their view of themselves and their interpersonal relationships.

Freud's approach to therapy

Psychoanalysis is a process of re-educating the ego (Nelson-Jones, 1982). During the development of his work Freud moved away from techniques such as hypnotism towards the techniques of dream analysis and free association.

Freud viewed dreams as disguised symbolic fulfilments of repressed unacceptable impulses that are primarily concerned with infantile sexuality (Storr, 1989). During sleep the ego reduces its repression and some unconscious material becomes conscious through dreams; however, the ego maintains some censorship and the material is distorted (Nelson-Jones, 1982).

In **free association** the patient traditionally lies on a couch and tells the analyst everything that occurs to them. This process helps to lift repressions and the material is interpreted to provide the therapist and patient with some understanding of the impulses of the id and the defence mechanisms used by the ego (Nelson-Jones, 1982). Armed with this new insight the patient may be more able to work through their own problems (Storr, 1989).

Relevance to creative therapies

The technique of free association acknowledges the importance of the client being allowed space to express themselves. This is a quality we attend to in detail in the practice of creative therapies, through creating the physical environment, selecting appropriate media and activities, the therapeutic style of the therapist and the management of group dynamics. Creating space for the individual is a particularly important aspect of this approach. Creative therapies also use the theory of **free association** in some activities. For example, as part of a creative writing exercise we might ask clients to write down anything that comes into their heads. The material can then be explored for common or related themes which provide insight into their unconscious material or defence mechanisms.

Storr (1989) acknowledges that in many cases the process of psychoanalysis does not rid the individual of the primary presenting problem but helps them to develop ways of coping with it. Individuals find the experience of therapy very enhancing, as having someone who will listen and provide a nurturing environment is of great psychological value. Both of these issues are also true of the experience of creative therapies.

Within the therapeutic relationship Freud came to recognise the importance of **transference**, in which the patient may transfer onto the therapist the emotional attitude they held or hold towards another figure in their life. **Counter-transference** arises out of the influences of the patient on the unconscious feelings of the therapist. Freud acknowledged this and recommended that analysts undergo what he called **training analysis** to help them deal with it (Storr, 1989).

Relevance to creative therapies

In creative therapies the therapist/client relationship is very important and **transference** and **counter-transference** can be issues. The therapist needs to be aware of this happening; the co-worker relationship and supervision can be useful in facilitating this awareness. Through developing awareness transference and counter-transference can be used and explored in the creative therapy process.

Creative therapies can be an intense approach to our work as occupational therapists and very demanding on the therapist. It is accepted as good practice for a therapist working in this way to receive supervision.

Summary

The work of Freud, as the founder of psychoanalysis, offers some useful theoretical foundations to creative therapies. Freud's work has provided us with an understanding of the significance of the unconscious and of early relationships in our work. It also offers a theory of personality and personality development that can be a useful framework for understanding our clients. Finally, Freud's work on free association may be adapted and applied in our practice. His insights into the dynamics of the therapist/client relationship are very significant in creative therapies as the approach draws heavily on this relationship.

Jung

The work of Carl Jung also lies within psychodynamic theory. Despite his close friendship with Freud, Jung found two of Freud's basic assumptions – that human motivation is exclusively sexual and that the unconscious is entirely personal to the individual – unacceptable (Stevens, 1994).

Jung's theories are heavily influenced by his work with psychotic patients whose delusions, hallucinations and actions he understood to be full of psychological meaning. His own experiences while growing up and through a period of illness also influenced his work (Stevens, 1994). Jung's theories can at times seem rather odd and based on the metaphysical. Aspects of his work can be supported to some extent by research and by the work of others but, like Freud, he basically presents a theory of human psychology.

The psyche

Instead of mind and mental activity Jung talked of **psyche** and psychic. He considered these terms more appropriate because they can refer to both the conscious and the unconscious. Jung saw the psyche as dynamic, referring to the psychic energy which emanates from it as **libido**, a non-sexual life force (Gross, 1996) that flows between two opposing poles termed **the opposites**. The natural movement of the libido is forwards (progression) and backwards (regression). Progression satisfies the demands of the conscious whilst regression satisfies the unconscious. Progression is therefore concerned with adaptation to the environment and regression with adaptation to inner needs. Jung also saw the psyche as self-regulatory. Regression could be a restorative phase to progression, and adaptation to the inner self and outer world are interdependent. If the natural flow of the libido is interrupted, neurosis, infantile behaviour, psychosis or aggression might result (Stevens, 1994).

Relevance to creative therapies

A key principle of the creative therapy approach is a recognition that the individual operates within a unique personal, physical, social and cultural environment. Operating successfully within this environment requires a reconciliation between the **inner needs of the individual** and the **demands of the environment**. Creative therapies can be used to help the individual to explore their situation and achieve an acceptable balance between inner needs and environmental demands.

Jung believed that the psyche has three levels:

- the collective unconscious;
- the personal unconscious;
- the conscious.

The collective unconscious

This is a deeper and more important level of the unconscious than the personal unconscious. It consists of memories established throughout the history of humanity, an inherited set of memories which are present in all humans, whatever their culture. The personal experience of each individual develops what is already there rather than occurring on an unstructured personality. This relates to what Jung calls the **number two personality** (Stevens, 1994). Jung described the functional units of the collective unconscious as **archetypes** – inherited psychic structures that are common to all individuals but which manifest themselves differently in every human as a result of environmental and historical changes. The archetypes initiate, control and mediate the common behavioural characteristics and typical experiences. They manifest themselves in the personal unconscious through **complexes**. Archetypes regulate the human life cycle, which is co-ordinated by the **Self** and includes the development of the persona, the shadow, the anima and the animus (Samuels, 1985; Stevens, 1994).

The personal unconscious

This equates with Freud's description of the unconscious. The personal unconscious belongs to the individual and is formed from repressed infantile impulses, subliminal perceptions and forgotten experiences. The memories of the personal unconscious can be recalled when repression is weakened. Within the personal unconscious are complexes; these are splinter parts of our personality with which we 'feel' (Samuels, Shorter and Plaut, 1986).

The conscious

What belongs to the conscious is not conscious all of the time as it may be repressed or suppressed. The ego remains at the centre of consciousness and relates to what Jung termed the **number one personality** – that part of us which is the son or daughter of the parents (Stevens, 1994).

Relevance to creative therapies

A key principle of creative therapies is that the unconscious has an important role to play in present conflicts. Jung presents an alternative view of the potential significance of the **unconscious**. Through using creative therapies we work to explore unconscious material that is having a negative impact on the individual's present situation.

Psychological types

Jung suggested that in the course of development people adopt different habitual attitudes which determine their experience of life. He considered that two main attitudes were apparent: **introversion** and **extroversion.** The individual is either predominantly one or the other. Introversion is characterised by a focus on the inner, subjective world rather than the outer world, so an introverted person is characteristically hesitant, reflective and defensive by nature. Extroversion is characterised by an outward movement of interest to the outer realm of objective reality. An extroverted person is generally outgoing, accommodating and readily able to adapt. As well as these two attitudes the individual will also utilise what Jung called the four functional types of **thinking, intuition, sensation** and **feeling** as a way of relating with the external world. Sensation tells us that something exists; thinking tells us what it is; feelings tell us whether it is agreeable or not; intuition tells us where it has come from and where it is going. In every individual the attitudes of either introversion or extroversion will predominate, but will link to one of the four functional types. For example, we can describe people as extroverted sensation types or introverted thinking types and so on (Stevens, 1994).

Relevance to creative therapies

An individual may have an awareness of their **psychological type**, or it may become apparent through creative therapies in their reactions to and perceptions of situations. The aim of creative therapies is to heighten awareness of the psychological type and to consider how it affects the way the individual copes with situations and interacts with their social and psychological environment. Through this increased awareness the individual may be able to identify specific areas of concern and work on them through using creative therapies.

Stages in life

Jung suggested that development occurs throughout life, not just in childhood and adolescence but continuing into old age. He called this process **individuation.** Archetypes regulate the human life cycle through seeking fulfilment in personality and behaviour. The components listed below become built into the psyche as complexes during the process of individuation. Each human makes use of them in unique ways but they perform the same functions in all individuals. Stevens (1994) describes the following components:

- **The Self** – individuation of the Self is the process by which the individual becomes what they were destined to be from the beginning. The predetermined pattern of human existence is achieved in an individual way within the life of the individual.
- **The ego** – the ego emerges out of the Self but is connected to it on the ego–

Self axis. It is the centre of consciousness and is what we refer to when we use 'I' or 'me'.

- **The persona** – the front we display to the outside world or how we would wish to be seen by others, thus a kind of mask. Acceptable traits are built into the persona and unacceptable ones are relegated to the personal unconscious, where they become associated with another part of the personality called the shadow.
- **The shadow** lies in the unconscious and much of the time it is ignored, but it may become apparent when the power of repression is weakened. The shadow gives rise to distrust, anger and fear – for example, a child's fear of strangers. To defend ourselves against the shadow we use defence mechanisms as a protection, so a demanding part of Jungian analysis occurs when the individual confronts their own shadow.
- **The animas and animus** – in developing our sexual identity we have masculine and feminine archetypes which provide the foundation upon which stereotypes develop. Relationships with the opposite sex also have their foundation in archetypes, the animus representing the masculine aspect in the female and the anima the feminine aspect in the male. Jung suggested that we marry our archetypal image of the opposite sex.

Jung suggested that in the first half of the life course the individual attends to the development of the number one personality (the ego) and in the second half to the number two personality (the Self). Through a process of individuation of the Self the individual undergoes progressive integration of the unconscious timeless self, and overcomes the divisions imposed by the parental and cultural environment. He or she sheds the false mask of the persona and abandons defence mechanisms (Stevens, 1994). To some extent this process is similar to that of self-actualisation described by the humanists.

Relevance to creative therapies

As detailed in Chapter 1 the focus of creative therapies is on the self: self-exploration, self-awareness, self-determination and self-help. Jung's detailed presentation of the self is helpful in providing a framework for which aspects this might involve. In addition, Jung's view of lifelong development provides us with the goals of our intervention through creative therapies. With the client we will work towards **development of the Self**, challenging the false mask of the persona, confronting the shadow and acknowledging the anima or animus.

The process of therapy

Jung viewed mental illness as an imbalance between the individual and the demands of the collective unconscious. He suggested that symptoms of mental illness occur as a result of the process of individuation not running smoothly, and that symptoms are developed as a form of adaptation to the demands of life (Stevens, 1994).

Like Freud, Jung recognised the value of dreams in therapy, seeing them as a route for connecting with the collective unconscious. However, rather than taking an interpretative approach Jung sought to amplify the material of the dream by entering into its atmosphere as if it were a private drama (Stevens, 1994).

Relevance to creative therapies

Although occupational therapists using creative therapies would not enter into Jungian analysis there are aspects of Jung's approach to therapy which can inform our practice. Jung suggested that when an individual does not know about something their **imagination** fills the void. They project their own psychic activity onto the gap to fill it with meaning and this enables them to become more aware of meanings arising from the unconscious. This concept underpins our approach in creative therapies, where we allow the opportunity for creativity through freedom and spontaneity unbound by constraining rules and conformity. This process allows meaning from the unconscious to emerge. The 'OH' Cards discussed in Chapter 5 provide a good example of this.

Jung viewed therapy very much as a two-way process, with both the therapist and the patient equally, fully and actively involved, each taking responsibility for themselves. He felt that every patient should be treated as an individual with no predetermined recipe for therapy (Stevens, 1994). Jung's intention was to equip his patients with the psychological knowledge to help themselves rather than relying on the therapist, and to this end he encouraged clients to actively use the time between consultations.

Relevance to creative therapies

Creative therapies require active and full involvement on the part of both client and therapist. Client centredness is integral to our approach; there is a respect for the **individual**, who is involved in identifying and prioritising their problems, setting goals for intervention and deciding on what form that intervention should take. Through this process, our involvement with each client is highly individual. A basic philosophy of occupational therapy is a focus on **enabling** the individual rather than promoting dependence on either therapy or the therapist. Working with creative therapies we help the client develop their own skills in resolving their problems to promote independence. We also encourage the client to make use of the time between sessions to explore issues that arose in the session in their own unique personal, physical, social and cultural environment.

Summary

Although at times difficult to grasp, the work of Jung offers a great deal to the theoretical foundations of creative therapies. Jung provides us with a perspective on the relationship between individuals and their environment and a view of the unconscious. His presentation of the lifelong development process directs us towards the goals of our intervention. Jung's approach to therapy mirrors many of the aspects that we would regard as highly important in creative therapy practice, such as client centredness and the promotion of independence.

Erikson

Erik Erikson trained as a Montessori teacher and then undertook psychoanalytic training under Anna Freud. His theory of personality development, like Freud's, is developmental but he differed greatly from Freud in how he viewed the stages of development. First of all he viewed them in psychosocial terms rather than in terms of sexuality and aggression (Glassman, 1995). Like Freud, Erikson believed that there is a biological basis to development, with the stages following a biologically predetermined sequence; however, he believed that progression through the stages requires interdependence between biology, psychology and social structures (Gross, 1996). Another difference between Erikson and Freud is that Erikson believed that the baby is born with an id, ego and superego and that the whole lifespan is important in personality development (Eysenck, 1998; Gross, 1996).

Erikson suggested that there are eight psychosocial stages of ego development. Each stage is named by two opposing outcomes: the adaptive and the maladaptive. At each stage there is a **normative crisis** between the two opposing outcomes. The normative crisis involves resolving conflict between the individual's sense of self and relationship to others (Glassman, 1995). Most people successfully deal with this crisis and healthy development continues. Successful resolution rarely involves an either/or outcome: the adaptive or the maladaptive. In most instances there is an element of both, but the adaptive quality outweighs the maladaptive one (Eysenck, 1998; Gross, 1996). In this process of ego development Erikson took a less deterministic view than Freud. He stated that it is possible to make up for unsatisfactory early experiences in later life and likewise that later detrimental experiences can shatter earlier positive ones (Gross, 1996).

The eight stages of psychosocial development are as follows.

Basic trust versus basic mistrust (0–1 years)

How the baby is treated and how its needs are met determine whether it develops a sense of trust or mistrust towards the surrounding world. If the baby is cuddled and responded to when it cries it will develop a sense of trust, perceiving the world as predictable and one in which it is important (Gross, 1996; Willson, 1983).

Autonomy versus shame and doubt (1–3 years)

Between these ages the child is becoming more physically mobile and cognitively developed. It begins to think of itself as a person in its own right and develops a sense of autonomy by trying to do things for itself. If the child is generally supported and encouraged in this it will be successful and achieve a sense of autonomy; if not, a sense of shame and doubt will develop (Gross, 1996).

Initiative versus guilt (3–5/6 years)
The child is developing physically, intellectually and socially and uses these skills to try to achieve new goals, through exploration and imagination. If it is helped in this a sense of initiative develops; however, if the parents discourage this behaviour by dismissing the child's imagination as silly or its exploration as a dangerous nuisance the child will develop feelings of guilt (Gross, 1996).

Industry versus inferiority (7–12 years)
The child becomes interested in how things work and in making things for themselves. They set out to achieve tasks, and their perception of their competence in this comes from the responses of teachers and peers as well as parents. If the child receives the necessary guidance, support and encouragement a sense of industry develops; if this is lacking a feeling of inferiority can develop (Gross, 1996).

Identity versus role confusion (12–18 years)
In the adolescent years the child's body is changing dramatically and it has to learn to live within this new image. It also has to decide upon its sexual identity. At a social level this is a time of confusion as the sense of when a child becomes an adult is very muddled. At this stage individuals develop a sense of themselves as individuals. To achieve this it might be necessary to challenge the views of others such as parents and teachers, adding to these feelings of conflict and confusion. Erikson believed that adolescence is one of the most important stages in psychosocial development (Gross, 1996).

Intimacy versus isolation (20s)
The development of a firm self-identity prepares the adult for the risk of combining that identity with another's within a lasting relationship. This relationship involves both giving and receiving intimacy: if this is not achieved a sense of isolation develops (Willson, 1983).

Generativity versus stagnation (20s–50s)
This stage involves a concern for growth of a new generation; this concern might be focused on rearing children but productivity and creativity can also be outlets leading to successful fulfilment of this stage. Failure to achieve generativity leads to a sense of stagnation (Willson, 1983).

Ego integrity versus despair (50+)
A greater feeling of success over failure in the preceding stages leads to a sense of ego strength and this allows a positive perspective to be taken on the entire life. Through this sense of self the individual achieves ego integrity and can see the

present and future, including death, with dignity. If ego integrity is not achieved a sense of despair is present (Willson, 1983).

Relevance to creative therapies

Erikson's theory of personality development provides us with another framework for viewing the individual. The less deterministic and lifelong perspective offered by Erikson is more congruent with the philosophy of occupational therapy than some of the other psychodynamic theories. His view that the individual exists on biological, social and psychological planes also fits with our concept of holism.

Erikson's eight stages of ego development can offer a useful way of exploring the experiences of the individual over the lifespan. Within creative therapies the emphasis would be on how past experiences influence the individual's present situation. The eight stages also provide a framework for exploring the role which conflict is playing.

Summary

Erikson presents a view of personality development that is more congruent with occupational therapy philosophy than some of the other psychodynamic theories. His lifelong perspective, with eight stages of personality development, provides us with a useful framework for viewing the individual's past experiences and present conflict.

Berne

Eric Berne's theory sits within the psychodynamic theory base but his suggestion that theories of internal psychodynamics have been unable to satisfactorily solve the problem of human relationships gives his theory a different flavour. Berne identified a theory of social dynamics and an approach to therapy called **Transactional Analysis** (TA) (Berne, 1964). Berne suggested TA as a broad approach that could be used on its own or as preparation for psychoanalysis or another specific approach (Patterson, 1986). As this theory has its origin in an understanding of human relationships much of this type of therapy is carried out in group situations. Berne's work is written in an accessible style, making a great deal of deliberate use of colloquialisms. Its popularity in the 1970s extended to the lay population as a result of the publication of some practical guides to TA, such as the one written by Harris (1969).

Man as a social being

Transactional theory is based on the understanding that infants deprived of handling over a long period sink into decline and ill health. In adults the equivalent can be observed in those placed in solitary confinement as punishment. This deprivation leads to what Berne termed **stimulus hunger**. The first form of this is **tactile hunger**, and the most favoured form of stimulus to satisfy this hunger is that provided through physical intimacy (Berne, 1964). As adults we no longer have the same physical closeness with our mother (or substitute parent) yet we still strive for this intimacy. Because physical, social and biological forces act against intimacy in the infant style we have to compromise and accept other forms of contact and so tactile hunger is substituted by **recognition hunger.** Satisfaction of recognition hunger is achieved through what Berne called **strokes.** A stroke is the basic unit of social interaction; it might be as simple as an acknowledgement of one's existence or it may be more intimate. An exchange of strokes constitutes a **transaction** (Berne, 1964; Patterson, 1986). Berne (1964) suggests that any form of social interaction is preferable to no interaction at all. Viewed like this it may provide part of the explanation as to why an individual will tolerate an abusive relationship.

Another form of stimulus hunger is **structure hunger.** This is the need of humans to structure their waking hours, thus avoiding boredom. This will be a familiar concept to occupational therapists. The process by which we do this is called **programming.** There are three types of programming: material, social and individual. **Material programming** is task oriented and arises from dealing with external reality through procedures. It provides a number of opportunities for strokes but these are secondary to the task in hand. **Social programming** includes traditional ritualistic behaviours; those commonly associated with good manners, such as greetings and table manners. Semi-ritualistic topical conversations are included here; these are what we commonly call 'small talk' and are termed by Berne (1964) as **pastimes. Individual programming** occurs when people become better acquainted. It tends to follow a definite pattern and, as the name suggests, occurs on a more individual basis. Individual programming occurs through games or real intimacy. **Games** are a substitute for real intimacy, which can occur only when the ulterior motives of games are discarded. Intimacy is the only completely satisfying way of addressing stimulus hunger, recognition hunger and structure hunger.

Relevance to creative therapies

Creative therapies view humans as social beings, acknowledging that many of the problems clients have can be framed in interpersonal terms. Through creative therapies the individual works towards resolution of **interpersonal** and **intrapersonal** conflict, thus effecting change. The work an individual does within creative therapies may involve exploring the games that are used in relationships and working towards discarding these so that real intimacy can be achieved.

Ego states

Berne (1964) suggested that in any given individual certain behaviour patterns correspond to a particular state of mind. This gave rise to the idea of **ego states.** An ego state can be defined as a coherent system of feelings and set of behaviour patterns. He proposed three ego states: the **Parent**, the **Adult** and the **Child.** At any given moment in a social interaction an individual will exhibit one of these ego states and individuals can shift with varying degrees of readiness from one to another.

The Parent ego state is exhibited in two forms: direct and indirect. When it is exhibited directly it is as an active ego state; the individual responds as his own mother or father would actually respond. An indirect ego state acts as an indirect influence and the individual responds as they know their parents would want them to. The Parent ego state is not the same as Freud's superego but the superego is an aspect of the Parent. The Parent enables the individual to act effectively and makes many responses automatic because 'that is the way they have always been done', thus saving a great deal of time and energy (Berne, 1964; Patterson, 1986).

The Adult ego state is concerned with the objective appraisal of reality – for example, on the basis of experience and knowledge it is able to evaluate whether the individual can take an appropriate and responsible decision. It is concerned with the survival of the individual and enables the individual to deal effectively with the outside world. As well as this the Adult regulates the activities of the Parent and Child and mediates between them (Berne, 1964; Patterson, 1986).

The Child ego state is responsible for intuition, creativity, spontaneity, drive and enjoyment. Every individual was once a child and aspects of childhood exist in later life. The Child is under the influence of the Parent but is distinct from it. The Child does not equate to Freud's id but it is influenced by the id. The Child ego state is exhibited in three forms: the **adapted Child**, which modifies behaviour under Parental influence; the **natural Child**, which is spontaneous and creative; the **rebellious Child**, which resists Parental control.

The Parent is the weakest, the Child the strongest and the Adult is concerned with reality. Each state is a separate and distinct entity; they are often inconsistent and react differently to stimuli. Each is important for the human organism and it is when the balance of these three ego states is disturbed that analysis and reorganisation is necessary (Berne, 1964; Patterson, 1986).

Relevance to creative therapies

The distinction of **three ego states** provides a useful model for understanding client behaviour. Through the use of creative media creative therapies provide opportunities for each of the ego states to play a role. Sessions can be used to explore the use of these states in the client's life outside the creative therapy environment. Creative therapies can also be used to provide an appropriate and safe environment for activation of the Child ego state.

Social interaction

Social interaction provides an opportunity for the satisfaction of hunger and gaining strokes. As the unit of social intercourse is a transaction this involves a

transactional stimulus, which elicits a **transactional response.** Transactions are analysed in terms of the source of the stimulus and the source of the response. For example, the Adult ego state of one person may have acted as a stimulus that elicited a response from the Child ego state of another. There are both complementary and crossed transactions.

- **Complementary transactions** enable communication to flow smoothly. Examples of complementary transactions are when the Parent ego state of one individual stimulates and elicits a response from the Child ego state of another individual or when the Adult ego state of one individual stimulates and gets a response from the Adult ego state of another.
- **Crossed transactions** result in the breakdown of communication. Examples of crossed transactions include when the Adult ego state stimulates the Adult ego state of another individual but the response comes from the Child. Alternatively, the response could come from the Child but be directed towards the Parent ego state of the individual who has initiated the transaction (Patterson, 1986).

Transactions occur in series and may involve the processes of material, social or individual programming. Simple or complementary transactions most often occur in social or working relationships through **procedures**, **rituals** or **pastimes.** Crossed transactions are the basis for **games** (Berne, 1964).

Relevance to creative therapies

Creative therapies are very commonly practised through groupwork. Groups provide a microcosm for **interpersonal dynamics** and **role playing.** Through the experience of the group, clients have the opportunity to demonstrate interpersonal dynamics and adopt roles as well as talk about and explore them. Berne's work on transactions offers therapist and client a framework for considering interpersonal dynamics and roles. This can be used either to unravel the interpersonal dynamics of the group within the therapy sessions or to help clients understand how they communicate with significant others and the roles they adopt outside the group therapy situation.

Games can be organised into **scripts**, which form the unconscious life plan, the sort of person we are going to be and the sort of destiny we make for ourselves. These are related to the four life positions:

- 'I'm okay, you're okay';
- 'I'm okay, you're not okay';
- 'I'm not okay, you're okay';
- 'I'm not okay, you're not okay'.

These life positions determine the way we view life and therefore contribute to our destiny.

- **I'm okay, you're okay** is a positive, healthy and successful position.
- **I'm okay, you're not okay** is somewhat arrogant and may be a position occupied by 'do gooders' for example.
- **I'm not okay, you're okay** is a position occupied by someone with low self-esteem and may be apparent in anyone with depression.
- **I'm not okay, you're not okay** is a despairing and futile position and may be held by people who commit suicide (Patterson, 1986).

Relevance to creative therapies

In creative therapies a client might be encouraged to explore their script in relation to the four **life positions.** If they have an unhealthy script creative therapies may be used to work towards its resolution.

Therapy

The goal of therapy is to achieve a position of 'I'm okay, you're okay'. Therapy is based on structural diagnosis, which involves identifying from which ego state a particular behaviour has originated. There is a series of stages to TA, and therapy may terminate with the success of any one stage or may go through the whole process.

Stage one: **structural analysis** – involves decontamination of the Adult boundaries, definition of the boundaries of the ego states and stabilisation of Adult control.

Stage two: **TA proper** – in a group situation transactions are analysed to see whether they are complementary or crossed.

Stage three: **Analysis of pastimes and games** – analysis of pastimes constitutes the early stages of group therapy. Games are analysed in terms of their gains; the goal is for the individual to be able to discard these in intimate relationships and choose which games to select, for how long and with whom in social relationships.

Stage four: **Social relationships** – scripts are acted out in the group setting. The intention of therapy is to help the individual adopt a better script by putting the Adult in control.

Stage five: **Analysis of relationships** – for example, marriage or very close relationships (Patterson, 1986).

Relevance to creative therapies

Unless the therapist leading the creative therapy session particularly favours Berne's theory and approach it is unlikely that the series of stages will be executed in this coherent order. However, aspects may be evident in the way the therapist interprets the **transactions** and **interactions** of the group members.

Summary

Berne provides a useful balance to the other theorists we have discussed because of his focus on human relationships and social dynamics. Creative therapies focus on interpersonal and intrapersonal conflict and thus human relationships and dynamics are a central concern. Berne's theory provides us with a model for understanding the social interactions and roles of the clients we work with as well as a framework for exploring them.

HUMANISTIC THEORY

Humanistic theory developed in the 1950s and 1960s as an alternative to psychodynamic theory and behaviourism. Humanistic theory takes the view that within each individual there is an active and creative force or self which seeks expression, development and growth. The therapist seeks to understand how individuals experience themselves, their world and others and helps them to actualise their potential. The focus of humanistic psychology is on the way humans strive to find meaning in life (Westen, 1999). From this outline one can see that humanistic theory offers a very positive view of the individual, one in which change and growth is inherent, becoming an integral part of the richness of life.

Maslow

Abraham Maslow was considered a founder of humanistic psychology (Gross, 1996), and so we have chosen to begin this section with a discussion of his work.

Needs

Maslow stressed acceptance of the person and believed in the positive evaluation of human nature with its potential for growth. He considered that individuals were subject to two sets of motivational needs or forces (Gross, 1996; Huizinga, 1970). The first set, **deficiency needs**, focused on survival through addressing basic physical and mental health needs. The second set promoted self-actualisation, encouraging a person to reach their full potential; these Maslow termed **growth needs**. Although these needs can be divided into two sets for understanding, it is important to recognise that they are not distinct. When one need level appears to be satisfied the individual moves on to the next in a hierarchical manner (Gross, 1996). This concept of wanting more, of not being satisfied, is a feature of human beings.

Maslow identifies four deficiency needs and we start at the bottom of the hierarchy:

- **Physiological needs** – the needs which sustain the person and which are vital to their existence; for example, food, water, sleep, and shelter. They are basic needs which have to be satisfied before moving on to the next level.
- **Safety needs** – these recognise the need for personal safety and security, including predictability and familiarity within life.

- **Social needs** – these encompass love, affection and belonging within society. They involve the individual feeling loved and having a sense of belonging and acceptance but also involve the more active needs of helping others, giving kindness and taking a responsible place within a community.
- **Esteem needs** – these deficiency needs are subdivided into the esteem which comes from within a person for his own self and the esteem which comes from others towards the person. Internal esteem considers aspects of confidence, achievement, competence and freedom, whereas external esteem focuses on reputation, recognition, importance and status (Huizinga, 1970).

These deficiency needs are viewed as the empty holes which must be filled for the individual to achieve a healthy state (Huizinga, 1970). When the deficiency needs have been achieved there is a move to growth needs, which lead to self-actualisation.

Relevance to creative therapies

The creative therapy approach also takes a positive view of the individual, recognising that they have the potential for development. **Viewing needs hierarchically** can be a useful concept to the therapy situation. Maslow states that the individual must address needs lower in the hierarchy before they can move on to higher needs. This view suggests that in creative therapies it would be inappropriate to expect an individual to be able to work towards achieving esteem needs if their physiological and safety needs are not being met because they are living in inadequate accommodation with an abusing partner. Likewise, it would be inappropriate to work towards growth needs when significant deficiency needs remain unmet.

Self-actualisation

Maslow (1954) explained self-actualisation as 'the desire to become more and more what one is, to become everything one is capable of becoming' (p. 92). This concept of psychological growth is central to Maslow's theory of motivation. Huizinga (1970) explains Maslow's characteristics of a self-actualised person, seeing these as the end product of psychological growth. The characteristics include the following.

- **That the person is able to resolve dichotomies.** Maslow did not mean that the self-actualised person could not see differences. For example, if we use the dichotomy of work and pleasure, the self-actualised person would find pleasure within work and work within pleasure.
- **That the individual is creative.** This creativity extends to the ways in which the person sees the world and is not concerned with the mastery of an artistic technique. It links with the child-like state for spontaneity, playfulness and lack of logic or rational behaviour. It is similar to the naive and universal creativeness of children and it touches whatever the individual is concerned with (Maslow, 1970).

- **There is a more efficient perception of reality.** The self-actualised person is able to see people with less bias, they welcome new and old experiences, and as they are less dependent on others to meet their needs they can explore their own perception of reality.
- **Problem centering.** The self-actualised person tends to focus on problems that are outside themselves, in contrast to the insecure or less motivated person who tends to have an introspective view.
- **Democratic character structure.** This characteristic sees people for what and who they really are, respecting and showing regard for others who are fulfilling their potential but showing scant regard for those who demonstrate their 'position' through financial status or power.
- **A sense of being at one with the world.** This characteristic concerns a desire to help others and to contribute to the world of others and extends both to the abstract sense of others and to the small circle of close friends with whom we develop in-depth relationships (Huizinga, 1970).

Maslow (1976) suggested that there were a number of ways of moving towards self-actualisation: through experiencing events fully, making progressive rather than regressive choices, listening to oneself, honesty in times of doubt, courage, applying intelligence, using what Maslow terms 'peak experiences' and by finding out who one is by identifying defences and opening oneself up. Maslow believed that only a few people achieve self-actualisation as the process could be blocked by a number of external and internal influences.

Relevance to creative therapies

Creative therapies may facilitate an understanding of this hierarchy of needs, enabling the individual to acknowledge their own journey within the different levels.

The ultimate aim of the creative therapy process might be to help individuals achieve the characteristics of the **self-actualised person.** As Maslow states, very few people achieve this, but through creative therapies we are able to help clients achieve a level of personal growth which is more functional for them and with which they are more satisfied.

Summary

Maslow's hierarchy of needs and the ultimate aim for the individual of self-actualisation can provide a framework for our approach in creative therapies. In assessment we can view the client's problems in terms of where they fit within the hierarchy and an awareness of deficiency and growth needs can help develop the agenda for the creative therapy process.

Rogers

Carl Rogers was perhaps the most influential humanist psychologist. He has developed a branch of psychology known as **client-centred therapy** or the **person-centred approach.**

Client-centred therapy works from the basic premise that every person has the capacity to **self-actualise** (Rogers, 1967); that is, to allow themselves to grow into a fully functioning, content and fulfilled individual, given the right conditions. In the therapeutic relationship Rogers aims to provide the conditions which enable this growth to take place. He defines specific qualities in the therapist of respect towards the client – **empathy, congruence** and **unconditional positive regard** – which enable the client to move from perhaps a static point engulfed with difficulties to a free, flexible point encompassing relationships and personal goals. He calls this **the organismic self** (Rogers, 1978). Rogers considered that psychological difficulties are caused by the self-actualising tendency being blocked. He believed that through a counselling relationship these blockages could be dissolved, giving the individual the motivation to take control of himself and to move away from evaluation and control by external influences. Thus self-actualisation becomes an active process of growth. Rogers' aim therefore is not to solve a particular problem with a client, as 'a problem' is not the focus for the work, but to concentrate on the individual, seeing him as the focus and thus freeing him to grow and develop.

Relevance to creative therapies

The client-centred approach is one of the three key elements of occupational therapy philosophy that we have identified as being specifically relevant to creative therapies. This focus on the individual within their world is fundamental in our use of creative therapies.

The therapist/client relationship

In his book *A Way of Being* Rogers (1980) states his central hypothesis:

> ***individuals have within themselves vast resources for self-understanding and for altering their self-concepts, basic attitudes, and self-directed behaviour; these resources can be tapped if a definable climate of facilitative psychological attitudes can be provided' (p. 115).***

Rogers therefore saw the basic relationship between the therapist and the client as the linchpin of client-centred therapy. Therapy would be optimised only if certain qualities were present within this relationship and these qualities present a different emphasis from those found in the psychodynamic approach.

Role of the therapist

Within the therapist/client relationship the therapist demonstrates deep respect for the client. This respect is shown in the acceptance of any material the client wishes to bring to the session to discuss and through empathic listening leading to accurate reflection. This material enables the world of the client to be explored and greater understanding gained. It is the view of the world held by the client which the therapist is seeking, and to elicit this the therapist has to put aside their own beliefs, values and perceptions and enter into the world of the client. Rogers identified three qualities which had to be present to enable the therapist to do this.

The first quality is **unconditional positive regard**. This involves perceiving another person without discrimination or judgement, prizing or accepting them – thus seeing the person as worthy (Rogers, 1978). This means that the therapist shows that they value the client, whatever or whoever they are, but it does not mean that they necessarily approve of all the client's behaviour. This may be a very new experience for the client; he or she may feel rejected and unloved by the world, and be very unused to anyone believing in their individual value as a person. This attitude can break the cycle of low self-esteem and self-defeating behaviours which may have been the client's way of being.

The second quality is **empathy**, which involves perceiving the client's internal frame of reference, including emotional components and meanings, accurately. It involves the therapist really getting on a level with the client and perceiving the situation 'as if' they were the client. It is important not to lose the 'as if' element (Patterson, 1986). To demonstrate empathy is to show an understanding of the client which communicates itself to the client. Empathy is about feeling and thinking yourself into another person's world without being drawn into it. To enable this to happen the therapist's own views and values must be laid aside in order to enter the other's world without prejudice. Throughout the process the therapist reflects back to the client clearly and accurately, showing listening based on respect.

Matching the outward responses of the therapist to their inner feelings demonstrates the third quality, **congruence** (Patterson, 1986). What they show is what they feel – there are no mixed messages, where the body language is saying one thing and the inner feelings are saying another. Mixed messages cause confusion and loss of communication, bringing a sense of insecurity and defensiveness. As the therapist shows congruence towards the client, so the client is able to develop a more congruent way of being for themselves, thus demonstrating growth. Congruence is about being genuine with the client – 'here I am, as I am' (Rogers, 1978) – stressing that it is feelings and attitudes which are important within the relationship rather than opinions or judgements.

Rogers (1978) believed that the therapeutic relationship would work if the client experienced these three qualities in the therapist, as the client would then begin to use them in thinking about the self, developing a sense of valuing, accepting and prizing. In this way a client is **received** (Rogers, 1967), understood, accepted and valued as a person. The safety developed enables the client to disclose painful issues and thus get behind and discard the mask, the front presented to the world, and become themselves.

Role of the client

Rogers (1967) states that once the therapist has created a relationship of acceptance, genuineness and understanding, the other person would

- *experience and understand aspects of himself which previously he has repressed;*
- *find himself becoming better integrated, more able to function effectively;*
- *become more similar to the person he would like to be;*
- *be more self-directing and self confident;*
- *become more of a person, more unique and more self expressive;*
- *be more understanding, more acceptant to others;*
- *be able to cope with the problems of everyday life more adequately and more comfortably' (p. 38).*

Rogers believed that every individual had the capacity to become a **fully functioning person** and that this state would be achieved by self-actualisation. This is the growth tendency, a desire to move forwards in life which can become buried under psychological defences (Rogers, 1967). This tendency is latent, if not evident, in all individuals. It is an active and positive process assuming the potential for growth, providing certain conditions exist.

Relevance to creative therapies

The creative therapy approach places a great emphasis on the therapist/client relationship and advocates a client-centred stance. In creative therapies we strive to understand the **personal meaning** of the client, to value them for who they are and to develop an honest, open and trusting relationship.

Change

Rogers saw change as a process within a client's life and that development of the therapeutic relationship enables this change to occur. The process of change moves along a continuum, 'from fixity to changingness, from rigid structure to flow, from stasis to process' (Rogers, 1967, p. 131). The person who emerges from this change is open to experience, trusting of self and with an internal locus of evaluation. The individual now obtains approval from within, rather than from seeking it from others, so bases decisions on their own feelings, values and needs rather than on the wants and expectations of others.

The start of therapy may be characterised by a person with rigid personal constructs but who is able to give some descriptions of feelings and personal meaning. As the client recognises that they are received and accepted, so there is a loosening and freeing of feelings and constructs, a development of self-responsibility towards problems and development of an ability to trust both themselves and others. Change is therefore seen as a process. There is no end product, as this would represent a fixity further along the continuum and the person would have merely moved from fixed, to change, to fixed again. Real change means that individuals continue to search to fulfil themselves, to actualise and to become; therefore there can be no final result, no reaching of a final fixed point (McLeod and Wheeler, 1996).

Relevance to creative therapies

The creative therapy approach is a dynamic process working towards change. The client is central within this and the aim is to help them to develop the **skills of personal evaluation** to create autonomy and a feeling of empowerment. This process is never-ending as development is always possible. To reflect this creative therapies can be used outside the clinical setting for addressing personal growth issues in what would be perceived as the 'well' population.

Summary

Of all the psychological theorists we review in this chapter Rogers is certainly the most influential to the creative therapy approach. His client-centred philosophy and the qualities of the therapist/client relationship are very strongly evident in creative therapies, where we believe in the client's ability to achieve self-growth through the use of media.

Perls

Fritz Perls was the founder of Gestalt therapy and was still developing the theory underpinning it at the time of his death. Perls was trained in psychoanalysis and, although Gestalt therapy has its foundation in this, it is flavoured by a number of other influences including Zen Buddhism and Taoism. Gestalt is a German word which means organised whole, form, shape and pattern. There is a basic premise that the organised whole is greater than the sum of its parts. Gestalt therapy is an existential therapy, which means that it does not support the concept of universal values that apply to all, but suggests that each individual creates their own values through action and through living each moment to the full.

View of man

Perls took a much more positive view of humans than the early psychoanalysts and rejected the theory that people are controlled by internal and external factors. There is an implicit assumption in Gestalt therapy that humans are capable of choice, are responsible for themselves and have the potential for change in that they contain the necessary resources to restore themselves (Patterson, 1986). Like Jung, Perls believed that such change and development is a lifelong process.

Perls viewed man as a whole person consisting of body, emotions, thoughts, sensations and perceptions. He rejected the principle that the mind, body and soul can be viewed as separate entities. He suggested that these are aspects of the whole person which function in an interrelated way – for example, that emotions have thinking and feeling aspects to them (Passons, 1975; Patterson, 1986). Here you can see the evidence of the basic premise that the whole is greater than the sum of its parts, as well as a link with the holistic principles of occupational therapy that mind, body and spirituality cannot be viewed as separate units.

Linked with this, Perls also believed that humans are very much part of their environment and cannot be viewed outside it as he considered that a person can be meaningfully understood only within their own context (Passons, 1975). Perls used the term 'environment' in its broadest sense to include the physical, social and cultural environment. He considered that maturity was reached when the individual was able to move away from relying on environmental support to taking responsibility for supporting themselves through their inner resources. This happens through what Perls terms **frustration**, which enables the individual to discover their potential to cope with the world (Patterson, 1986). This development of maturity does not happen to a predetermined time frame but will be different in each individual (Passons, 1975). If the individual cannot cope with the demands placed on them from inner needs or environmental demands they will manipulate the environment by playing neurotic roles. Introjection, projection, confluence and retroflection are methods of resistance used at a time when the individual cannot cope.

- **Introjection** is the uncritical acceptance of concepts, standards of behaviour and values. The person who habitually introjects fails to develop their own personality.
- **Projection** is the process by which the individual displaces aspects of their self which they find unacceptable.
- **Confluence** occurs when the boundaries between the self and the environment become undifferentiated and the individual loses touch with where these end and where the environment begins.
- **Retroflection** is when a function originally directed at the environment is turned in on the self, for example self-hatred. The suppression of emotions is sometimes necessary but can become habitual (Patterson, 1986).

All of these may be positive methods but they can constitute neurosis when they become chronic or are used inappropriately.

Perls believed that man could only experience himself in the present, so Gestalt therapy operates very much in the here and now. It states that the past and future can be experienced in the present only through remembering and anticipating (Passons, 1975). Gestalt therapy deals with these memories or anticipations in terms of how they impact on the individual now.

Perls suggested that throughout life the individual tries to maintain a state of balance or homeostasis (he termed this state **organismic homeostasis**). When the individual is faced with needs, either internally or through external demands, the state of balance is upset. The continuous process of restoring this balance is called **organismic self restoration**, and occurs as identified needs are met. A new or unmet need results in a state of unbalance which constitutes an **incomplete Gestalt** or unfinished business. The process of meeting a physical or psychological need is called **assimilation**, when the balance is restored and the Gestalt is complete. The dominant need at any time becomes the **foreground figure,** allowing other needs to recede into the background. Perls considered that the individual interacts with the environment to meet needs using sensory and motor processes; thus the point of interaction between the individual and the environment is called the **contact boundary**. Therefore thoughts, actions and emotions are ways of dealing with events at the contact boundary (Patterson, 1986).

The overall motivation of the individual is to achieve the primary need of **self-actualisation**, for the individual to become himself; however, there are other biological and social needs and whichever is the most pressing will be in the foreground. According to Perls there is no universal hierarchy of needs; each individual will have their own formula which will adjust depending on whatever unique situation they find themselves in (Passons, 1975). This process of completing Gestalts is the process through which growth occurs. Perls views neurosis as a stagnation of growth or a disturbance of development, which occurs from conflict between the individual's needs and the demands of the environment. The development of a neurosis is an effort to maintain equilibrium when the environment is demanding too much of the individual (Patterson, 1986).

Relevance to creative therapies

Perls' positive view of the individual mirrors a key principle of the creative therapy approach. In creative therapies we recognise that each individual is capable of choice, responsible for themselves and has the potential for their own development.

Perls' view of the environment and the importance of understanding the **individual within their own context** is also evident in the creative therapy approach. We recognise that the individual operates within a unique personal, physical, social and cultural environment. In our practice we have to consider that the person needs to return to and function within their own social milieu, and that their situations and problems must always be viewed within this context.

All the occupational therapy models recognise the significance of and potential tension in the individual interacting with their environment and responding to its demands. Our role, through approaches like creative therapies, is to help the individual find appropriate ways of interacting with and meeting the demands of the environment.

Creative therapies are not as strongly focused on the present as Gestalt therapy. In creative therapies, when appropriate, we would allow the individual to dwell on past experiences and anticipate the future but a focus on how the past and future impact on the present would be used as a valuable grounding influence.

Therapy

Gestalt therapy can be performed on an individual basis but more usually occurs in groups. The therapist will often work with one person at a time in a group setting, and this frequently turns into a group experience as others identify with the process (Nelson-Jones, 1982).

> ### *Relevance to creative therapies*
>
> This is a different focus to the groupwork experience of creative therapies, where the emphasis is on using the group dynamics and the group experience to achieve both individual and group aims. We would usually strive to avoid working with one person at a time in a group as active participation of everyone involved with the intervention is a key aspect.

The overall aim of therapy is to help the client to mature. There are two key elements within this process. The first is achieving integration, which involves helping the client to acquire organismic balance through making effective Gestalts with their environment. The client is helped to replace the abnormal resistances of introjection, projection, confluence and retroflection by the process of assimilation. The second key element is helping the client to move from relying on the environment for support to being able to utilise their own resources effectively to support and develop the self. The client is encouraged to take responsibility for themselves rather than blame events on others, the situation or the illness (Nelson-Jones, 1982; Passons, 1975; Patterson, 1986).

> ### *Relevance to creative therapies*
>
> In the practice of creative therapies the therapist would always try to **centre the situation with the individual** rather than allow them to blame events on others. The individual has to learn to cope with or accept the situation they find themselves within and understand that that apportioning blame is generally unhelpful to this process.

The focus of Gestalt therapy is on the here and now, and on **how** the client is feeling rather than **why** they feel the way they do. This is very much a present-centred approach. The therapist will use questions such as 'what are you feeling?', 'what do you want?' and 'are you aware of what you are doing?' to help the client focus in the present (Patterson, 1986).

There is no systematic approach to Gestalt therapy because it is tailored to the needs of each client and different therapists develop their own approaches. However, there are some standard techniques which may be adapted for use in creative therapies such as 'topdog/underdog', 'the empty-chair' and dreamwork.

- The topdog is equivalent to Freud's superego and consists of the 'shoulds' that are internalised by the individual. The underdog is equivalent to Freud's id and sabotages the efforts of the topdog. The client alternately takes the topdog and underdog roles and enters into a dialogue between them. Through this process these two parts of the personality become integrated.

- The empty-chair technique is another way of facilitating the dialogue between the two parts of the personality or between the client and another individual. Two chairs are placed facing one another, each representing either a different part of the personality or the client and another individual. The client can then move from one to another to engage in the dialogue in a different role.
- In Gestalt therapy dreams are considered to represent unassimilated situations. Through dreamwork the client relives the dream in the therapy situation by acting it out and interpreting it (Patterson, 1986).

The role of the therapist is not to support the client and provide solutions to their problems but to frustrate their efforts to seek support within a nurturing and caring environment. In this way clients develop and learn to use the resources within themselves to facilitate the process termed by Perls as frustration. The therapist does not offer interpretations but may direct the client's attention towards certain things which may be significant. Working with Gestalt therapy requires the therapist to be actively involved, able to use themselves and their own emotional reactions within the therapy situation and be able to be flexible in their approach in order to react to the client's changing needs (Passons, 1975).

Relevance to creative therapies

In creative therapies the therapist would not offer interpretations but would bring something to the client's attention and pose some hypotheses for the client to consider. The therapist is actively involved in the therapy process. An important tool available to the therapist in creative therapies is the therapeutic use of the self.

Summary

It is evident that the work of Perls, in his development of Gestalt therapy, has a great deal of influence on the approach of creative therapies. The positive view of the individual and real recognition of the significance of the unique environmental context of the individual are key. The active, non-interpretative role of the therapist also mirrors the creative therapy emphasis on the therapist's use of self in the therapy process. The use of non-verbal as well as verbal techniques in therapy is also evident within creative therapies.

COGNITIVE AND BEHAVIOURAL THEORY

Cognitive and behavioural theory are evident in the practice of creative therapies although they are not a primary influence. Our experience has been that they are most notable in this approach when we are working at a level lower down the activity continuum in Figure 1.2. These theory bases also provide us with another perspective on understanding the cognitions and behaviours of the clients we work with through creative therapies, no matter what level of the activity continuum we are operating at.

Cognitive theory

Cognitive psychology does not have the name of a single theorist attached to it but the works of Beck and Ellis are very significant. Cognitive psychology is an approach which has grown since the 1960s and it has become part of the language when looking at theories for understanding people. It is concerned with the processes involved in making sense of the environment and interacting within it (Eysenck, 1993).

The cognitive approach is concerned with thinking and the mental processes associated with this (Glassman, 1995). It is therefore an internal process, which cannot be directly observed, although an outsider may infer that they know what a person is thinking. Cognitively healthy people are able to cope with change and challenge, as they live within a world of meaning which they construct. An unhealthy cognitive state results in a distorted sense of meaning which in turn reflects on the person's ability to cope with the demands of life.

The principal cognitive processes that are involved in making sense of the environment are memory, attention, psycholinguistics, thinking and perception (French and Colman, 1995). These are internal processes which come between a stimulus and a response, and will affect the response the individual makes to a stimulus. For example, the response will be based on past experience (memory), whether the individual is preoccupied (attention), whether the verbal stimulus was heard (perception) and understood (psycholinguistics), and finally what decision is taken on the response (thinking). Responses are explored to enable an understanding of inappropriate thoughts and behaviours.

Relevance to creative therapies

When people are ill, under stress or troubled their cognitive processes can be affected. This can distort the meaning of the world in which they live and in turn interfere with the individual's ability to fulfil their life roles. An ill, stressed or troubled individual is likely to be preoccupied and unable to attend properly; this poor attention will impact on memory as information is not stored properly. **Thinking and perception become distorted** as the cognitive processes in making decisions, judging situations and reasoning are affected. Psycholinguistics may also be affected as the individual may misinterpret what is said, inappropriately interpreting verbal and non-verbal cues and they may be unable to express themselves effectively.

Creative therapies are not fundamentally a cognitive approach, but we need an awareness of the above processes and how they can be affected. This awareness gives us a better understanding of the client's situation and it may be appropriate to challenge these cognitive processes and encourage their replacement with more healthy ones. Both occupational therapy and the practice of creative therapies aim to help the client achieve mastery over their self and their environment. Learning how thinking and reactions to situations can influence emotional functioning is important in this (Willson, 1996).

Behavioural theory

The key focus of the behavioural approach is the emphasis on **learning**, the factor which changes behaviour as the result of experience (Glassman, 1995). In essence, behaviour therapy isolates certain forms of behaviour and effects change through a programme of relearning. Thus it identifies problem behaviours and focuses on developing functional skills (Bruce and Borg, 1993). Watson is considered to be the founder of behaviourism, attempting to link psychology more closely with biology and redefining it as an objective science of behaviour (Gross, 1996). The behavioural movement is also heavily influenced by the work of Pavlov and Skinner, who conducted experiments on stimulus–response learning in animals (Glassman, 1995; Patterson, 1986).

From the behavioural perspective, a person is able to learn to change through experience, which is linked to goals or reinforcers. This perspective suggests that the reaction or response to any behaviour determines the likelihood of it being repeated. Learning has to take place through exposure to stimuli in the environment, so that new ways of reacting can be developed. The process of relearning is an attempt to directly change this behaviour, as it is seen as learned behaviour, influenced by past events and experiences. The focus is on current behaviour, where specific aspects are identified for change and a systematic treatment programme is established with interventions to manipulate behaviour. The individual is involved in monitoring progress and evaluating change. As the emphasis is on observation rather than empathy the therapist working in this way is required to be objective and focused on specific behaviours rather than on a full range of behaviour.

Any programme of behavioural change involves breaking the task down into simple and achievable stages, which are goal oriented and supported by clear instruction (Hagedorn, 1997). Behaviour modification can be used both to encourage desired behaviour and to reduce undesirable behaviour. This usually involves an approach of rewarding good behaviour and withdrawing privileges when bad behaviour is in evidence.

Relevance to creative therapies

Aspects of the behavioural approach are evident in the practice of creative therapies but they are not a strong influence. It is unlikely that the therapist working through creative therapies would work from a strongly behavioural stance, as it does not sit comfortably with the psychodynamic approach. However, creative therapies are about effecting change, so learning and behavioural change are often important. Through creative therapies we may help the client to explore learned patterns of behaviour and test out alternatives. This is where groupwork can be particularly helpful, as the group is a social microcosm and can provide a safe environment for exhibiting and challenging social behaviour. The group itself also has its own behavioural norms which the members agree and are expected to adhere to. These are evident in ground rules and boundaries.

Summary

Neither the cognitive nor the behavioural approaches are key influences on the practice of creative therapies. However, an understanding of these is valuable in offering a perspective on the thought processes and behaviours of our clients. An awareness of the cognitive and behavioural approaches also provides us with some useful tools for working with clients within the creative therapy approach.

CONCLUSION

In this chapter we have summarised some psychodynamic and humanistic theory bases. Creative therapies are a psychodynamic approach to practice but their application is heavily influenced by humanistic theory because of its centrality to occupational therapy philosophy. We have also provided a very brief overview of cognitive and behavioural theory. Each of these theoretical foundations provides us with a different perspective on the client and the process of therapy and there are times when the influence of one theory base over another will change the focus of our work.

In presenting these theory bases we have provided information on some specific theorists, as the different perspectives provide us with useful insights into our clients and the process of creative therapies. Dealing with the work of specific theorists allows us to build a more detailed picture of the psychological theory base underpinning creative therapies. Understanding the complexities of the work of each of these theorists is not easy, so the summary table clearly outlines the significant features of each, and traces their influence on creative therapies.

We are aware that we have presented the theories briefly, and would urge readers who are particularly interested to explore some of the texts we have used to develop their knowledge further. We hope that this overview, when considered in conjunction with Chapter 1, will provide a sound theoretical underpinning which both informs and grounds our approach of creative therapy. Only by knowing where our approach is coming from can we justify using this intervention with our clients.

As we leave this chapter it is useful to reflect on our original summary, which reminds us how the important components link together to give a sound theory base, and leads us towards the next chapter, which will focus on the process of achieving a creative therapy intervention (see Figure 2.1).

Table 2.1 Summary of the theoretical foundations

	Understanding of the individual	**View of mental illness**	**Methods of therapy**	**Therapist/client relationship**	**Outcome of therapy**	**Influence on creative therapies**
Psychodynamic theory:						
Freud	Deterministic view – under the control of instincts. The unconscious has an important role in the psyche. Three subsystems – id, ego and superego. Personality develops in childhood through stages of sexual development.	Conflict between id, ego and superego resulting in repressed unconscious material. Problems arise from early childhood experiences. Failure to move through the stages of psychosexual development.	Early in Freud's work hypnotism, later dream analysis and free association. Classical psychoanalysis. Long term, often daily contact. Two stages: (i) express unconscious feeling; (ii) explore and work through conflicts by gaining insight and so strengthening the ego.	Therapist is superior and offers interpretations. Complex relationship. Patient appears more active in the process than the therapist. Transference and counter-transference.	Harmony between id, ego and superego. Repressed material brought into the conscious and assimilated.	Offers an understanding of the role of the unconscious and early relationships. A way of viewing the personality as three subsystems developing through a series of stages. Understanding of defence mechanisms and thus a view on dysfunctional interactions. Possible application of techniques such as free-association. Raises an awareness of the potential significance of transference and counter-transference in the therapist/client relationship

Jung	Constant tension between adapting to inner needs (regression) and responding to the demands of the environment (progression). The psyche consists of three levels – collective unconscious, personal unconscious and the conscious. Personality develops throughout the lifespan, the complexes of the Self, the ego, the persona, the shadow and the anima and animus have a role to play in this process which is termed individuation.	Imbalance between the individual and the demands of the collective unconscious. A problem in the process of individuation. A way of adapting to the demands of life.	Dream analysis. Analysis of transference. Talking. Acknowledgement and confrontation of suffering, accessing healing powers of the unconscious. Contact once or twice a week with breaks approximately every 12 weeks.	Equal and full involvement. Very active process.	Bring patient/client into contact with the collective unconscious. Development of Self. Sheds false mask of persona, confronts shadow and defence mechanisms. Equipped with psychological understanding to be self-reliant.	Relationship between individual and the environment. An understanding of the role of the unconscious. A way of viewing the personality and personality types. Significance of lifelong developmental process which provides potential goals for therapy. Emphasis on unique process for each client and promoting independence.
Erikson	Eight stages of psychosocial development occurring over the lifespan. Interdependence between biology, psychology and social structures.	Outcome of normative crisis towards maladaptive pole.	Positive view of the individual, possible to overcome early unsatisfactory life experiences later in the lifespan.		Achievement of balance towards adaptive pole in each stage of psychosocial development.	Optimistic view that earlier negative experiences can be resolved later in life. Eight stages of psychosocial development provide a lifespan framework for exploring conflict.

Table 2.1 Continued

	Understanding of the individual	**View of mental illness**	**Methods of therapy**	**Therapist/client relationship**	**Outcome of therapy**	**Influence on creative therapies**
Berne	Positive view of individuals. Social beings who strive for intimacy. Three ego states – Parent, Adult and Child.	Disturbance of balance between the three ego states. Structural or functional pathology in the ego states. Unhealthy life script.	Group work. Transactional analysis.	Participatory.	Balance between three ego states. Position of 'I'm okay, you're okay'.	Provides a structure for understanding social interactions and roles.
Humanistic theory:						
Maslow	Driven by two forces – deficiency needs, growth needs. Ability to achieve hierarchy of needs, to self-actualise.	Concerned with mental health, not illness. Self-actualisation blocked by experiences.	Verbal exploration of presenting symptoms. Facilitates working through the defences, understanding the barriers to growth.	Acceptance and positive view of the person. Facilitates working through the defences, understanding the barriers to growth.	Intrinsic learning = process of growing into the best person one can be. Ultimate aim is self-actualisation.	Creativity sets you free. Person can move towards self-actualisation. Understanding of difficulties on a deficiency/growth hierarchy.
Rogers	Every person has an Inherent capacity for growth. Deep respect for the person. The concept of self-awareness.	The individual, not the problem, is the focus. Prevents growth and self-esteem. The psychology of becoming.	Conversation and dialogue. Individual/group counselling. Conscious process. Optimism.	Non-directive. Reflection. Linchpin of person-centred counselling – respect based on empathy, unconditional positive regard and congruence.	Independent self. Growth of the individual. Acceptance. The organismic self.	Client centred. Creativity is encouraged. Emphasis on process. Personal responsibility. Honesty. Holistic.

				Acceptance of the individual. Valuing the individual. Non-judgmental. An equal relationship.		Qualities of therapist/client relationship. Person sets own agenda. Belief in the individual's capacity for growth and change.
Perls	Positive view of individuals. Holistic. Individual's environment is important. Present time centred. Individuals strive for organismic homeostasis. Overall, motivation is for self-actualisation.	Disturbance in organismic homeostasis and ineffective organismic self-restoration because the environment is demanding too much of the individual.	No systematic approach. Frustration. Uses non-verbal as well as verbal techniques. Techniques such as 'topdog/underdog', 'empty-chair'. Flexible approach.	Very active involvement of both therapist and client. Therapist uses self and own emotional reactions in the therapy situation.	Enable client to mature through achieving organismic balance through the process of making effective Gestalts with their environment. Help client use own resources effectively rather than relying on the environment for support.	Positive, holistic view. Importance of clients interaction with their own environment. Use of the therapist's self within the therapy situation. Encourage client to utilise own resources for their own support and development.
Cognitive and behavioural theory:						
Cognitive	A thinking conscious being with a range of cognitive processes affecting the individual world view.	Disturbance in cognitive process between a stimulus and a response. Unhealthy cognitions.	Explanation and understanding of cognitive process. Altering cognitive processes to more healthy ones.	Supportive/suggestive.	Change in cognitions to a more accurate and healthy world view.	An understanding of cognitive processes, how these can be affected and how they can affect functioning.
Behavioural	Appropriate or inappropriate behaviour.	Exhibiting inappropriate behaviour as a result of faulty learning.	Analysis of behaviour. Behaviour broken down into small achievable pieces. Goal oriented.	'Teacher' relationship. Objective relationship.	Change in inappropriate behaviour towards more acceptable behaviour.	An understanding of behaviour and learning both in the self and in others.

Psychodynamic theory + Occupational therapy 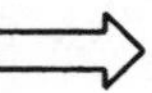 **Creative therapies**

Figure 2.1 The constitution of creative therapies

REFERENCES

Berne, E. (1964) *Games People Play. The Psychology of Human Relationships,* Penguin, Harmondsworth.
Brown, D. and Peddar, J. (1991) *Introduction to Psychotherapy*, 2nd edn, Routledge, London.
Bruce, M.A. and Borg, B. (1993) *Psychosocial Occupational Therapy*, 2nd edn, Slack Inc., Thorofare, NJ.
Eysenck, M. (1993) *Principles of Cognitive Psychology*, Lawrence Erlbaum, Sussex.
French, C. and Colman, A. (eds) (1995) *Cognitive Psychology*, Longman, London.
Glassman, W. (1995) *Approaches to Psychology*, Open University Press, Buckingham.
Gross, R. (1996) *Psychology The Science of Mind and Behaviour*, 3rd edn, Hodder and Stoughton, London.
Hagedorn, R. (1997) *Occupational Therapy: Foundations for Practice*, 2nd edn, Churchill Livingstone, Edinburgh.
Harris, T.A. (1969) *I'm OK – You're OK*, Pan Books, London.
Huizinga, G. (1970) *Maslow's Need Hierarchy in the Work Situation,* Wolters-Noordhoff, Netherlands.
Maslow, A. (1954) *Motivation and Personality,* Harper & Row, New York.
Maslow, A. (1970) *Motivation and Personality*, 2nd edn, Harper & Row, New York.
Maslow, A. (1976) *The Farther Reaches of Human Nature,* Penguin, Harmondsworth.
McLeod, J. and Wheeler, S. (1996) Person Centred and Psychodynamic Counselling: A Dialogue. In: *Counselling The BAC Counselling Reader* (eds Palmer, S., Dainow, S. and Milner, P.), Sage, London.
Nelson-Jones, R. (1982) *The Theory and Practice of Counselling Psychology,* Holt, Rinehart and Winston, London.
Passons, W.R. (1975) *Gestalt Approaches in Counselling*, Holt, Rinehart and Winston, USA.
Patterson, C.H. (1986) *Theories of Counselling and Psychotherapy,* 4th edn, HarperCollins, New York.
Rogers, C.R. (1967) *On Becoming a Person,* Constable, London.
Rogers, C.R. (1978) *On Personal Power,* Constable, London.
Rogers, C.R. (1980) *A Way of Being,* Houghton Mifflin Co, Boston.
Samuels, A. (1985) *Jung and the Post-Jungians*, Routledge and Kegan Paul, London.
Samuels, A., Shorter, B. and Plaut, F. (1986) *A Critical Dictionary of Jungian Analysis,* Routledge and Kegan Paul, London.
Stevens, A. (1994) *Jung*, Oxford University Press, Oxford.
Storr, A. (1989) *Freud,* Oxford University Press, Oxford.
Westen, D. (1999) *Psychology, Mind, Brain and Culture*, 2nd edn, John Wiley & Sons, Canada.

Willson, M. (1983) *Occupational Therapy in Long-Term Psychiatry*, Churchill Livingstone, Edinburgh.
Willson, M. (1996) Cognitive Change. In: *Occupational Therapy in Short-term Psychiatry* (ed. Willson, M.), Churchill Livingstone, Edinburgh.

3 THE SEVEN DIMENSIONS OF CREATIVE WORKING

INTRODUCTION

In this chapter we consider the processes which take place before, during and after creative therapy sessions, the processes which turn creative activity into therapy. When presenting any aspect of theory or practice it has to be placed within a structure. What follows is the structure we have chosen, one of seven interlinking, interdependent dimensions. This is not a hierarchy of those processes we consider most important, nor is it a chronological structure of the order in which we think things occur. What it represents is our thinking, at present, regarding a way of expressing what is occurring in this highly dynamic and creative way of working. Within the practice of creative therapies creativity does not only arise from the media we use, it is very much inherent in the way in which the therapist uses artistry to juggle, address and react to these seven dimensions of creative working.

- The Environment – the where
- Membership – the who
- Working relationships – the with
- Working processes – the how
- The Underneath – the hidden
- Making therapeutic sense – the reason
- Effectiveness – the outcome

Only by paying attention to each can the key factor of effectiveness be achieved.

We start by addressing some of the more fundamental aspects, such as the **environment** we use and the **membership** of sessions, which includes both client membership and therapist membership. We then go on to consider **working relationships**, in which we address much of the core theory of group dynamics, ground rules and leadership roles. Following this we return to the more practical issues that have to be considered in the light of these dynamics. These are the **working processes**, aspects such as the duration of sessions, the structure of sessions through a beginning, middle and end, and recording and reporting issues. We then explore some of the less tangible processes which occur **underneath** the surface of these sessions. These may not always be overt and will challenge both the therapist and the client in **making therapeutic sense** of them. However, these aspects are key to the therapeutic process. It is when working with and addressing these processes that creative activity really becomes therapy and we are truly achieving **effectiveness** in our work.

Generally we consider the seven dimensions of creative working in relation to group therapy. We have done this because creative therapies are most often conducted on a group basis due to the inherent value of groupwork and because this has been our main practical experience. However, many of the principles and processes can be applied to individual work.

We include a case study from a clinical setting, which illustrates the ways in which these dimensions thread through our work; they should not be seen as discrete parts as each informs and contributes to the whole. The case study shows the importance of paying attention to each of the processes and provides an opportunity to make each dimension explicit. Readers might find it helpful to refer to the illustrations presented at the end of each section in Chapter 5. These are illustrations of sessions which our occupational therapy students have led and participated in, and they form part of our teaching of the creative therapy approach to practice. Aspects of the seven dimensions are evident within these sessions, so they provide useful examples.

THE ENVIRONMENT

It is essential to consider the environment, which is a main tool in facilitating the practice of creative therapies. Your first thoughts when considering what 'environment' means probably focus around a room in which to work, but this term is far wider than physical space. This section will focus on environment from three main aspects:

- the wider environment, which impacts on the process of planning and carrying out a creative therapy group;
- the physical environment within which the work takes place (indoors or outside);
- the psychological environment, the abstract features that need to be present to enable this type of work to happen.

This section will explore these three aspects in depth, and will consider how they are integrated into a whole approach, thus forming the first of our seven dimensions of creative working.

At times this section will state seemingly simple detail. This is important, as there is a need for the novice practitioner to actively consider the 'minor' issues that play a role within the creation of a session. Each issue functions as a part of the interlocking jigsaw and only by paying attention to the detail will the whole be achieved.

The wider environment

Few occupational therapists work in isolation. They are usually members of a multidisciplinary team where the range of professional members have different priorities and approaches to practice. In order for creative therapies to be incorporated into the therapeutic programme offered by a service there has to be an acknowledgement of the wider environment which will affect the therapist's ability to work in this way.

It is important that the need for creative therapy is recognised by other staff members, that they support its functioning and will therefore facilitate members attending the sessions (Bertcher and Maple, 1996). Careful planning on the part of the therapist is essential at this early stage, to ensure that the intervention is understood, that there is a space in which it can take place and that there is support for it within a wider service. This support protects the outer boundary of the sessions from external sabotage (Brown, 1994), enabling them to work as planned.

Preparation ensures that a room is available on a regular basis. It is rarely possible to use a dedicated room and so negotiation must take place with other room users to ensure that the space is reserved for the session. Creative therapies require space to use the media and we have found that the consistent use of one room supports and strengthens the dynamics of the group, making familiarity of the surroundings an important aspect, particularly in the early stages of group forming. Regular access to a room involves discussion with others, who might not understand the need for this consistent approach. Only by gaining the respect and understanding of others will the value of the intervention be apparent and room usage easier to negotiate.

There is a need to consider whether creative therapies can take place in the space available. Will it affect others outside the group through noise, use of materials or simply by the time the session takes? Creative therapies have to fit not only into the programme of the surrounding environment but also into the personal programme of the programme's members. Will they be available at the chosen time, or does the session conflict with treatment by other members of the multidisciplinary team, visitors and transport arrangements? All of these factors can affect attendance and prevent a consistent approach. Careful consideration of these issues enables the sessions to fit into the therapeutic programme, an essential aspect within the planning stage.

The wider environment also impacts on the running of the creative therapy session as any intervention has a financial cost, as well as a cost in time and space. For this reason it is essential to consider the need for using creative therapies, to be clear about justifying this approach and to gain co-operation and support for this way of working. If the group is ill prepared and misunderstood, then there will be a loss of credibility and less support to use resources in this way. Active thinking at this stage prevents a static programme and ensures that the impact the intervention will make has been considered from all angles.

The physical environment

Few therapists are fortunate enough to be involved in planning and designing a room solely for creative therapies. Indeed, they are far more likely to be involved in enabling creative therapies to function successfully in multipurpose rooms, with few specific facilities. The provision of facilities has changed with the move away from institutional care, where space tended to be plentiful and dedicated rooms made up part of a large and well used department. Now an aspect of institutionalisation is avoided through using resources in the community, making use of smaller treatment centres, public rooms, church halls and other meeting rooms (Wells, 1995). These rooms may provide space in which creative therapies can take place, but they succeed as an environment only if attention is paid to the detail of working in them, so that the created space is responsive to both aspects of need: physical and psychological.

The location of the place where the creative therapies group is to function should be considered. The room needs to be easily accessible to all group members. With the increased use of community resources, public transport, parking and convenience need to be thought about. There may also be issues surrounding a person's attendance at an identified treatment area, particularly if this is within the public arena: it is important to preserve confidentiality and to understand that a group member's motivation to attend is likely to be influenced by a wide range of factors. Issues about attending a hospital, or returning to one for an intervention, may influence the location of the session. Some settings have strong memories attached to them, for instance, a group planned within a hospital environment may remind former inpatients of distressing experiences at an acute phase of their illness, making it difficult for them to return to the same place. Even a room can remind a group member of past events, and their feelings should be recognised and attended to where possible (Brown, 1994). This point is clearly illustrated by the case study, where the client was reluctant to return to the acute hospital setting. Whilst the agreed location may not be ideal for all, owning and exploring the issues which influenced the choice will play an important role within the group's work and should not remain unaddressed.

Rooms are many and various, so an essential skill when considering room use from a physical perspective is the ability to adapt. The therapist will often have little choice about the room but may have considerable opportunity to alter things, to consider how best to arrange resources to address the needs of the session. These needs will vary depending on the creative media to be used, making the imaginative use of resources doubly important.

With our students, and in recognition of constraints within a clinical environment, we plan for a single room to be used for all the indoor creative therapy sessions. This is a large room, well equipped with tables, chairs, shelves and cupboards, a sink and a linoleum floor. It can, however, be considered to be a soulless room, with hard shiny surfaces and practical furnishings, not unlike many others we have visited on clinical practice. The room gives students a starting point from which to consider their environment. First, how are they going to make the room work for the activity? Secondly, how are they going to make the activity work within the room? Creative thinking and problem-solving abilities soon come to the fore: spare furniture is stacked, tables shifted, mats brought in to allow for floor work and a general feeling of appropriate space and preparedness evolves. Finlay (1993) and Brown (1994) draw attention to the need for the physical environment to look prepared and welcoming, recognising this as an important starting point for the session.

The time boundary at both the beginning and the end of a creative therapy session influences the planning and the actual group session, but it also has important connotations regarding shared access to facilities. If others are using the room before the session, then time should be available for setting up and making the environment ready for the group's use. Equally, at the end of the session time is required to leave the room ready for others. Although these may appear obvious issues we have perhaps all made the mistake of over-zealous timetabling, thinking that we can move to another commitment without allowing time for preparing or rearranging a room. This action devalues the group's work, gives the wrong message to other room users and leaves the therapist open to criticism. In an area of work which is often misinterpreted, attention to such detail is essential, not only for effective practice but also to retain credibility and obtain co-operation from other professionals.

The size of the room influences its use, with positive and negative factors to consider (Brandler and Roman, 1991). A large room may seem daunting; members are scattered around, leading to disparate functioning of the group, and making it difficult for the therapist to retain the group's focus, direction and cohesion. A small room may provide a greater feeling of security, but can also become oppressive; too many people will overwhelm the space available. Although there may be no choice, the important issue is to consider the space and to plan its use in a way which will enhance the process rather than detract from it.

The room should provide a physically functional environment. There should be space for each person and attention should be paid to how the group members position themselves. The chosen activity will dictate certain positioning arrangements – around a table, in groups, on the floor. A room that allows a variety of arrangements will lend itself to the dynamics of creative therapy. Each new position requires some adjustment from the group members, as working groups are set up and disbanded, physical props are introduced and withdrawn. If the session is using tables, then they should be the right height for the chairs provided and should have sufficient space to allow each person to work freely. If the floor is used, then carpeting, floor cushions or mats provide a warm and comfortable physical environment which does not have the restrictions of chairs and tables. Access to the positions chosen for the activity also requires careful thought to ensure they are achievable by all. The issue of positioning was significant in the following experience. In one group a member was not able to sit on the floor and her need for a chair resulted in an isolating position. She towered above the other group members and was ignored when materials were shared or groups were reformed. Her isolation thus became both physical and psychological: she was marginalised within the session and found the experience to be both lonely and uncomfortable.

Fixtures and fittings present a different aspect of the physical environment. A sink with running water is a real bonus: this provides not only quick and easy access to water but also a clearing up area, where materials can be cleaned and stored for future use. To find a solution to the 'no sink' problem you have to be very well prepared. You need to have a supply of suitable materials ready in order not to compromise a chosen activity or lose the cohesiveness of the group as members come and go in search of the sink. It is hard to protect the physical and psychological boundaries of the session if other areas have to be accessed to enable the media to be used. This results in the outside world imposing on the process, thus reminding members of other issues and compromising the security of the group's interaction.

As most activities used within creative therapies will require some equipment or materials, then their safekeeping and storage requires attention. Lockable cupboards and dedicated shelving are useful, but in their absence the problem may be considered more creatively, especially if shared rooms are used. Storage boxes and free-standing shelf kits can provide cheap options, which have an advantage in being portable and thus storable elsewhere. A visit to the local DIY store may provide some useful ideas for alternative storage, but whatever options are used it is important that tools and materials are ready for use.

Safety is an important feature of any environment, both from a physical and a psychological view. It is obvious that the room should provide a safe physical environment, with a sensible approach to the storage and maintenance of tools. Ensure that disposable aprons and gloves are available and that there is an adequate First Aid box. Creative therapies requires more use of body parts than many approaches and it is irritating if the creativity of expression is compromised by the lack of a plaster for an injured finger. Activities which involve physical movement should be carefully thought through, especially in relation to footwear and non-slip floor surfaces. Any electrical appliances used to enhance the environment should be tested for safety. We have a professional responsibility as therapists to ensure the safety of our clients and to follow the health and safety procedures of our working areas.

The environment influences the physical boundaries of the working area. There is a need to think beyond the single room used for creative therapies. The therapist should consider the need for and availability of additional facilities such as waiting space, toilets, refreshment areas and alternative rooms which can be used if a member needs some private space. All of these issues play a part when considering the physical environment and, whilst a compromise is usually necessary, should be taken into account.

The psychological environment

Once the physical boundaries of the group have been established a psychological environment should be created to enable the group to function effectively (Aveline and Dryden, 1988). This psychological environment affects creative therapies as an intervention and includes factors which are common to most therapeutic groups. They are the elements which cannot be seen, yet need to be in place and which are just as vital to group functioning as the provision of an accessible room with suitable fixtures and fittings.

Creative therapies require privacy (Finlay, 1993). This may be obviously achieved by closing the door and displaying an 'engaged' sign. We have found in our work that, despite such precautions, sessions do get interrupted by people inadvertently opening the door and that this has a disruptive influence on our work. It is important to give a clear message to others in the surrounding environment that the group is functioning in a certain room for a certain time. If this message is ignored, then time should be spent with those who have misconstrued it. Exposing the work of the session inadvertently to outside eyes is disruptive and destroys the trust and cohesion that has been established within a safe psychological boundary.

There are times when privacy has to be assumed. One clinical area we use has open-plan space for creative therapy, as no other is available. This raised all sorts of questions in our minds and challenged our beliefs regarding the need for privacy within which the creative therapy group could function. The answer to the dilemma was apparent in the close multidisciplinary working of the unit and the respect which was evident for the different professionals working within it. Other staff and patients understood the purpose of the creative therapy group and so a safe place to function existed as if within invisible walls.

Comfort is part of the psychological environment. It is provided physically by suitable chairs and cushions but psychologically by a warm and accepting atmosphere. The state of preparedness for a group and the planning which has taken place in the pre-group stage engender this feeling: it creates a welcoming atmosphere, thus making it easier for the members to start work and to become involved in the session. People feel more valued when trouble has been taken to make 'their' environment feel attractive (Brown, 1994). Although the therapist may have little choice about the physical shape, size and content of the room, he or she may be able to influence the atmosphere of the room by providing small touches: a vase of fresh flowers, pictures, a tablecloth or brightly coloured rug all influence the environment and change a clinically impersonal room into a conducive group room. Warmth should also be apparent in the therapist as the leader of the session. Whilst acknowledging the ever-increasing stress and workload, the need for personal time management is important to enable the therapist to be present to welcome group members and protect their time for the group. These result in group members feeling valued in their own right, as they are expected and prepared for.

A feeling of psychological safety may be established by the use of ground rules, which enable members to define what they have agreed as acceptable behaviour. This gives confidence to the members, as the rules provide boundaries which are shared and understood, thus forming a safety net around the functioning of the session. This safety net will be tested throughout the life of the group but the therapist needs to ensure it remains intact to keep the sense of psychological safety. The case study illustrates that ground rules provide not only an etiquette of behaviour but also real security for members to work within. Their presence made attendance at the creative therapy group possible for the client as they were negotiated to support all the group members.

The balance of space is an important aspect to consider from a psychological perspective. The room may dictate how many members will participate in a group at any one time. This definition extends beyond the physical resources, such as the amount of available chairs, to how many people 'feel' right within the room. The need for personal space is also important. The therapist needs to consider the proximity of one person to another and the potential need for a variety of group formations. Proximity and group formation may be dictated by the activities chosen for the session; members may be required to work individually or as small groups, in pairs or all together. There should be flexibility and scope for moving around and using the balance of space appropriately to enhance and capitalise on the psychological environment.

Summary

We have raised issues concerning the wider environment, the physical environment and the psychological environment in relation to the process of a creative therapy group. However, concern for the environment should not be a static process. It may be that something is getting in the way of the group functioning and that the environment may not be conducive to the process of psychodynamic working in some way. It is important to reflect on what is happening, as a small change – such as altering the seating arrangements or presenting the media differently – may be all that is required. Our feeling is that the environment, if it is to reflect the work of the group, should never be static; it should be adapted and changed as required. This can only be achieved if the therapist is able to think flexibly, to put things into place and is prepared to change and alter arrangements to facilitate the optimal functioning of the group. The most valuable environment is created through attending to detail in such a way as to make this level of preparation almost imperceptible.

Key points

- Consideration of the environment is a fundamental stage in planning a creative therapy group
- There are three aspects to the environment which should be thought about – the wider environment, the physical environment and the psychological environment
- The wider environment includes the issues of working within a multi-disciplinary team such as gaining credibility for this approach and access to rooms and resources
- The physical environment considers the use of facilities, fixtures and fittings and aspects of safety
- The psychological environment includes the preparation, privacy and processes which need to be in place to provide the security for a group to function

MEMBERSHIP

Membership is the next dimension we choose to explore as perhaps the first active stage of planning a creative therapy group revolves around this issue – who is the group for? Our students frequently ask us this question as if there is a formula for who to include. Our answer is that each group is an individual experience; there are criteria which we need to consider but the membership is unique and each group has a life of its own. In planning the membership of a creative therapy group we need to consider not just the group members but also the practitioners who will be part of the day-to-day running of the group. The membership can be powerful in either facilitating or inhibiting the progress of a group towards its goals, so appropriate selection is very important (Benson, 1987). Selection of membership is a complicated process as many factors, which all deserve consideration, come into play but there are no hard and fast rules and no recipe for success. We will start by reviewing some of the issues of client selection and move on to address staff membership.

Client selection

In most cases the membership of a creative therapy group will be actively selected. The selection process serves to ensure that those attending the group have an identified need that will benefit from intervention through creative therapies, and which is sufficiently shared by group members for them all to gain from working together.

Aveline and Dryden (1988) suggest that most people join therapy groups because they are experiencing problems which are framed in interpersonal terms. The actual problem may take many forms but the common element is that they affect the individual's interpersonal relationships. This is the case in the practice of creative therapies, where we are principally concerned with the individual's functioning in **interpersonal relationships** and how **intrapersonal processes** may impact on this. Because of this focus on interpersonal relationships the value of group working becomes apparent as groups can be used as a microcosm for exploring interpersonal dynamics.

Whitaker (1985) suggests that in forming the membership of a group the therapist is aiming for two things:

- to include those members who are likely to benefit from the group and exclude those who may be damaged by the group or be damaging to the group;
- to form a group which provides both support and challenge to its members.

Members who are likely to benefit from a creative therapy group need to have the willingness and potential ability to explore intrapersonal and interpersonal issues through the use of creative media. They also need to be sufficiently motivated to engage in the group therapy experience as a high level of involvement is required. Although the creative therapy sessions themselves are challenging it should be acknowledged that much of the therapy achieved actually occurs outside the times of the group meeting. The group experience serves as a catalyst to thinking, enabling individuals to develop and apply it to their life outside the session. Each individual needs to be committed to taking part, thus demonstrating personal motivation to work in this way; anyone who has been 'sent' by someone else is unlikely to benefit greatly.

When considering the exclusion of those who may be damaged by, or be damaging to, the group Whitaker (1985) suggests that one needs to exclude highly vulnerable people who are unlikely to have the defences to withstand a group approach. An example might be an individual in acute crisis, as such a person is in a state of shock and will be using all their defence mechanisms and energy to get through daily life. At this stage he or she has no energy to spare for the inclusion in a psychodynamic group because their defence mechanisms are serving a useful purpose. Whitaker (1985) also suggests that one should discriminate against individuals who are very disorganised or who clearly have the potential to be disruptive. This may include a person who is confused about themselves, who is self-absorbed to the point of being largely unaware of the needs of other people or who perceives the world in a fragmented or distorted way. Yalom (1975) supports this view by suggesting the exclusion of individuals who make unrealistic demands for instant intimacy, those with a schizoid type of withdrawal from the social–emotional environment, those whose level of disclosure is inappropriate and those who have a fear of emotional contagion. This final category refers to those who are fearful of being adversely affected by the problems of other group members.

To achieve Whitaker's second aim (that of forming a group composition which provides support and challenge to the group members) one is striving to create an appropriate balance between what many texts present as the dichotomy between homogeneity and heterogeneity. **Homogeneity** means that the group members have sufficient shared needs to ensure commonality and compatibility among group members, for example in the type or severity of the presenting problem or the level of vulnerability. This homogeneity fosters the development of group cohesion. **Heterogeneity** means that there should be sufficient differences between group members to provide a stimulating and challenging environment, where group members have a range of attributes and skills which can be useful to others, thus providing the forces for change. For example, group members may use a range of ways of expressing themselves or may adopt different coping styles, enabling them to observe and learn from one another's experience. Behavioural attributes such as the role the individual is likely to take or how talkative, dominant or introverted they are likely to be within the group should also be considered (Aveline and Dryden, 1988; Benson, 1987; Brown, 1994; Whitaker, 1985). The balance in homogeneity and heterogeneity will depend on whether the primary aim of the group is to provide support or to promote change (Brown, 1994). In creative therapies our ultimate aim is usually to promote change within a sufficiently supportive environment, so we can see that the balance between homogeneity and heterogeneity might be delicate.

The selection of group membership should also take into account characteristics such as age, gender and race, ensuring that no one person is isolated and unable to identify to some extent with another group member (Finlay, 1993). There are times when mixed membership may be a very positive attribute and better than excluding someone just because they are different. The way in which this is dealt with is crucial and links back to the motivation of the individual and their willingness to be actively involved.

Another aspect to consider when selecting group members is whether any practical or external factors are likely to impinge on the experience of being included in the group. These factors might be as basic as whether the group will be meeting at a suitable time or venue to enable the individual to attend. It is obvious that an individual's commitment to a group is likely to be adversely affected if they have to make complicated arrangements at work or drive across the city centre at rush hour in order to attend. These issues need to be raised before a member commits to the group, as at this stage compromises can be explored and changes made. However, a level of commitment is required and most potential members who are sufficiently motivated will be prepared to deal with some inconvenience in order to attend the sessions.

We stated in Chapter 1 that creativity is a core element which exists on four levels: one of these is especially pertinent in informing the selection process – **creativity exists within each individual involved in the creative therapy process.** In selecting members for creative therapy groups we have to consider whether the potential member will benefit from using creativity as a tool to help them explore their issues. Often this approach is useful for people who find verbalising problems difficult. The creative medium offers a third party to the therapist/client relationship (Hagedorn, 1992; Hagedorn, 1995) and can provide a vehicle for the individual to express themselves, helping them to find the words to frame their situation, or offering an alternative medium where words seem difficult to access (for whatever reason).

Each client will have an individual response to the different creative media. There is no universal guide for this and no way of predicting what the individual client's response will be. The decision to use or exclude any medium should be explored with the client. An obvious consideration in creative therapies relates to the individual who has a particular skill with a specific medium such as art or music. Sometimes it can be difficult for an individual with more traditional skills in a medium to throw away the rules and use the medium freely in the way required in creative therapies. It is important to remember that the focus of the session is on the process of the work rather than on producing an end product. Alternatively, the person might have used the medium successfully in the past to express themselves on an emotional level so it is useful or reassuring to use this familiar medium again in creative therapies. The ease with which a medium is used for expression is highly individual. A very visual person may respond well to the use of paper and paint, whilst a more physical person will interact through the use of body and movement. Part of the initial interview for group inclusion will involve finding out what sorts of activities the client does in their life and what they have found helpful in the past. This will assist in the selection process as it builds a rich picture of each individual.

We have seen that establishing an appropriate group membership involves taking a number of factors into consideration and that there is no formula for selection criteria. We have suggested some general principles and pointed out that the skills of the therapist in assessment and helping the client to clarify personal aims are paramount. However, once the therapist has become familiar with this way of working, a great deal will rest on an intuitive feeling that a particular individual will fit well within a group, benefiting and contributing to it.

We now need to discuss how, in practice, the therapist conducts this selection process. The most common way is through referral and the pre-group interview.

Referral and the pre-group interview

The way in which referrals are received for a creative therapies group will depend to some extent on the service in which the therapist is based. This in turn will affect how the planned group is advertised. It is important to be as clear as possible about the purpose and intentions of the group and the inclusion and exclusion criteria. Clarity at this stage will ensure the most appropriate referrals. Following receipt of a referral for the group the therapist will make an initial judgement about its appropriateness and will then engage in some form of pre-group interview with the prospective member.

The pre-group interview can take many forms depending on the setting and system in which the therapist works. In some places there is a clearly identifiable and fairly structured process; a specific referral for the group is received, the individual is sent an appointment for a pre-group interview and from this the decision is taken about inclusion. Alternatively, a more general referral might be received by the service as a whole, the patient is seen for an initial interview and from this a range of interventions which might include involvement in a creative therapy group will be considered. A third form of pre-group interview is where the service or the therapist might already know the patient and through this prior knowledge suggest inclusion in the group. In this instance no specific or identifiable 'interview' may take place but the objectives of the pre-group interview will have been achieved through an informal and unstructured process over an undefined time scale.

Benson (1987) suggests that the objectives of the pre-group interview are:

- For the therapist to introduce himself or herself to the potential group member. How much information it is appropriate to offer here will need to be considered.
- To provide information about the group and its purpose. This will include practical information such as the time and venue as well as information on how the group will run and what is likely to be expected of participants.
- To relate the purpose of the group to the prospective member's perception of need. As discussed earlier there should be some commonality of need among the group members; in this way there will be a shared group purpose to work towards meeting those individual and collective goals.
- Possibly to negotiate an individual contract with the prospective group member. This may involve identifying specific outcomes that the individual wishes to achieve through the creative therapy experience or might focus on setting ground rules for involvement in the group. The negotiation may be achieved through verbal agreement or it might be supported by written statements. The process of negotiation, involving both the therapist and the client, is important within this client-centred approach. It assures ownership of

outcome and assists the group member to develop a sense of active involvement.

The pre-group interview is likely to take the form of a semi-structured discussion and will probably be conducted by the person who will be the leader or facilitator of the group. If there is going to be a co-therapist in the group he or she may also participate or another professional, such as the client's key worker or a student, might be involved. Involving two professionals can be of value as they will bring different perspectives to the interview and will both be able to contribute to the decision regarding inclusion. However, a balance always has to be struck and a client should not be overwhelmed by the presence of professionals.

The pre-group interview should be a two-way process between the prospective group member and the therapist or therapists involved. It should provide the therapists with enough information to decide how the prospective member will fit into the composition of the group and whether inclusion would be appropriate. It should help the prospective member prepare for the group experience by providing an opportunity to raise and explore any anxieties, curiosities or expectations. Having received adequate information about the group the prospective member should be encouraged to play a role in the selection process, exploring whether they think the group may be of value to them (Whitaker, 1985; Yalom, 1975). This is very important as it fosters a sense of self-responsibility as well as an expectation of taking an active role, both of which are important processes in creative therapy. Yalom (1975) also suggests that it is much better for a client to self-deselect before entering the group than for them, and the group, to undergo the discomfort of dropping out.

The issue of membership can make us question whether there is a clear understanding of this strategy, as was evident in the example below.

> In the final stage of the undergraduate course, creative therapies is an optional experience, and we can usually predict fairly accurately who will join us for it. One year the group membership was very different from expectations, and we wondered if the purpose of the experience had been misconstrued. We decided to ask the members to identify and then share their personal aims for attending creative therapies, using time within the session to do this. The process ensured that the students developed explicit aims, and therefore understood the opportunity which creative therapy offers. A similar strategy could be used within a clinical environment. Although the selection process will consider individual aims, it is useful to return to them from the client's perspective, encouraging ownership of the aims by stating them to the other group members.

Open/closed groups

One aspect of group membership, which has to be decided at the planning stage of creative therapies, is whether it is to be an open group or a closed group.

Open groups allow members to join and leave at any stage within the life of the group. The length of membership is primarily determined by need; new members join when there is a vacancy and leave when their difficulty is resolved or their situation alters to make membership no longer appropriate. The time span over which the group meets may be set in advance, for example eight weeks, or it may be indeterminate. Open groups allow members to work at their own pace and can take account of the differing severity of problems of the various members. Open groups can also have the advantage of providing an opportunity for newcomers to see where those who have been attending for a while have progressed to and, conversely, for those who have been attending for some time to judge how much progress they have made (Aveline and Dryden, 1988; Benson, 1987; Finlay, 1993). Through evolving group membership, open groups can also offer a real variety of resources and skills as each new member brings different attributes. The changing membership can be useful in helping members work on issues of initiating and terminating relationships as well as issues of change, adaptability, separation and moving on. Balanced against these advantages, a group with changing membership can inevitably result in less stability and predictability. This in turn makes it difficult to achieve depth and intimacy of relationships within the group (Benson, 1987). However, if appropriate, it can be possible to achieve an acceptable balance by engineering a slow evolution of the group membership.

In **closed groups** members make a commitment to stay together for the life of the group, which is usually for a predetermined number of sessions. In reality there are often some changes in group membership because people break this commitment or circumstances interfere with attendance. Despite this, closed groups provide a stable, more secure and cohesive group environment in which increased levels of trust can be developed (Aveline and Dryden, 1988). Disadvantages of closed groups are that there can be a strong tendency to conform with the group, they lack the variety of open groups and may provide less opportunity to deal with issues of change, adaptability and termination (Benson, 1987). The termination of the closed group itself can be a problem, as members may be reluctant to give up the security and stability which the group offers. The therapist should be aware of this risk and address the ultimate termination of the group throughout its lifespan.

A variation to the open/closed group format is what Brown (1994) terms **re-formed groups**. In these, the group meets for an agreed period with a set group of members and no new members are allowed to join. At the end of the agreed period the group breaks for a number of weeks and later re-forms, with some members from the original group and some new members. This format offers a useful combination of the advantages of both open and closed groups. It offers a set point of discharge for those who have met their needs and an opportunity for those who are still benefiting from the group to continue. An agreed point of breaking the group for review can also be a useful advantage over open groups, where there can be a tendency for members to continue attending without specifically reviewing their individual progress and needs.

Creative therapy groups may adopt any one of these formats. The choice will be influenced by a number of factors, which include the setting in which the therapist works, the needs of the client group and the availability of therapists. Consideration of the appropriate format is very important as it will significantly affect the potential level of functioning and thus the effectiveness of the group.

Size of the group

Just as constancy of membership can affect the degree of cohesiveness and trust which develops in a group so too can the size of the group. It is commonly suggested that, for therapy groups with an emphasis on self-disclosure, intimacy and support, membership should be in the range of five to ten members (Benson, 1987; Finlay, 1993; Yalom, 1975). At this size the group is small enough to be intimate and safe yet large enough to operate as a group.

If the group is too large members might get 'lost' within it; it can be more difficult to draw out quieter members and communication can be inhibited. However, with fewer than five members there is a tendency for interaction to diminish and for the therapist to find themselves engaged in individual therapy with members within the group (Yalom, 1975). Closed groups might start with a slightly higher number, allowing for the potential loss of some members (Yalom, 1975). Practical factors should also be taken into account – for example, as the size of the group increases more time will required for activities and discussion and may have implications on the size of the room needed, equipment and staff resources (Finlay, 1993).

Staff membership

In discussing group membership we also need to consider staff membership issues. A major point here is that of **co-leadership.** The decision to work within a co-leadership relationship needs to be considered very carefully. On face value, and particularly to an inexperienced practitioner, it could be viewed as easier to plan and run a group in which the responsibility is shared. In some instances this may be the case but co-leadership is a sophisticated way of working, which can be very effective and rewarding if successful. However, it can lead to ineffective or even damaging group work and can undermine the confidence of both the leaders and the group members if it is not properly planned and practised. Co-leadership is also an expensive option – it involves two therapists in a group – and this has to be justified.

Much of the success of co-leadership depends upon the partnership. On a fundamental level the two leaders need to like and feel comfortable with one another and should respect the contribution that the other has to make (Finlay, 1993).

When deciding on co-leadership the following issues need to be considered:

- The most appropriate pattern of co-leadership for the therapists involved and the group. The therapists need to consider whether to take equal responsibility or for one to take a more dominant role (Finlay, 1993).

- The gender mix of the leaders (Brown, 1994). This may be a significant factor in some groups – for example a 'Mother's Group' – while in others it is unimportant.
- The status of the two leaders. It is often more appropriate for the leaders to have equal status and experience as difficulties can arise if group members perceive an inequality (Finlay, 1993). An exception to this might be within a learning role, where one leader is gaining valuable experience through an opportunity to co-lead with a more experienced therapist although accepting less responsibility.
- The skills and personality of the leaders should not fully duplicate one another. In the co-leader relationship the aim is to achieve a difference in role, life experiences, group work skills, knowledge and ideas. In this way the group benefits from the variety of attributes and skills and the two leaders gain from mutual feedback and stimulation (Finlay, 1993).
- The beliefs, values and theoretical stances of the co-leaders should complement each other (Finlay, 1993).

Many of the above issues are particularly significant when considering a co-leadership relationship with someone from another professional group. Sometimes we might run a creative therapies group with a creative arts therapist or a psychiatric nurse, for example. Here professional socialisation issues need addressing as we tend to run groups differently and would certainly approach using creative therapies from a different perspective.

Developing the co-leader relationship needs to be an integral part of the planning stage of the group. Each leader needs to be clear about the purpose and style of the group and their own role and contribution within it. Many co-leaders, particularly those who are unfamiliar with working together, use the supervision process to help them prepare for this way of working. Supervision provides an opportunity for the co-leaders to explore how they feel about working with one another, to address any anxieties and to confirm potential roles and contributions.

Throughout the life of the group the co-leader relationship needs careful nurturing. At regular intervals time should be set aside for communication, sharing ideas and feelings and providing one another with feedback and support. It is essential that the two leaders should be willing to discuss conflicts and to engage in open and frank communication with one another, a process which can be assisted through effective supervision.

From this it can be seen that co-leadership is not an easy option but one which may be very rewarding and which can help to develop the therapeutic skills of the leaders if communication and reflection on practice take place. Successful co-leadership will also be advantageous to the group. The presence of two leaders not only offers a variety of style, personality and attributes but also provides professional support. This is particularly useful in times of unease as the presence of two leaders enables one to focus on an individual member while the other holds the group together. A second advantage of co-leadership is the opportunity to explore how the two leaders perceive the group experience, which in turn allows for a more credible evaluation of the group. It might be that the two leaders hold different perceptions. This is not a negative outcome but rather opens up new avenues for exploration, as these differences may be explored within the group or kept within the co-leader relationship. The exploration of these different perceptions will help to increase the effectiveness of the group.

Another aspect of staff membership which needs to be discussed is the presence of students. Many health professionals work in settings which are involved in taking students on clinical experience. There are times when it is appropriate to involve a student in a creative therapy group, whether it takes an open or closed group format, if the length of their clinical experience enables them to offer the necessary level of commitment. If students are included on a supernumerary basis the staff to patient ratio needs to be carefully considered to ensure that there is still an appropriate balance. The student may gain experience as a co-leader, especially if a final-year student, in which case the issues outlined above, particularly the one relating to status, need to be regarded.

The presence of any colleagues who are not actively involved in the group raises some issues. This may occur in certain clinical settings, perhaps where patients need an escort to the group for security reasons. Generally one should avoid the presence of any staff members who are not willing to actively engage in the group as fully as possible within the constraints of their other responsibilities. This is not always easy to achieve, especially when working across professional boundaries, but obviously someone sitting on the periphery of a group watching proceedings is likely to be off-putting and detrimental to creativity and the potential group experience.

We practise a system of co-leadership in our work with students. Each of us has a background in mental health, but we bring different skills to our sessions. We both have experience of working in this way, but one of us is a sound theorist and the other is more of an 'ideas' person. In collaboration we make a team, as each works to the strength of the other. We use our different approaches to extend the opportunities that arise from this way of working. We are also able to rely on each other for support, but we particularly value the reflections that we share after the sessions, where we explore what went on and where the experience might be going.

Leaving the group

Issues surrounding leaving the group need careful consideration. What these issues are will depend on whether the departure is planned and possibly collective, as might occur in a closed group, or an unexpected departure of an individual. In open groups a steady turnover of membership is a feature and the opportunity to deal with this is an advantage of this format. However, even in closed groups some members may want to leave before the agreed end and on occasions one of the leaders has to leave.

In a closed group, where the life has been agreed in advance, this must be adhered to except in exceptional circumstances. The termination of the group should be addressed throughout its life and in the final few sessions this emphasis should increase, the focus of the sessions being on leaving the group and moving forwards. The last session will focus on issues of leaving, with the therapist helping the group members to consolidate their experience. We discuss more fully the whole issue of endings, and how to facilitate them, in Chapter 7.

If the situation involves an individual person leaving, ideally they will give some notice of their intention and should be encouraged to discuss their departure within the group (Hyde, 1988). An individual leaving a group can be a very powerful and demanding experience for both the person concerned and the group members who are left behind. The departure may bring to the fore issues of rejection or abandonment in other areas of life and creative therapies provide a forum for addressing these issues. If an individual leaves unexpectedly with little or no explanation of their reasons, or with some kind of blame placed on the group, these issues may be particularly significant.

The situation of a therapist having to leave should not occur in a closed group except in very exceptional circumstances; however, it does happen and this issue might also arise in open groups which can have a lengthy life. If the therapist has to leave, it is preferable for them to give some warning and offer an explanation for their departure so that group members have an opportunity to disengage with the therapist. If possible, the new therapist should be introduced and have an opportunity to work alongside the therapist who will be leaving for one or two sessions.

Summary

The effectiveness of creative therapy as an intervention is dependent on the careful selection of those who will be working together. There is no recipe to ensure that membership selection is successful but careful consideration of key issues such as client selection, format, size, staffing and continuity will facilitate the process. Membership links with environment in informing the process of creative therapies, and therefore forms another of the dimensions of creative working which we have chosen to explore.

Key points

- Interpersonal problems are usually the identified issue which influences membership selection
- Membership of a group should be selective, to include those who will benefit from the creative therapy approach
- A balance will be sought between homogeneity and heterogeneity
- Clients need to be capable of using creative media to work through their issues
- The pre-group interview should be a two-way process between the therapist(s) and the client

- Open groups and closed groups offer different characteristics which need to be considered when planning a group
- Attention should be paid to the optimum size of the group
- The decision to work in a co-leader relationship requires careful consideration and the relationship needs nurturing
- Issues surrounding members leaving the group should be addressed within the group

WORKING RELATIONSHIPS

This third dimension explores the relationships within creative therapies. We have considered the environment that must be in place to enable intervention to take place and we have considered the issues which influence the formation of creative therapy groups: now we need to move on to thinking about the interpersonal activity which must occur to allow creative working to become effective. This activity will concern the roles of the key players – the therapist and the group members – but it will go beyond this to address less tangible factors which facilitate a working relationship; issues of trust, confidentiality, disclosure and security.

We should begin by defining what we mean by working relationships. A relationship implies a sense of connection, an association, one to another. Relationships are the currency with which we work. They are the focus for the dynamic interpersonal exchanges, the 'living part' of the group. Think for a moment of any group with which you have been involved – this thought will immediately remind you of the people, the interactions, the things which took place. You will be able to recapture some of the energy and sense of involvement. The process is complex; interactions are happening on a number of levels and each situation takes on an identity of its own. It is this energy which makes each group unique, which cannot be exactly recreated. Although this energy is a vital part of the group processes it needs to be contained so that it can be used effectively in a therapeutic way. There is a need to 'know where one is' within any group, to feel a sense of security and safety to allow the relationships to develop, to explore, change and grow with the experience. Relationships require a safety net in therapeutic use, a structure which wraps around the process people are engaged in, making the space safe for interaction. This safety net enables the group to develop trust – trust in each other, trust in the therapist and trust in the process of the work.

At the first meeting of a creative therapies group the key players have been identified but the process has not really begun. As the group begins to function interaction takes place, supported by the structure which defines a safe boundary for the group's work. At this time, as it shifts from the planning stage to the active stage, the group becomes dynamic, using relationships as its force. We are not concerned here with the ways in which we use media to facilitate group action, this is addressed in Chapter 5, but we are concerned with the action that develops through relationships. What are these relationships about, who makes them and what needs to be in place to facilitate their happening?

The working relationships of a creative therapy group are multifaceted. An understanding of the group process enables us to see that the therapist develops working relationships both within the group, internally interacting with the group members and the co-therapist and externally with other professionals. At the same time the group members develop internal relationships with other members and the therapist, but they also have working relationships which reach outside the group boundary. This becomes a complicated picture, with the group at the centre, providing the forum for all these connecting relationships – see Figure 3.1.

To see how these take place we need to examine the roles of each in greater detail.

External working relationships of the therapist

Externally the therapist is communicating and connecting beyond the boundary of the group with other involved professionals who need to understand and respect the group process and the work of the individuals within the group. However, they are not involved in running the group or the minutiae of the sessions. (Here we are referring to other professionals who are involved with the group members – the psychiatrist, the general practitioner, the nurse or the social worker, for example.) Feedback to, and liaison with, these professionals ensures

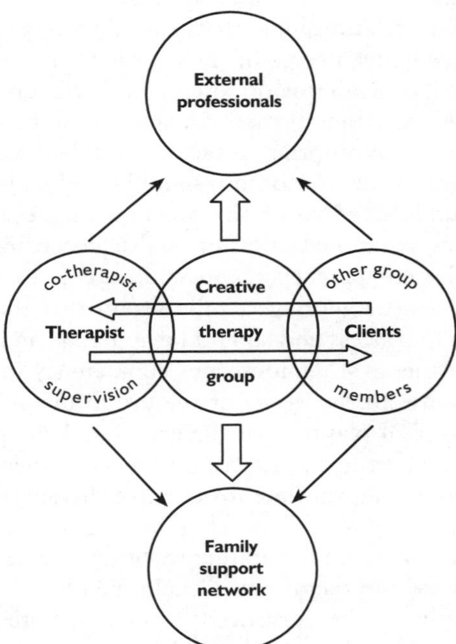

Figure 3.1 The multifaceted working relationships of a creative therapy group

that the group process is evaluated in relation to the client. The role of the therapist here will be as a communicator who ensures that connections are made to those who need to know. It is the responsibility of the therapist to explain the intentions and the process of the group, so that it can be understood and respected. The therapist is engaged in using the general skills suggested by Brown (1994) of reporting on the group creation, its maintenance, its achievements and the unique culture which it has developed. This task links back to some of the issues about the environment, where respect was gained from others to enable the group to function. This external communication may take place as a face-to-face encounter, by attending case reviews and ward rounds, or through written reporting on the work of the group.

The need for this level of external communication reflects the fact that no therapist works in isolation with clients and that each group member will be supported by a multidisciplinary team. Relationships to and from the team ensure that everyone is kept informed and that a full clinical picture of the client is available.

Internal working relationships of the therapist

Here we consider the issues of leadership, co-working and supervision. These are all working relationships of the therapist which fall inside the boundary of the group.

Qualities of leadership

The internal working relationships that the therapist develops all have a connection to the group members. In most groups, the usual function of the therapist is as the leader, facilitator or conductor of the group – the position the group members expect the therapist to take. Leadership, with its specific tasks and qualities, becomes an appropriate professional role which connects the group members and the therapist. A relationship should develop, built upon the security of the role and an understanding of the function of the role within the group process. The qualities of good leadership skills, according to Benson (1987), focus around three C's: competency, compassion and commitment.

Competency gives a clear message to the group that they can trust both the therapist and the group process and should be apparent on a number of levels. In the first instance, the therapist demonstrates competency in creating the concept of the group in response to the needs of the group members. This competency will extend to the physical planning of the group and the practical details to be addressed. It will then move to the selection process, ensuring that those who are selected for the group are appropriate for creative therapies. As the group begins to function this competency will allow relationships to develop as the skill of the therapist in communicating and facilitating the group process becomes apparent. Throughout this process the therapist will help members to work towards their individual goals. Finally the therapist needs to demonstrate competency with the selected creative media (this refers to the safe and effective handling of the media rather than to specific expertise). A sense of familiarity with the group process and the activities within it will instil a feeling of confidence in the group members, a feeling of competency of practice.

Compassion refers to the relationships which are established with all the group members, including the co-therapist if present. This extends to recognising that each member plays a unique role within the group and that, although each person's ability to contribute will be different, everyone has a significant place within the group. Through achieving a secure relationship the leader is able to observe and recognise when a group member is finding the process difficult, when they may be feeling marginalised or ignored by others. This skill includes working with a co-leader, recognising times when the co-leader's role may be difficult, acknowledging and valuing their contribution, and feeling comfortable working together. Compassion is an extended observation skill, demonstrating an awareness of the distress or discomfort of others, and the ability to unify the group whilst recognising and acknowledging the worth of the individual.

Commitment to the group is evident in different ways. There are the practical levels of commitment, where the therapist makes the group a priority, attending on time and being suitably prepared. There is the emotional commitment which seeks active engagement with the work of the group and through which the leader devotes the time to focus on group interactions, putting other issues aside for the duration. Benson (1987) reminds us of the need to believe in what we are doing. If the therapist doubts the group process, or shows an ambivalent attitude when introducing the activity of the group, then this will quickly result in anxiety and lack of security for the group members. The leader needs to instil a feeling of confidence through appearing committed to the activities which the group is to undertake, and therefore nothing should be introduced that has unclear intentions. Only by thinking through the purpose and worth of the activity selected can the therapist present it with confidence, knowing what can be achieved by it. As leaders, we may find ourselves introducing activities that raise our own anxieties and feelings of self-consciousness. Later in the group process this may be an appropriate feeling to share with members, but only when the group is firmly established.

We would add a fourth C to Benson's list: **communication**. To be a good communicator is a fundamental quality for any leader, one so obvious that it risks being unstated. Indeed, communication skills are more often commented on when they are lacking than when they are being effectively used. In our work with students we have observed incidents where a student's leadership style showed hesitant, apologetic communication, which failed to generate commitment in the group, or authoritative communication which prevented the group members from functioning for themselves. Muddled communication leads to anxiety and lack of purpose, whilst an excessive amount by the leader limits the interactions which the members can make. The right amount of communication, carried out in an appropriate manner, gains the confidence of the group, allows the feeling of trust to develop and eases the work of the group.

As the leader of the group the therapist also communicates non-verbal messages to the group through appearance, dress, manner and expression

(Brown, 1994; Yalom, 1975). The way the therapist presents himself or herself to the group conveys personal messages, which are seen by group members in relation to their worth. Arriving for the session looking untidy and scruffy may convey an unprofessional image or may be translated as not being bothered with the group. Facial and body expressions also give clear clues to the way the therapist is feeling. Leadership skills involve developing an awareness of both verbal and non-verbal messages.

Appropriate use of competency, commitment, compassion and communication promotes the growth of working relationships between the therapist, the co-therapist and the group members. Confidence grows on all sides and the roles of the leader, the co-therapist and the group members develop and are better understood.

Roles of leadership

Ratigan and Aveline (1988) have developed a comprehensive list of the major functions of the group leader in interpersonal groups. The leader takes the following roles.

Establish and sustain the group boundaries

This is seen as creating the structure of the group, the selection of members, room allocation, time, frequency, type of group. The leader is creating the space for the group to happen, taking responsibility for its initial creation and sustaining boundaries to allow the group to continue.

Model and maintain a therapeutic group culture

The leader's role is to enable the group to function in a therapeutic way. Not only is the leader responsible for providing a role model for the group, using observable behaviour and interactive skills, but he or she also maintains the working of the group by ensuring that it is shaped towards its stated purpose. The therapeutic group culture is achieved by paying attention to interpersonal interactions. The leader should ensure that the creative media used make these interactions easier and that they happen in a way which is acceptable to all group members, meeting the remit of the group process and working towards the achievement of personal aims.

Provide an understanding of the events of the session

The leader's role is to watch, listen and think about the group process in order to develop an understanding of the meaning of events as they occur (Whitaker, 1985). This process is easier for the leader as they are taking a different role from the group members, they have a different level of personal involvement and are able to more objectively observe the whole picture. The skills of a co-therapist are valuable here, as he or she is also able to offer an interpretation of what has occurred. For the group member the meanings tend to be more subjective, limited in part to their personal involvement, and may not reflect the whole event. From a rather more external stance, the leader can help to explore and share the meanings of the processes the group engages in.

Note and reward member gain

Creative therapies, like all interpersonal groups, are about facilitating self-growth and self-discovery. To do this the group members take individual risks which lead to change. The leader should be alert to this risk taking and provide the opportunity for it to happen, offering support and encouragement. He or she should recognise that the process of change is a difficult one and provide verbal and non-verbal messages to help group members take the risks involved in achieving self-growth.

Encourage members to take responsibility for their actions

Therapeutic groups operate on two levels at the same time. One level relates to the aims of the group as a collective process, the other relates to the aims of the individuals within the group. Members are therefore responsible for maintaining the process of the group through active, purposeful involvement. They are also expected to take responsibility for their individual learning; part of the development that occurs through a group process concerns taking responsibility for oneself. For some members this will be a new and scary concept, one which will take some time to adjust to. If the leader instils feelings of security and trust within the group, then the atmosphere encourages members to take this step, to expose themselves therapeutically rather than seek anonymity within the shadows of others.

Predict (and possibly prevent) undesirable developments

Groups are always unpredictable. The most skilful and experienced leader will on occasion be surprised by an outcome and will reflect afterwards about the chain of events that led to the development. The leader's role is helped by returning to Whitaker's (1985) key points of watching, listening and thinking to explore the meaning of the event. It is important to acknowledge that the undesirable can and does happen in group processes, as it does in other areas of life. Strategies can be learned to prepare for, and to develop learning through, an unexpected process. Undesirable events do not always result in a negative outcome; they can be worked with and turned around by a skilled therapist, so that they become a useful experience for the group.

Involve silent members

This is a tricky issue within any group, as there will always be a difference in the amount which individual members contribute. Inappropriate verbal contributions that need to be addressed extend beyond silence and can be recognised on three levels:

- Firstly there is the very vocal contribution of those group members who like to take a central role and perhaps dominate the proceedings.
- There is a middle position, where members are engaged and participating in the group process, but who do not make a verbal contribution. They may be gaining from the dynamics of the group, but feel unable to seize an oppor-

tunity to speak, to risk voicing their feelings. This is the position occupied by Ann in the case study presented at the end of this chapter.
- Finally there are those members who remain silent, who are present physically but are not engaged with the process and who make no contribution.

The role of the leader is to use the group to address these levels of communication. The leader takes an active role in facilitating change in communication, helping group members to recognise their behaviour by encouraging appropriate involvement. Behaviour can be reflected back to the individual, enabling them to understand that they are habitually using one level of communication and introducing the opportunity to change. Thus the vocal member should be encouraged to make space for others, to recognise the value of listening to and respecting their contributions. The silent but engaged member is encouraged to contribute through verbal participation and given the opportunity to do so. The role of the silent group member who finds involvement difficult is explored, as their silence may signify a number of complex messages.

Group cohesiveness and instillation of hope
Two other roles of the leader which Ratigan and Aveline (1988) suggest concern group cohesiveness and the instillation of hope. Cohesiveness will be addressed in this dimension of working as one of the factors which relates to the internal working relationships of the group. The instillation of hope is referred to later in the chapter, being one of Yalom's (1975) eleven curative factors within group work.

All of these factors play a part within creative therapies. They link to the effective use of the intervention and strengthen the role of the therapist in furthering the work of the group.

Self-disclosure within leadership
One area that often presents a dilemma for practitioners, and which is something our students tend to raise, is the issue of self-disclosure. Therapists need to bring something of themselves to the therapy situation or they risk appearing detached and insincere to the client group. Self-disclosure concerns the appropriate level of personal contribution, using ourselves in our work. The use of oneself is something we have suggested as fundamental to the practice of creative therapies, but the leader always has to decide how much to disclose within an individual situation. Brown (1994) suggests that self-disclosure can take three forms:

- **'Here and now' disclosures** usually consist of comments or feelings about the group or about individual members within it. This type of disclosure can be very useful in helping the group to develop an analytic and reflective approach to the group processes.
- **'There and then'** disclosures tend to be about past experiences.
- **Self-disclosure about personal values or beliefs.**

The last two types of self-disclosure should be considered very carefully before being offered because they bring something personal into the group, and can result in group members focusing on the therapist's situation or beliefs rather than their own. A fundamental rule of self-disclosure is that it should always be used to help members achieve their personal goals (Brown, 1994).

The level of self-disclosure varies in different situations as it is not a learned technique but relies on the intuition of the therapist. It is influenced by issues such as the length of time the group has been working together, how well the group is functioning, and how comfortable the therapist feels within the situation. There are times when the amount of self-disclosure offered by group members leads to a feeling of obligation on the part of the leader to share in meaningful disclosures. However, there is an important distinction between the disclosures within a friendship role and those within a therapeutic role. At all times the therapist should feel comfortable with the amount and level of personal disclosure, ensuring that it is purposeful and enhances the working of the group. As this relates to the way we use ourselves within creative therapies we will return to this topic in Chapter 4 when considering the art of the therapist.

Working relationships with a co-therapist

It is important that the working relationships between the group leader and the co-leader facilitate the group process, and this will form part of the decision to work in this way. The advantages of a successful co-working relationship relate to the ways in which they further the work of the group, through effective involvement, provision of support and the opportunity to develop professional skills (Finlay, 1993). The relationships that develop between leader and co-therapist roles will work with these advantages, using the different skills and contributions to enhance the group process. By involving another person at a leadership level there is a greater opportunity to share understandings and reflections of the events that take place within the group, all of which contribute to the effectiveness of working in this way. There are practical issues which reflect good working relationships; for instance, one can lead in the absence of the other as both are fully conversant with the group's work and each can support the other, both during and after the group process. The co-therapist relationship will enhance the use of creative therapies as an intervention, as this approach can be particularly challenging and testing to a therapist working alone.

Supervision

Working as a leader within a therapeutic group is demanding of professional and personal skills. One aspect of our work that enables us to address our own needs is that of supervision, a process which provides both support and the opportunity to learn. Supervision is a relationship that is specifically established to provide an opportunity to talk through, and reflect upon, the experience of working within the group. It can be provided in a number of ways, but it is important to ensure that supervision is in place. This encourages good practice, which in turn protects the interests of the members of the group.

Although supervision can be provided by a professional who is outside the therapeutic group, we still consider it to be a working relationship within the boundaries of the group as it is primarily concerned with the group processes. Supervision may take place on a one-to-one basis, between a group of professionals who are working in similar ways or through peer support, using a co-therapist. The supervision relationship offers encouragement whilst sharing some of the responsibilities of the work. During supervision there is time to talk through exactly what is happening within the group, to explore difficulties, question actions and reflect upon the process. This sharing enables a sense of perspective to emerge; it helps the therapist to test out thoughts and suggestions and allows different interpretations to be made. The process may also focus on the needs of the therapist, rather than the needs of the group, enabling them to be made explicit so that they are acknowledged and can be worked with. These needs might include inner conflicts, hidden feelings or the need for psychological refreshment and nourishment (Benson, 1987).

Whatever the style of supervision, it encourages the development of therapeutic competence and enables the leader to receive personal support. Planning for the process of supervision in the early stages of the group is important as it requires time and space, so there are financial and practical costs to consider. Planning for individual supervision sessions is also important: it can be useful to make a note of issues to be discussed and set an agenda. The use of a reflective journal can enhance the process as it enables the therapist to take control of the opportunity by identifying and then working with those needs which have been made explicit.

It is now appropriate to consider the relationships that are present for the group members – relationships between group members but also extending to others outside the group.

Working relationships of the group members

The relationships the group members develop with each other, with the group as a whole and with the therapist contribute material which informs this dimension of working. It is useful to observe who communicates with whom, and whether any members seem isolated or marginalised. These practical observations give clues about personal relationships, which may be reflected in the group's internal process. In some groups, as in our work with the students, friendships are very apparent and a 'pecking order' is quick to emerge. However, in therapeutic groups the members may be strangers to each other, and the therapist the only person who knows each group member, so the relationships that emerge are different. As friendships develop and relationships between group members become more explicit there is a need to protect the working of the group, to ensure that it has a structure and boundary between it and the outside world. This is a stage where members may suggest meeting outside the group, an initiative which can be healthy and desirable, but which raises difficulties in defining how to leave the work of the group behind. Clear ground rules can help the members to understand and respect the need for confidentiality, providing a firm boundary for any interaction outside group meetings.

Roles

All group members have roles or functions that affect the working relationships of any group, including creative therapy groups. Benson (1987) defines a role as 'a series of actions which guide and determine our behaviour, according to what is expected of us in a certain situation' (p. 68).

Just as in life we have many roles (mother, teacher, daughter, etc.) so the group situation gives an opportunity for different roles to be enacted and explored. For the therapist to understand these roles we need to return to the principles of gaining meaning from a situation – watch, listen and think (Whitaker, 1985). In this way we can see how role-playing connects to the working relationships developing in the group. All roles the group members take are functional and are commonly categorised as task roles, maintenance roles and individual roles (Finlay, 1993; Howe and Schwartzberg, 1986).

The **task roles** of a group are defined as those which facilitate group effort. Finlay (1993) considers that these roles are taken by members who bring suggestions, ask questions, check out their understanding, try new ideas and look at what the group is accomplishing. These roles energise the group, moving it forward. An example might be where the group members are involved in planning their own programme. In their final year, our students join us in planning a series of creative therapy sessions, an exercise that is dependent on them having ideas, sharing suggestions, listening to and acknowledging the needs of others whilst developing a specific programme. There may be incidences in your own experience which provide examples of when the group process used task roles and action took place.

The **maintenance roles** are focused on the interactions within the group in relation to the feelings that are being expressed as the group unfolds. Roles here encompass the encourager, the mediator, the compromiser and the follower (Finlay, 1993; Howe and Schwartzberg, 1986). These roles are part of the group functioning; they are often positive roles which assist in engaging the group with the activity, as they facilitate working together and therefore develop the group process.

Individual roles refer to roles that address the specific needs of each group member rather than roles which relate to the whole group function. Examples of these are the playboy, the blocker, the dominator, the recognition seeker, the aggressor and the self-confessor (Finlay, 1993; Howe and Schwartzberg, 1986). All of these roles involve using the group process to address a personal need, some part of the personality which is being played into the group process. Individual roles tend to be more negative, reflecting the fact that the group members have been selected for a specific purpose and interpersonal groups do tend to explore roles and relationships which are unfulfilling and detrimental to the individual.

The action of the group will be to recognise specific behaviours and to confront rather than challenge a role which is being played consistently. This action will help the role player to address the behaviour and the underlying need which dictates the action. Some roles may be problematic as they exert a considerable influence on the group process. For example, the member who constantly jokes about issues may be relieving commonly felt tensions in the early stage of the group's life, but this behaviour becomes irritating as the group gains cohesiveness. Then joking may be an avoidance strategy, used to prevent the recognition of other issues, both for the individual and the group. Others who are ready to address issues may resent this role and the relationships that have developed between members become the pathway for exposing and changing behaviour.

Making roles explicit

We are used to working with our students, and before an initial session of creative therapies we were concerned that we were allocating roles to them almost subconsciously, expecting them to behave in predictable ways. To challenge our thinking, and to help them grasp the roles they were playing we prepared a number of small cards, each with one role written upon it. There was a wide range, with common roles having a number of cards. We spread the cards out on a work surface and asked each student to collect five roles which they felt were most appropriate to them. We asked them to think about these roles, and to keep the cards with them. In the final session of the group we revisited this activity, spreading out the cards again and asking the students to change or retain the roles they had originally chosen. This exercise was followed by a discussion, which enabled each person to identify the roles they had selected, and to consider whether they had changed through the sessions. This approach could be used with clients to help them understand the roles they habitually undertake, and to explore the concept of changing them.

The working relationships that are a part of the group may be influenced by the perceived status of individual roles. Some are held in more respect than others and have a more powerful influence. In one of our sessions a student who was taking the unofficial leadership role almost succeeded in bringing the session to a halt: she held a powerful position amongst her fellow students and her verbal and non-verbal dismissal of the group process was a very strong message for the others. Another role that arouses powerful feelings is that of the scapegoat. Benson (1987) suggests that scapegoating is a transfer of anger from the real object to a weaker and more acceptable target. Perhaps the group is angry over an action of the therapist, but feels unable to make a direct confrontation. Instead the angry feelings are expressed against a group member who is singled out for this purpose: this may be a person who appears not to contribute to the group, or one who is caught up with their own agenda and does not seem to have the group's best interests at heart. This brings into question the role of the scapegoat – is the person the obvious scapegoat, allowing themselves to take the role, or does it happen almost at random? It is important to explore the role of scapegoating and try to work out what is actually being expressed in an apparent attack upon another group member.

There are times when members of the group become stuck with a role they no longer wish to own. Finlay (1993) terms this 'role lock'; the behaviour or role the individual expresses becomes expected, both by them and the group. Role lock prevents a person moving forward, thus denying them the experience of different aspects within the group. An example can be provided by the more mature group member, who may have the unofficial role of leader thrust upon them simply because they have more life experience than others. Within the group this role may be capitalised on, as members collude with the fact that someone else will act as leader, making the decisions and taking the group forwards. On the one hand this facilitates the action of the group, but conversely it locks that individual into a role they may not wish to own. He or she may not need the responsibility of leadership and might want to feel able to express their vulnerabilities.

Members also have working relationships with others outside the group, other professionals as well as their family and social network. Interactions within these relationships can contribute to and inform the group process. Individuals may adopt the same roles within these relationships as they take within the group or may present in a different way. This information gives some clues to relationships in a broader context, exploring whether behaviour follows a defined pattern or varies in different situations.

This section has looked at working relationships that are formed and which underpin group behaviour. These interactions cannot take place unless a structure is present within the group, a structure which enfolds the group and enables it to function. Because so many of the interactions are based on a feeling of trust we are looking for a safety net beneath and around the group to enable dynamic interchanges to take place, a cohesiveness within which the group functions. If this structure is absent, then the group will remain static, members will not feel able to take risks and will be unable to make changes. The group will be sterile and ineffective on a therapeutic level. The structure is developed using ground rules, group norms and group cohesion.

Ground rules

A starting point for this structure and safety net is to look at the ground rules that are part of the negotiations which take place as a group begins to define its existence. Ground rules are an explicit code of behaviour which the group puts into place and expects all members to follow (Brown, 1994). They are usually negotiated during the first session of the group and are reached by consensus. Ground rules that are imposed on group members are unlikely to enhance interpersonal working, as the group needs to have a sense of ownership and negotiation develops cohesiveness as it is based on respecting the opinions of all.

Brown (1994) states that ground rules should be realistic and practical in their expectations so that they are achievable. However, they remain open to renegotiation during the life of the group as aspects may change as other issues arise (Bertcher and Maple, 1996). The following set of ground rules was negotiated for a creative therapy group between our students and ourselves.

- Attendance – this concerned individual commitment to the group and attendance was to be a priority. The group must be notified if a member was unable to attend.
- Timing – it was the responsibility of all members to attend on time and to stay for the length of the session.
- Confidentiality – what happened within the group stayed within the group; the video material of the sessions was to be viewed *only* by group members.
- Role of student leaders – to plan and undertake the session, arranging the room and managing the time.
- Role of lecturers – to be active group members, but not to be responsible for the student-led part of the session.
- Participation – active participation was expected, any subgrouping or non-involvement was to be discouraged.
- Displacement activities – any form of these (e.g. drinking, chewing gum) would be discouraged.

Our experience was that through bringing these issues into the open for discussion by the whole group we clarified the expectations and the structure of the group. This gave a secure basis upon which the group process could build, as everyone knew and owned the code of behaviour we were working within.

Although **confidentiality** has been briefly referred to in the ground rules it plays such a vital role in underpinning the trust of the group that it deserves more consideration. Confidentiality is implicit in a therapeutic group situation as it is inherent to the security that underlies working relationships. Creative therapy groups use the chosen medium to facilitate personal growth, and risk taking is part of this process. Risks need to be taken within the security of the group; they involve individual exposure so they must remain the business of the group. Think of this issue from your own perspective for a moment. If you were working hard to address, and possibly change, an aspect of your own understanding and behaviour would you want your action commented on and talked about by people who were not part of the process, or who might not have a real understanding of and empathy for what was taking place? If this happens there is a danger of misunderstanding, as the action has been taken out of context, without the group structure to provide support. It also impinges on the rights of the members – idle talk away from the group gives them no opportunity to speak for themselves. It is easy to see that if the group members do not trust each other over the personal material which is generated then that material, before it is even stated, will be severely censored, becoming bland and impersonal.

The issue of confidentiality, however, raises a dilemma. We talked earlier of the need for the therapist and the group members to connect with other professionals and this need makes the issue of confidentiality less clear. As part of negotiating the ground rules on confidentiality, the therapist should be clear about the people to whom they need to communicate group business. This might include the supervision relationship or other professionals involved with a client. Generally, in these relationships the therapist seeks to report a broad overview, keeping the specific issues private, unless permission is obtained. Another route to explore is that of encouraging the group member to take responsibility for disclosing their own personal information to another professional; by confining the feedback to themselves they are not breaking the corporate confidentiality of the group.

The client within our case study had particular difficulty in coming to terms with issues of confidentiality. She wanted everything to stay within the group, and it took careful negotiation by the therapist to help her to see that other professionals needed to be informed of her progress.

Group norms

When a group of people begin to work together they need some behavioural rules, or norms, to enable them to function in a therapeutic way (Finlay, 1993; Yalom, 1975). These often simply occur and are not developed explicitly. Once they are in place they do not have to be re-negotiated even on an implicit level each time the group meets, as they become part of the 'how' of the group, the way in which it finds itself functioning in an acceptable manner. These norms fall into categories relating to different aspects of group behaviour: presentation norms, behaviour norms, communication norms, participation norms and practical norms.

Presentation norms

At the very start of the sessions there are norms relating to the ways in which group members present themselves for activity. These norms will cover personal presentation – the expectancy that people will comply with a code of dress, be clean and not under the influence of alcohol or drugs. These expectations relate to the respect which group members generate for each other; a person who attended in a dirty or drunken state would find difficulty integrating into the group and there would be some sense of pressure to change and conform to the expectations of others.

Behaviour norms

These relate to what the group considers acceptable behaviour, for example the group might not tolerate swearing. Behaviour norms may extend to sharing materials, perhaps taking turns with instruments or passing paints, but will also relate to the ways of reacting when others are disclosing information. For example, it is not appropriate to laugh at a group member when they are exploring some material which may have an amusing side unless that person starts the humour. Norms are established to cope with the way the group reacts to a member in distress, or to a person who is finding it hard to contribute for the first time. These norms provide a refuge within which disclosure takes place, as all the members are seen as worthwhile and are valued for themselves.

Communication norms
Communication norms relate to the use of conversation between all members of the group. Conversation includes the unspoken agreement that each person has the right to make a contribution, that no one dominates a discussion to the exclusion of others and that there is observation of non-verbal clues. This agreement allows members to respond to each other, preventing everyone from communicating at once and ensuring that each person has a chance to make their view known. Imagine for a moment the chaos which would ensue if these conversational norms were not in place – the group would become an arena for the loudest voice, no one would listen to anyone else and alternative views would be dismissed even if they were heard. The group provides a venue for observing respect for all the members, enabling each to contribute and to be valued as an individual.

Participation norms
Creative therapies rely on active participation, so a norm becomes established which encourages all group members to take part. It is inhibiting to the group to have non-participant observers who remain on the periphery and do not take the risks associated with active involvement. The opportunity for personal experience is lost and other group members will be wary of taking this step if they feel that personal exposure may lead to criticism or mockery.

Practical norms
These relate to some of the procedures which surround the group process. For example, it may be expected that group members help to tidy up the room following a session, putting materials away and making the space ready for other room users.

Although norms have a unifying role within the group they may also result in areas of conflict (Finlay, 1993). This conflict becomes evident when group members take a deviant position, resisting the pressures to conform to the rest of the group's behaviour (Whitaker, 1985). In turn this provides material for the group to explore as part of its process, moving towards people taking responsibility for and developing an understanding of their own behaviour.

It is a useful exercise to consider the norms within a group of which you are a member. Some norms are clearly stated and explicit; some will be implicitly understood in the way the group behaves. All norms serve a purpose in providing the rules and security within which a group functions.

Cohesiveness
The process of working within a creative therapy group creates a sense of belonging for the members, which is one of the most important therapeutic

factors. This sense of belonging cannot be achieved unless the members of the group feel accepted, both as individuals and as a group. As this happens the group develops a sense of cohesion, which holds it together at times of challenge and stress (Bloch and Crouch, 1985). Achieving cohesiveness within the group becomes an important working process, but one which is difficult to grasp, simply through the vagueness of the concept.

Cohesiveness is an invisible factor, which has a life of its own within a group yet which is unstable. It is influenced by the group leader and the group members as well as by the group as an entity in its own right. Finlay (1993) suggests that there are explicit ways by which cohesiveness can be encouraged, strategies which stress equal interaction, risk taking and self-disclosure, thus encouraging participation amongst all group members. These encourage the group to respond as a whole and to take ownership for its actions.

Within creative therapies we are able to use various media to develop this process. We might introduce a group sculpture to involve everyone within a new group, or use our own bodies to portray a physical message of cohesiveness. For example, in a disparate group students held hands and threaded themselves in and around their colleagues. This was a strong way of drawing the group together, as each person was involved both in taking action and in being drawn into the tangle. The activity introduced trust, touch and unity as well as lightening up a difficult session. As a group develops this closeness of working so the individuals who are a part of it become more accepted by the group. They achieve a sense of belonging, which generates warmth, friendliness and a strong feeling of support and understanding. As the level of acceptance grows, so does the security of the individual, which enables them to use the group for self-disclosure without fear of rejection. Bloch and Crouch (1985) make the point that cohesiveness and acceptance do not always work in tandem, but that within a cohesive group there is room for different degrees of acceptance of individuals, allowing interpersonal learning to take place through judging the reactions of others. There is the security to do this when the group is acting cohesively and the boundaries for the group are clear and specific.

Summary

This section has explored the working relationships that develop within the group for both the therapist and the group members. It has also considered the need to extend these relationships beyond the boundaries of the group. Attention has been drawn to the safety net which must encompass the group, providing a structure and security within which these relationships can grow.

Key points

- The working relationships of a group form part of the dynamic forces of the group process
- Working relationships involve the therapist(s) and group members but also extend outside the group to other professionals and family and social contacts

- The group leader needs to demonstrate the qualities of competency, compassion, commitment and communication and should be able to undertake a number of roles to facilitate the group process
- Group members will demonstrate task roles, maintenance roles and individual roles within the group. These may be positive or negative for the individual or for the group and can form the material for the work of the group
- Establishing ground rules, norms and cohesiveness are an important part of working relationships in providing a secure base from which the group can function

WORKING PROCESSES

This section will look at the very functional processes that take place within creative working. These processes form the structure of this approach and in group work they help 'the group' develop as an entity in its own right, a collective which is greater than the sum of the individuals within it. Working processes include the practical issues that have to be considered, such as time, frequency and content. Although these will have formed part of the individual selection process, they become the basis of the group structure and therefore provide an important dimension which supports the use of creative therapies.

Timing of sessions

Creative therapy groups require structure and form, so the first practical issue we will address relates to the time frame of the group. Deciding on a time slot involves taking a number of factors into account. There are external constraints, such as room availability, staff time and ease of member attendance, and these must be balanced against the intentions of the group. The time slot needs to reflect the rest of each group member's programme, existing arrangements which will influence their ability to fully participate in the therapeutic group. Although it may not be possible to find a convenient time for everyone it is important to consider the intentions of the group to ensure that the time is appropriate.

Being involved in creative therapies is personally very challenging and may lead to feelings of unease, conflict or distress. For these reasons there may be times in the week when it would be inappropriate for a group to meet. For example, we rarely run a creative therapies group on a Friday afternoon because there may be few support networks for members to access over a weekend. Obviously the decision of precisely when the group will run has been taken before the first meeting begins and will often be influenced by discussion in the pre-group interview. The first session gives the therapist an opportunity to explain the thinking behind the time slot chosen and acknowledge that, although this may not be ideal for everybody, there are sound reasons behind the choice.

The second aspect is the timing of the specific sessions – when they will start and finish. The pre-group planning will consider the group members' ability to arrive at a certain time, but the first session puts this arrangement into place and considers the implications of punctuality with the group as a whole. The group might negotiate a ground rule of starting at the agreed hour, as it is very difficult to establish group cohesion when members drift in at differing times. Lack of punctuality causes disruption within the group as verbal messages have to be repeated and space has to be made for the latecomer. This has the effect of shifting the focus of the members from their work to that person, thus delaying the process of the group. Persistent lateness indicates a problem relating to the value which the individual invests in being part of the group, it gives a message about commitment which needs to be addressed as soon as a regular pattern develops.

If both start and finish times are clearly stated and agreed at the early stage, then discussion can usefully take place if this agreement is not being kept. Vague messages about what is acceptable for attendance do not place boundaries around the group; they create anxiety and result in lack of structure. A clear time for the end of the session helps members to use the available time and ensures that, generally, members stay until the group closes. An important role for the therapist is to wrap up the business of the group before the closing time. This provides an opportunity to summarise the session, to share with the group members what occurred and to clarify the points reached. If a discussion is unfinished there is an opportunity to suggest that the group members work on this as 'homework', and bring their thoughts to the next session. In this way issues that are not concluded can form the starting point for further discussion.

The actual length of the session should be clearly thought through and agreed with the group members. The session has to be long enough to be valuable, yet not so long that it is hard to sustain or its purpose becomes vague. Obviously there may be practical constraints – pressure on room usage, therapist's time and the group members' time. However, the proposed time slot needs to be sufficient to enable the group to work through the format of a warm-up activity, the main content and a closing activity with quality time for both the chosen media and the personal interactions. Time needs to be balanced with care and this can only be successfully achieved if planning and thinking has taken place ahead of the session. Our experience with creative therapy groups suggests that a session lasting 1·5–2 hours seems to work well, depending on the concentration abilities of the group members. This gives enough time to engage everyone in the business of the group, to actively use the media and to work towards achieving the goals of the session, whilst maintaining the motivation and interest of the group members. However, this is the group contact time, and there is a need to remember the vital functions of group planning, preparation and tidying up, feedback and evaluation. The media involved in creative therapies often require time to set out and, more particularly, to clear away, a process which cannot be ignored and which may be part of the session or can occur outside the session boundaries. If this is the case the time commitment of the therapist will have to extend beyond the stated session, something that should be remembered. The whole time commitment of the therapist should be recognised, rather than just that part which takes place during the group session.

Frequency of sessions

The next working process to be considered is the frequency of the group meetings. This is a practical process as creative therapy groups often work to a certain number of sessions. The group is given boundaries, the period within which to work is made explicit and the fact that the sessions will come to an end is clearly stated at the beginning. This prevents any misunderstandings and lets everyone involved know what the lifespan of the group will be. The actual decision on the number of sessions will depend on the nature of the problems presented by the group members, but an average group life tends to be between eight and ten sessions. In our final chapter we consider the need to address the disbanding of a group even as it begins, making it clear to the members that the group experience is not for ever, that there is a moving off point from it and a finite number of sessions in which to work.

The time, length and frequency of the meetings provide a framework for the content of the sessions. We do not intend to address specific content here, but we will look at the format for a group session, to clarify the working processes that are undertaken. This format will include the welcome, the warm up, the main activity and the closure. These are the explicit parts of the group session, the structure within which the work takes place.

Content of sessions

A working process at the beginning of any session is the welcome that is extended to the group. This is usually undertaken by the therapist, as the leader of the group, but it may be shared amongst members. A welcome defines the start of the process, creating a boundary between the world outside the door and the world within the group. It should be evident, not only in verbal communication but also through the preparedness of the room and the therapist. It introduces, establishes and acknowledges the presence of the group members, making them feel at ease and expected. The welcome also gives the therapist time to make some early judgements about the mood of the individual members and the mood that is likely to permeate the group. This early observation enables adjustments to be made to the planning of the session in response to a group or an individual mood, thus helping to ensure that the session addresses the perceived needs. Creative media offer scope for change and adjustment, as one of their qualities lies within their diversity. The group may be presenting a message that a complex activity is not going to work, enabling the therapist to simplify or substitute a medium which is more appropriate.

In the early stage the therapist may be the only person who knows everyone by name so the welcome is a chance to greet people, using their names to help the group to identify itself. This communication will draw attention to anyone that is missing, giving an opportunity for explanation and making a person, even in their absence, part of the group process. A verbal welcome plays a part in settling the group, it signals that the work is about to begin and establishes some interpersonal interaction. Often the content of the welcome includes some small talk, as this bridges the gap between the sessions and enables members to gradually involve themselves in the new session. There is an implicit message here – the leader is showing that the group is valued, both as a whole and as individuals. It acknowledges the effort that some members will have made just to attend and reinforces the fact that there is a safe space within which to work. This short interaction relieves anxieties, nurturing and creating a warm atmosphere which inspires trust (Benson, 1987).

The life of a creative therapy group will have a beginning, a main part (which is likely to extend over a number of weeks or sessions) and finally a closing, when the work of the group terminates. This life cycle is mirrored in miniature as we plan the content of a single group session when we tend to think in terms of a warm-up activity, a main part and a closing activity (Finlay, 1993). Each of these parts has a specific function, they are not just brief activities which are included for variety or to fill the time! We will look at each stage of this process in greater detail.

Warm-up activities

Warm-up activities, also known as ice breakers, take place at the start of the group (Benson, 1987; Howe and Schwartzberg, 1986). Their purpose is principally to encourage the process of member interaction, to get the group working together. This has the effect of establishing the group in the first session and of re-establishing the group in subsequent sessions. When working with creative therapies the warm up also serves to introduce the members to the medium, linking it to the main activity and establishing the level at which the medium will be used. Warm-up activities aim to do what they say – warm up individuals and the group. This cannot happen if the activity chosen is complex, with a risk of failure: this would inhibit involvement and increase anxiety levels. Warm-up activities should be engaging, require no special skills and be accessible by all. The following is a simple example of part of a sound and rhythm session.

Sound and rhythm warm up

The group members sat in a circle on a large rug on the floor. In the centre was a selection of musical instruments. Each person was encouraged to select an instrument, and to experiment with the sound it made. Then, in turn, each group member said their own name, and imitated its sound through playing the instrument. As the activity moved around the circle the members became familiar with the names, and were able to introduce their neighbour, again saying the name and playing it on the instrument.

When we explore this exercise we can see that it achieved quite a lot for the group.

- First, the group members formed a circle, establishing themselves on a level and placing themselves close to each other. This draws members into the group and has a unifying function. It gives a visible picture of the group, establishing the boundaries between it and the outside world.
- Secondly, it introduced the musical instruments in a non-threatening way. Experimenting with sound gives permission for noise to take place, making sound rather than performing a tune. Choosing an instrument required some negotiation – not everyone could take the tambourine!
- Then there was room for individual contributions, but on a very safe level. Our name is one thing that is most familiar to us and we are used to saying it. Combine saying the name with a musical interpretation of the sound and a double purpose has been achieved – the group members know something about one another and each member has used the instrument creatively.
- Finally, by introducing a neighbour the individual is taking responsibility for knowing and attending to someone else, moving the focus away from just themselves. Sharing each member's name with the group reinforces it for others and still gives an opportunity for a musical interpretation.

At the end of the activity names were known, contact had been made and the medium had been introduced in a way which involved and encouraged everybody. The group was then ready to move on to the main activity.

Warm-up activities may also have a role in preparing the body for physical activity. They may literally be used to 'warm up' the body, using gentle movement and exercises in preparation for a more strenuous main activity. In this way they provide a safety role, as well as enabling the group members to connect with their bodies (Rogers, 1993).

Main activities

The main activity will take most of the time within the session and it is important to consider what it should achieve in terms of the group process and the individual aims of group members. As the group is likely to meet over a number of weeks the media and activities chosen for the main part of the session will vary. Our students often ask us whether a specific activity can be used within creative therapies and seem bemused by the activities we suggest in our discussions as our ideas challenge their conventional thinking. Through activity analysis we can ascertain whether an activity has the necessary qualities to be appropriate for use in creative therapies. These qualities are the potential within the activity for spontaneous expression, self-exploration, emotional communication and active involvement (Steward, 1996). We have considered creativity as a core element and therefore use creativity not only within the activities we offer but also within our therapeutic style which enables us to expand activities to address these qualities.

The opportunity to express oneself spontaneously through an activity moves its use away from a 'right or wrong' approach to one surrounded by freedom. It is this spontaneity which we seek within the sessions as it often contains the surprise, the self-discovery, for the group member. The need for conformity can be left aside, making space for creativity (Rogers, 1993).

Self-exploration involves discovering and accepting parts of oneself that may have been hidden or unaccepted, including both positive and negative traits. Once these are acknowledged they can be brought to the fore and acted upon. It can be important to know whence these feelings or difficulties originate, so the other aspect of self-exploration involves learning the cause and source of the conflict. Through this process the group member learns about their self, facilitated by the group activity.

Jones (1972) suggests that creativity lies within everyone, that we all have a creative potential which can be realised within the right environment. This creativity exists within emotional communication, an original statement that is made through using the media. It is the choice of activity which provides the scope for this communication to take place, securely grounded within the group environment and structures. It is important that the medium allows this freedom and it is for this reason that we are not concerned with the technical aspects of using the medium in creative therapies.

Active involvement is key to the creative therapy approach and the main activity should encourage this whilst recognising that the degree of involvement will vary from member to member. This means that the group should be prepared to use the activity as a means of emotional exploration, involving themselves and working to communicate the emotions aroused through the process. The chosen activity should encourage participation though involvement on both emotional and physical levels.

Closing activities

Closing activities are the short interactions which take place at the end of a session. Their purpose is to provide a stepping stone between the work of the main activity and rejoining the world outside the group. They often encourage the members to reflect on what has taken place within the session, to think about this in relation to themselves and to identify what was meaningful within the session. Closing activities may also be used to relax the group, recognising the amount of work which has taken place and its emotional cost.

A group closing activity

The group members stand in a circle holding hands. They are encouraged to close their eyes, and to take a relaxed stance. Slowly a hand squeeze is passed from member to member. When this has moved around the circle a few times the group is asked to think of one thing which they wish to remember from the session and which they will take away with them. Each group member is encouraged to verbalise this memory, making it explicit for the rest of the group to hear. Finally the group joins in a collective hand squeeze, before disengaging and moving away from the room.

This apparently simple closing activity achieves a number of different purposes. First, there is a feeling of group unity as each person is a part of the circle. There are no leaders, no followers, each has an equal part to play. Closing the eyes enables the members to focus on the group, avoids distractions and reinforces the feeling of trust the group has generated. Holding hands is an acceptable form of touch; it communicates a sense of belonging and of reaching out to another. By passing on a squeeze this communication becomes a non-verbal message; there is some anticipation in waiting for it to arrive and a sense of ownership as the group member decides when to pass it on. Following this clear example of the group working together as a whole, a space of time for each person to think about a specific critical incident allows reflection of the session to take place. The process of sharing this memory gives it to the group, so that each contribution is heard. This can be an exposing moment for a group member, accompanied by feelings of anxiety, so it is important to regain the group's confidence through the final squeeze, which signifies acceptance and belonging. Finally the group can disengage, moving away from the circle and preparing both emotionally and physically to leave the work of the group behind and to rejoin the outside world.

Working with media

Within the working processes we have tended to consider the issues that affect the people involved in the process, and so we now turn to a consideration of the media, which provides a thread running through this entire chapter. Later in the book we give examples of the media we have used, but we should also address some of the practicalities of working with media and the issues surrounding it.

Acquiring the materials

We need a budget to be able to work with creative therapies because some basic materials have to be bought if we are intending to use them as our tools. However, one of the freeing aspects of working creatively means that sophisticated materials are not required; media tend to be far more adaptable if they are basic and sound. The creativity comes from the use we make of them, and there are times when posh new materials can be inhibiting. To work effectively we need sufficient materials to support our activities but also to be adaptable, making use of almost anything that comes our way. This involves creativity within the therapist, one of the key aspects of our approach to creative therapy.

When planning the sessions for a group it is important to think not only about what you are going to be doing but also about what materials will be required. Sensible stock control is important, as nothing is more irritating than running out of things, and an absence of materials is frustrating in terms of self-expression. There are times when it is appropriate for the members to bring in items from their homes. You might use this approach to provide a theme within creative writing, or when you are collecting 'rubbish', such as the cartons which were required for the island session described in our final chapter. In some ways this makes the involvement of the group members stronger: they feel they have some materials to contribute even if they find it difficult to contribute to the process; it assists in making the group 'theirs' rather than something supplied by the therapist.

Disposing of material

Materials bring with them the issue of disposal. We have stressed that the focus within creative therapies is on the process of the work, rather than on any product, yet we have to acknowledge that there are times when an end product is created, and decisions have to be taken relating to its disposal. The disposal of an individual's piece of work is easier, as the person concerned can choose to take it away or destroy it. Our case study illustrates some of the difficulties which may surround this action: the client was more involved with destruction than disposal, and this was a key feature which the therapist chose to address. A collective piece is harder to dispose of, as one has to achieve a consensus for action. As an occupational therapist you may attempt to be explicit about the issue of keeping or disposing of work, so that there are no mixed messages. However, it is difficult to have a rigid rule, as there are times when the piece of work is too close to the creators to be disposed of immediately. Discussing the issues that arise with disposal provides some useful material to work with in the sessions, (Patrick and Winship, 1994). The closing picture in Chapter 7 illustrates the importance of occasionally retaining items. This symbolic picture of butterfly's wings was far too meaningful for both the therapist and the person who created it to destroy.

Recording, reporting and evaluating

Recording, reporting and evaluation are processes which accompany this dimension of creative working as there is a responsibility to document our intervention and provide evidence of our work. All of these are essential components of any therapeutic group work and should be recognised as a vital part of the group process. For the group leader the work of the group does not finish as the session ends, there must be time allocated for completing these tasks.

Recording

Recording the work of the group involves gathering evidence of what happened within the group experience, so that a record exists which does not rely on the memory of the therapist. There are a number of reasons for this. The first relates to our responsibility within the group to provide an account of the procedure that could be legally examined. This might address the use of resources, the way in which individuals behaved within the group and the aims and objectives of the selection of creative therapy for the group. This record may need to be accessed by people who were not a part of the group, a co-therapist perhaps who missed a session or other professionals who are involved with group members. Records also serve as useful reminders for the therapist of the actual events, refreshing the memory and informing the working of the next session.

Records can be gathered using a number of tools but important precursors to recording are the skills of active observation and reflection. These skills rely on the ability of the therapist to observe and interpret the actions and interactions of the whole group, focusing on individuals but also on the effect of events on the group as a whole. This is a skill requiring concentration and active involvement. The co-leader has an important role to play here: in conjunction with the leader they can contribute to a more comprehensive observation of the group processes and the co-leader relationship can add objectivity to the reflection process.

Possible tools for recording include video or tape recorders. Permission from the group members should be sought when either of these recording devices are used (Brown, 1994) and there needs to be a clear understanding about who will have access to the tapes. The tools provide some opportunity to return to the action of the group, but they are limited in their value as they fail to provide a comprehensive recording. Tape recording the session may produce a verbal account, but fails to capture non-verbal behaviours. The video likewise may pick up the interactions of some group members, but is unlikely to be able to provide a picture of everyone. These tools can provide useful *aides-mémoire*, but they do not take the place of the active role the therapist undertakes. Another recording 'tool' is a non-participant observer, perhaps behind a one-way mirror. This individual may contribute to the observation process but their perception will be different as they are not actively involved in the group. The non-participant observer is also in a position to use tools such as sociograms to record interactions.

So far we have considered ways of recording as the session is happening; however, the most common practice is to record after the session and there are many ways in which this can be done. Most commonly the therapist will make a record in the client's notes with a few sentences about their involvement and progress towards their own personal aims. In addition to this the therapist may want to record details on the group process, in a diary or notebook relating purely to the group sessions. A useful record will note the media and activities used, information on interactions and dynamics and detail on group as well as individual progress. A tool that supplements this type of recording is the interaction chronogram described by Cox (1973). This uses a circle for each individual in the group; inside the circle the therapist indicates significant behaviour or achievements and uses arrows between circles to indicate interactions or relationships.

Recording information is an important part of the group process and has a significant role in ensuring effectiveness. Formulating thoughts about the session sufficiently clearly to record them is useful to clarify, in the therapist's own mind, what actually occurred.

Reporting

Reporting is the process that follows on from recording. We have stressed that no therapist is likely to be working in isolation and that there will probably be other professionals involved with the group members. There is a need to report to these practitioners, through verbal or written means, so that they receive information following the process of the group. Again, this is a professional responsibility and if we are to expect credibility for our work we need to take responsibility for reporting our practice. This may be particularly important for interventions such as creative therapies, which can easily be misunderstood. For these reasons reporting should be taken seriously and undertaken in a clear and accurate manner.

Evaluating the outcome

Evaluating the outcome of the group is the final part of the working process. There are two distinct parts to this activity, which relate to what is actually being evaluated. First, the individual group member – what effect did the group process have on the individual, what evidence of change is apparent within that individual? Secondly, the group process – did it fulfil its aims and intentions and what contributed to the success or failure to achieve them? This evaluation considers all the working processes already outlined and provides evidence for the creative therapy approach. We consider the issues of outcomes and evidence more fully in Chapter 6.

Summary

This section has enabled us to consider the working processes which are necessary for creative therapies to occur. Some of these give a framework to the sessions, by providing boundaries within which the work can take place. We have considered a typical structure for a session, recognising each aspect as a part of the whole. The specific medium used has not been the focus of this discussion, but we have addressed issues of acquiring and disposing of materials, an important practical consideration. Finally we have considered communication issues through recording and reporting the process of the group. Attention to all these practical aspects is necessary to enable creative therapies to function at a therapeutic level.

Key points

- Working processes involve clarifying the practical aspects of sessions: the timing, frequency and planning. These processes are important in ensuring the effectiveness of creative working
- Sessions usually follow a format of a warm-up activity, a main activity and a closure activity and each of these elements has valuable functions
- Attention should be paid to the role the creative medium plays, particularly disposal issues
- Recording, reporting and evaluation are important parts of the working process as they provide evidence and contribute to the effectiveness of the creative therapy approach

THE UNDERNEATH

We have termed this part of the seven dimensions of creative working 'the underneath', an unusual title but one we feel expresses best what we are trying to convey. The underneath refers to the hidden part of creative therapies, processes which take place beneath the surface. These processes are not obvious through glimpses of a session from the outside as they occur on the psychological level and take energy and effort on the part of the therapist and group members to acknowledge and work with them. It is through these processes and making sense of them that we really turn creative *activity* into creative *therapy*. This is a very important issue as we must ensure that we are effective on a therapeutic level. The concept of processes occurring beneath the surface of our intervention is a difficult one to express because what we are looking at here are the underlying forces of the therapeutic experience. These may remain hidden and unacknowledged, but for the experience to be truly effective and therapeutic they *must* be acknowledged, made explicit and explored.

Occurring processes

The first point which needs to be outlined when considering the processes which occur through creative working is what therapy is actually about. The key principles that each individual is capable of choice, responsible for themselves and has the potential for their own development enables creative therapy to occur on an individual or a group basis. **Individual therapy** takes place in a one-to-one situation, making use of a creative interpersonal relationship between the therapist and client and exploring the forces operating within the client. We recognise that each individual operates within a unique personal, physical, social and cultural environment. Therefore these forces form part of the therapeutic experience which occurs with the use of the creative media. **Group therapy** can take two forms: it can be a collection of individuals gathered together for therapeutic sessions or it can be a planned and facilitated endeavour to develop group forces (Bion, 1961). This second form of group therapy becomes a very powerful therapeutic tool. Creative therapies are most commonly practised through group work and in this we aim to actively foster the group experience, the process of working creatively together. We set out to make use of group forces through intrapersonal and interpersonal exploration within and through the group, using these in conjunction with the creative media to create the therapeutic experience.

Groups provide a microcosm for interpersonal dynamics and most of the clients we see have problems which are framed in interpersonal terms. Groups therefore provide members with an opportunity not only to talk about or explore their problems but also to demonstrate them through the experience of working collectively with others. This provides an immediacy and accessibility to the issue; something is happening in the here and now. This has a powerful potential to be therapeutic, but it is also a very challenging experience. To maximise on this the group members have to be prepared to be physically and emotionally present for one another. They need to work together to provide the energy to help each other explore their difficulties, a process which is facilitated through the group experience. The therapist is pivotal in this but all the group members have a part to play and must be prepared to be sufficiently engaged to fulfil this aim.

An advantage of this group experience is that groups operate on two levels at the same time: on one level the group is working towards the achievement of collective goals whilst on another level it is working towards the achievement of the goals of individual members. The selection process should identify some commonality of goals but on occasions other members may not share individual goals or may be at cross-purposes with the goals of the group. This is often termed a hidden agenda (Benson, 1987) and can lead to some interesting dynamics within the group. An example of this occurs when a member sabotages or rubbishes the process of the group to achieve attention.

The therapeutic experience of the group occurs through:

- disclosure;
- feedback;
- acceptance; and
- risk taking.

In **disclosure** the individual discloses issues from the past and present to the group, a process which usually leads to a feeling of release of emotional tension and of being unburdened. The leader develops this process by offering **feedback** to the person, and encourages other group members to do so. This serves to increase the self-awareness of the individual as they may become more aware of aspects of themselves, the way in which they present and helpful or unhelpful strategies which they use. Once the individual has a heightened level of self-awareness they are then in a position to make changes. **Acceptance** refers to whether feedback offered by the group is accepted, and to some extent this will be influenced by the way in which it is presented and whether the timing is right. The individual has to be receptive to the feedback. Within all of this, there is a large element of **risk taking**, which is why therapy is such a challenging experience. The process of disclosure and exposing oneself to feedback feels very risky, as does being in a position of offering feedback (Hinksman, 1988; Ratigan and Aveline, 1988). The whole process is a vital one to grasp actively, as it plays a significant part in moving creative activity to creative therapy.

In addition to this, the group offers further therapeutic advantages. While an individual is going through the therapeutic experience other group members witness it and are actively involved through the process of offering feedback. If they are sufficiently emotionally present and engaged they will be touched by the experience and identify with it in some way. This process is termed 'vicarious participation' by Hinksman (1988) and it has the potential to make groups highly effective as it enables group members to learn from the experience of others.

Group forces, which contribute part of the occurring processes of creative therapy work, are highly dynamic, they are interrelated and constantly changing.

They operate on many levels including the internal structure, organisation and culture of the whole group, parts of the group and individual members (Benson, 1987). Thus group forces can be very complicated and helping a group to work effectively is a skill that has to be learned and refined over time and through experience. Benson (1987) offers a useful structure for considering these group forces in suggesting that they can be expressed structurally, behaviourally and psychologically.

Group forces are expressed **structurally** through

- effectiveness of communication;
- quality of decision making;
- allocation of roles;
- quality of power and authority in the group;
- calibre of group culture, norms, values and goals.

Group forces are expressed **behaviourally** through

- the quality of interaction;
- silence, anger, tears, avoidance;
- lateness, absenteeism, getting stuck;
- gesture, posture and seating arrangement.

Group forces are expressed **psychologically** through

- the degree of trust, cohesion and intimacy;
- the extent to which individuals feel valued, included, able to contribute, defensive rather than open or split rather than integrated.

When working with a group the therapist is observing and interpreting these forces as it is their role to influence, direct and control the energy of the group as it operates. The therapist will, to a varying extent, help members become part of this process by encouraging them to look at and explore both what is occurring and how it is occurring (Benson, 1987).

We have said that a main function of creative therapies is to help clients work towards the resolution of interpersonal conflict and communication is a key issue here as it is the basis for successful interpersonal relationships. Communication can be very complex; it occurs both verbally and non-verbally and arises from both conscious and unconscious levels. Non-verbal communication in particular often stems from the unconscious and requires particular attention. The therapist needs to attend to the verbal language used by clients, encouraging them to speak in the first person as the use of 'I' or 'me' implies ownership of the experience. The therapist also needs to try to avoid situations where the communication of the group is channelled through them; each member should take responsibility for their role within the group and demonstrate a willingness to speak from their own feelings and thoughts. If everything is channelled through the therapist this valuable element of group work is lost and members will feel that therapy occurs only when they are talking to the therapist. In this situation the therapist is conducting individual therapy within the group rather than capitalising on the therapeutic potential of the group experience. All communications, whether spoken or unspoken, are potentially the subject of enquiry in creative therapy practice and it is the therapist's task to help group members explore and understand the communications which occur (Bion, 1961; Finlay, 1993; Ratigan and Aveline, 1988).

Yalom's (1975) eleven curative factors provide a useful framework for exploring how group therapy can help individuals. They are present beneath the surface of the group and help turn the experience of creative activity into creative therapy. These factors can be present in all therapeutic group work if the appropriate physical and psychological environment is created.

1. Instillation of hope

The individual is motivated to participate in the group and has faith in the treatment media. The pre-group interview has an important role to play here in instilling sufficient hope to motivate the client to attend in the first instance and in providing enough information about creative therapy group work. The attitude and manner of the therapist is critical in giving the client faith. If group members are at varying stages of improvement this can be useful as members see each other make progress.

2. Universality

This refers to that element of coming together in a group where members realise that others are experiencing very similar situations or feelings. It provides the feeling of not being alone or of not being the only one to feel a certain way. To achieve this sufficient homogeneity has to be present within the group. Universality helps the individual feel less isolated with their problem.

3. Imparting of information

This occurs on two levels: information provided by the therapist and information provided by group members. The therapist may offer information about the illness, interpersonal or group dynamics or the creative media, for example. Such information giving can empower the group as it reduces uncertainty. Members will frequently offer one another advice, particularly in the early stages of the life of the group. In many instances this advice is of limited value but the process of offering it is important as it conveys a sense of interest and caring. How group members receive and act on advice can also be significant – we have all experienced the 'yes ... but' individual for whom moving forwards is difficult.

4. Altruism

Group work disperses the focus of therapy from the individual, as there is a clear group process with individuals operating within it. Working within a group requires the members to show a regard for one another and through this occurs a process of receiving through giving. This can be particularly useful for some individuals as it helps them to realise that they have something to offer others.

5. Corrective recapitulation of primary family group

Most people come to group therapy because of problems on an interpersonal level. Very often these problems have their roots in the first and most important interpersonal relationships they developed – those of their primary family group. The group can be used to go over family conflicts and work to resolve them and their impact on the individual.

6. Development of socialising techniques

Some therapeutic groups set out to achieve this more specifically than others; for example, social skills groups would state this as a main aim. In creative therapies we are encouraging the individual to explore their intrapersonal processes as well as interpersonal relationships. Through this, group members can learn about their own behaviour and adapt it. For example, we may help an individual explore the way they express how they are feeling or how they ask for help.

7. Imitative behaviour

This is where having some heterogeneity among group members is useful, as members may have different coping styles and different ways of expressing themselves. Membership of a group offers an opportunity to learn from one another and from the therapist, as strategies can be imitated or tried out to see how useful they are within the individual's personal situation.

8. Interpersonal learning

Because of the central importance of interpersonal relationships a crucial element of therapeutic group work is providing the client with an opportunity to explore and learn about these relationships, thus working towards correcting problems. In time, each group member will act within a group in the way they would normally act in their own social universe; they will exhibit their own interpersonal behaviours. These can be brought to the person's attention, enabling them to explore new behaviours to replace maladaptive ones, testing them out and receiving feedback. There is a strong emotional element to this process, which has the aim of helping the individual interact with others more deeply and honestly. The emotional experience is uncomfortable and the process of interpersonal learning requires skilled facilitation by the therapist.

9. Group cohesiveness

This is a precondition for the effectiveness of a group, as there needs to be a sense of belonging and identity within the group. Members perceive that acceptance by other group members tends to be more credible than acceptance by the therapist. This is because often members are accepting the individual for their own sake, whilst they see the therapist as only doing this as part of their work. If an individual feels accepted by others they are moving towards the development of their own self-acceptance and self-esteem.

10. Catharsis
Catharsis involves releasing emotion and expressing feeling. Catharsis provides a sense of liberation; it clears the intensity of emotion and defences from the individual, opening the way for them to move towards change. This alone is not enough; it needs to occur as part of the interpersonal process and be complemented by the experience of other members. Exploring emotion is important to the group process; it shows members are really in touch with what is occurring and not just intellectualising the experience.

11. Existential factors
These are factors relating to the reality of existing. They include factors like accepting that at times life is unjust and unfair, that there is no escape from pain and that we are ultimately responsible for our own lives. In this way we stop blaming others and become more accepting of ourselves.

The therapist's role in occurring processes

The therapist obviously has a central role to play in facilitating the processes which take place within the creative therapy group. We addressed these earlier (pp. 82–88); however, the therapist needs to establish with the group specifically what their role will be and it is often useful to clarify this at the first session. It is important that there is no disparity between the therapist's perception of their role and what the group expects of them. To be effective in group work the therapist needs constantly to evaluate their role and explore how it meets their own expectations and those of the group. The supervision process, reflection with the co-worker and discussion with the client group concerned can all help with this evaluation.

In facilitating the processes of the group the therapist's role is likely to evolve over the sessions, a process which we explore in more detail.

Stages in group development

The dynamic forces operating within a group will vary over its course and it is suggested that this evolution follows a fairly common pattern. The most well known theorist on this process is Tuckman (1965), who suggests four developmental stages: forming, storming, norming and performing. A second theorist, Schultz (1958), defines the process in three stages: inclusion, control and affection. Of particular relevance to creative therapies, because of her specific reference to activity groups, is the work of Mosey (1986). She describes five phases: orientation, dissatisfaction, resolution, production and the terminal phase. Each of these theorists has something useful to offer to our understanding of the processes occurring over the lifespan of a creative therapy group. Knowledge of these processes is useful to the practising therapist as they provide some understanding of what is taking place within a group. Although each theorist defines the processes of each discrete stage there are commonalities between them, which, viewed together, provide a general overview of the processes occurring over the lifespan of a group. This can be conceptualised on a

Stage 1	Stage 2	Stage 3	Stage 4	Stage 5	
Forming	Storming	Norming	Performing		(Tuckman, 1965)
Inclusion	Control	Affection			(Schultz, 1958)
Orientation	Dissatisfaction	Resolution	Production	Terminal	(Mosey, 1986)

Figure 3.2 Stages in group development

linear scale in stages which represent the progressing lifespan of the group – as shown in Figure 3.2.

Stage 1

Stage 1 is a settling-in period, where group members decide on their degree of inclusion and commitment, begin to develop relationships, determine their role, establish structures and routines, formulate aims and identify ground rules for the group. The therapist can facilitate this stage by using activities which encourage group members to participate, interact and communicate with one another, helping them to discover what they have in common (Finlay, 1993). Activities should also be selected that minimise anxiety, reinforce the desire of members to join in and acknowledge the fear presented by a new situation (Benson, 1987). We used to begin a series of creative therapy sessions with the use of paper and paint but discovered that our students found this a daunting initial medium, as they were still unsure of the relationship between process and product. We now start with sound and rhythm: somehow this seems less threatening, perhaps because of the transitory nature of sound and the definite lack of an end product. It was useful for us to reflect on the influence one medium has for a range of reasons. Attention to the physical environment can help this stage of forming, inclusion and orientation. The therapist should carefully consider aspects such as the seating arrangements, greeting members on arrival and having the materials for the session prepared. At this stage in the life of the group the therapist takes an active role in leading and guiding the group.

Stage 2

Stage 2 is a time of conflict. This may be between the group members and the therapist over their leadership style or competence, or between the group members over issues of belonging, roles or power. Individual group members may also be experiencing conflict within themselves over personal issues and needs which arise through the group process. At this stage the therapist should be able to tolerate and permit a degree of conflict and even rebellion. The leadership role is to keep sight of the aims of the group, provide protection where necessary and offer reassurance. The therapist should help the group members explore what is taking place. This can be achieved through a short statement outlining perceptions, asking members to look at the issues involved, inviting contributions to secure a mutual definition of the issue and then fostering problem solving and decision making (Benson, 1987). This can be a difficult stage for the therapist, who may not immediately recognise or understand what is occurring within the group. The presence of a co-leader and/or the use of supervision can be invaluable as it is at this stage that the leader themselves may be under attack from the group.

Stage 3

This is the stage at which the group begins to settle down, moving towards a position where it can start to function effectively. The group develops an identity, becomes more cohesive and trusting. The therapist strives to promote teamwork by encouraging the group to perceive itself as a cohesive whole rather than as a collection of individuals. Members are encouraged to work together in a way which utilises their diversity to strengthen the group as well as meet their individual needs. It is important to encourage the participation of all group members as any regular non-participants are likely to get stuck in the observer role, from which it may be difficult to move. This stage, and those that follow, rely on effective communication, so the therapist will work to encourage it by challenging unhelpful communication, fostering open exchanges and identifying practical issues which might prevent it from happening (Benson, 1987).

Stage 4

Stage 4 is the productive stage of the group. The group as a whole, and the individual members within it, are able to work effectively towards achieving their goals. Here the therapist is less directive, offering support and reassurance. Feedback will be offered to group members, encouraging them to be honest and to manage the feelings they experience (Finlay, 1993). By helping members adopt a problem-solving approach and encouraging them to think creatively about possible ways of dealing with their situation the therapist facilitates the group and the individual members within it. The therapist helps group members to perceive the choices available to them and to take appropriate courses of action (Benson, 1987). This is the stage when the group may venture away from the security of the usual meeting room, accessing some of the media we explore within our section on the use of the environment and new ideas (Chapter 5). The group is cohesive and has sufficiently defined itself to make this transition.

Stage 5

Stage 5 is the closing stage of the group, the time of endings. The group has to come to terms with its eventual end and prepare for it. This is a time for taking stock of achievements, tying up the group processes, completing tasks and helping members to prepare to function without this support. The imminent end of a group may lead to denial and regression among group members, which may be manifested in prolonging behaviours such as introducing new material or personal aims. A very clear role for the therapist at this stage is to be consistent about when the group will end and to reinforce this (Finlay, 1993). Activities should be used that help the group prepare for the ending; ones for saying 'goodbye', for dealing with unfinished business and ones which encourage ritual and celebration. Group members should be given permission to express their feelings about the ending, and it is also important that the therapist considers their position, as the group is coming to a close for the leader too, albeit in a different way than for the group members (Benson, 1987). This stage in the life of the group is very important, as it is the springboard for the client towards independence from the group. Sometimes it is not given the attention it deserves and we offer further thoughts regarding endings in our final chapter.

Difficult situations

It is very common for our students to be concerned about dealing with difficult situations that might arise when working with clients through creative therapies, most notably dealing with silences, strong emotions and non-participation. These difficult situations usually arise from processes taking place beneath the surface of therapeutic intervention. They are usually meaningful and are manifestations of the client being affected in some way by the experience. In expressing their concern, our students seem to be looking for a magical recipe for dealing with such situations, often stating that they 'do not want to get it wrong'. The reality is that there is no right or wrong and certainly no recipe for success. However, it is possible to discuss these issues and this, along with the application of clinical reasoning and reflective skills, can help the therapist to judge the situation and decide on an appropriate course of action.

Silences

Silences in a group can be difficult. Most of us find them uncomfortable and a natural reaction is to think of something to say. The therapist needs to judge what to do about silences and this involves considering what the silence might be about.

The silence might be a natural lull in the conversation or the activity and feel perfectly comfortable. In this instance nothing needs to be done and the therapist should allow the silence to take its course. It is useful to pay attention to the process of breaking a silence, to see if it is the same person who takes this action and to observe how silence is tolerated within the group.

Some silences may feel awkward and if these occur frequently it is appropriate to explore them with the group. They may be a result of anger, resentment or fear or the group may be confused, perhaps about the instructions they have been given, and therefore feel unable to contribute. In the early stages the therapist might choose a less direct approach to addressing silence, using subtle means such as making more use of direct eye contact or using activities which force the group to talk, perhaps working in pairs or small groups. If silences become established behaviour the therapist may choose to phrase a direct question to identify the cause of the silence and thus enable the group to move forward. An example might be: 'We seem to frequently fall into these silences. To me they feel slightly awkward. I'm just wondering what they are about.' This gives the group an opportunity to think about the role the silence is taking, acknowledges that the atmosphere feels difficult and makes the issue of silence explicit.

Observing the behaviour of the group enables the therapist to recognise whether silence is a habitual stance for one member. It is usually easier to challenge this early in the life of the group before it can become an established role for that individual: a change of role becomes more difficult over time and any challenge becomes more confrontational. Sometimes it is appropriate for the therapist to do nothing and wait for the other group members to challenge silent members.

The complexity of this difficult situation is illustrated in our case study, where silence played a major role. Eventually the group members chose to challenge the behaviour, bringing it into focus and allowing it to be worked with. Exploring some of the reasons behind the silence developed the group's understanding of the individual's behaviour.

The therapist's judgement, co-working relationship and clinical reasoning skills are all valuable in helping to decide on the most appropriate course of action when dealing with silence. As creative therapies are concerned with interpersonal relationships it is inevitable that periods of silence will occur. By developing confidence in dealing with these, silence can become a useful aspect of group working, one which gives valuable information and enables the group to move forwards.

Anger

Anger is usually expressed at the second stage of the group development and, whilst it is still uncomfortable and requires management, it remains a natural part of the development of the group and should be acknowledged as such. It may be an individual reaction, one to another, or a collective action where the group displays their anger.

Anger is a very powerful emotion and can be destructive to the work of the group. One way of dealing with it is to acknowledge it, allow time within the group for its expression and ensure that all concerned have a fair opportunity to contribute to the discussion. The therapist should be prepared and able to listen to what the individual or group has to say. The primary task of the therapist is to work to maintain the security of the group. If the anger is directed towards one group member the therapist should support that individual, ensuring that ground rules are maintained. Direct questioning, or the use of activities to explore the anger, might be appropriate.

We have vivid recollections of working with a group who became angry with us as leaders. This manifested itself through non-co-operation towards the end of one session and the situation became very uncomfortable with no time for its resolution. The following week we approached the session with trepidation, having spent considerable lengths of time thinking and talking about what had taken place. We had experienced an unexpected show of anger and we had to find a way of working with it. We planned a completely different type of activity, which shifted the focus of the group to a more practical task level, in this instance making pizzas. This activity served to involve the group co-operatively in a task which, on the surface, appeared removed from the business of the group. As leaders we were equally involved and there was a social element as we ate the finished pizzas together. This choice of activity served to defuse the atmosphere and develop a level of cohesiveness which was sufficient to enable us to discuss the situation with the group and reach some understanding about what was occurring. It was important at this stage that we abandoned our previous plan for the session, reacting to the messages we were receiving and reflecting on our behaviour. The strategy for dealing with this situation resulted in us using an activity which was much lower down the activity continuum presented in Chapter 1. However, having regained the confidence and cohesion of the group, we were able to move up the continuum again in subsequent sessions. The ability to alter plans in response to changing circumstances is part of the essential artistry of the therapist. This experience was a key learning process for us and for the group but it was vital that we dealt with it to enable the group to regain security and move forwards.

Because of the nature of the emotion, anger can be particularly challenging for the therapist to deal with. As well as managing the group and maintaining its security the therapist also has to manage their own feelings. They may feel threatened, responsible or uncertain. The therapist needs to use the co-working relationship and/or supervision to help them understand what the anger of the group is about and to acknowledge how they personally are affected.

Crying

Crying, like anger, is a very powerful expression of emotion. In our culture crying in public seems unacceptable and in a group session it may be embarrassing for both the individual and the other group members. When this happens the therapist has a real opportunity to be a role model to the group by demonstrating that expression of emotion is acceptable and can be worked with. There is a need to acknowledge that an individual is crying: simply offering them a tissue is a useful first step. Following this with a straightforward statement such as 'you seem to find this very upsetting' can help to provide them with an opportunity to talk about why they are crying. It is usually inappropriate to dismiss the crying by pretending it hasn't been noticed or by using humour.

If the individual who is upset leaves the room, the therapist is faced with the dilemma of whether to follow them or to stay with the group. Someone leaving the group is likely to unsettle the other members and may be vulnerable and possibly a risk to themselves. In such a situation the therapist has to consider a range of factors and make judgements about why the person has chosen to leave and their emotional state. These judgements will help determine the most appropriate course of action. If a co-therapist is present one could stay with the group while the other follows the member who has left. A sole therapist may choose to follow the individual, clearly stating to the group why they are going and for how long. A brief absence may be possible depending on the stage the group is at, and signifies concern for a member, a commitment which is an important message for others to receive. We would stress that only a *brief* absence is acceptable, as the whole group remains the therapist's responsibility. Alternatively, it might be appropriate to contact someone else by phone to follow up the individual. However, sometimes we have to allow the individual to go, letting them take this opportunity of personal expression and space. The issue, after someone has removed themselves from the group, is how to enable their return should they wish it.

Non-participation

Non-participation can be a challenging dynamic to work with. It mainly becomes an issue when an individual regularly attends a group but does not engage in the experience. They are physically present but not emotionally connected. In creative therapies the individual may not be prepared to engage with the media, perhaps rubbishing the activity or saying they are no good at art or music and using this as an excuse to disengage. Alternatively, they may go through the motions with the activities but remain untouched on a psychological level, unreceptive to the intrapersonal or interpersonal forces. Such non-participation should be explored. Initially it might be appropriate to do this in an indirect way, trying other media, making the purpose of the activities really explicit in relation to the individual's identified aims and asking direct questions. If the behaviour continues it might be appropriate to challenge it directly and to explore within the group the issue of non-participation.

It is important to address non-participation as it is a behaviour which has ramifications beyond the individual concerned. Not only is that person missing the therapeutic experience but their behaviour undermines the security of the group which relies on co-operation, involvement and trust. If a member is persistently failing to engage in the experience then they are really acting as a non-participant observer and this is not a comfortable environment for other group members to disclose sensitive information or lower their personal defences.

Summary

The processes occurring during therapeutic intervention, whether on an individual basis or through group work, can be very challenging. The forces or dynamics present are powerful, sensitive, deep and multifaceted. They might not be obvious as they take place beneath the surface on a psychological level. This section has focused on the processes of the therapeutic experience of the group, the underlying group forces and stages of development, the curative factors and the management of difficult situations. All of these need to be explored, understood and worked with to make the experience therapeutically effective. This is key in turning creative activity into creative therapy.

Key points

- The hidden processes must be acknowledged for the group to be effective
- Creative therapy groups work on two levels: towards the achievement of group goals and towards the achievement of individual goals
- The forces of the group and the curative factors of group work are used to foster intrapersonal and interpersonal exploration and resolution
- Group forces operate over the life of the group and take a characteristic development
- The therapist has a vital role to play in helping the group work with the processes occurring, thus promoting effectiveness of the group experience

MAKING THERAPEUTIC SENSE

We have considered the processes that take place within creative therapy practice; these are present beneath the surface and constitute the therapeutic forces of the group. However, for creative therapies to be effective such processes need to be acknowledged and worked with. The therapist has to be able to make sense of what is happening in order to help the group and its individual members to achieve their aims. It is through this process that creative activity is moved along the activity continuum presented in Chapter 1.

The primary skills involved in this process are reflection and clinical reasoning. These are very active and rich processes, which start with observation and listening. However, the therapist is involved in much more than just observing what takes place and listening to what is said. He or she uses clinical reasoning skills and the skills of reflection to interpret those observations. The therapist cues into *how* things are said, observes non-verbal language, listens to what *isn't* said, notes engagement in the activity and many other outward manifestations of the processes. In tandem with such observations the therapist uses clinical reasoning skills to interpret what these behaviours might mean. Clinical reasoning provides the underpinning knowledge and experience of the creative media, drawing on occupational therapy theory, psychological theory and group work theory to inform interpretations of the processes. Each therapist will use some psychological theory bases more heavily than others, and this will influence how the client and their problems are viewed. The interpretations are re-examined against other observations which might provide evidence to support or dismiss the interpretation. This is an ongoing and often very rapid process. It takes place within two time frames. The first is called 'reflection in action' and occurs during the session. The second is 'reflection on action', which takes place at the end of the session (Schon, 1987).

Reflection in action requires the therapist to have the ability to make sense of complex and shifting situations on the spot. This enables them to alter their approach during the session in order to maximise the effectiveness of the therapeutic experience. Reflection on action involves looking back over the session, with distance provided by no longer being immersed in the situation, to examine what has occurred in detail. These reflections are used to inform the planning of subsequent sessions and the approach of the therapist within them. Reflection on action requires a level of pre-planning, so time needs to be reserved for this, ideally as soon as possible after the session. It is preferable to involve another therapist in this reflection, perhaps a co-therapist if there has been one, an observer or a supervisor, as this provides an alternative perspective and sharpens reflective skills. The simplest form of post-session reflection is an open discussion based on the recollections of those present but this runs the risk of selective recall; it may be unfocused and might not make the best use of the time available (Whitaker, 1985). It can be useful to add some structure to the discussion by deciding in advance what issues should be examined, perhaps focusing on the aims of each group member. Reflection of this kind also enables the therapist to consider their own role in the session and how it may influence what is happening.

Summary

The therapist needs to use clinical reasoning and reflective skills to acknowledge and interpret the processes occurring beneath the surface of the therapeutic experience. The process of making therapeutic sense is essential to justify the effectiveness of creative therapy practice. It is valuable to involve another professional in this process as this provides a mechanism for checking understanding and refining the skills of reasoning and reflection.

Key points

- Making therapeutic sense of occurring processes is essential for effective creative therapy practice
- The primary skills involved in making therapeutic sense are those of clinical reasoning and reflection
- Clinical reasoning provides the theoretical knowledge and experience to inform the interpretation of occurring processes
- Reflection involves examining the experience. It occurs in action and on action and is used to inform subsequent work

EFFECTIVENESS

The final dimension we consider is that of effectiveness, which is informed by and linked to all the earlier dimensions we have addressed. Effectiveness is a very important aspect of creative working, as it means that we achieve what we set out to do. In creative therapies our aim is to help the individual explore and express conscious and unconscious feelings and to resolve interpersonal and intrapersonal conflict, thus effecting change. Effectiveness in creative therapy practice involves achieving this in response to each client's personal aims which

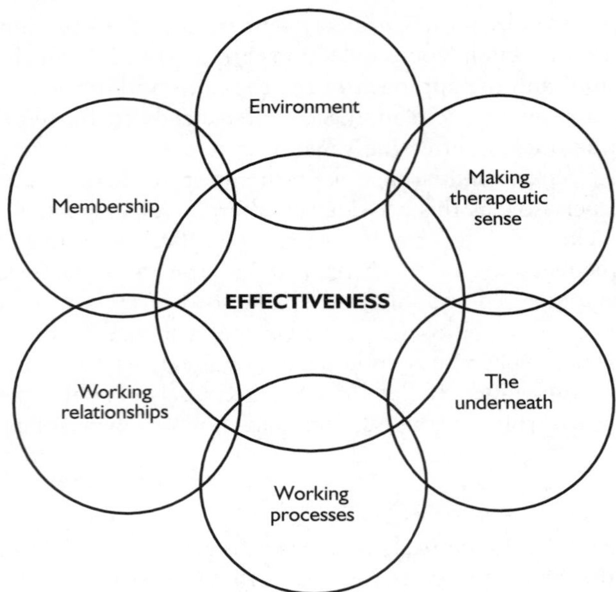

Figure 3.3 Effectiveness in the seven dimensions of creative working

relate to the processes of self-discovery, self-exploration, self-determination and self-help. For this a baseline is required; it is then possible to monitor movement from this baseline (Spreadbury, 1998). It can also be appropriate to follow up a client at some point after the end of intervention to ascertain if the change has been maintained (Benson, 1987). The client's perception, as well as that of the therapist, is important in measuring effectiveness.

Although an important theme in its own right, effectiveness runs through each of the dimensions of creative working. The processes that occur contribute to the overall effectiveness of our creative therapy intervention; this relationship is illustrated in Figure 3.3. In making decisions at each of these dimensions of creative working – for example, who to include in a group, the timing of a session or the use of a co-leader – the therapist is always considering which option will enhance the effectiveness of creative therapies.

To be credible we must be demonstrably effective in our practice. We achieve this through monitoring quality standards, evaluating our intervention, gathering outcome measures and demonstrating evidence-based practice. These strategies are discussed fully in Chapter 6, but here we illustrate how each of the dimensions of creative working play their part in the process of achieving effective practice.

The environment

In this section we consider how environmental factors contribute to the effectiveness of creative therapies. To achieve this we need adequate access to rooms which are physically suitable. We should also ensure that the environment is appropriate for the type of work we plan, with sufficient space, appropriate seating arrangements and plentiful resources of creative media. The psychological environment needs to be conducive to personal disclosure, feeling secure, warm and accepting. Unless we attend to all of these environmental factors the effective practice of creative therapies will be impeded.

Membership

The membership of creative therapy sessions is important for enhancing effectiveness. In individual work membership refers to the therapist/client relationship. The therapist should be the right person with a balance of skills appropriate for the client's needs. In group work we aim to achieve a balance of homogeneity and heterogeneity between group members, which allows members to benefit from mutual support as well as experiencing a range of coping styles and strategies. The format of the group appropriately addresses the shared aims of the group members. If the group is going to focus on highly personal and sensitive issues a closed group format might be most appropriate. Alternatively, if the group has been established for individuals who would benefit from ongoing support but who might be at risk of becoming dependent, then an open group format might be most appropriate. The size of the group will also have an impact on its effectiveness: a group that is too large may feel insecure or there may not be sufficient time to give all members attention. Conversely, a group that is too small may feel inhibiting or too pressured for personal disclosure.

The co-leader relationship can be particularly significant in the effectiveness of creative therapies. Two leaders may be able to work more skilfully with the group forces and occurring processes than one, thus ensuring that the evaluation is credible as it arises from more than one source.

How we deal with termination of a group, or members leaving a group, can also influence effectiveness. The cessation of group membership is the point at which the individual starts coping entirely on their own resources outside the group. It is important that this essential transition is facilitated competently. Occupational therapy is concerned with promoting independence so achieving this is a prime aim within our practice.

Working relationships

Successful working relationships in creative therapy practice enhance the effectiveness of this approach. These working relationships extend beyond the therapist/client relationship, as there is a need to communicate effectively with others who are involved with the client group. By effective communication we ensure that the work of the various professionals is complementary and directed towards a similar end point. It is also important that the occupational therapist is successful in fulfilling the roles expected and required of them. If this is not the case, creative therapies will fail to help the client meet their personal aims and the effectiveness of the approach will be compromised. The supervisory relationship can provide a more objective view on the therapy process as it assists the therapist in reflecting on their practice, enabling them to be more effective.

The working relationships of group members also have an important part to play in effectiveness. The group members need to feel sufficiently secure with one another for personal disclosure, exploration and change to take place. Group roles, norms, ground rules and cohesiveness all contribute to the feeling of security.

Working processes

These are the functional processes that form the structure of creative therapies. Time is an important working process: it relates to the timing of sessions within an individual's programme or week, the length of each session and the duration of intervention. If any of these aspects is not carefully considered effectiveness can be impaired. If the session takes place at an inappropriate time or is too short for the necessary work to take place then the outcome will be compromised. The duration of creative therapy intervention is also important. In some cases a client may need flexibility in the number of sessions offered so they have time to build up a sufficient feeling of security to begin to address their personal issues. Alternatively offering a client a finite number of sessions can help to focus their attention on achieving specific aims.

The structure of sessions is also important. This includes the use of warm-up activities, main activities and closing activities. Through the warm-up activities clients make the transition from the outside world to the group experience, become familiar with the creative media and prepare to address personal issues. In the main activity they really begin to work on their individual aims and the collective aims of the group. In the closing activities clients prepare for the ending of the group and for re-entering the outside world. This structure enhances effectiveness by fostering the **process** of creative therapies. It prepares clients for work, facilitates that work and then helps the clients to make the link between the experiences of the session and the outside world.

The working process of recording ensures that the therapist is well informed for subsequent sessions and can build on previous work; it also encourages thorough reflection. Reporting on our practice to other professionals ensures that the intervention which has occurred through creative therapies is justified and acknowledged. All of these factors contribute to the overall effectiveness of creative therapies.

The underneath

It is within this dimension of creative working that we are really reaching the core of effective practice. The first four areas we consider have put the necessary structures and processes in place. These all contribute to the whole picture but without really engaging at this 'underneath' dimension of creative work the effectiveness of practice will be severely compromised. Here the therapist works with and addresses the processes occurring and the dynamic forces which arise through therapeutic intervention, on an individual or a group basis. Operating in this dimension requires a commitment of engagement and emotional involvement. The therapist uses their knowledge, clinical reasoning and reflective skills to recognise the processes occurring and dynamic forces but also have to be prepared to invest enough of themselves to work through what can sometimes be challenging situations.

In group work the therapist can facilitate the group experience, thus enhancing its effectiveness for the members. The therapist assists this process through the stages of group development and helps the members use the interpersonal and intrapersonal dynamics of the group experience to meet their personal aims.

At this point the therapist uses their artistry to select creative media to increase effectiveness. Here the skills of grading and adaptation are used to turn activity into therapy. Grading involves adjusting the level of difficulty (Finlay, 1993) to the clients' individual needs, for example gradually introducing physical touch into sessions or increasing the range of roles each client is expected to take within a group. Adaptation involves changing the activity to take into account the situation or individual needs, and provides the background upon which grading can occur (Finlay, 1993).

Making therapeutic sense

This involves putting the whole process together. The therapist draws from theory bases, applying clinical reasoning skills and reflective skills to make therapeutic sense of the occurring processes, thus achieving an outcome. The outcome will link back to the aims which were identified at the start of the process. These aims will relate to the individual, the group as an intervention and the expertise of the therapist, as each of these interlocking processes will contribute to the effectiveness of the whole.

Summary

Each of the dimensions of creative working contributes to the effectiveness of creative therapies and this becomes the therapist's focus in making decisions about their practice at each stage. Processes and mechanisms are put into place which will enhance effectiveness. However, the most significant tool at the disposal of the therapist is his or her own artistry. This is the key thread of effective practice which runs through each of the dimensions. Achieving effective practice is an important issue for every intervention, although for creative therapies it is vitally important that we are effective and demonstrably so. If we fail in this final process we risk our work being misunderstood and reduced to the level of 'having fun and playing games'. We need to inform others of the purpose of our practice, its process and outcomes. Therefore we need to be able to succinctly justify our use of creative therapies, understanding each of the dimensions which play a part in contributing to the overall perspective.

Key points

- It is essential to demonstrate effectiveness in creative therapy practice
- Each dimension of creative working contributes to the effectiveness of creative therapies
- The therapist has a key role to play in ensuring effectiveness

CASE STUDY

We have chosen to illustrate the seven dimensions of creative working which contribute to effective practice through the following case study. This case study is based on a creative therapy group with Ann, a 45-year-old single woman who had suffered from periods of deep depression for the past 25 years.

Although the case has been compartmentalised into the dimensions we have considered within this chapter it is evident that there are no firm boundaries. One aspect will inform and flow into another, and all will cumulate to ensure effective practice, enabling the process of using creative activity to become creative therapy.

The environment

The creative therapy group was planned to take place within a community mental health centre which was located in the centre of town. This resource provided a base which was used by a range of health professionals, and comprised a converted house with a range of rooms, kitchen, garden and parking spaces. The house was about 5 miles from the local mental health hospital, but was specifically maintained as a community resource, with no outward indication that it formed part of the mental health service.

The environment formed one of the crucial considerations for working effectively with Ann. She had experienced long periods of inpatient admission over a number of years. Although when discharged she agreed to return to the hospital for appointments with her consultant, she refused to consider accessing any of the outpatient services based within the hospital. The community resource provided an acceptable neutral base within which to plan her treatment.

There were implications of access which needed to be considered to enable Ann to attend the group sessions. As her depression was compounded by an eating disorder she was at a low body weight and found it very difficult to motivate herself in the mornings. The option of hospital transport was discussed, as she lived a few miles from town and public transport was limited. However, Ann was a very private person, who did not want any aspect of her illness to be obvious to her neighbours. She chose to travel independently, walking some distance to catch the bus. This indicated her motivation and her aim to keep her personal life private, although at times travel became physically and emotionally demanding.

The irregularity of public transport meant that Ann often arrived for the sessions early and stayed after the group had finished. The house provided a kitchen where clients could make hot drinks, and a comfortable and accessible waiting area. During the early stages of the group these facilities were important, although in later stages Ann was able to use facilities within the city centre, meeting others for a drink or doing some shopping.

The room allocated for creative therapies was not ideal. It was a large group room on the ground floor, but had no running water or built-in storage areas. The room was used for a variety of purposes, but provided large table space, chairs, and a pleasing outlook onto the private gardens. It was important that there was time for the therapist to set out the media that would be involved in the session and time for clearing away at the end, simply because the room was heavily booked and would be needed by another professional. Despite these practical constraints the room had a welcoming atmosphere and was sufficiently adaptable to allow it to be used for creative therapy groups.

The provision of psychological safety played a very important part in engaging Ann in the creative therapy group. Her traumatic history of admissions, and the way in which 'treatment' was linked in her mind to the pain of these experiences, meant that she found it very difficult to agree to involve herself in further interventions. However, there was some ambivalence around this. This reflected some of the thinking linked to her eating disorder, her wish for change yet her inability to take an active role in achieving it, and her depressive thinking which developed a negative cycle of not expecting anything to be successful. As these forces were very strong within Ann it was important to ensure that the environment provided the psychological safety which gave security to her attendance.

Membership

Ann was referred to the occupational therapy team by her consultant following her discharge from the acute ward. The referral was considered at the regular weekly planning meeting, and it was decided that creative therapies might provide a suitable treatment intervention. The therapist who was planning the next group agreed to contact Ann to arrange an initial interview to explore whether creative therapies would be an appropriate choice, and whether she would engage with the group. At the initial assessment Ann was able to articulate her difficulties. She showed an interest in creative media and was interested in, although hesitant about, being part of a group process, which would be a new experience for her. She was able to consider the practicalities of attendance, and to discuss the commitment the group required – regular attendance, active participation and the ability to work spontaneously and creatively with the chosen media. Ann was interested in working creatively, and saw this as a positive change from interventions which focused on verbalising her difficulties, as she found it really difficult to access her thoughts and feelings in this way. Her presentation showed a need to work on both interpersonal and intrapersonal skills. She had a complex history of damaging relationships and was currently living a very isolated life with a very rigid control system. It was indicative of her despair that she was sufficiently motivated to take part in the process of the group although she indicated that this was more to please her consultant than to please herself. Again this reflected her 'anorectic' thinking, where she was unable to value herself sufficiently to strive for anything for herself, seeing it as more acceptable to please a significant other person.

The initial assessment enabled the therapist to link Ann's individual goals into the goals of the creative therapy group, where the focus of the work would address self-discovery, self-exploration, self-determination and self-help. The other group members had identified needs which reflected Ann's, making membership homogenous whilst still respecting the personal differences that provide a stimulating environment.

The outcome of the referral was that Ann was to attend a series of twelve creative therapy sessions, with a membership of six clients and one therapist. The group would take place on a Wednesday afternoon for two hours, and would be a closed group with no further referrals accepted. The aspect of a closed group was really important to Ann. She had little experience of working in this way, and was apprehensive about the experience. As she was a very private person, with few friends and no close family, she had little opportunity for sharing issues, and the prospect of accessing her feelings through the use of creative activity was both daunting and exciting. She needed the security of a closed and bounded group to enable her to participate. This, plus the initial contact with the therapist, enabled her to see attending the group as a manageable goal, built on a secure base.

Working relationships

This section explores the connections which were made between the individuals who were involved in Ann's treatment. These relationships occurred both within and outside the group, and needed to be explicit to enable creative therapies to be an effective intervention for Ann.

Externally the therapist needed to communicate with a number of professionals outside the group boundary. These were people who were involved in other aspects of Ann's care, as no professional was working in isolation. There was a need for regular feedback with the consultant who took medical responsibility for the case, and who provided a source of supervision and evaluation of the intervention. It was important to liaise with Ann's general practitioner, who was involved in monitoring her medication, with the community psychiatric nurse who visited Ann, and with the manager of the day centre that Ann occasionally attended.

Within the group the role of leadership the therapist undertook was an important safety factor for Ann. As her attendance was surrounded by many ambivalent feelings it was vital to build up a secure and trusting environment, based on effective leadership skills. These ensured that Ann's contribution was valued, that she found the activities manageable, and that the group worked together in a therapeutic manner. Ann's acceptance of the occupational therapist into her very limited circle of contact was a significant step, and this influenced the decision for the group to work with one therapist rather than having a co-leader. The small size of the group enabled Ann to relate to each member, and not to feel overwhelmed by new contact.

During the early sessions of creative therapies Ann found it difficult to integrate and engage herself in the group. She was comfortable with the media chosen, and enjoyed the range which was available to her, but she found it very difficult to verbalise and take part in the group discussions. However, she used the media actively, and appeared absorbed in her tasks, quietly collecting the things she needed, sharing equipment with others and actively listening. It was this level of participation which encouraged the therapist to tolerate her silence and lack of verbal contribution. The fourth session developed a discussion about roles and the customary roles which group members assumed. It was during this discussion that a group member challenged Ann's silence, asking her why she did not contribute anything. Ann was not able to respond to this direct comment, but the therapist used the opportunity to explore the meanings which might lie behind a silence. This action 'gave permission' for Ann to speak and her role was changed – from someone who was wrongly perceived as not bothering to contribute anything to a person who was finding it difficult to speak, but who just needed the space and encouragement to do so.

Change for Ann occurred very slowly, and was dependent on feelings of trust and security. During the first session the group formulated some ground rules which they agreed together. Again this was a new experience for Ann: she had not been part of establishing an explicit contract which referred to the behaviour of herself and others during her previous experiences of the service. As she was a person who needed to keep a very firm sense of control she welcomed the ground rules, because they provided a structure for her to work within. However, one rule she found very difficult referred to confidentiality. She was sure that the minutiae of the sessions would be fed back to her general practitioner, with whom she perceived a negative relationship. The therapist spent time reassuring her that, although contact would be maintained with this professional, the detail of the sessions would belong to the group and that only a general review of her progress would be communicated. Ann did not show the same level of concern for the feedback to her consultant: she had established a different level of rapport with him, and was very open to him receiving more information. As the consultant was providing supervision for the therapist this enabled issues to be discussed and did not compromise client confidentiality.

Working processes

Ann chose to travel to the sessions independently using public transport rather than requesting a hospital car. This confirmed her personal commitment and her ability to start to take control of an aspect of her life. It was important that she was able to claim the cost of her fares, as she had a limited income. A seemingly small point such as this may be a crucial factor for a person who is struggling with the issues surrounding engagement in treatment, and financial constraints may provide a reason for not attending. The centre's receptionist was aware of the group's programme, and so was available to welcome people to the building, particularly in the early sessions when attendance may be daunting.

The creative therapy sessions followed the format of a warm up, main activity and a closure. Throughout the weeks the members were encouraged to explore different media creatively, participating as fully as they were able and engaging in discussion during the session. They were encouraged to reflect on the experience, both verbally at the time and by keeping a diary to refer to outside the sessions. Ann found using the diary very helpful, as she could explore her own thoughts and feelings in a tangible way and at her own pace. As the sessions progressed she was able to share some material from her diary with the group, and this helped her to see the changes in her own performance.

Part of the reflection addressed the use of the media and personal preferences. Ann responded easily to the use of paper and paint, and to the text and verse, which focused on creative writing. The use of clay was a further challenge: it was cold and wet, and messy to work with. Although Ann wore exactly the same clothes to each of the sessions these were always scrupulously clean and she was carefully presented. The use of clay presented a threat to her clean and tidy persona, part of her control system which linked to her anorectic tendencies. Another area which Ann found particularly difficult related to touch. Her privacy and living alone meant that touch had become taboo for her: she was aware that the only touch she had experienced recently was invasive, that of holding her to give her medication, and restraining her when necessary. Her lack of self-esteem and distorted body image made the giving and receiving of touch a scary process, one which needed to be worked with in a very gradual and non-threatening way. The therapist introduced touch almost as a by-product of a closing activity where the group held hands with one another. This activity was brief, non-threatening, and occurred after the main work of the session, thus reinforcing trust and security. In subsequent sessions touch played more of a role, but was always sensitively introduced and time was available to discuss issues surrounding its use.

Another area which Ann worked on related to the issue of disposal. The group were working together to experience the process of creative therapies, but there were times when using paint and clay when there was an end product. Ann chose to destroy anything she created as soon as she was able to. There was no sense of valuing the product for the experience it had brought, as it was rapidly destroyed in a deliberate manner. Through discussion Ann was able to explore her inability to allow herself to share, keep or appreciate anything she had created which was not purely functional or necessary. She also prevented others from considering her product, projecting the image that it was worthless (rather like her perception of herself). This presented an interesting dilemma for the process and product debate. In Ann's case there were times when the product *did* seem important, and it was through recognising this that she eventually became sufficiently interested in painting to take it as a day course within the community. This acceptance of the product addressed her need to value herself and her ability to keep what she had created, enabling it to become part of the wider process of working in this way.

The underneath

This was an important dimension in ensuring that the creative activity planned during a series of sessions actually became creative therapy. Ann was unfamiliar with working in a group environment, and this presented a challenge to her as she had to develop interpersonal skills of communicating and considering the behaviour of others. She had to learn to accept feedback, and to formulate her own responses to it. As many of her previous interventions had involved one-to-one counselling approaches the opportunity for using activity in a different way brought feelings of anxiety as well as of freedom.

At one level Ann was working as an individual within the group, addressing her own aims and intentions, whilst on another she was playing a part in the group process, influencing the way in which it collectively worked together. Disclosure and risk taking were very difficult for her, and required a real sense of trust before they began to occur. Ann played the role of a powerful member of the group as she used behaviour which could be seen to be negative, almost sabotaging the group activity. She rarely spoke, she removed anything she had created, and she remained very tense in her non-verbal communication. Yet she was always present, on time and prepared for the work. She presented a very needy image, but initially rejected help when it was offered. This mirrored her anorectic behaviour and reflected the depression she had experienced for so long. It was important to enable Ann to recognise the roles she was playing within the group, and to address the force of these roles to allow her positive self-esteem to develop. The therapist played an important part in this interaction. Ann felt isolated from the other group members, feeling that she had nothing in common with them and expecting rejection to occur here as it had in most other areas of her life. The therapist's task was to prevent rejection from happening, and to use the situations that arose to help Ann see that other reactions could occur. The group members were helped to work with Ann, as much as she was encouraged to work with them. At times of conflict the ground rules provided a useful safety net, re-establishing the group and drawing it together as a whole.

The issue of ending became an important factor for Ann. It linked with her feelings of rejection, and made explicit her home situation where she had little contact with others. The group became a mainstay of her week, providing her with company as well as a sense of purpose and involvement. Her anxiety was that the group would finish and she would return to a very restricted existence. With such an enduring presentation as Ann's an improved quality of life was the intention rather than the concept of 'cure'. There was a need for the therapist to plan with her to move towards health-orientated activities within the community, and to detach herself from activities which focused around sickness. Ann expressed an interest in swimming, t'ai chi and art. These were incorporated into a discharge plan which involved liaising with community facilities to manage the transition from a therapeutic environment to a more social one. Ann was able to take part in this, gradually developing her social skills to enable her to enrol for classes and allowing herself to become involved in other things. This was a very healthy stage, especially as there were financial implications to doing this, which Ann readily accepted; a very different attitude to that which she brought to the group in the initial stages.

Making therapeutic sense

This complex case study involved the need to develop an understanding of the processes which were occurring for Ann, so a knowledge of occupational therapy theory, psychological theory and group dynamics provided some foundation for both her behaviour and that of the group. Adjusting these theory bases in action to use the therapeutic activity fully involved accessing the clinical reasoning skills that are developed within the therapist. There was a need to understand Ann's previous experience, how she was presenting and the impact of using creative therapy as an intervention. This skill demanded observation, communication and understanding, and particularly the ability to reflect on a situation both in and following action. The therapist was constantly adjusting her input to engage Ann in developing self-growth, reflecting on the sessions and critically analysing them. This reflection informed the pace of the session, the element of risk taking involved and the intention to be achieved through the process of using an activity. A knowledge of Ann's pathology, her family history and her lifestyle informed this process and ensured that the activities chosen were at the right level.

It was important for the therapist to make therapeutic sense in relation to Ann, the other group members and with herself. This personal understanding was achieved through active supervision with the consultant, who provided a forum for exchanging ideas and thoughts and for sharing perceptions about the work of Ann within the group.

Effectiveness

The effectiveness of using a creative therapy intervention with Ann was dependent on the relationship between each of the six dimensions suggested above. Each contributed a valuable part of the whole, and none was exclusive of another. Ann's complex case required each dimension to be carefully explored to ensure that her needs were being addressed. On the surface it seemed that Ann had agreed to take part in a series of activity afternoons with others: only by exploring the complexity of the task could it become an effective treatment intervention. The responsibility of the therapist was to ensure that each detail was evaluated as a part of the whole, and that the intentions of using creative therapy, from both a group and an individual perspective, were being met. It is this task which relies on the artistry of the therapist and the investment of self which accompanies working in this way. The effectiveness of the sessions was shown when Ann undertook a process of change, working towards her personal goals. This was uncomfortable and painful at times, but the therapist recognised that change is never easy and was able to ease Ann's change within the safe structure of the group. By critically analysing the process the therapist was able to recognise Ann's difficulties, using herself to push Ann further or to allow her to withdraw in response to her perception of the situation.

In Ann's case it was particularly important to demonstrate effective practice as she had had such a long history of interventions and was so ambivalent about engaging in yet another treatment strategy. Following the final group session each member was seen individually by the therapist, a process which involved reflecting on the group experience and considering the extent to which the individual aims had been met. Through this very tangible process Ann was able to chart her own progress, identifying times of change and movement for her, comparing her interactions at the end of the sessions with those at the start. The therapist was able to reinforce the progress Ann had made, giving her the confidence to accept that there had been significant change.

It was important that the other professionals involved with Ann's treatment were informed of the outcome of the creative therapy intervention. This was achieved through written and verbal reporting, informed by the perceptions of both the therapist and Ann of her progress. This joint approach ensured that the reporting was accurate and that there was a shared understanding of Ann's experience. The effectiveness of the intervention was evident by recognising change in the following areas:

- the ability to attend sessions both regularly and punctually;
- an increased level of participation within creative activity;
- communication with both the therapist and the other group members;
- an increased ability to recognise and explore difficult issues;
- an increased sense of trust, both of herself and of others;
- a move towards community activities and a shift away from those linked with treatment;
- a greater acceptance of herself, her past and her ability to take responsibility for her future.

Creativity played a central role in this case study. Ann was able to engage with the creative media, and to use them to develop her personal growth. Although this did not mean that Ann was discharged from the system she was able to accept a considerable shift in her ability to develop both interpersonal and intrapersonal issues. She was motivated to work in this way, and achieved a greater quality of life through engaging in the intervention.

CONCLUSION

This chapter has considered the seven dimensions of creative working, each of which makes an important contribution to the whole experience of creative therapies and has to be addressed to turn creative *activity* into creative *therapy*. We have presented these dimensions in a format of seven sections for ease of understanding but the reality is that they are all connected and each is dependent on another. Throughout the chapter we have developed links with our original concept of creativity and the way we use it throughout our work. We have also considered the key principles of the creative therapy approach, linking them through the dimensions to provide a unifying structure. At times the content of the sections becomes applicable to any group intervention, so we have highlighted specific relationships to creative therapy through the use of examples. Finally we clarify effectiveness, the principle which underlines our practice and from which we achieve the outcome of an intervention.

The ways in which these dimensions impact upon our work is illustrated through a case study. Creative therapies provide the therapeutic intervention for a client who was referred to a community mental health team. The case gives us an opportunity to link theory to practice, making each dimension a specific part of our approach. This overview enables us to see that practice was effective in achieving the desired outcomes for the client.

REFERENCES

Aveline, M. and Dryden, W. (1988) Group Therapy in Britain: An Introduction. In: *Group Therapy in Britain* (eds Aveline, M. and Dryden, W.), Open University Press, Milton Keynes.

Benson, J.F. (1987) *Working More Creatively With Groups*, Tavistock Publications, London.

Bertcher, H. and Maple, F. (1996) *Creating Groups,* Sage Publications, London.

Bion, W.R. (1961) *Experiences in Groups and Other Papers*, Routledge, London.

Bloch, S. and Crouch, E. (1985) *Therapeutic Factors in Group Psychotherapy*, Oxford University Press, Oxford.

Brandler, S. and Roman, C. (1991) *Group Work – Skills and Strategies for Effective Interventions*, Haworth Press, London.

Brown, A. (1994) *Groupwork*, 3rd edn, Arena Publishing, Aldershot.

Cox, M. (1973) The Group Therapy Interaction Chronogram, *British Journal of Social Work*, 3(2), 243–256.

Finlay, L. (1993) *Groupwork in Occupational Therapy,* Chapman & Hall, London.

Hagedorn, R. (1992) *Occupational Therapy: Foundations for Practice*, Churchill Livingstone, Edinburgh.

Hagedorn, R. (1995) *Occupational Therapy, Perspectives and Processes*, Churchill Livingstone, Edinburgh.

Hinksman, B. (1988) Gestalt Group Therapy. In: *Group Therapy in Britain* (eds Aveline, M. and Dryden, W.), Open University Press, Milton Keynes.

Howe, M. and Schwartzberg, S. (1986) *A Functional Approach to Group Work in Occupational Therapy,* Lippincott Company, Philadelphia.

Jones, T.P. (1972) *Creative Learning in Perspective,* University of London Press, London.

Hyde, K. (1988) Analytic Group Psychotherapies. In: *Group Therapy in Britain* (eds Aveline, M. and Dryden, W.), Open University Press, Milton Keynes.

Mosey, A.C. (1986) *Psychosocial Components of Occupational Therapy*, Raven Press, New York.

Patrick, J. and Winship, G. (1994) Creative Therapy and the Question of Disposal: What Happens to Created Pieces Following the Session? *British Journal of Occupational Therapy*, 57(1), 20–22.

Ratigan, B. and Aveline, M. (1988) Interpersonal Group Therapy. In: *Group Therapy in Britain* (eds Aveline, M. and Dryden, W.), Open University Press, Milton Keynes.

Rogers, N. (1993) *The Creative Connection: Expressive Arts as Healing,* Science and Behaviour Books, California.

Schon, D.A. (1987) *Educating the Reflective Practitioner*, Jossey-Bass, California.

Schultz, W. (1958) *FIRO: a Three-Dimensional Theory of Interpersonal Behaviour*, Holt, Rinehart and Winston, New York.

Spreadbury, P. (1998) 'You will measure outcomes'. In: *Occupational Therapy New Perspectives* (ed. Creek, J.), Whurr Publishing Ltd, London.

Steward, B. (1996) Creative Therapies. In: *Occupational Therapy in Short Term Psychiatry,* 3rd edn (ed. Willson, M.), Churchill Livingstone, Edinburgh.

Tuckman, B.W. (1965) Developmental Sequences in Small Groups, *Psychological Bulletin*, 63, 389–99.

Wells, C. (1995) Maintaining Mental Health. In: *Community Practice,* (ed. Bumphrey, E.E.), Prentice Hall Harvester Wheatsheaf, London.

Whitaker, D.S. (1985) *Using Groups to Help People*, Routledge and Kegan Paul, London.

Yalom, I. (1975) *The Theory and Practice of Group Psychotherapy,* Basic Books, New York.

4 THE ART OF THE THERAPIST

INTRODUCTION

This chapter attempts to ground some of the less tangible aspects of working with creative therapies. Our ideas began with a discussion about this intervention, how it worked and why it worked, what we enjoyed about it, why it really excited us and what actually occurred. This led us to consider the use of ourselves within the dynamic, realising that within all of the action we, as therapists and session leaders, hold a pivotal place, a central role around which the therapeutic process occurs. We are responsible for creating the opportunity of working with creative therapies in the first instance: we plan the sessions, select the members, and take professional responsibility for the outcomes of the intervention. This places us in a unique position – one which will always be different from that experienced by a client, and one which is dependent on a different commitment of the self. To achieve this we must know ourselves and the qualities we have, and be comfortable with this knowledge.

Each of you approaching working with creative therapies will have experienced an individual journey, enabling you to bring different perspectives to the situation which need to be recognised and understood in order to work effectively with creative therapies. This investment of the self is crucial, as it provides a balance to the more ephemeral, transient sense of the experience. The nature of creative therapies is that they will be a creative experience, one which is imaginative, freeing, planned yet unplanned, unknown and therefore challenging in unexpected ways. This fluidity of approach requires an anchor, a central point upon which your clients can depend for security, as only from a secure base can the creativity of discovery begin.

Yet the therapist does far more than provide an anchor for the group. Earlier in this book we considered the concept of creativity and the ways in which it entwines itself though the creative therapy approach. In our definition of creative therapies we suggest that 'creativity exists and is fundamental within the style of the therapist', a point which is further emphasised by Stein and Cutler (1998), who explore the role of the therapist as a creative treatment agent who uses these skills to facilitate change within the client.

This chapter will focus on this aspect of creativity, how we use *ourselves* as a medium with which to achieve therapeutic change in our clients. We consider that there is an artistry in achieving this; it is not a way of working which feels comfortable for, or even appeals to, some of our colleagues, perhaps due to the greater investment of self, the risk taking and the unpredictability of working in this way. For this reason we have called the chapter 'the art of the therapist', a title which ensures that our focus is on recognising the personal investment of the therapist. To enable us to develop this focus we are placing the therapist in the central role, exploring their ability to use the self within the therapeutic process. This central position gives an opportunity for the therapist to gather information from the whole process of the session, information which provides evidence to justify this way of working. If this evidence is not gathered there will be little recognition of the potential for using creative therapies. To obtain the evidence the therapist develops an end product, using themselves to collect information throughout the session which reflects the process that has occurred. Therefore the outcome of the intervention can be defined as the end product. Achieving an outcome has to be a creative experience, as it is the part of using the self which energises the actions, words and situations within the process of creative therapies to achieve a creative therapy product. To help consolidate this, text boxes summarising the use of self draw together the key points relating to the therapeutic use of self.

THE RELATIONSHIP BETWEEN PROCESS AND PRODUCT

May (1975) discusses creativity as a **process** of bringing something new into being, so our initial thoughts when considering creative therapies might consider an end product: a painting, a sculpture, a poem. There is an assumption that something is going to be 'made', and perhaps taken away. Casual conversation amongst colleagues leads to comments such as 'I couldn't do that. I'm not creative', making the assumption that to work in this way we have to be able to create an artistic end product. However, this is not our concern as for us the creativity we seek lies within the ability of the therapist to use the **process** of the work to create an end **product**. At this stage we should carefully consider what we mean by product, because we have to be able to define an end product to justify our intervention. This is a key point within this chapter. We suggest that the product we are aiming for in this way of working is created through the process of using the activity. Therefore our end product refers to the change and growth within each individual rather than to any created artefact. This is a really important concept, which is illustrated in Figure 4.1.

In creative therapy the end product is *not* a created object. It is the achievement of the desired outcome of the client's aims. For example, an activity using ceramics may provide a route for a client to be able to develop self-esteem. The aim of the session will not be to create a perfect pot, but to create the opportunity to work on issues surrounding self-esteem. The outcome will be whether the client's aim has been achieved, and to what extent. This is the goal to which we are working, which will be evident in the way changes and the self-growth relate to the original aim, thus creating the end product.

If the therapist fails to recognise the investment of themselves in facilitating an outcome from the process, the intervention will remain activity based, and will not achieve its psychodynamic potential. The difficult part of working in this way is to recognise that the media merely provide the opportunity to facilitate change, but that the emphasis is on observing that change in relation to

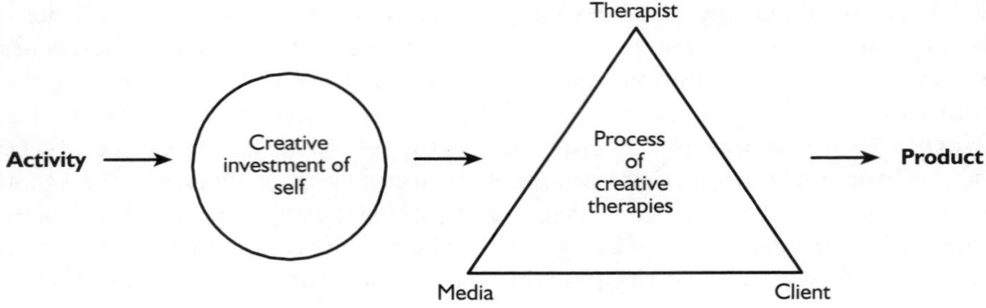

Figure 4.1 Creating the product

the identified aims of the client using the intervention. From the therapist's perspective the end product will also reflect a refinement of their practice – an enhanced artistry which enables them to work with creative therapies.

A number of aspects of creativity underpin our art as therapists to move the process of our work towards achieving this end product:

- the creativity of the therapist in interpreting and moving towards both group outcomes and individual aims, as for every therapeutic encounter something new will be created;
- the creativity of the therapist in being both flexible and reflexive in this way of working. There is a need to work with an open mind, not knowing what will happen or where the session will go. The therapist may be prepared for one thing, yet find that something quite different will occur;
- creativity through knowing ourselves and feeling comfortable within this knowledge, as this way of working is dependent on using the self as a therapeutic tool;
- creativity in working alongside creative media, feeling comfortable with them, exploring through artistry rather than technical expertise.

To make this concept of using creative artistry a little clearer we ask you to imagine a group based around music as the medium. There may be a collection of objects or instruments with which to make sound. The sound is momentary; it has a life of its own and cannot be recaptured or replayed in exactly the same way. The group members are involved with creating the music through patterns of noise and silence, sound and no sound. There is interaction, not only between the group members but also between the group and the instruments. There is involvement, exploration, experimentation and contribution, so that the group process becomes an experience that is unique for each individual. There is no judgement of the material product of the group, because the sound has gone, and there is no element of 'performance'. As therapists we need to seek **evidence** that the music session has been a therapeutic intervention, achieving an outcome. There is a need for us to work with this group process, the entire experience which touches us and the group members. It is this role within the therapist which moves an activity based around music into a product, a highly skilled interpretation of the whole therapeutic process that has occurred through using a creative therapy.

In order to reach this interpretation we need to consider the factors that lead towards creating the product, this end result which often seems difficult to measure or quantify. We need to consider what will inform the interpretation, and from where evidence will be gathered. Some of the information will come from exploring aspects of a psychodynamic approach, which produces evidence through understanding behaviour. Some will be gathered from the application of theory, using our knowledge base to provide us with evidence. By creatively combining evidence from different sources we are able to define our end product, and therefore justify our intervention.

Let us explore this concept in a creative manner, with reference to Figure 4.2. We will begin by imagining a therapist placed within the core of the session. The therapist plays an active role, gathering in the one hand explicit threads which relate to the dynamics of human behaviour: observation, communication, action and reaction, integration and the environment. In the other hand are gathered the implicit threads, those which are less obvious; the theoretical underpinnings, clinical reasoning, reflective practice. In this model the therapist creates the end product from the process of the experience through using their self, interweaving the threads to form a tapestry which reflects the work of the group. This interweaving makes a pattern, not a preplanned or conceptualised one, but one which will be different on every occasion, reflecting the unique therapeutic experience. The therapist as the creator of the tapestry involves themselves with the process, and contributes to it. Their artistry is apparent in the ways in which the threads are selected, understood, interpreted, included or discarded and finally acknowledged as being a part of a whole. This becomes an ongoing process, which is constantly re-evaluated.

This process cannot happen without considerable personal commitment as it is dependent on the individual involvement of the therapist, their role in the communication process, actions, interpretations and choices. It will be the thera-

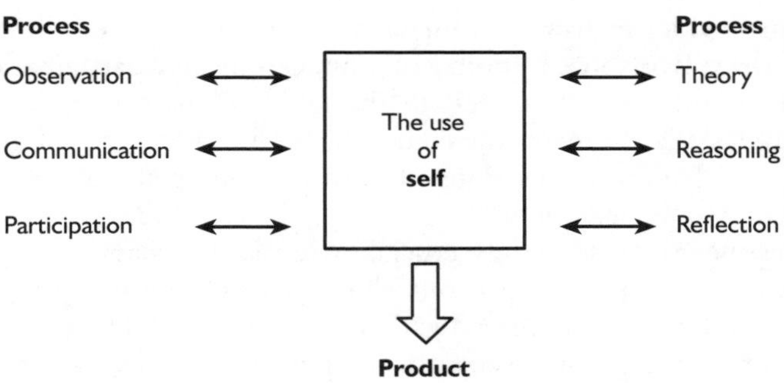

Figure 4.2 The threads of evidence

pist's expertise which skilfully moves the process towards becoming a product. Their ability to achieve this reflects aspects of themselves which are important within the creative process, the tolerance of ambiguity, openness to experience, confidence, curiosity and the propensity for risk taking (Russ, 1993).

It should be remembered that, as we attempt to consider, unravel and understand a creative process, we cannot be bound by a 'checklist' approach. We will explore factors which we consider to form part of the process, explicit and implicit threads which we can expect to be evident. These can be woven within the tapestry to create an end product that is greater than the sum of its parts. This will not be a finite collection of factors, as for every situation they will be present in differing strengths. They will also depend on the selection process of the therapist themselves, recognising that we work in different ways. Think back to the concept of interweaving threads, and allow yourself to explore some images which come to mind. They might be about the media used, the composition of the group, the evidence of problems, the ability of people to function within a given situation. These images may be based on actions or feelings, which within creative therapies can change a situation so quickly that you can almost miss it happening, leaving you with the feeling that the group has altered and moved, whilst probably looking just the same. A process took place that was not rehearsed or expected but provided material which will be woven into the completed tapestry through the art of the therapist. Because these threads can be so intangible, so transitory, unexpected and fragile you have to be receptive to gathering them, using observation and awareness to draw them together to create the end product.

There is a risk to working in this way. It is all too easy to become absorbed in the activity, to focus on a fragment of a group and to miss something which is happening elsewhere. In this case your hands may be almost empty, there will be few threads to weave and the pattern created will not be a reflection of the therapeutic process. It will be difficult to gather evidence to show that the intervention achieved its aims. To return to our earlier example, you will be unable to explain that you were doing more than 'playing about with music'.

To work in this way involves identification and exploration of the threads we seek to gain evidence from within creative therapies. We will explore the more evident threads of observation, communication and participation, linking them through the creative use of self to the less obvious threads of theoretical foundations, the skills of reasoning and reflection. These are all parts of the process which involve the interactions of both the therapist and the clients, and which contribute to the final picture.

As the investment of the self is crucial, within this chapter we will try to outline the ways in which we use ourselves to achieve the evidence in each section. These equate to the thread-gathering process of the therapist at the centre of the intervention, and recognise the personal artistry which is involved in the process. We do not provide a finite list, but suggest areas which may be applicable to individual practice.

OBSERVATION

Observation is a key skill which involves using a clear body of knowledge upon which to base valuable insights into the process of therapy (Bloch and Crouch, 1985). It is an active task, concerned with gathering messages from a situation. Many of us find ourselves within situations where we tend to think we 'observe' but the quality of this casual awareness lacks the depth and focus of real observation, which involves paying attention on both deep and superficial levels because with any therapeutic intervention a great deal is going on at once (Whitaker, 1985). Our theoretical knowledge, skills and expertise refine the process of observation, enabling us to cue into effective and significant occurrences, filtering out those which do not require further attention. It is the task of the therapist to use these observations, which fall into three main categories:

- observations about the behaviour of clients;
- observations about the therapist and their own behaviour;
- observations about the session as a therapeutic medium.

For the purposes of this chapter we will focus on the first two categories, as much of the material which surrounds the session itself is addressed in Chapter 3.

Observations about the behaviour of clients

We need to break this process down into two sections: how to undertake observation and what to observe. However, for both aspects the therapist needs to understand the importance of the task, help it to happen and store the information gathered for future use. The process enables the therapist to assess what takes place within the session to give clues to the behaviour of those involved. This will result in a mass of material from which threads are skilfully selected to be interwoven into the tapestry of our end product. Some of these threads may be key aspects of emotion – for example, an outburst of anger or distressed sobbing, which are easily observed. Others will be small nuances of behaviour; a glimpse of eye contact or an unexpected smile. Each will provide evidence to inform the process of the group.

The process of observation can be carried out in a number of ways, all of which rely on the attention and engagement of the therapist. If you are working within a session it is not good practice to write down occurrences as they happen: this inhibits interaction and conversation and becomes disruptive. The skill is to recognise significant happenings, remember them, and allow yourself time at the end of the session to reflect back on them and develop understanding through them. This is reflecting on the action (Schon, 1983) that has taken place within the session, and informs the final tapestry. As well as using yourselves there are other ways of observing behaviour, for example a co-therapist or recording the session with a video or tape recorder both contribute to the process of gathering information.

Whichever strategy is employed the purpose of the activity remains the same – to gather information to help you to address what is to be observed. There are some key factors which reflect the dynamics of human behaviour and therefore provide messages about the ability of members to function within a creative therapy session. These include

- **openness** to the whole experience of working in this way;
- **interaction** – from the moment clients arrive you will be gathering messages from the ways they interact both with each other and with you as the therapist;
- **communication** – both verbal and non-verbal, the content and timing, the balance between social and formal communication, and the pattern within the session;
- **positioning** – you will notice where clients choose to position themselves in relation to each other and to you, the ease with which this pattern changes and appropriate and inappropriate stances;
- **emotions and moods** – the ways in which these are apparent within the session and changes that occur in relation to the creative media or through verbalisation;
- **involvement** – the degree of participation, and whether it alters at different stages of the session;
- **use of the creative media** – the ease with which a medium is used, involvement with it and individual preferences;
- **roles** – the ways these affect the session, whether they are changing or static, the use of positive and negative role taking.

These observations will provide evidence of the ways in which clients are engaging in a creative therapy session, but they can also be compared with observations made outside the session. It is useful to consider whether behaviour alters within the session, whether clients react differently within a group than in individual contact, or even whether different times of day affect behaviour. These observations give you clues to inform your intervention, whether to change your approach to push a client on or to withdraw slightly, knowing that a challenge would be inappropriate. Finlay (1997) stresses the importance of being specific about observations rather than using vague comments, so refining observation skills within the whole spectrum of your work enables you to gain a clearer picture of the whole person, and to use this knowledge to inform your end product.

Use of self

- An active process of watching, listening, and reflecting on actions
- Looking for both superficial and deeper reactions
- Gathering previous information and knowledge to inform observations
- Facilitating the process to enable observations to be made

Observations about the therapist and their behaviour

The second aspect of observation concerns what therapists observe about themselves and their own behaviour, as within any creative environment there is the need to know oneself (Warren, 1984). Thinking and feeling are personal emotions involved in the process of watching and listening to others (Whitaker, 1985) so it is important to acknowledge their affect upon your sense of self. Only by being comfortable within your knowledge of yourself can you develop the trust in your abilities to work in this way.

Stockwell (1984) summarises qualities that support the therapist's ability to use themselves in a therapeutic environment. These include:

- **Self-understanding** – this involves knowing your own needs and abilities, the aspects of your work and your life which give you satisfaction, the things which are difficult and the things which are easy, your personal strengths and weaknesses. It provides an awareness of situations within a therapeutic environment that cause you a personal challenge, topics which reflect a past experience or are particularly sensitive to you as a person.
- **Warmth, genuineness and acceptance** – these principles link back to the client-centred approach, and need to be apparent in your interventions. They enable you to engage your clients through showing personal commitment to working with them.
- **Personal security** – only by achieving a sound personal base can you expect to become involved with others and to work with them in a therapeutic manner. This security needs to be explicit in the ways you deal with situations, respond to challenges, engage in disclosure and maintain the boundaries of the session.
- **Knowledge of the dynamics of behaviour** – you need to understand what aspects of behaviour are telling you, to know what to look for and to remain responsive to changes.

It is important to ensure that these qualities are apparent, as through them the clients develop the confidence to take risks with their behaviour, knowing that they can rely on the therapist to provide the central stable base for the intervention which is built on understanding. This makes explicit the therapist's ability to deal with situations as they arise, ensuring that the session will not get out of control and become damaging to those involved.

As well as observing external behaviour of your clients you need to be aware of your internal functioning. Observing personal behaviour also involves considering where your thoughts are at any one time (Rogers, 1993), a process which recognises that these will be on all sorts of interrelated topics almost at once. You may be thinking about the clients, about the room and the general ambience, about whether you are physically comfortable, too hot or too cold, whether you are distracted by something from outside the session. All of these thoughts are personal observations, which are a part of knowing yourself and which contribute to the behaviours you will use. It is only honest to acknowledge that these thoughts will creep into your mind at times, so it is important to recognise them and be able to consciously place them to one side.

It is important to remember that observation of yourself and your behaviour is only one part of the process: the clients will be closely watching the therapist's reactions, especially when something challenging or unexpected occurs. The therapist who gives a message of being preoccupied, distracted or unprepared will be observed by the clients as not being involved, not being present for them, and thus less engaged in the process. This will result in a lack of trust, and therefore a lack of risk taking to move forward, which may reduce the effectiveness of the session.

The use of supervision or a co-therapist can greatly help the therapist to achieve a depth of self-knowledge, as they provide an opportunity for you to safely explore the issues that have arisen through the experience of working in this particular way. These issues are considered in more detail in Chapter 3.

Use of self

- Develop a clear understanding of 'where you are coming from'
- Know your vulnerability
- Recognise traits within your behaviour
- Be aware that you are not only observing but also being observed
- Use yourself to provide a secure anchor

COMMUNICATION

The second aspect of Figure 4.2 that continuously informs the outcome of the session and therefore contributes to the end product is that of communication. This is an inevitable and essential part of human life (Minardi and Riley, 1997), so we will consider the roles of both verbal and non-verbal communication that provide meaning within creative therapies.

Verbal communication

The occupational therapist within their central role in the therapeutic process will use verbal communication for a number of purposes.

- To develop interaction between themselves and the clients. This will be evident not only in the ways in which verbalisation takes place but also in the way communication is facilitated by positioning the members to encourage interaction.
- To engage the clients in the chosen activity. Some of this communication will be task orientated, explaining the use of the medium, but other communication will encourage involvement of the participants.
- To facilitate understanding of the process. This reassures the clients throughout the session, ensuring understanding not only of the activity but also of the purpose of working in this way.

- To explore issues – understanding who is active within the process, the balance and level of communication, the ways issues are accepted or avoided.
- To reflect back – to check understanding with the client and the co-therapist to inform the end product.

This process involves sending and receiving messages effectively, and giving appropriate feedback in response to messages received (Benson, 1987), so it becomes a fundamental part of any therapeutic relationship.

Observing the pattern of verbal communication gives information about individuals and the session as a whole. Firstly there is the informal, social communication which occurs through the use of small talk, chatter, jokes and casual remarks. This gives information about who is conversing with whom, and who is isolated from the process through not being a part of it. Informal conversation provides an indication of the mood of the session and the individuals within it, which is also apparent through the body language the clients display. This is a necessary part of any communication process, providing the 'light relief' to balance the more weighty aspect of formal communication.

The formal part of therapeutic communication involves giving instructions, expressing feelings, searching for understanding through using the media and using verbal clues to facilitate the therapeutic process. This dialogue forms the 'weight' of the session, providing clues about any member's individual abilities to work with the dynamics they have uncovered. This can often be a hesitant, painful process, and it is useful to focus not only on the person who is articulating the problems but also on those who are listening to and receiving them.

Both formal and informal communication is dependent on being heard, making it a two-way process. Listening involves closely attending to another person to receive information which is evident on three levels: the content of the actual words, the ways in which words are expressed, and the non-verbal communication which accompanies the conversation (Burnard, 1992). For the therapist, this process rests on the ability to empathise with the client, not to judge or criticise, and to demonstrate a warmth and sincerity which encourages the conversation to become a meaningful experience. The ability to listen to others, to give them space and support, is a vital part of the communication process. As well as observing the quality of really hearing another person, the therapist will also be observing the behaviours which accompany listening, a point where there will be an overlapping of the strands of evidence being collected. The therapist will be noting those members who want to talk all the time, who find it difficult to make space for another. There are times of interruptions, or of one person finishing a sentence for another. Equally there will be clients who are unable to communicate verbally but who demonstrate their engagement or lack of it through their body language. These communication behaviours provide information, and can be reflected back within the session as well as being gathered to take forward to the end product.

As a therapist you are using your communication skills to achieve different purposes within a session. At the beginning your communication will be welcoming and reassuring, making the members feel valued and accepted. As the session moves on so your communication becomes involved with exploring, interpreting, challenging and acknowledging difficulties. In the final phase of the session you are affirming the client's work, reflecting your understanding, and giving encouragement for the next session. One part of the artistry of the therapist is to adapt communication skills appropriately, so that they support and strengthen their role, enabling the process to move forward to a therapeutic outcome.

The topic of communication provides threads which relate not only to the ways words are used but also to how communication is being used within a session. If conversation is occurring on the periphery of the session it indicates that something is taking place to prevent the work from being done within the main work area. An example of this occurred within the second of a series of creative therapy groups held in a mental health setting.

> The therapists prepared the room for the group by placing some small tables together to form a large rectangle. There were chairs along each side, and the therapist leading the group positioned herself at a short end. The members filled the chairs on either side, and by chance the co-therapist ended up sitting at the other short end, opposite the leader. The session began with the leader welcoming the group, then introducing the materials and the activities which were planned for the session. The group members soon engaged in the task, but there was little discussion accompanying the activities. The session appeared to be stilted and hesitant, with long silences and a lack of interaction, until the members left their seats, moving to the sinks to wash the materials. Whilst washing up the group talked openly about the activity and their involvement in it, exchanging views and conversing freely.

It was observation of and reflection on what was actually occurring within the session which enabled the therapists to see the key role that positioning of the group was taking. The group members were facing each other in two long rows, with any cohesiveness of the arrangement being broken by the presence of the leaders at either end. By strategically placing themselves separately within the body of the group, both leaders could have integrated themselves, resulting in a more interactive and cohesive group. This might have encouraged the discussion and interaction to take place around the table where the work occurred, rather than on the periphery of the activity. Therefore information gathered on this particular session related to the fact that the group was not sufficiently cohesive at this stage to work with this seating arrangement. They avoided issues within the session, preferring to deal with them in the less formal arena of the periphery.

Another thread which contributes to our understanding of communication is the role of silence, as within any session of creative therapies there will be times when this occurs. Silence has an invisible presence which takes many forms, making it important to understand what it is saying, as silence can reflect not just a lack of speech or sound but also the whole mood of a situation. It can be calm and peaceful, a thinking time which is welcomed when the clients are absorbed in the task, or it can be bold and threatening, a mixed message which begs exploration yet challenges those who seek to break it. In a world surrounded by noise and sound, silence can be an uncomfortable presence, one which starts in a small way yet as it grows engages everyone within it. It may be broken by deliberate action, through a client not being able to tolerate it any longer (which is usually an emotional moment) or can be allowed to fade away and lose its importance. One student talked of 'silence slowing down', where he saw silence being used in a positive way, giving time for private self-exploration and then gently fading into the background of the session.

As a therapist you are observing a silence to gain yet more information, asking yourself a number of questions about the roles silence is taking, who is able to cope with it, who breaks it and why it is occurring. You may choose to stay with the situation, observing how others will look to you to take the responsibility of breaking it to relieve their discomfort, whilst recognising their need to address the problem for themselves. Your ability to extract information about behaviour from this non-vocal message gives you another thread to weave into the tapestry.

Use of self

- Recognising the role of your verbal communication
- Engaging in active listening
- Understanding communication within your clients
- Staying with silence

Non-verbal communication

Verbal communication provides evidence from a creative therapy session which contributes to the end product. However, the evidence of words is also accompanied by a significant amount of evidence which is gained through non-verbal communication, which can replace or reinforce speech. Therefore we need to think about the messages which this behaviour gives to the therapist. Aspects of non-verbal communication we consider here are body language, touch, and eye contact.

Body language

As a therapist gathering strands of information we can explore body language as a form of physical communication. The way in which clients present themselves through their body language gives some indication about their moods, responses and self-management. This is particularly important within creative therapies, where the therapist depends on clues from numerous sources. These may be evident in the way a client arrives and engages with others or in the way they respond when presented with an activity. Many of the clients with whom we work have difficulty voicing their feelings, so watching their body language provides important information about likes and dislikes, which may conflict with what they are saying.

The body language of posture adds another strand of information about mood or engagement. The firmly crossed arms of a client suggest a barrier to involvement, as they are demonstrating a negative or defensive stance to becoming engaged in the activity. Posture and appearance are apparent as soon as the group members enter the room, giving initial clues about the state of the group that day. These clues allow the therapist to adjust both the content of the session and their approach to it, ensuring that the session is appropriate. This fluid decision making is part of the artistry of the therapist, where the plan for the session is changed or adapted in response to non-verbal messages.

Touch

Touch is an aspect of non-verbal communication which can be informally present within a creative therapy session or can take a lead role. It requires a sensitive approach, as it may be wrongly perceived or resented, and so is dependent on careful communication. The ways in which we use touch will relate to the individual aims we have identified with our clients, and the information gathered from the experience of touching will inform us of their ability to engage in the process. It is useful to consider the different ways touch can be incorporated to provide the focus of the activity, for example by holding hands with others, or incidentally through sharing materials and using spontaneous gestures. Touch can also be used to give and receive comfort, and a client's ability to engage in touching provides further evidence for our end product.

Eye contact

The ability to look at someone or something directly is another important aspect of non-verbal communication. Eye contact is a social skill which gives messages of interest, of involvement and of interaction. We use our eyes as part of our conversational skills, indicating with them when it is the turn of another to speak, or drawing someone into the discussion by engaging them in eye contact. Equally, if we wish to withdraw from a situation we disengage through ceasing to maintain eye contact, and many of you will be familiar with the patterns on the carpet when a volunteer is sought for an unpopular task! As a therapist you will be considering whether eye contact changes during the course of your intervention, looking for the reasons behind the change and developing an awareness of the pattern which unfolds within and between individuals.

The therapist plays a very active role in gathering information from non-verbal clues. These will be considered within the total picture of the client, but creative therapies provide us with an intervention that we can adapt to focus on specific aspects of behaviour. The art of the therapist is involved in recognising this need in the first instance, and then creating the opportunity for these issues to be worked with. The scope of media which we can use provides a flexible working environment within which to explore this dynamic.

Use of self

- Paying attention to the messages of body language
- Changing the emphasis of the session in response to these
- Involving touch when appropriate
- Demonstrating that clients are valued through preparing for them
- Being aware of the messages within your own behaviour

PARTICIPATION

The final explicit thread we intend to explore is that of participation. One aspect of creativity that is evident in the process of our work is the ability to work with creative media, requiring active participation from therapist and clients. The ease with which this is practised is evidence for our final product.

Participation indicates a commitment by the client to become engaged in a therapeutic process through the medium of creative therapy. It demonstrates the ability to use the media as the tools for self-exploration, and to take the challenges that are part of working in this way. Participation gives first-hand experience upon which to draw, and shows an ability to choose to change, recognising that change requires a degree of risk taking. The therapist gathering information will be considering the ease with which a client is involved in the creative therapy process, the times when it is too hard, and their ability to overcome the difficulties of working in this way. Within creative therapies we often work with clients for whom risk taking and change are threatening concepts, yet they are necessary to achieve self-growth. The confidence to take risks or make changes can be gained through active participation with the process where understanding happens through a creative route, trusting the support within the session. The therapist is using their artistry to enable these steps to be taken, to encourage participation and to observe the client's ability to become involved.

Information is also gathered from non-participation, a complex dynamic that needs to be recognised and explored. Non-participation occurs for a number of reasons, making it important for the therapist to check their understanding of the situation to uncover the real reason. There may be a straightforward explanation of the behaviour, which occurred in the following example.

Two students were involved in planning and leading a session based on the use of clay. They had excellent ideas, and were soon actively engaged in working with the medium. They were unaware that a member of the group had withdrawn from the session, sitting quietly but not engaging in the activity. When the group reached the discussion phase they were surprised when this group member stated that she hated using clay, as the texture was cold and wet and it was messy. She expressed her feelings about the material, and added that she felt abandoned by the leaders, who had not noticed her discomfort.

This reason for non-participation appeared straightforward and easily explained, although others are complex messages about mood, feelings, emotions and past experiences. The behaviour is reinforced by the accompanying body language, providing clues to increase our understanding. It is important to remember that active participation is not always required for links to be made from situations (Whitaker, 1985). In the above example the individual may have been more affected by her feelings of withdrawal than if she had been actively involved, as she was required to consider and express her discomfort, thus learning from the experience.

For the therapist an issue of participation relates to self-disclosure, the act of revealing personal information about oneself to the group (Bloch and Crouch, 1985). Brown (1994) states that this can be a verbal or non-verbal process, suggesting that verbal self-disclosure encompasses personal feelings, personal information and personal values whilst non-verbal disclosure is apparent through appearance and manner. The ability to use self-disclosure can help clients to achieve their goals, as it allows them to recognise that the therapist is genuinely involved, and that their disclosures will not be entirely one-sided. However, there is a need for balance, to ensure that the therapist's communications do not distract the clients from their work. The extent of this self-disclosure is a choice which will vary according to the time and mood, making firm rules unviable. There is a need to define boundaries both for oneself and for others, so that they are not encroached upon (Glassman and Kates, 1990), ensuring that dignity and privacy are respected. This process will be assisted through knowing oneself and being able to use this knowledge creatively to move the process forwards, which in turn provides information for our end product.

Use of self

- Observing active participation of others throughout the session
- Recognising and understanding reasons for non-participation
- Observing changes in personal behaviour, involvement and non-involvement
- Considering the place of self-disclosure, the way it is used and its content

So far we have looked at the aspects of behaviour which are apparent within creative therapies, which the therapist is able to observe and make sense of. To use our original illustration (Figure 4.2), the therapist is gathering these threads of information into one hand. These threads all contribute to the end product, but only if their meanings are explored and understood. This is the process of interpreting the group, working out the issues which underpin the behaviour. To achieve this the therapist draws upon the skills of reasoning and reflection, skills which are informed through theory to become an integral part of the process.

THEORY

There are three theory bases which inform creative therapies.

- Occupational therapy theory – explored within Chapter 1
- Psychological theory – explored within Chapter 2
- Group dynamic theory – explored within Chapter 3

The therapist uses these theory bases in a fluid and interchangeable way throughout the whole process of creative therapies to gather further threads of evidence to weave into the end product. Revisiting these theories will enable you to draw out the key issues of each, helping you to recognise factors that underpin the creative therapy approach. It might be helpful to return to our initial figure, (presented again in Figure 4.3) to remind you of the basic structure which we use our artistry to develop.

Psychodynamic theory + Occupational therapy ⇨ **Creative therapies**

Figure 4.3 The constitution of creative therapies

Despite a sound theory base the task of the therapist working within creative therapies may appear deceptively simple, and it is this simplicity which is open to misunderstanding. There is a difficulty in finding the right language to convey the complexity of the approach – which we hope this book addresses. Fleming (1994) describes 'an elegance of practice' achieved through being able to 'do' an activity such as creative therapies, which links to the artistry of the therapist in working creatively within the medium. However, we need to develop the language to explain this practice, externalising the knowledge and reasoning process to produce the evidence which is required for the outcome of the group.

REASONING SKILLS

Clinical reasoning provides a structure to thinking that both organises and supports the thought processes which are used to understand and evaluate a therapeutic experience (Neistadt, 1998). It is suggested that this process uses several forms of reasoning – procedural, interactive, conditional and narrative – all of which contribute different aspects of information (Mattingly and Fleming, 1994). As therapists we are involved in searching for an understanding of the client's problem, and so may use this process of reasoning to assist us in the task.

In creative therapies we initially seek information from a theory base, relating to a clinical presentation or to a dynamic of behaviour, which gives a greater understanding of the presenting situation. Let us take an example of a client with an eating disorder, and attempt to follow through the reasoning process in relation to this presentation.

Our thinking is informed by **procedural reasoning**, which defines the problem and selects the method of intervention, ensuring that the decision to use creative therapies as a therapeutic strategy is carefully considered. We may decide that creative therapies provide an approach which focuses on interpersonal skills and the opportunities to explore underlying behaviour, thus making it an appropriate choice.

This level of understanding and decision making is further informed by **interactive reasoning**, a process which takes place between the therapist and the client, enabling a greater understanding of the person. As trust is likely to be a significant issue within the therapeutic involvement we need to ensure that the structures are in place to ensure trust, and that it is open and explicit. Creative therapy facilitates a level of interaction and provides a forum for contact through using a creative activity.

Conditional reasoning is a type of thinking between the client and the therapist in which the therapist and the client are able to consider ways of moving forward, recognising problems that may remain but developing a sound base upon which to build despite previous experience. This will involve trying out new strategies and behaviours, understanding responses which have become habitual and acknowledging the part these are playing within the presentation.

Finally, **narrative reasoning** explores the story both from the client's perspective and from the shared experience of the client and the therapist. Creative therapies provide an opportunity for this through the use of the media, which may be more acceptable than some of the purely verbal therapeutic approaches. There is the dynamic of this being a shared experience, as the therapist is also engaged in the activity, and will be contributing their own perceptions. This builds and consolidates the relationship between the client and the therapist.

The theory of using clinical reasoning to facilitate the understanding of a creative therapy process partly explains the art of the therapist in being able to access knowledge and information from different perspectives within a clinical situation. We have acknowledged that this approach is different each time we use it, and that it is dependent on interaction which cannot be preplanned or rehearsed, so there is a need to get in touch with the thinking that enables us to use our information in the ways that we do. This thinking is complex as it occurs on different levels (Finlay, 1997). Fleming (1994) proposes that therapists think and work in three parallel tracts: a **procedural** tract, which draws information from the presenting problem, an **interactional** tract, which encompasses images relating to the client, and finally a **conditional** tract, which informs actions in relation to the client. She suggests that there is a dynamic process of interaction between these tracts, yet each provides evidence for the way we work and the decisions we take within a session.

Reasoning remains an essential skill for the therapist, one that is constantly being employed, yet it takes place beneath the surface of our work. It is the thinking which enables us to qualify the actions, questions or interactions which we took at any one moment, as there is a need to ensure that these decisions are based on reasoning ability, rather than taking place at a whim. The artistry of the therapist is evident in the way this thinking becomes refined and seemingly effortless as it focuses on the key issues that unfold within the session. The ability to make our reasoning processes explicit justifies our therapeutic intervention.

Use of self

- Reflect on your practice
- Recognise the thinking which took place at a particular time
- Observe what was informing it
- Check your ability to make this reasoning explicit

REFLECTION

A strand of information which encompasses all these aspects of our practice and which informs our final end product is gained through a process of reflection. Reflection enables the therapist not only to think about what has occurred within a creative therapy session, using this to inform the end product, but also to examine practice within the process, learning from the experience and thus making changes for the future.

Tickle (1994) suggests thoughtful deliberation as a straightforward definition of reflection. This suits the process of achieving an end product from a creative therapy session as the therapist uses her artistry to reflect on the experience, using this thinking to inform the end result. Examples of reflection are given following each of the sections in Chapter 5. In these examples the looking back and thoughtful deliberation which constitute reflection have enabled us to gain evidence from the group itself and from the behaviour of each person within the group. Thus we have explored practical aspects such as the choice of activity, the leadership skills, length of the group's life and preparation for action. This reflection provided examples of practice, clues to the way the group worked and situations which may have influenced outcomes. It enabled us to consider whether a group met its intentions and how this knowledge could be built upon when planning another session.

Reflecting on the behaviour of each client allows us to gain an understanding of their experience of the session. This thinking would encompass all the issues which impact on this experience: participation, interaction, involvement, motivation, the display of mood and emotion. Using the information gathered will enable us to create an end product in relation to the individual which will inform decision making. It will provide evidence which is shared with other involved practitioners as well as with the client and will justify the therapeutic choice.

Finally the therapist will reflect on their own performance, using it as a means of developing and improving practice. This process requires both cognitive and affective skills which enable the therapist to be aware of their own performance, to describe and critically analyse the experience, to synthesise ideas and to assess and appraise the situation to allow judgements to be made (Spalding, 1998). Only by critically reflecting on the process can the therapist develop an in-depth awareness of the experience from which to develop new understandings and improve practice. Schon (1983, p. 295) describes a 'reflective conversation with a situation', which provides a framework for this practice. The ability to work reflectively demonstrates an aspect of the art of the therapist to question and explore whilst at the same time being honest and self-critical.

One of the most useful aids to reflection is to develop the habit of keeping a reflective diary (Alsop, 1995). This practice encourages the therapist not just to write up the structure of a creative therapy session but to really delve beneath the surface, to explore the issues which were significant not only to the clients but also to themselves. In this way you are able to monitor and become aware of your own performance. The process may be assisted by asking reflective questions which break down the experience. Examples might be:

- What actually occurred at that point?
- Why did I respond in that way?
- What was I trying to achieve?
- How could I have intervened differently?

These questions can be used to examine your own behaviour within the session. In this way you can develop a greater understanding of yourself, through considering your actions and thinking through how they affected the process of the session. This understanding will support your central role, as an increased understanding of your own behaviour will give you a greater ability to understand and interpret the behaviour of your clients.

Use of self

- Reflect in action as well as on the action
- Reflect on your own performance as well as that of your clients
- Think deeply about the session as a whole
- Use tools to assist this process, for example a reflective diary
- Identify aspects from the reflective process which need greater exploration
- Implement different strategies as a result of your reflections
- Use the experience to inform the end product
- Become a reflective practitioner

We now have the threads of theory, reasoning and reflection which the therapist gathers in the second hand. As both hands come together the process of creating an outcome becomes tangible. Each thread brings information which can be included or discarded as, layer upon layer, they build the **process** into the end **product.**

CONCLUSION

This chapter has placed the therapist within the central role of a creative therapy intervention. It has explored the artistry upon which this role depends if there is to be an outcome from the process of working. We have suggested the creative model of gathering threads of evidence which inform the final outcome, recognising that each outcome will be an individual perspective. Although we have explored some of the more obvious threads in some depth we do not see this as a comprehensive collection. The creativity inherent within the creative therapy approach ensures that there is no finite list, but that there is an adaptability to respond to the clues which become apparent as the process of the work unfolds. To achieve this there has to be an investment of the self which may present both professional and personal challenges, and we have attempted to outline some of these within the theme of the use of self.

In summary, this chapter suggests that the therapist uses their artistry to create:

The process:
- The reality of a creative therapy session.
- A central core of stability from which clients can experience self-growth.
- An opportunity to use media in a creative way.
- An investment of the self.

The product:
- Information gained through using strategies such as observation, communication and participation.
- Information gained through using underlying knowledge, theory, reasoning skills and reflective practice.
- Collection of evidence → the **end product.**

REFERENCES

Alsop, A. (1995) The Professional Portfolio – Purpose, Process and Practice, Part 2, *British Journal of Occupational Therapy,* **58**(8), 337–340.

Benson, J.F. (1987) Working More Creatively with Groups, Tavistock Publications, London.

Bloch, S. and Crouch, E. (1985) *Therapeutic Factors in Group Psychotherapy,* Oxford University Press, Oxford.

Brown, A. (1994) *Groupwork,* 3rd edn, Ashgate Publishing, Hampshire.

Burnard, P. (1992) *Effective Communication Skills for Health Professionals,* Chapman & Hall, London.

Finlay, L. (1997) *The Practice of Psychosocial Occupational Therapy*, 2nd edn, Stanley Thornes, Cheltenham.

Fleming, C.H. (1994) The Search for Tacit Knowledge. In: *Clinical Reasoning: Forms of Inquiry in a Therapeutic Practice* (eds Mattingly, C. and Fleming, C.H.), Davis Co., Philadelphia.

Glassman, U. and Kates, L. (1990) *Group Work: A Humanistic Approach,* Sage Publications, London.

Mattingly, C. and Fleming, M.H. (eds) (1994) Giving Language to Practice. In: *Clinical Reasoning: Forms of Inquiry in a Therapeutic Practice,* Davis Co., Philadelphia.

May, R. (1975) *The Courage To Create*, Norton and Co., London.

Minardi, H.A. and Riley, M.J. (1997) *Communication in Healthcare,* Butterworth-Heinemann, Oxford.

Neistadt, M.E. (1998) Teaching Clinical Reasoning as a Thinking Frame, *The American Journal of Occupational Therapy,* **52**(3), 221–229.

Rogers, N. (1993) *The Creative Connection: Expressive Arts as Healing,* Science and Behaviour Books, California.

Russ, S.W. (1993) *Affect and Creativity,* Lawrence Erlbaum Associates, New Jersey.

Schon, D.A. (1983) *The Reflective Practitioner: How Professionals Think in Action,* Basic Books, Harper Collins, America.

Spalding, N.J. (1998) Reflection in Professional Development: a personal experience, *British Journal of Therapy and Rehabilitation*, 5(7), 379–382.

Stein, F. and Cutler, S.K. (1998) *Psychosocial Occupational Therapy,* Singular Publishing Group Inc, San Diego.

Stockwell, R. (1984) Creative Therapies. In: *Occupational Therapy in Short term Psychiatry* (ed. Willson, M.), Churchill Livingstone, Edinburgh.

Tickle, L. (1994) *The Induction of New Teachers*, Cassell, London.

Warren, B. (1984) *Using the Creative Arts in Therapy,* Croom Helm, London.

Whitaker, D.S. (1985) *Using Groups to Help People,* Routledge, London.

Part Two

Creative media

5 THE CREATIVE MEDIA AND THEIR APPLICATION

INTRODUCTION

In creative therapies we select activities for their creative potential. The use of activity forms part of the occupational therapy triad, which consists of the relationship between the therapist, the client and the creative media (Hagedorn, 1992). In this chapter we do not set out to offer a series of recipes – ideas of creative activities to use and how to use them. We hope that by now it has become evident that the creative therapy approach is far too dynamic, responsive, flexible and creative for that! To explore creative activity we have used themes based on the creative media. These themes are:

- the use of paper and paint;
- the use of body and movement;
- the use of clay and sculpture;
- the use of sound and rhythm;
- the use of text and verse;
- the use of the environment and new ideas.

What we aim to provide here is an analysis of the potential use of these media in creative therapies. We hope that this analysis conveys a sense of how we can use the media freely: a use which is not bound by expectations of the product, which allows us to be responsive to the needs of our clients and provides opportunities for the therapist to apply their artistry to enhance the effectiveness of the therapeutic experience. We achieve this analysis by exploring four aspects of the use of each creative medium. We consider the **resources** required – things like space, consumables and equipment. We then discuss the **qualities** of the medium, such as whether it has permanence or fluidity or whether it is physically demanding. We go on to explore the **process** involved in using the medium, issues such as the scope and structure of sessions, how we turn ideas into reality through experience. Finally we offer **illustrations** of the use of the media.

These illustrations have come from our work with second-year undergraduate occupational therapy students in student-led sessions which are established as learning experiences. These sessions occur over a period of five weeks. The usual arrangement is for two students to lead the group and two to act as non-participant observers focusing on a predetermined aspect of group dynamics such as roles or group forming. The remaining members, approximately eight, participate in the activities. The student-led creative therapy sessions last for 1–1.5 hours and we as lecturers also take part, relinquishing our usual leadership role. The student-led session is followed by a further hour of discussion. The non-participant observers initiate the discussion by contributing their material, which is supported by background reading on the specific group dynamic. The other students are involved by reflecting on what has occurred, exploring any pertinent issues arising out of each session and linking them across the experiences of previous sessions in conjunction with psychodynamic, occupational therapy and group work theory.

The intention of these sessions is *not* that the students undergo a therapeutic process. By participating in the sessions, having an opportunity to be a leader and an observer, and by being involved in the discussion through reflection, they learn about psychodynamic practice, group work and using creative media. These skills can then be transferred to the clinical setting. We therefore see the primary aim of their involvement as a learning experience. As with all learning, a by-product is that the students are touched by the experience in some way. They become more aware of their personal involvement, of their willingness to explore their style, their ability to be dynamic and flexible and their place within the group.

The illustrations provided of the student-led sessions contain examples of both excellent and less developed practice. They can be read individually alongside the relevant section on the creative media. However, read collectively they serve to illustrate a number of issues which relate to the use of creative media in therapy, they can be used effectively to support the information provided in Chapter 3 about the seven dimensions of creative working.

By discussing the use of the creative media in themes we are not suggesting media should be used in isolation. There is no reason why any one session, series of sessions, or indeed individual activity should not use a range of media. We do not explicitly discuss how to choose which medium to use; this would be an impossible task as so many factors influence this and there are so many permutations on what might be the appropriate course of action. Knowledge of the qualities of the different media, the client and of oneself as therapist all contribute to the selection. With the client the therapist would explore which creative media they have used in the past, what they enjoy and what kind of person they are. The therapist may also make use of the centring process described by Natalie Rogers (1993). This is a strategy used at the beginning of the session and involves acknowledging what the client is expressing and bases the selection of the media on this. If the client is looking physically tense or making use of gesture while talking, the use of body or movement might be appropriate; alternatively if they involve imagery in their language they might respond well to the use of paper and paint. From the therapist's viewpoint, we are all more comfortable with some media than with others. While retaining an open mind, personal preferences should be acknowledged in our work, as these are manifestations of our own psyche.

Before discussing the creative media in detail, we want to emphasise that their use in creative therapies does not rely on achieving competency in technical or traditional skills. Inherent to the creative therapy approach is a free use of the medium, one where traditional skills are laid aside, rules are abandoned and where there are no judgements of right or wrong, good or bad.

So, to the use of the creative media – enjoy, consider, be inspired and experiment!

THE USE OF PAPER AND PAINT

The use of art is a familiar medium within creative therapies, it takes its place amongst other creative media and provides a route for creative therapies. However, the word 'art' appears to conjure up the need to be able to draw, to make a picture or an acceptable image or to produce an end product. This is not the remit of the use of art in creative therapies. We are concerned with the process which takes place whilst using this medium, a process which enables exploration of the past as it lives on and affects the present. For this reason we have chosen to call this theme the use of paper and paint: we feel that this reflects a broader concept of using art in therapy. The use of paper and paint in teaching sessions with our undergraduate occupational therapy students has equipped us with examples from their work which we use here to illustrate or emphasise particular points.

The choice of this creative medium, as of others, involves planning and preparing a session, exploring its content from a psychodynamic perspective, and then evaluating it afterwards. All aspects of group and individual dynamics give us material upon which to build, and yet nothing can be predicted, repeated or recreated in exactly the same way. Each session is a snapshot of experience, a fragment of growth which stands alone. As Cameron (1996) suggests, this may be used as a route to provide healing, insight, creative problem solving and the resolution of conflict.

Art has been a powerful medium which has accompanied society through the ages. It is a visual form of expression which surrounds our environment. Gombrich (1960) suggests that the early cave paintings dating from the Ice Age, some 15,000 years ago, show man's need to exert power over animals by recreating them. In this way the animals, upon which they were dependent for survival, remained present and would not desert them; they were captured through the drawings. In a similar way the Egyptians depicted their kings and creatures in a powerful but stereotypical manner, so that the images left on the walls of the tombs and temples portrayed a fantasy of importance and strength. Today, images are still created which link the world inside the person to the world outside. Jung considered imagination and creativity as healing forces (Feder and Feder, 1981); he was concerned with symbolic messages from the unconscious which the approach of creative therapies moves towards the conscious. It is this process of making explicit unconscious or forgotten thoughts, and thus exploring them to facilitate growth, which we use within an art process. The image is created almost as if by accident; it is externalised and can then be explored. Art gives opportunities to know more about yourself because, to some degree, it is within everyone's capacity to reinterpret their own experience and to share in the experience of others through an involvement with the world of art (The Attenborough Report, 1985).

Occupational therapy and art therapy

Occupational therapists use the activity of art differently from other allied professionals, particularly art therapists. We have a different training, background and professional identity and therefore view the medium as a tool to be used and explored in different ways. It is important to clarify our approach from the start as, although we may work in conjunction with art therapists, our approach is not the same and should not be confused.

Art therapists are artists in their own right. They will normally have completed an art degree and have some postgraduate experience before they undertake further training to enable them to qualify as an art therapist. This training is accompanied by personal therapy and is a balance of theory and practice. Students undertake clinical practice in a manner similar to occupational therapy education. An obvious difference is the length of the process, which therefore results in more mature students both training and qualifying as art therapists. Art therapists remain a smaller profession numerically and at times share management or working space with occupational therapists. This issue may contribute to the potential confusion of roles, particularly as the two professions can act as co-leaders within group work.

A valuable discussion with an art therapist colleague enabled us to explore some major differences between the professions in the use of the media and the use of themselves. It seems that the main differences lie in two areas: the significance given to the created image and the emphasis placed on the dynamic process which occurs.

Art therapists work within the medium of 'art' and are focused within it. Art is their tool for helping clients to explore and express conscious and unconscious thoughts. This inner world is made visible through an image or a picture. The image is owned by the client; it has been expressed by them and is a conscious portrayal of that moment of time. The permanence of the expressed image gives a pictorial expression of the inner experience of the client. The work of the session is often kept, giving it an individual value because the meaning of the image may not become explicit until a later time. The focus of the session is therefore on the process of the work and on the completed image, the visual expression or the product.

Within the process Schaverien (1987) explores the change that takes place between the therapist, the client and the medium. She calls this 'the embodied image' which is dependent on the trust and relationship that develops between the therapist and their client. Only when this relationship of trust is firmly established can the 'real' work of art therapy begin. The strength of the relationship is the factor which allows the image to lead, the image that emerges from the client's unconscious and which has an energy and force of its own. So there is not necessarily a visually descriptive picture but an image which is unpredictable, unplanned and very free. The reality of the expression is returned to through verbal exploration, requiring specific professional skills. For both occupational therapists and art therapists the process of reaching a point of consciously expressing an unconscious inner thought is important, but for art therapists this process leads on to exploration of the image, and understanding and growth is achieved through the analysis of the work produced. Is the 'embodied image' (Schaverien, 1987) the key to the differences in our approach? The more we thought about the approach of psychodynamic work within occupational therapy the more we felt we needed to clarify this point.

The occupational therapy approach is credible in that it explores the process of change which occurs through using a medium, but we almost deliberately turn our focus away from the 'end product'. The image produced may be more superficial, more directed, less of a gut reaction. In this way the importance of the image is not as significant. It is no less valuable because it is still expressive, but it is a different route towards exploring personal growth. Occupational therapists will be more concerned with the dynamic process which is undertaken to reach this point of understanding and growth and will focus on many other aspects of behaviour within the session. For this reason they tend to participate in the activity but retain an overview of the dynamics of the session. A great deal of emphasis is placed on setting up both the activity and the session to explore the intrapersonal and interpersonal dynamic relationships, and it is here that the specific professional skills of the occupational therapist come to the fore. It is primarily through this process that the occupational therapist works to facilitate understanding and self-development within the group members.

A very simple example may help to clarify this point. The occupational therapist, in preparation for a session to be led by an art therapist, paid specific attention to setting up the physical environment – in particular gathering the tables together to create a group space within which to work. In the occupational therapist's eyes the environment had been arranged to facilitate the dynamic processes of the group. On arrival the art therapist promptly separated the tables, enabling each individual to work on their own. The session took place in supportive silence. There was a focused discussion at the end of the session which was based on the paintings produced, with little attention paid to the dynamic process. Whilst this simplistic example should not be taken in isolation it illustrates a different relationship within the work.

Inevitably there is blurring between professional roles and ways of working. This is a positive feature, with the subtle differences of one expertise enhancing the other. We have come to feel that the crux of these differences lies in the significance given to the created image and the emphasis placed on the dynamic process. Added to these philosophical differences are the individual ways of working of each therapist, and these add their own perspective to the blurring of professional boundaries. The two professional groups of art therapy and occupational therapy have a great deal to contribute to one another and we have referred to art therapy literature in this section where it supports understanding of our approach in creative therapies.

Resources

For many people an experience of using paper and paint will bring back memories of a childhood activity, perhaps within a school room which provided a certain range of facilities. This is similar to a therapeutic approach in that attention has to be paid to people, materials and physical space. It may, however, create preconceived ideas about using the medium, an anxiety that it will be childish, or that it will be product focused. To use paper and paint creatively and therapeutically requires preparation and attention to detail to enable participants to gain the maximum benefit from the experience.

The occupational therapist is a fundamental resource within a creative session. The interrelationship of the medium, the person and the therapist provides the basic structure for the work. Thus the role of the therapist may be seen as 'a knowledgeable empathetic guide who develops a collaborative relationship with the patient and maintains the frame work of treatment' (Bruce and Borg, 1987, p. 54). Empathy in this statement links back to the humanist approach of showing an understanding of the person, which communicates itself to the person and demonstrates acceptance. The framework provides a security to begin to express and explore issues that have remained unacknowledged, perhaps hidden. These link to resources in terms of providing a safe environment from both a physical and a psychological perspective. The need for caring and respect towards the people who are to be involved with the process is defined by attention to this environment (Liebmann, 1986).

The use of paper and paint does not require artistic ability from the occupational therapist but it is an exciting medium to use and explore. It does require knowledge of resources and materials that will enable the participants to use the materials with confidence. This may be different from the client's previous experiences of art, working within a teacher/pupil dynamic, where the teacher was usually seen as 'the expert' and judge. Experience of the ways in which materials interact, the grading between a simple activity and a more complex one, are qualities the therapist will bring to the session. This knowledge contributes to the state of preparedness.

The usual considerations regarding the physical space available should be taken into account when preparing for a session. The room should provide flexibility, so that there is an opportunity for each person to work within an area of space – alone, in small groups or together on a joint project. The room should afford some privacy with access to a range of materials. A starting point when discussing materials is to consider what is meant by paper. As the purpose of using art in creative therapies is not about producing a masterpiece, ready for mounting and framing, it could be argued that the quality of paper and materials do not matter. However, this attitude belittles the importance of the process, rendering it unsatisfactory as an experience. If the activity has been chosen to fulfil an aim, a purpose within the treatment approach, then it should be adequately resourced. There is a place for good quality paper as well as cheaper sugar paper and even for waste paper, old newspapers, magazines, and other textures such as tissue and crepe. Each will provide a different choice for the individual and can be explored in different ways. Being presented with a choice at this stage may be a challenge for an individual, and will indicate a level of confidence, or the ability to make a decision.

The range of materials with which to work is endless, making it a very flexible creative medium. Materials should be carefully considered to meet different needs and may change from session to session. A variety should be available to inspire and capture the imagination (Jones, 1972). Pencil, crayon, pastels and charcoal can be considered to be the less permanent materials, as they can be erased and changed. They may provide a more tentative approach, one which is not as definite as paint and which encourages an individual to explore the medium. It is obvious that these should be stored with care, and that tidying them away is an integral part of their use.

Paints are many and various. Cheap instant ready-mixed colours which can be stored easily lend themselves to the creative therapy approach. They can be decanted into smaller palettes or containers to prevent waste and to keep colours pure. Even this level of choice gives an indication of a client's functioning. Brushes also come in all sorts and sizes, again adding an element of personal choice to the selection process. Good brushes tend to be expensive and should be cleaned and stored with care.

Art can be messy and to use the materials expressively usually means there is an element of mess involved. Having permission to make a mess can be significant for some clients. A sink with running water is a real asset, disposable aprons and plenty of towels encourage participants to feel that it is acceptable to make a mess and preparing for mess is a way of implicitly giving permission for it to happen. The messiness may extend to the floor and to the work surfaces, which need to be easily cleaned. Rooms often have to be used for other purposes, which can dictate the choice of materials, but time should be available for clearing up, so that it is seen as part of the process and not as an additional activity. One of the constraints in community work may be the need for the therapist to access premises which are only used on a sessional basis. As with most of the creative media, the content of the sessions can be adapted to fit the room available, but it should be acknowledged that the use of paper and paint may present practical difficulties that need to be overcome.

It is important to consider the issue of storage, both of the materials that are gathered in preparation for a session and of the products of the session. What message is conveyed if paper is torn and dirty, paints dried up and brushes caked with glue? Care for the equipment and materials within the session can be a ground rule of the group, but storage before and between sessions requires some thought at the planning stage. Whilst stressing that the use of paper and paint in creative therapies is focused on the creative process it is acknowledged that this medium may result in a tangible end product, one which needs to be disposed of, stored or displayed. Wall space, an accommodating waste bin and areas of safe storage are all important options within the decision of disposal and should be available.

Time is a resource which needs consideration, as it provides structure to the activity and gives permission for creative expression. As within any creative therapy group it should be clear how long the session will be, whether it is a single session or part of a series, and how the content will be planned to ensure that each part receives appropriate attention. Art materials take time to assemble, to explore and use and a considerable amount of time to clear up. All of these stages are important in their own right, as they introduce different dynamics within the session, so the time frame should be agreed.

The client who is referred to the session is a resource from both a psychological and a physical perspective. To be able to use these two perspectives they need to be clear about the purpose of using a paper and paint medium and their responsibilities within this process. Steward (1996) explores spontaneous expression, self-exploration, the communication of emotions, both to oneself and to others, and active involvement as aspects of therapy upon which creative work depends. These form a baseline for the interaction of the client with the media and the therapist. From another perspective the client may bring physical resources, in that they move around the room, choose where and with whom to sit, collect materials, wash up and clear away. If these physical resources are not present the therapist must ensure that choice is taken to the individual, so that the experience is not limited through physical difficulty. Psychomotor skills will be used in manipulating the materials, and can also be used directly in creative expression, for example finger painting can extend the experience and may be included in the session. The use of unexpected materials such as fingers or feet becomes a freeing opportunity in relation to spontaneous expression, and gives a physical as well as a psychological slant to communication. This is a quality as well as a resource within the media, and indeed physical resources may be introduced deliberately to effect a change within a session.

As an illustration we offer this example. At one stage within our work we found ourselves within a group who were very passive, failing to communicate with each other and reluctant to become involved in the session. We decided to use barefoot painting on a large area of paper. This not only got people moving around but also encouraged them to converse, make eye contact, choose colours and generally interact on a level which was inaccessible before the activity – it is almost impossible *not* to communicate when dipping your feet in squidgy paint and making footprints all over the paper! The process of this, from the physical sensation to the interactive dynamic, led to a quality of discussion which had not previously been achieved within the group.

Qualities

Here we consider why we might choose paper and paint as a medium for creative activities, the potential it has to facilitate the creative core within this approach to practice.

Individual or group involvement

Planning a session around paper and paint gives the opportunity to work alone or with others in a variety of ways. In the early stages, group projects may be chosen simply to introduce members to media in a non-threatening way. This recognises that beginning to make a statement on a piece of paper can be very personal and quite difficult. Joint expression might feel much more comfortable, especially if the activity chosen is very free, like blowing paint or conversing in crayon. As the confidence of the group grows, so individual activities can be included, although often these are dependent on the co-operation of others, for example sharing materials or passing equipment. This may be the more physically static stage, where the group members stay relatively still to complete the activity. More action and interaction can be introduced through deliberately planning a group project, a quality of which can be compared to 'taking the temperature of the group' (Liebmann, 1996, p. 155) as the process used will reflect the way in which the group is functioning at a given moment. The purpose and demands of working collectively are very different, yet both approaches provide the opportunity to gain insight into specific behaviour.

Visual quality

Paper and paint is a visual medium, it can be used to commit something of the inner self to paper where it can be seen by the outside world. Its use is a visual communication which is not dependent on words and this may be very refreshing for a group member. As a visual communication it is open to interpretation, enabling the unspoken inside world to become explicit and tangible. It gives an opportunity for each person to explore thoughts and feelings, which may not have previously been clarified or understood. In forming a visual image ill-defined feelings can become more explicit. Through discussion they can be challenged for their effect on the individual, and this may offer further clarity

The flexibility found within paper and paint demonstrates how it lends itself to grading. Take an example of simple flow painting, where paint is dropped onto a sheet of paper and is allowed to flow in whatever shape it forms. The colours for the paint have to be chosen and the consistency has to be right, but otherwise there is little decision making. It can be a solitary activity or one carried out within a group. The pathways the paint has taken may then be discussed with the person. This paint flow is not preplanned, it requires minimal skill and yet creates a visual image. It may remain a simple activity, merely an explanation of coloured lines and associated shapes, or it may shift to a more complex activity, one where the lines, shapes and colours become significant and meaningful and where the experience of working with others in the group is explored. There is no advanced skill required and yet the paint bridges the gap between the thoughts and the conversation.

A quality of pleasure

Using paper and paint can also be enjoyable. This is an important aspect of therapeutic intervention and may provide a balance within the illness and therapy experience. Liebmann (1986) links elements of exploration and experimenting with this medium to play, seeing that the rediscovery or development of play in adults can facilitate personal growth and health. Playing frees us from normal constraints and so elements of it can be used to free a person to take opportunities or to tackle the problems that are a part of their life experience.

As with any of the creative media there are going to be personal preferences regarding the materials. This is an issue in its own right and may be one to be explored within the therapist/client relationship or the group. Exploring people's likes and dislikes, the element of surprise created by a medium both positively and negatively provides useful material with which to work; it tells us something about the person.

The quality of colour

Colour is a principal quality in the use of paper and paint and it may be singled out as a theme for the work of a session. Colour links to emotion and mood and we are familiar with it being used as a descriptor, for example, green with envy, white with fear. Colours also have associations. There are warm colours and cold colours, enabling selections for each category to be made almost automatically. We cannot assume a universal perception: individuals will view colours in different ways, so red does not always mean anger! However, a dark sombre painting or a cacophony of colours are likely to send non-verbal messages about the painter and it can be useful to explore the choice of colour with the client.

As well as a theme in its own right, colour may be part of a picture. It can be used as the central focus, a supporting focus or a means of joining images together. An example of colour taking a central role might be a collage created from a single colour. Perhaps an individual for whom an open choice may prove too difficult could be asked to create a 'yellow' collage. This enables a whole range of shades to be selected and used to create a picture focused on that theme. Alternatively, colour may provide a supporting focus, the theme of the session might be 'seasons' and colour would be used to support this, autumnal colours or fresh spring shades. Colour can also be useful in joining images in shared pictures, when one person's space links up to another's. These are pictures constructed from large pieces of paper with each person taking a section for themselves, building towards the whole. With our students we have noticed that as each individual area becomes filled the selection of colour is altered to tone into another's frame, the next segment. As the edges merge so the colours tend to be adjusted to join the separate pieces of work together. Sometimes this results in an unspoken demand for one person to alter the colour they are using in order to fit the picture together, which may lead to an expression of feeling and emotion.

The quality of texture

Texture brings a three-dimensional aspect to the medium. It can be used either on its own or to support the use of traditional materials – paper, pencils, paint. Some people find it easier to start creating a picture with textiles rather than with paint. The materials may be more familiar or be perceived as requiring less artistic ability as they have a form of their own. In conjunction with paint they emphasise, stress or draw attention to aspects of the work. Texture also extends creative thinking in the choice of materials: the aesthetic feel of sunflower seeds, knobbly wool, crunchy tissue paper, foil, all create different visual and sensual experiences. Many people will not have considered using materials in this way, so a junk box filled with scraps becomes a treasure trove of expressive material. Texture can be used as an addition to a painting, developing its richness, or it can be used to create in its own right. It becomes three dimensional in its use perhaps for a puppet, a mask or a sculpt. These products begin to move art towards the other creative media of drama or clay and sculpture, connecting one medium with another.

The use of collage gives another dimension to using paper and paint, which incorporates both texture and colour. Collage is an art form in which a composition is created from a collection of objects that are stuck onto a sheet of paper. The most common form is to use pieces cut from old magazines or newspapers, although a different effect can be created by including scraps of material, wool, seeds, pasta: indeed, anything that will readily stick onto the base paper. Collage can be used as an individual or a group project, but its choice as a psychodynamic tool will focus on the experience of the medium. Collage often tends to be a spontaneous medium. The picture rarely has a pre-conceived plan but is created from finding images which hold significance, thus developing a theme. Collage within creative therapies is usually created around a theme which encourages self-exploration, and which may be concrete or abstract. An example of this would be a theme of 'summer' moving to a theme of 'expectation'. Exploring the theme involves thinking about what was cut out and why, how the pieces were placed on the sheet and what the final picture is expressing.

One example from our work is a collage focused on the theme of Christmas.

> Christmas was expressed by pictures of tree baubles carefully cut and positioned as if they were broken. It included some gifts that were symbolic of Christmas and each object was linked to another by a swirl of red paint. Words associated with the festive feeling were cut from magazines and carefully placed to make a statement. The explanation ranged around shattered dreams, and the hopes that were created by the Christmas event, but the tensions surrounding them led to the symbolic breaking of the decorations. The angry red line, which predominated, showed the emotional impact of the event.

The use of themes

Paper and paint is a medium which lends itself to the use of themes, and these can weld a group together providing a shared focus. A theme can also offer a starting point for expression, this can be useful to a client who might find a completely open remit threatening. We consider the themes of identity, mood and journeys as these have emerged from our work. These are only starting points; the range of potential themes is endless.

The theme of identity

Identity lends itself as a theme within creative therapies as each person involved has an identity of their own, even if it may be difficult to get in touch with because of illness or experience. This can be established right at the start of the session through a warm-up activity. An example might be drawing features within face-shaped outlines to acknowledge each person's presence within the group. This task relies on observation, colour and shape, enabling the faces to depict the group members. These faces can then be joined together to explore collective and individual identity. Names can also be useful within an identity theme because they are very individual, special, and strongly associated with personal identity. They are also aspects of our identity already within the public domain. In the first instance initials might be used in identity theme work to diffuse anxiety, as they are only a small part of personal identity. Initials can be expressed in a variety of ways, using colour, shape, size and texture to develop a theme which can become complex or remain very simple. Having consciously acknowledged the initial, each person might explore their own name, their thoughts and feelings regarding it, memories it evokes, changes, nicknames, pet names and angry names. In this way a visual focus is used to move towards a verbal dialogue.

The theme of identity can extend to self portraits, which portray an internal as well as an external picture. The internal side of us contains aspects of the self which it may be difficult to acknowledge, positive as well as negative aspects, and so paper and paint provide the medium for getting in touch with these and making them explicit. The imagery can extend to the actual portrayal of feelings. Examples suggested by Liebmann (1986) include using the inside of a paper bag and collecting images within a box. Handling identity in this way gives a visual image of feelings hidden away, internalised, which are now being made conscious by using an external object that still allows for a secret or unobserved element. How much these elements of the self are discovered, shared and exposed to other members will indicate self-discovery and personal growth, as a tangible form has been provided to allow the internal exploration to take place.

The theme of mood

The explicit statement of mood is another commonly expressed theme. Subconsciously colours, shapes and brush strokes are linked to mood, and are visual indicators of feelings. The expression of mood in this way can be a cathartic and healing process, transferring the inner feelings to the paper. It may be difficult for people to access their mood, and to feel safe enough to expose it. This may be helped by music, which fills the silence and provides a background. This is an example of deciding to merge two creative media together, one to support the other. As moods are abstract images their portrayal will be symbolic. Feder and Feder (1981) suggest that colour preference is a more sensitive indicator of emotions than form or shape, using colour choice as a diagnostic tool within personality. Thus the colour chosen to portray an emotion or mood may be a more spontaneous reaction than the thinking which goes into creating a shape or pattern. Perhaps the colour comes before the shape, demonstrating how swiftly a colour choice for an emotion can be made explicit, whereas the shape for an emotion requires thinking time and is harder to capture. Observation of our work with students supports this theory. When moods have been suggested to students to portray they choose the colours they are going to use before they commit a shape to paper. The expressive communication of a mood needs to be handled with sensitivity by the therapist. Interpretations should be checked out as there is not necessarily a universal meaning to colour, shape or form. This emphasises the need for therapists not only to be secure with the materials and the groups members but also to be secure with their own feelings.

The theme of journeys

Every person attending a paper and paint session will bring with them an individual journey, which provides material for another theme to emerge. Journeys are personal and unique, they can be explained as the significant experiences and events that have happened to us. They can be called lifelines, personal maps, family trees – the name is really not important. The medium is the important thing as it enables this journey to be expressed in a visual form. It traces the experience and makes it explicit on paper. A group, which had an enforced break, used their pictures to explore what had happened within the interim. They recaptured the group experience from the previous sessions, using the journey as a bridge to link the present with the past. The journey expressed the issues that had occurred for them, the unconscious happenings that had affected the way in which they were able to settle into the group identity again. It acknowledged the importance of exploring the gap time, seeing it as contributing to the feelings of unease about starting again. There was a lot of group bonding within this activity, as individuals thought they were the only ones to be finding the restart difficult, so it was important to share these feelings in a visual way, giving reassurance that similar difficulties were being experienced by everyone. Journeys provide a theme which can be interpreted on many levels. It is the person who selects what is to be included, and what significance these inclusions have. In this way they are a safe form of exploration, and provide evidence of what a person feels able to communicate to others and to acknowledge to himself.

Process

The process of using paper and paint encourages us to get in touch with our own healing and creative solutions. Feder and Feder (1981) consider that the process of art in itself is healing, whilst Cameron (1996, p. 185) suggests that 'art as therapy provides healing, insight, creative problem solving and conflict resolution'. She considers that insight is gained during a movement from poor thought processes, through a creative thought process which makes itself known by using the medium, thus leading to verbal communication which in turn addresses problem solving and the resolution of conflict. Although this opportunity is present within the media, taking part, and therefore taking the risk of involvement to see where the actions lead, enables access to it.

Steward (1996) considers that a vital criterion for creative therapies is participation of the group members and the therapist. Participation means involvement, and in this way there is sharing of the experience and a collective creative approach. The self-exposure through communication, both verbal and non-verbal, is only possible by everyone participating, as all have been involved with the experience although it will be different for each. This involvement raises issues for the therapist in terms of disclosure. As a facilitator and participant, rather than a leader or observer, it is important to acknowledge the personal experience and the impression that certain aspects of the work have made. The dividing line between professional and personal disclosure needs careful consideration, and should be worked with rather than rigidly observed. Non-participation of group members remains just as difficult a problem as in other forms of creative therapies and is not encouraged. The need for participation should be clearly expressed at the start, as it provides the material, the personal experience with which to work. Participation can be encouraged through the selection of activities that acknowledge a person's difficulty, and which give them a safe starting point. Making a beginning is very significant in creative therapy: a blank sheet of paper is daunting. The 'conversation in crayon' between two people, suggested by Liebmann (1996, p. 156), provides a simple yet structured starting point. As one line explores the paper it meets the other, colours and shapes mirror spoken communication as they explore the paper together. It is a warm-up activity that encourages a member into the group, breaks down apprehension and anxiety, and results in active involvement.

As a visual medium there is something at the end of a paper and paint session to be seen. There is a permanent quality in this medium in that the image is captured in a definite form. Liebmann (1986) describes art as a fluid experience, a phrase which really captures not only the quality of the medium but the quality of the process. How do you evaluate such a fluid activity when the emphasis is not on creating an end product but on creating an experience? To justify our use of the medium as occupational therapists we need to attend to evidence and the way in which we use it to support the choice of activity. Some evidence is visual; a group collage, for example, might be used to explore the dynamics of people working together on a shared project but could create a dilemma in terms of ownership, storage and disposal. It may be used to decorate the area, pinned to the wall as part of the atmosphere of the room, fulfilling a different purpose. It is open to misinterpretation – 'what a lovely rainbow' replaces all the unseen issues of group dynamics that led to the creation of the rainbow, leading to confusion in the outcome of the session and thus to a misunderstanding of the therapeutic process.

The way in which we evaluate the use of paper and paint provides evidence of what actually occurred, what incidents changed the group or moved it on. Some people will have difficulty with the medium, which is worth consideration, and equally others will be very comfortable using the wide expanses of it in a psychodynamic way. To justify the resources used within the medium of paper and paint – materials, time, people or expertise – feedback must be recorded in a tangible way which does not depend on people's visual statements.

How to dispose of a piece of creative work is a deliberate decision, and one which may require time to reach. The process of creating something may have been so intense and meaningful that there is a need for the end product to remain, at least for a time, as recognition of the experience. These feelings often fade, and the product becomes less important as the experiences build. In the interim, work should be stored carefully, with respect for the individual and the work involved. There are some issues of privacy which extend beyond anonymity, so that created pieces are not available for casual inspection by others who have not been involved in the session. Patrick and Winship (1994) and Schaverien (1987) consider the different options of disposal, the routes between keeping and destroying, and we discuss these in Chapter 3 as a working process. The ground rules for the sessions should address the issues of disposal, ownership, and whether pictures will be kept. Our feeling is that, as the creation of an artistic statement is such a personal experience, the choice for the 'life' of this statement rests with the creator.

Illustration

Here we offer a description and analysis of a paper and paint session led by second-year undergraduate occupational therapy students on a group of fellow students. This session formed part of a series established as a learning experience rather than a therapeutic process. For this reason, the psychodynamic process was not a primary focus but occurred as a secondary gain.

Description

This student-led group provided an interesting example of using two media to support each other. Rogers (1993) draws attention to the ways in which creative media flow into one another, so this group session provided an opportunity to link the qualities of paper and paint with music. This session occurred towards the end of the series and involved three group leaders and a total of eight participants.

As we entered the room there were obvious signs of preparation. The tables had been gathered together into a square shape, and were covered with newspaper. Chairs were arranged around this large table, paints and papers were ready on one side, and the room looked welcoming and ready for the session.

The group members arrived and sat down around the table, talking easily with each other. One member did not arrive with the rest, and the talk quietened as everyone waited. On her arrival one of the group leaders welcomed the group, and outlined the plan for the session. She reassured everyone that there was no expectation to produce any masterpieces, but that the purpose of the session was to explore the opportunity of linking music with art, which she hoped would be a pleasurable experience. She stated that there would be plenty of time for discussion, and handed over to another leader to introduce the first activity.

Warm-up activity

The leader explained that the warm up activity – 'Musical Handprints' – was in the form of a game, where a pot of paint would be passed around the circle. When the music stopped the person with the paint would dip a hand into it and make a handprint on a large sheet of paper. When you had made two handprints you were 'out', and dropped from the circle. As this was a messy activity there were disposable aprons for everyone, and plastic gloves for those who preferred not to have paint on their skin.

The leader asked whether everyone was clear about the activity and ready to start. On receiving confirmation the music was turned on, and the activity began. There was a lively selection of music, and the paint was freely passed from person to person, amidst some laughter and feelings of anticipation. As the hand prints were made there were exclamations about the feel of the cold wet paint. Gradually the size of the group diminished as people dropped out, having completed their prints, and the activity ended with one person remaining. There was a break as everyone washed their hands and fresh paper and paints were placed on the table.

First main activity
The leader explained that music would provide a theme for this activity – 'Musical Fragments'. A selection of different pieces, depicting different tempos, moods and expressions had been collected on a tape, and each person was asked to express how the music made them feel on their paper, using any of the materials which were available. The activity started with some lively '60s music, moving to a very sombre choral piece. A modern, unmelodic piece and rhythmic guitar music followed. Everyone worked on their own piece of paper, varying their images as the music varied, attempting to express the moods and feelings the music raised. There was no stated time limit for the activity, which ceased as the last piece of music ended. The activity was followed by a period of discussion.

Second main activity
This activity was called 'Multi Media Painting'. The members were asked to form three groups, and to move to different work areas which had been prepared by providing paper and paints. The groups formed easily with one leader working in each. We were asked to complete a group painting, which we could enhance with any of the materials in the room. These materials included dipping into the 'scrap box', collecting pasta shapes, sequins, raffia, tissue paper – even potatoes cut into shapes. A musical piece had been chosen as the theme for the group painting but no suggestions were made of possible titles. The time for this activity was clearly stated, and the leader offered to remind us when this was nearing the end.

The groups moved to their work areas, and sat quietly listening to the music. They started to discuss themes which were inspired by the melody, and began to work, getting up to collect extra materials as they were required. The leaders reminded the group of the time scale, and an industrious period of activity followed. As the music finished the leader suggested collecting the paintings together for some group discussion. This was difficult to achieve as the paintings were wet, and quite heavy with their three-dimensional objects stuck on them. The groups therefore moved around the different workstations, looking at the completed pictures and asking about the theme and construction. There was some comment about the ease of working together and enjoyment of the freedom of the media. There was a discussion about keeping or discarding the paintings, and a group consensus was reached to bin them, as they were fragile and very messy. The paints and brushes were washed up.

Closing activity
The original table and seating arrangement was recreated, but the papers were removed and a cloth covered the surface. The final activity was to make a bow tie from a £10 note. Each group member received a photocopied note, and the third leader started the process of showing how to do it, taking the group stage by stage through the activity. This was very carefully done with both verbal and visual instructions. The musical accompaniment was casino style!

The final activity was followed by a discussion on the whole session, and then the leaders closed the group and, as there was no clearing up to complete, the members dispersed.

Reflection
This session achieved an interesting link between the two principal media. This is not always easy to manage and it reflected the interest and knowledge one leader had in music. The planning that had been undertaken to prepare the music was very apparent, as at each stage there was an appropriate selection, providing a theme for the painting activity. The success of the activity was dependent on this successful partnership, as in this case the music was not a background but provided a supporting theme in its own right.

The leaders managed the logistics of the session successfully. They paid attention to the small details, which are so important when planning a series of activities. Their preparation was obvious in the arrangements within the room: materials were provided, aprons and gloves were ready, and there was a strong sense of valuing the group and the activities planned. At each stage the leaders guided the group, using time for discussions and clarifying the timing, whilst still being involved in the activities. This gave a feeling of confidence to the session, as the leadership styles were supportive rather than dominant.

The ways in which the activities worked together was also successful. Some student-led sessions tend to be composed of a series of activities, rather than achieving a cohesive whole. In part it was the presence of the music which enabled each aspect of this session to link to the next, although the planning and skill of the leaders was obvious in the way this was achieved. A key aspect of achieving creative therapy, rather than creative activity, occurs when the medium provides a unifying theme for the session, giving opportunities within it for self-exploration. This requires a clear focus which is provided by careful consideration of the medium, and the ways it can be used to ensure the purpose of using it are met.

The session provided different ways of working. The first and final activities were undertaken in a circle, involving the whole group and giving a strong feeling of unity. There was a nice sense of balance as the beginning and ending activities took place around the same table, and it was interesting that each person took their original seat. Within the body of the session there was both individual and small group work, which introduced another dimension. Quite a lot of physical activity was involved at the group painting stage, as members collected extra materials, shared resources and generally gathered the props needed to complete their paintings. This was a co-operative stage, where each subgroup was communicating with another over sharing materials yet were working independently. The arrangement reflected the general feeling of group unity, as there was interaction whilst still working separately.

At each stage of the session there was time for discussion, when the group gathered together and exchanged thoughts and feelings. These comments were readily forthcoming, and there were none of the long silences that can occur when suggesting feedback. Most members clearly stated their likes and dislikes, talking about the music as well as the painting, and compared one activity with another. There was consideration of the issue of disposing of the three group paintings, which were not kept. This was useful discussion, which ensured that the experience of working in this way was explored.

This group was familiar with working together, yet there was one member who chose not to contribute to any of the discussions. The leaders did not explore this point, and no one else in the group raised it as an issue. Creative therapies provide an opportunity to look at individual behaviour, especially that forming a pattern, such as members who regularly choose not to contribute verbally. There may be a number of reasons for a person staying silent, which can be usefully explored in a non-confrontational manner. Creative therapy sessions rely on interaction with the media and openness to the experience offered through this involvement. A regular unwillingness or inability to contribute becomes a dynamic which is important to work with.

Reflecting on this session enabled us to see how effectively it had been managed. The activities had been selected carefully, with a clear purpose. The accompanying theme of music added another dimension, which encouraged everyone to involve themselves in the activities. The freedom to use all the materials that the room offered gave scope for exploring the media fully. The leaders reassured the group at each stage, clarifying that no skill was required, and the music helped to remove any tension. The attention to detail ensured that the different parts of the session fitted together to create a whole experience, and there was an effective balance between activity and discussion. There was evidence throughout that the group was enjoying the session, there was commitment and involvement, and a general atmosphere of working hard, both as a group and as individuals.

Summary

This section has explored some of the ways in which paper and paint can be used within creative therapies. It has glanced at the history of painting, tracing its familiarity, and continued by exploring the medium as a theme in its own right.

We have considered the relationship between art therapy and occupational therapy as a positive opportunity to develop an understanding of the roles and backgrounds of these professions which link closely in the therapeutic use of this medium.

The use of paper and paint provides a flexible, highly adaptable route for creativity. It offers single and multidimensional work, and the opportunity to explore imagery through colour and texture. Paint has a tactile feel to it, and a fluidity within its structure which allows it to be used in many different ways, from the simplicity of blow painting and hand prints to the complexities of collage and group paintings. We have considered the scope and range of the medium, and the need to pay attention to the tools we use. Paper and paint can provide a very freeing experience, one which should not be constrained by technique or convention, so we have acknowledged the need to make a mess, to really engage in the medium and to use our creativity to adapt its qualities in numerous ways. There is an end product with this work, and therefore there are issues around its disposal and the need to focus on the process of achieving an experience through using paper and paint rather than producing an end product. Finally we have used an example of a student-led session where two media were merged – music and paint. The music provided the theme to enable the use of paper and paint to become a creative experience.

THE USE OF BODY AND MOVEMENT

This section will explore the way we use our bodies and their movement as a therapeutic strategy through dance, sculpture, drama – the expressive arts of movement. Using our bodies expressively is considered as a primary use of body and movement; however, movement and body language contribute information to all the other media and activities we might use within creative therapies. These clues assist us at every stage of our work and so could be considered a secondary aspect of their use. Whatever we are doing, our bodies become an integral part; they are a central prop for the creative therapy session. Bodies are never still, so movement becomes a creative aspect of life, creative in that it adjusts and adapts to any circumstance and environment, and in that it maintains our life functions, pumping the heart, expanding the lungs, giving us sight, touch and direction.

There is a clearly defined connection between motion and emotion and a concept that physical activity promotes a deeper level of emotional release than purely verbal expression (Feder and Feder, 1981; Payne, 1990). Using body and movement in creative therapies acknowledges this and the media are used to give us clues to a person's inner and outer health.

Movement is inherent within us and takes on specific meanings throughout our lives, from before we are born until we die. An identical mechanical structure lives under each human skin, but for every person movements are individual and unique. Think of how you recognise a person through their movements. You may see them at a distance and yet be able to identify them – not because you can see who they are, but because you can recognise the specific pattern of movements they make. A child moves very differently from an adult, jumping, rolling, falling and generally using their whole body in exploration of the environment. A person who is in pain moves in a constrained way, adjusting the balance of their body to relieve the symptoms and being physically restricted through the pain. Emotions are reflected through body movement, particularly in posture, which shows exhaustion, distress, excitement or fear. Tension is observable through the presentation of the body and can become so automatic that someone has to learn to achieve a more healthy body stance. So the behaviour of the body changes to reflect not only our age and physical abilities but also our emotions and inner thoughts. Our body can respond to verbal instruction, or to the non-verbal instructions given by another through the use of their body. Movements can be correct or incorrect depending on the context of the task. If the task is functional, dependent on a specific movement to achieve an identified end – like entering these words into the computer – then the posture, arm and finger movements have to be correct to achieve the end product. If movement is used in an expressive way then there are no rights and wrongs. It is about free expression and the ability to change the body in a non-directed way.

Movement is a complex and multifaceted activity. It is the expression of ourselves and yet it is a basic requirement for everyday life. It involves the functional as well as the recreational parts of our lives. Think of the complexity of movements which you have taken part in before reading this chapter. You probably got up from sleeping, and undertook all those personal activities which prepare us physically for the day. You have eaten, moved from place to place, relaxed, created words and received them. You have used your eyes and your limbs. You have touched all sorts of things and responded to a range of stimuli. You may have used your body for recreation, deciding to put it through a series of movements to achieve physical and mental health. All of these actions show just how complex movement can be and how dependent we are upon it to achieve a fully functioning state both physically and emotionally.

Resources

The resources required for a creative therapy session focused on body and movement are generally minimal: the greatest resource at our disposal in such sessions is our own body. It is as if the use of bodies and their movements require no other resource than a place to be, as it is the group members who create their own resources. Rogers (1993, p. 50) refers to the work of movement therapist Barbara Mettler when she states: 'in every other medium our inner experience is externalised in some material apart from ourselves. In movement expression, the movement of our own body is the material.' We do not have to provide other material, we just need to facilitate the use of our bodies to express ourselves.

Space is one resource which enables movement. This may be indoors or outside, so that the environment complements the need for expression. A group who used the framework of a nature trail for one session evidenced the importance of this. The session involved exploring the outside environment and the movement of the group from point to point on the trail. It gave legitimate space to group processes, released energy, identified and gave ownership to feelings aroused by the environment and facilitated a process of self-discovery through the medium. We become so removed from nature through our lifestyles, our buildings, our mobility that we become disconnected from what Rogers (1993) refers to as 'our inner nature'. This is exacerbated through illness, where life becomes an indoor experience, making the disconnection even more intense. The freedom of the open air can be contrasted to the physical restrictions of a room.

As with all the expressive arts, the room used for indoor work should afford privacy and safety to allow exploration. It should be large enough and sufficiently uncluttered to allow a degree of free movement. The activity may be supported by props – such as music, masks, a scrap box of odds and ends – which can be transformed to help create an image or to enhance an expression. It may require floor mats or a carpet if some of the activities are to be carried out in bare feet or sitting on the floor.

Another resource we usually have available is that of other people's bodies. These provide the material to create a structure such as a sculpt, which is a physical rather than a verbal description of an abstract concept. We may ask other people's bodies to be involved in role play or as partners within dance expression. Using another person in this way gives a physical form to an unstated thought process. People are placed deliberately to reflect a situation, which therefore gives clarity and explicitness to encourage growth and understanding. Bodies are flexible and dynamic; they can be moved around until the image is as close as it can be to the desired effect. Because the body is dynamic it can provide a moving image, one where the initial image dissolves when another movement takes place, providing a series of images that may be separate entities or which form parts of an interconnected whole. Because of this dynamic element an image can quickly be lost. This transience may be desirable, or there may be a need to give it more permanence through the use of video recording or photography. This changes the process as it captures the 'product' of an expression, which may or may not be appropriate for the session.

As special materials are not required to explore body and movement this medium is inexpensive and easily resourced. It is also mobile, and can be used in a variety of venues with the minimum of effort. There are no extra tools needed, no materials to be prepared or supplied, and the element of clearing up is probably confined to rearranging the furniture following a session.

Bodies are most able to express themselves when they can move most freely and this is only possible when they are not constricted. It is important to emphasise to group members the advantage of wearing loosely fitting clothing which will allow for freedom of movement. Safety should also be considered and either bare feet or stable shoes are required to ensure that the group members can fully engage themselves in expressive movement. These seem obvious points, but they are the practical resources which the group brings to the session, and they can either facilitate or impede the process of the session.

Qualities

Perhaps the greatest quality of body and movement as a creative medium is the fact that it is always available, should we choose to use it. Its use, however, is twofold: as a primary medium where it is the main focus of the session, and as a tool of expression which we take to any other creative medium. The observation of this expression provides information about the physical and mental wellbeing of the client.

Potential for grading

A quality of using body and movement as the focus of a session is that the medium can be graded, both in the amount of the activity and the way in which it is carried out. It is such a flexible creative route that it can move from the very gentle to the most strenuous, and can use the whole, or merely parts of, the body. A simple amount of movement can be introduced to instil confidence in the activity because suggesting a 'body and movement' session sometimes leads the group members to think that they are going to have to 'perform', raising anxieties about completing an end product rather than experiencing the process.

To enable you to think how some apparently simple movements can become more complex compare the following two examples which were part of a session with our occupational therapy students.

In the first example each person mirrored the movements of a partner in a simple warm up. This encouraged concentration to copy the activities performed and gradually got parts of the body moving in a safe and controlled manner. It relied on close observation, non-verbal communication and co-operation. After a time the partners changed roles, so that the second person had an opportunity to lead and the first to follow.

The second example involved all the group members. One person took the role of the 'untier' and distanced herself from the group. The activity involved the members linking hands to form a long chain and then threading themselves around one another to form a knot or a tangle of bodies and body parts. This knot had to be untied by the one person who had volunteered for this role. The subsequent unravelling became quite complex. It involved carrying out the instructions of the untier, touching, bending and reaching to overcome others' bodies and being led through the process of the initial activity in reverse to allow the knot to be untied.

The second activity relied on the trust that had been established in the group as it involved close contact and certainly invaded body space. Involvement became a complex affair, requiring much more interaction than the first example.

These activities can be built upon, adding props of music, stories, other people's bodies, until a more complex use of body and movement is achieved.

Individual or group work

Movement can be explored alone, in partnership, or as a group theme. Often there will be space for these combinations within the session. The qualities of moving alone are very different from the qualities of moving as a group, and one can lead on to exploration of the other. There are times when a movement is dependent on another person, or when the whole emphasis demands a group approach. Group movement may be less inhibiting than moving individually and it is reassuring if others are taking part, as there is less exposure of the individual. Working in this way requires relinquishment of defences – there is no equipment or material to hide behind – and is physically dependent on the active involvement of all group members.

Touch

A quality of use of body and movement is that it reaches across barriers, as it is a tool which is inherent within all of us as a means of emotional expression. An issue of the freedom of the media is the presence of touch, as many of the activities used in these sessions are dependent on touching others. In this way it differs from some of the other media we have chosen to explore. Touch carries unspoken rules that relate to culture, age and language, all of which should be considered before including it within a session. Touch is a sensitive topic as it may result in feelings of discomfort or even distress. It can be abused by society, reminding the group of past incidents, or it may emphasise the loneliness of an individual. It is a sad reflection that many people touch an animal more often than they touch another person, so introducing touch within a session carries certain risks and creates anxieties. Again this part of the activity can be graded: holding hands seems an acceptable place to start, whilst moving another's body into a desired shape involves more intimate touching.

It is quite difficult for a group of people to move about without touching, so touch can be incorporated without being the prime focus of the activity. This may be more acceptable to some of the participants. Many therapeutic interventions have the effect of isolating the person into a world which relies on communication through speech, but not through touch. Barriers grow up to protect, to form a 'bell jar' where the person seems bounded and enclosed by a transparent, impenetrable shell. At this stage touch is feared and avoided.

Movement is so freeing as an activity that touch happens intentionally as well as unintentionally. Acting out a story, moving around a room, using role play or sculpture, may incorporate touch in an unintentional manner. Unstated permission is given that it is safe to touch in this way, and that use of touch will be built on the trust of the group. There are times when touch needs to be introduced more explicitly to change a situation and the use of body and movement provides a forum for this. An example is colour touching, where the group moves around and is then told to stop and touch a named colour. This can start with inanimate objects which cannot move, and can be extended to ask the group to touch each other's clothing. Clothes provide a multitude of colours, and asking group members to touch (for example) the colours red and green on another's clothing encourages a number of positions, movement and makes touch more personal. The basic principles of movement – what, how, where and with whom – are incorporated into the activity. It also introduces humour, an aspect of movement whose importance is often ignored. It is almost impossible to be in a group, touching tiny items of colour through stretching, entwining and generally wriggling, without it becoming a humorous activity. Laughter has its place, and laughing at one another trying to achieve such physical contortions can be a healthy group dynamic.

Touch becomes explicit in activities which rely on it to function. Leading a person, leaning on them, allowing someone else to control your body through touch are actions which rely on trust and which give an opportunity to explore the feeling of allowing another person to take control. This might be a very scary use of movement, and requires careful preparation. Many people remain so in control of themselves that it becomes a burden which they are unable to let go. Asking them to let another take charge gives space to explore how this feels, and a variety of emotions will be expressed. The trust which is required for this is a non-verbal trust, provided not in the usual way through communication dependent on words but through their bodies.

Touch can be misused and wrongly interpreted (Totenbier, 1995), thus the purpose of the movement should be explained so that it becomes a safe activity. Society is becoming touch-deprived, with less and less physical contact occurring as the contact with machines and inanimate objects grows (Rogers, 1993). So touch becomes related to sexuality or aggression rather than an expression of concern, friendship or appreciation. Appreciation links to clapping, and here we are making a 'creative connection' (Rogers, 1993) as clapping is a wonderful form of touch within movement for warming up the session – it can be safely done with yourself, can extend to another, and can move around the whole group. It gives sound and rhythm, and expression through movement moves into the expression of music. Perhaps the greatest quality of movement is its ability to move around in its own right.

So far we have considered the general qualities of body and movement, but there are some specific approaches which this medium offers. We have chosen to explore some of these in greater detail – dance, role play, sculpture and drama.

Dance

Warren (1984, p. 88) describes dance as 'the mirror of the soul' and suggests that the movements involved express feelings more accurately than words. He goes on to define dance as 'a statement of emotion expressed through movement'. This definition sits comfortably with the ways in which we might use dance within creative therapies. It is not the formal, correct sequencing of movements, which has more to do with technique and performance, but is the spontaneous release of expression through movement. It is about self-discovery, which Rogers (1993) suggests can begin from any one of four points – a feeling, an image, a concept or an impulse.

Using dance as an expression of a feeling makes the actual feeling become explicit; it becomes owned by the person. Dancing as if you are sad, excited, grieving or happy enables the body to be used to depict those emotions. It brings self-realisation and understanding through getting in touch with those physical feelings. Similarly, if you dance an image – a sunflower, a caterpillar, a muddy bank – then the freedom of expression allows you to use your body freely in a creative way and to feel the image. Dancing a concept may create an experience – a powerful dance, a shy dance, a dainty dance. This is empowering; it gives an experience of how these concepts feel and allows for self-growth. Finally there is allowing the body to be impulsive, to take on whatever form of dancing it wants, just to get in touch with important emotions and to go with them through the movement.

We need to ask ourselves why this movement experience is so powerful. First, it is valuable in that it establishes freedom of expression, anything goes, it is all right. There are no rights and wrongs to dancing like a bulldozer. It gives freedom to the expression which comes from inside each of us. If these dances are observed without understanding they can be labelled as 'silly, childlike, just plain stupid', and indeed some clients will identify with these feelings when they begin. Why, then, do we feel so different after the session that has enabled self-expression in this way? Using movement freely is so experiential that it becomes difficult to put into words. It is about paying attention to the inner feelings that are present throughout the process. It is not about looking at the product. You do not look like a bulldozer, but you are able to experience the tensions of moving forwards over rough ground, of remaining steady, of being powerfully driven, of being able to surmount anything in your path. You reflect on how that felt, the freedom it gave, the way you got in touch with parts of yourself which you hardly knew you had, the way in which you were able, for those few moments, to live the experience and express it. All of these things are part of the healing process, as they empower and facilitate personal growth.

Whilst it is easy to explore the use of dance in this way it is important to recognise that this level of interaction is very difficult for some people. There are complex issues around projecting oneself in a different way, issues which focus on self- exposure, inhibitions and an inability to free oneself to become at ease with the medium. The physical tensions that may be present mirror the anxieties of the group; the body as well as the mind expresses resistance. Wilhelm Reich, whose ideas contributed to the development of a group of theories known as 'body therapies', explored the link between physical tension and mental tension, believing that one reflected the presence of the other. He used the terms 'body armour' and 'muscular armour' to describe defence mechanisms employed against threatening situations. Thus a group member may show resistance to involvement through crossed arms or a tense body, which Reich suggests reflects their inner feelings of anxiety. This message should be recognised and acknowledged to encourage involvement. Reich's work contributed to the theory that physical activity promotes a deeper emotional release than verbal activity and that there are links between movement and emotions which can be explored through the use of this medium (Feder and Feder, 1981).

Rudolf Laban was a significant figure in the development of dance and movement (Wethered, 1973). He not only promoted the use of creative dance but also developed a means for observing and categorising movement, using it to inform the joint processes of diagnosis and assessment. He explored movement through considering the body, the effort, the space used and the relationship of the movement. In other words, he looked at what is moved, how movement happens, where it takes place and with whom. He viewed movement holistically, seeing that the whole is greater than the sum of the parts. Laban placed a great deal of emphasis on the quality of movement, so he looked at how a movement occurred, the process and form of that movement and what the movement achieved (Payne, 1990). This focuses on the relationship which develops during movement. It may be a relationship with an inanimate object, floating a parachute for example, or it may be with another person, a movement which is dependent on interaction like mirroring specific movements in a partnership. This holistic view of dance movement is reflected in the creative therapy approach where participation through movement shifts the focus from the functional to the expressive.

Role play

Role play is literally playing a role. This may be the role of yourself or may involve taking on the role of another, imagining being this person within a given situation and creating that situation by actively expressing it.

The use of role play follows a specific plan. It is not just an activity which interjects into a session without due attention being given to the whole process beyond the active stage. The activity begins with a defined goal – what are you aiming to achieve from using movement in this way? The problem needs to be made explicit, so that the main aspects are clearly outlined to form a framework within which to create the scenario.

Van Ments (1994) refers to three key factors within this scenario:

- the role player;
- the situation;
- the learning which takes place.

To develop our understanding of working psychodynamically with this technique we will explore each of these in turn.

The role player

The session might begin with defining the roles which the group members are enacting – imaginary people, a defined other person, or the player himself. These options have to be clarified and explored in relation to the purpose of the activity. Specific roles may be allocated at random or may follow the stereotypes of the situation; a male, for example, playing the father role gives a clearly defined figure but does not move the experience away from the expectation of male playing male. This can increase the effectiveness of the activity if participants are inexperienced at using this medium, providing a known structure within which to relate. People may be anxious, may have bad memories of previous role plays, or may simply not wish to expose themselves in this way. Taking on any of these diverse roles requires preparation and a certain amount of risk taking. Time should be spent explaining the process, allowing a person to 'feel' themselves into a role and to understand that everyone involved with the activity is working towards it being a useful and constructive experience. Taking a role should therefore be framed by a preparation stage, an active stage and a de-roling stage, where the role is left behind and the person moves back into being themselves. Using role play effectively depends on attention being paid to each of these stages – and especially to the de-roling, as it is easy for the active stage to end with the participants returning to their chairs still carrying the roles they were playing.

The situation
Role playing adapts itself to a wide range of situations, making it a very flexible activity. The situation can be simple and familiar or a complex one which moves into new territory. At this stage it may be important for the therapist to help the instigator to decide whether to provide a detailed scenario within which to work or whether a brief outline may suffice. The framework for the activity explores how many participants are required, what time span is appropriate, whether it will move from scene to scene to create the situation. When the parts have been allocated and the situation explored the language of the scenario may be explicit or left to unfold on its own. Participants are prepared, involved and active in this planning process, which then leads into running the session. Role play is dependent on interaction and observation; it provides a framework within which to try out a range of different behaviours.

The learning
If learning is achieved through participation it will focus on the feelings associated with the action. An understanding will develop of different roles within the scenario. Active participation leads to being affected by the role, feeling what it is like to be ignored or misunderstood – for example, the boss of the company or the most junior employee. Students are often surprised by the intensity of these feelings, especially if they are placing themselves within an unfamiliar role, and it is reflection on this action which is a key to the learning process. The role play may involve only a few participants, allowing the remainder of the group to be active observers. They are able to see the action as a whole, to explore the different parts of it and to provide rapid feedback on the process. The successful use of role play is dependent on it being as accurate as possible, allowing it to achieve its goal. De-briefing follows the role play, beginning with enabling the participants to de-role and to return to being themselves. Finally the experience of the session is reflected upon, from the perspective of both the participant and the observer, to give an opportunity for learning, understanding, exploring and changing behaviour.

The initial goal should be revisited, to see if it has been achieved. This will provide a focus for future learning.

We can see that role play has the potential for grading, shifting it from a behavioural level (as might be used in social skills training) to a more psychodynamic level. The role play is used to actively work with the experience, to explore its personal meaning and to facilitate change and understanding. It shifts from a focus on the product to attention to the process.

Sculpting

Sculpting involves creating a 'snapshot' of a situation which is static for that moment: a frozen picture (Gobey, 1996). It can be a very powerful method of enabling a person or group to explore an issue which is significant and has feelings associated with it. Sculpting is a versatile activity as it can be used to depict a real situation or an abstract theme. Once the theme of the sculpt has been determined the process follows in an ordered way.

One member takes the role of 'director'. This person will both create and own the sculpture, which is dependent on other participants to take roles within it. The director places the participants into positions which are the most meaningful. This creates a visual image which closely portrays the goal of the sculpture. The participants are placed carefully, but usually in silence. Their positions are clarified through mirroring or modelling. In mirroring the participant copies as accurately as possible the position shown to them by the director: this is a non-contact technique which requires the director to take the position first, giving them first-hand experience of the feeling of it, which is in turn reproduced by the participant. Alternatively the director moves the participant's body into the required shape or stance: this involves physical contact, and introduces touch into the session. Gradually the layers of the 'snapshot' build up, as people take their place within it. The very silence of the activity reflects the frozen nature of the image, it is as if verbal communication, upon which we depend so heavily, is frozen also. Once the participants have been placed as correctly as possible the director moves outside the scene, surveying it for accuracy. The image is held for a few moments, allowing its story to be told, and then the group de-sculpts and the image melts away.

There are times when interpretation of the sculpt is not a silent affair. A space of time follows the action to give the observers, participants and director time to consider the process of the image. The director may choose to share the meaning behind the sculpture, or others may contribute interpretations to clarify their understanding. In either case it is a powerful way of working – as can be seen from the following examples.

To facilitate understanding of some aspects of the dynamics of a family situation a group might be asked to portray a sculpt entitled 'my family relaxing during an evening'. The director takes the role of placing people to convey this image. When everyone is in place the sculpt is closely observed. This observation might lead to a verbal interpretation, as the director is able to explain the roles taken and the focus of the scene. This can raise an intensity of feeling, and discussion ranges around the ownership of seats around the television, the lack of variation so that the same people claim the same spaces, and then the disruption should the pattern be broken by an imposed change. Even the pets seem to have an established place, and a pattern of communication – both verbal and non-verbal – is established. It may be useful to think of your own family, and see if you can identify with the routine that has been established without anyone ever remembering being told where to sit. Depicting a family in this way clarifies a familiar situation. Who touches whom, who shares space with whom, who has the best view of the television, the warmest place, the place near the telephone? So much meaning is made explicit from just focusing on the ways in which people sit on a routine basis and yet this arrangement happens so normally that it is hardly ever considered, and rarely discussed.

Sculpture can be used to capture an abstract concept: for example, we sometimes ask our students to sculpt their feelings about the course they are undertaking. In turn, one student directs the other members of the group to depict aspects of the course – the study topics, the support systems, friends, entertainment, practical pressures, the balance with home life all may play a part. Such sculpting usually involves some touching to depict closeness of feeling. An aspect which is popular tends to be placed close to the person representing the director, probably linked to them through touch, whereas an area of difficulty or conflict goes to the extremity of the group, distancing it from the rest. Once the sculpt has been completed to the satisfaction of the person in control the positions are held for a few moments to allow time to absorb the visual image.

The discussion and explanation which follows a sculpt is revealing. Working with an abstract theme enables thoughts and feelings to become concrete, real and open for exploration. It addresses issues such as why one part was disconnected from the rest, what the thinking was which led to the selection of positions, what was included and what ignored. It gives a safe route for exploring relationships, and the fact that the action is non-verbal and static changes the demands on the participants. Just as in role play, attention should be paid to de-roling, ensuring a space between holding the image and returning as a group member. Although the focus of the discussion is with the person who created the sculpture it is valuable to explore the feelings of those involved as participants or observers. If a group member has been asked to depict an unpopular aspect, and have been marginalised or isolated from the rest of the participants through this, they will have a contribution to make as to how that experience actually felt. They may have strong feelings about the role they have taken in relation to the aspect portrayed, perhaps reminders of previous situations where the same feelings arose, and these will need owning through exploration. In any of these situations personal insight is gained through the portrayal of a silent, static image.

Both role play and sculpting are techniques which arise within a range of treatment approaches, behavioural, cognitive–behavioural, humanistic and psychodynamic for example, and an equally wide range of professions use them. To focus on creative therapies the psychodynamic and humanistic approaches of giving ownership to the person, enabling them to explore feelings and suggestions, believing in their ability to grow through self-discovery and self-exploration, provide the framework. The process of bringing the unconscious to the conscious through using the activity of movement in this way provides the link between motion and emotion, and it is the reflection on this process which enables growth and personal change to take place.

Steward (1996) refers to the need for the therapist to tolerate uncertainty, to resist imposing order or structure upon a group, which is vital in using these movement activities. The pictures portrayed have to be those the client is portraying; the uncertainty of action has to be tolerated to allow the final picture to emerge. The method is valueless unless it captures the importance for the person.

Drama

Whilst writing these sections we debated how and where we were going to address drama. The activities addressed seemed to live clearly in one chapter or another until we reached drama, an expressive art which appears to have a number of homes. Rogers (1993) uses the 'creative connection' of the expressive arts to allow them to be worked with together, or to be considered as parts of a whole, each supporting the other. We have placed drama within body and movement, acknowledging that it has links to writing, music and the environment, whilst the sheer drama of movement may be present in any session.

Drama is an example of a creative activity in therapy that has become a specialism in its own right. Drama therapists, like art and music therapists, seek specialist theoretical and practical training at a postgraduate level, accompanied by personal therapy to achieve a professional qualification. This specialism is a relatively recent addition to health care, found working in conjunction with other professionals whilst contributing specialist qualities. For our purpose as occupational therapists this section will consider the ways in which we can use drama in creative therapies, the qualities which are present for our use, recognising the boundary between our work and that of the drama therapist.

Jennings (1987, p. xv) suggests that 'drama is not an absolute entity, and as such defies an absolute definition'. This is a reassuring and very valid statement. Our practice using 'drama' has focused on active doing in all sorts of ways – linking touch, movement, imagination, narrative and mime. Our use of drama does not link to performance, production or theatre, and there are no rights and wrongs surrounding it. However, the sessions reflect the central issues of self-discovery, self-exploration, self-determination and self-help through a creative experience that is free from constraints.

Narrative and story telling are aspects of drama that reach into the imagination, and in doing so they create a space within which to reflect. The process of imagining creates a separation between an actual situation and an alternative, imagined, one. Gersie and King (1990) see this space as being the place where reflection on both the current situation and the imagined one can take place. It gives space to re-examine, to explore and thoroughly consider these alternatives by distancing the person. It becomes an intensely personal and private process, or one which can be shared. Think of the function of 'daydreams', where we fantasise about a change to our lives created by our imagination. The activity gives space to look at the actuality of life, to consider how it is and to see if change can be effected in a more reasoned manner. The joy of imagination is its freedom, the flights of fancy, the lack of practical constraints, its creativity. It is multidimensional and multifunctional, so it adapts itself to be used on many planes, in many ways.

There are times, particularly when coping with mental ill health, when the moves between reality and imagination become too difficult. Thinking is restricted to one plane or the other, simply as a means of survival, blocking out the other. If this is the situation, then the interactions that take place when using imagination therapeutically do not happen. There is no energy for the space between, where the action can be taken to change, to grow, to achieve something of the imagined state. Yet we need to consider how to translate our dreams into actions. Humanist theories stress the ability of the individual to self-actualise, to have the power to make changes, which may begin within an imagined state and then be used in an actual situation. The energy for this change may begin through stories and narrative which capture the imagination, making them effective tools to use within a psychodynamic approach.

The use of props within a drama session focusing on imagination gives structure to the exploration, and provides a theme for the session. Take the example of a collection of objects from which a story is told. The objects may be ones the group members choose to bring to the session, they may be a random collection and they can be obvious or hidden. Placing a group of objects into a paper bag introduces the dimension of discovery and surprise whilst telling the story, but collecting something from a display means the props are visually shared and have been specifically selected. Objects might not even be there, the invisible suitcase of holiday treasures, using a story created entirely from the imagination, and not dependent on material things. The objects form a theme for the story; they encourage participation, fantasy, interaction and structure. They create a space for imagination, thus beginning a process of change.

The power and history of stories is considered within the section on text and verse, where the focus is on the words, but within this section the movement which is involved with stories gives them a separate dimension. Movement provides a chance for the participant to enter even more fully into the story, to reach the subtext which is beneath the words. Again, this can be clarified through the following example.

The focus of one session was the portrayal of a boring lecture to a group of students who left no doubt as to their feelings of being on the receiving end. They enacted their boredom and lack of interest. In the discussion that followed they explored alternative methods of delivering this particular topic, a difficult one which defies creative approaches. They imagined being the lecturer faced with the task, and developed greater insight into how it felt for her. They explored their own behaviour, looking at their reactions and linking them with other events. There were issues of power, numbers, compliance, and unity which had escaped earlier consideration. Movement within the drama gave an intense understanding of the dynamics of the situation, so the process of reflection became more meaningful than any evaluation sheet!

Process

We have referred to the fact that planning a creative therapy session requires a balance of a warm-up activity, a main session and then a closing activity. When movement is the main focus of the session the warm up is important from both a physical and an emotional perspective. Leary (1994, p. 42) describes this part as 'framing the session' in that it sets the tone for what is to follow and generates both physical and mental energy for the activity. A short gentle session that explores using the body, stretching, bending, generally moving around and touching, prepares the body for further activity and initiates movement without risking physical injury. These warm ups can follow the structure of the body, making sure that each part is mobilised in turn, thus freeing the body of tension and stiffness. No one should attempt movements that cause strain, and the therapist should be particularly observant to identify any physical difficulties throughout the session.

The closing part of the session may include some relaxation: it is important to wind-down and prepare for the closure. Because movement requires little clearing up, there are no brushes to wash, no instruments to collect, no products to store, reducing the opportunity for casual conversation and adjustment that tends to take place during the tasks. For this reason it is important to finish the session appropriately, allowing space and time for participants to move away from the experience.

Illustration

We go on here to provide a description and reflection of a body and movement session run by year-two undergraduate occupational therapy students on a group of fellow students. This session was one of a series of five established as learning experiences for the students. The aim of these sessions was not for the students to undergo a therapeutic process and for this reason the psychodynamic issues which might occur are secondary, arising as a by-product of the learning experience.

Description

This group was based on the use of body and movement in its broadest sense. Some activities focused on physical movement whilst others enabled the participants to decide how much movement would be involved and the form it would take. In this way the session was planned to involve all the members yet to have a variety of action.

This group met towards the end of a series of sessions. The room had been prepared by moving the tables to give plenty of floor space and arranging a circle of chairs around a colourful rug. There was music playing in the background, which added to the warm and welcoming atmosphere. As group members arrived they were asked to take off their shoes, and they took their places around the circle, chatting freely to each other. The two leaders were aware that one member had not arrived, but after a short waiting period they decided to start the session. At this stage the music was turned off and the members focused on the leaders, one of whom checked to see if anyone knew why the non-attendee had not arrived. No further information was forthcoming, and so they decided to begin.

One of the leaders introduced the session by acknowledging that some people find the whole topic of using body and movement quite daunting, and she reassured the group that there would be no element of judging their performance. She outlined the plan of the session, which would include some group work and some work with partners, stressing that she hoped everyone would find it an enjoyable and useful afternoon.

First warm-up activity

A series of short warm ups had been planned. In the first, the leader asked us to start a circular process of greeting each other by saying 'hello' to our neighbour, who then said 'hello' to the next person, moving round the circle. This was then varied by the greeting being in any form the participants chose – verbal, non-verbal, phrases, foreign languages – which was accompanied by an increase in volume. The leaders then gestured for a decrease in noise, and the process quietened until the greetings were passed in a wholly non-verbal manner. This activity involved quite a lot of eye contact, turning the body to the neighbour and using body parts for communication.

Second warm-up activity

This involved communicating with our partner through mime. We were asked to mime some activities that we had taken part in over the weekend, which our partners would then share with the group. At this stage the leader asked us to work with the person on our right, and the pairs easily rearranged themselves to enable this to happen. The leader stood up and illustrated a mime, using lots of movement and floor space. Each pair then spent a few minutes miming activities to the other and guessing the meanings, which were then shared verbally with the group.

First main activity

This activity required us to leave the circle of chairs and to move to an empty floor space. We were asked to take a partner, and to form an inner and an outer circle, with each person facing a partner. Thus we had a small circle of people facing outwards, and a larger circle of their partners, surrounding them facing inwards. Those within the inner circle were asked to make small movements, gradually getting larger, which would be mirrored as closely as possible by those in the outer circle. The leader explained the process very clearly, using gestures to demonstrate the process, and then put the music on to accompany the activity. After the partners had mirrored each other for a while they were asked to move to the right, thus collecting a new partner. When this process had been completed around the whole circle, meeting up with the original partner again there was an exchange of roles, with the outer circle taking the inner place and vice versa. This gave everyone an opportunity to lead and to follow, exploring a wide range of movement in the process, until we were asked to finish the activity with the smallest movements possible. The music was turned off to signal the end of the activity.

Second main activity

This activity was led by the second leader, who asked the group members to select a filled carrier bag from the table and to return to the circle of chairs. The bags were placed, unopened, under the chairs and the group was asked to separate into two teams. We were given 25 minutes to create a story entitled 'The Bus Which Would Not Stop' using the objects from the bags. The leaders reassured the group that they could create the story in any way that they wished, and pens and paper were available if they wanted to write things down. The leaders then told us to open our bags, and to use the objects we found in our story. The items were very mixed – one group found a silk scarf, a shoe, a set of Russian dolls, an imitation snake and a balloon; the props for the other group were a colander, an empty picture frame, a rolling pin, a tee shirt and some knitting. Each group was involved in formulating their story and then acting it out. This process took quite some time. There were tentative suggestions of a theme, and gradually everyone reached a point of freely contributing ideas. Often the group had to remind itself of the boundaries set by the props and the title, and had to be quite creative to fit everything in, thus giving each person a part. Both groups rehearsed their story before presenting it, both verbally and with movement, and although they were working in the same room there was no involvement across the groups or any element of watching the rehearsal stage. Each group finally acted out their story, which was received with applause. The interpretations of the stories were completely different, and everyone played a role within the performance.

At this point the chairs were re-formed into a circle around the rug, and the leader opened discussion about the previous activity. There was some laughter as members reflected on the visual images; a bus driver with a colander on his head, 'his brain like a sieve', and the richness of the silk scarf which formed a robe for the princess. Some items had been difficult to incorporate and the group shared their thoughts about creating the story and then acting it out to others.

Closing activity

The leaders handed each person a pen and piece of paper with a circle drawn upon it. The circle had a cross at the centre. We were asked to consider the cross as the central point of the group, and to mark our involvement in the session in relation to it. The leader suggested we worked in pairs, sharing our perception with the person sitting on our right, who would comment on the position and then offer their circle for discussion. This quiet and contemplative activity in partnership completed the session. The group leaders thanked everyone for their participation and the furniture was returned to the original positions before the group members dispersed.

Reflection

The preparation for the session was evident in the way the leaders had arranged the room to facilitate the group. This gave a feeling of reassurance and welcome to the members as they arrived, and having the music quietly playing in the background removed some of the silent spaces that occur when a group is assembling.

There were two potentially difficult moments at the beginning of the group. The first was asking the members to remove their shoes. Asking people to do this can raise anxieties, so it is the role of the leader to explain why such an action is required, and how this links to the activities planned for the session. As this was the first body and movement session the group members were wondering about the content and what might be expected of them. Removing shoes raises an expectation that the session will be different from those focusing on other media. At this point it is important to carefully observe the comfort levels as participants comply with the request. The leaders demonstrated an awareness of these issues, they removed their own shoes and explained the safety factors which justified the action.

The second point related to the absent member. Although ground rules had been agreed which clarified the responsibility amongst members to inform the leaders if they were unable to attend, no message had been received. This left the leaders in the uncomfortable position of not knowing whether to proceed. In this instance the leaders handled the dilemma appropriately, extending the informal talk, welcoming those who were present, asking for information about the missing member and then making a clear decision to start. It is important to address the issue in this way, as it clearly identifies that one person is absent, and therefore concern is expressed about them as a part of the group membership. If attention is not paid it makes a member feel devalued, that their commitment and presence within the group is not important. The loss of a session will be apparent in the next meeting, where experiences will be different for the person who was absent.

The first two warm-up activities developed the theme of body and movement. Using a greeting around the circle reinforced people's presence, and introduced an element of touch. The gradual increase of noise also gave confidence to the group in using their voices, exploring the boundaries of the room through sound and then allowing it to diminish. This is a freeing aspect of the activity, but one which involves risk taking and might be difficult for a group in the early stages. The use of mime is quite demanding, as it involves using the body rather than the voice. However, the choice of the topic encouraged everyone, as it was relatively simple to think of things that had occurred over the weekend. There is an element of safety in using activities to which everyone can contribute, as the group may meet this choice of medium with apprehension.

Mirroring with a partner involves a range of complex skills. This activity took quite a long time, but the plan was made clear to the group and the leaders were prepared to demonstrate themselves initially. The activity requires eye contact, concentration, movement and touch. As we were encouraged to start with small movements, so confidence developed. Throughout the activity the leaders took control of the moving on, giving clear instructions to change partners or to change roles. This clarity provided support within what was potentially an exposing activity, but the way it was handled enabled movement to be creative and energising.

The story around the bus was a challenging activity for the group; however, they were already comfortable working together and so split easily into two smaller subgroups. There was a sense of mystery about the filled carrier bags, which also made the group feel valued and prepared for, as there was a bag for each person. The leaders had written the title for the story on the blackboard, forming a focus for the task, and they clearly stated the time allowed for the activity. These aspects formed a boundary for the activity, enabling the group to involve themselves and allow their imaginations to develop their story. This activity was a demanding one, made safer through the artefacts and the title, as they provided a theme for the story. Both groups chose to act out their story, using a range of movement to achieve it. This did lead to an element of performance, but not to a feeling of being judged, which was evident through the level of involvement and enjoyment that was obvious within the activity.

This group session demonstrated leadership skills both in the balance of the content and the management of the activities. The leaders provided a structure to the session, which is important with a demanding media base. They paid attention to detail through clear instruction, timing, involvement and preparation, all of which encouraged the participants to involve themselves in the experience.

The group members appeared to be thoroughly involved in the session. This was apparent through their concentration and the level of their contributions. They moved freely from one scenario to another, and were able to develop their themed stories in a harmonious and co-operative manner. This may reflect the length of time the group had been working together – they felt safe to make suggestions, and to use themselves as a part of the activity.

The closing activity was dependent on trust and confidence within the group. This was apparent as the members had worked together, but sharing personal reflections with a partner and owning one's position within the group are sophisticated activities which rely on a sense of security. In this example contemplating the activity provided a peaceful end for an active session and encouraged members to get in touch with the whole process. At this stage some privacy was retained around the activity as it was shared with a partner rather than with the whole group.

Summary

This section has considered the use of body and movement, recognising that there is movement within everything we do and exploring the ways that we can make this theme the main focus of a session. The section has explored the simple and complex uses of movement, from mirroring actions to enacting stories. We have considered the space that may be needed for movement and the need to pay attention to the body, enabling it to safely warm up within the session. We have explored some specific forms of movement, dance, role play, sculpting and drama, all of which provide useful routes for self-expression and self-discovery. We have also looked at the significance of touch within movement, seeing it as a means of communication and considering the role its plays within our society.

There is no end product to body and movement; the medium is transitory and cannot be captured except through the experience of involvement or watching. This places further emphasis on the value of the experience and the creativity inherent within it. Finally, we gave an example of a student-led session to provide an opportunity to explore the scope of the medium, using individual and group work to develop the activities in a creative manner.

THE USE OF CLAY AND SCULPTURE

This section addresses the use of three-dimensional media which we see as a main difference between sculpture and the other media used in creative therapies. Clay may be used to create a sculpture but is only one of a wide variety of materials available. Clay and sculpture sessions offer huge opportunity for creativity, perhaps because the medium is so varied and the range of materials available for use so wide.

The use of clay and sculpture within creative therapies provides two routes for exploration. Firstly, the activity relates to creating something with the medium, where the emphasis is on the process that occurs during creation; secondly it might make use of sculptures which have already been made. The emphasis is not on skills in sculpture or appreciation but on using the creative medium to facilitate expression, self-discovery, self-determination and self-help (Finlay, 1997; Steward, 1996).

Many of the media we use in creative therapies we have experienced during our schooldays, when the emphasis was on achieving a certain level of competence. Those of us who are less talented may have negative memories of this, of dreading the art class because we weren't very 'good' at it (the teacher, the national curriculum, our peers or ourselves defined 'good' in this case). Perhaps this medium is the least tainted by negative previous experiences: sculpture will have constituted only a small part of most of our formal art education and the way we use sculpture in creative therapies often bears very little resemblance to any form that this might have taken. All of these factors help to make sculpture quite accessible to the clients we work with in creative therapies and contribute to the feelings of opportunity, variety, enjoyment and fun that this medium brings.

We begin by describing an experience of using sculpture in a creative therapy session. This will serve as an illustration to many of the points we make in this section.

Figure 5.1 The owl and the pussycat went to sea

The 'Owl and the Pussycat'

The group members walked into the room and were met by the group leaders standing in front of a pile of cardboard boxes and armed with staple guns and masking tape. After an initial warm-up activity, the members decided to make a boat with these materials. From this point the group took on a life of its own, with the leaders having to offer very little direction. It seemed that the imagination of the group had really been fired and they were working co-operatively to provide an outlet for each of the members' own fantasies. A period of industrious activity followed, with everyone very much working together to achieve the overall project within the time limit allowed; however, a great deal of negotiation had to take place. A boat – complete with mast, sails, seats for all and with a seagull flying overhead – was finally created. A short time of surveying and admiring ensued. The leaders then prompted us to get into the boat and simply offered the opportunity to talk about where this boat would be going. Most of us talked about our own little fantasies but the general agreement became that we would like to all go somewhere together, thus agreeing a final destination. It seemed that making our boat had been very much a collective experience and none of us felt it would be right to use it for our own individual journeys.

Resources

Almost by definition, the use of clay and sculpture requires some resources – materials or consumables with which to sculpt. The materials may be conventional ones like clay, which is ideal because it is readily malleable and can be moulded quite easily. However, it is also cold and wet and not everyone enjoys its texture. Other conventional materials such as wood or metal need to be selected with care. Two main principles about choosing materials for use in creative therapy sessions are that they should not require technical skill and that it should be possible to yield a result within a reasonably short time. In most cases the sculpting of wood or metal requires quite an advanced degree of skill and time (Steward, 1996). Clay may be purchased relatively cheaply through a local supplier, and as the aim is not for a technical and product-focused result the quality of the clay used is less important. Clay should be stored in an airtight container because it has a limited lifespan and needs to be discarded or reconstituted when it becomes unfit for use. When using clay for sculpture it is useful to have as well a supply of wooden boards to work on, cheese wires, modelling tools and a water supply.

One of the more freeing or creative aspects of using sculpture is the possibility of using less conventional materials. These can really be anything that you can think of – bric-a-brac, old cartons, cardboard boxes, sand, natural materials such as branches and leaves and so on – the list is as endless as your imagination! When we think of the sculpture sessions we have been involved in images enter our minds of students arriving by taxi laden down with cardboard boxes and bags of sand, and of ourselves spending Sunday afternoons wandering in the forest searching for fallen branches, fir cones and leaves while trying not to look too suspicious. The range of materials can be very freeing and the process of entering a room for a session and meeting an unexpected and unusual pile of materials sparks a sense of excitement, interest and creative imagination.

As well as a selection of materials that will form the main part of the sculpture, other materials are normally required to fix things together. A good supply of sticky tape, glue, masking tape, staple guns, etc. is useful. Paints and large brushes may also be required to decorate the sculpture.

A collection of 'junk' may be built up over a period of time but its storage requires a lot of space. In the days when most occupational therapists worked from a department base these were real gold mines, but fewer of us work in this sort of environment nowadays. Space is at a premium and storage of materials might be difficult. A good range and amount of material is required to allow people choice and contribute to the freeing aspect of using sculpture, but collecting this together for a one-off session can be time consuming. The group may choose to keep the end product and storage of a three-dimensional object or objects also has implications for space, which becomes a consideration to put to a group when discussing what to do with the product.

Qualities

In this section we will explore some of the qualities of clay and sculpture which make this medium well suited to use in creative therapies.

The first and most obvious quality of sculpture is that it is inherently three dimensional. This alone gives it a different quality to some of the other creative media we use. There can be a front and a back to an object, or an inside and an outside, one of which we may wish to keep unseen. We have used cardboard boxes of various shapes and sizes to help group members project their sense of self. The outside of the box forms that part of themselves they want the world to see, the inside of the box projects that more private, internal part, enabling members to choose how much of this 'hidden self' they wish to discuss with the group. Alternatively the fact that there is an inside and an outside may mean that group members can actually get inside the sculpture, as we saw in 'The Owl and the Pussycat'.

Working with sculpture may be a messy process, particularly if clay, glue or paint is involved. Messiness itself may be part of the freeing nature of using sculpture; as adults we are rarely allowed to be messy and having permission to do so can be a new experience, although for some this might be difficult. Some people dislike getting their hands dirty and really object to this aspect of using clay. Depending on the aims of intervention, it might be appropriate to expose the client to this and help them work through this problem; it might be appropriate to avoid placing others in such a situation.

This medium enables one to work on a large scale, which can be a different experience, through the appropriate selection of materials: cardboard boxes or rolls of chicken wire easily and cheaply form large structures. Working on a large scale can again be a freeing aspect of using sculpture. Doing something big is a bold act and enables the group and its members to make a bold statement. The opportunity to make something which takes up a huge amount of space within a room, or which is perhaps big enough for the whole group to sit in, is exciting and serves to spark enthusiasm, creativity and imagination. While particularly lending itself to large-scale work, sculpture can also be used on a small scale and this may be the choice in instances when an individual needs to gradually build up their confidence by working on smaller, more manageable pieces before using larger scale work.

Sculpture is very flexible: it can be added to or taken away from. This gives a different quality. With art there is a sense of permanence: a paint stroke has been made on the paper, it can be changed or painted over but it cannot be taken away; with sound a noise is made, it cannot be taken back, it has happened. In clay and sculpture the material can be moulded and adjusted and it is likely to remain in this flexible state for some time. This may be a desirable quality for some clients – perhaps someone who is in the early stages of their treatment, who is tentative and unsure, would welcome this flexibility. There is not the pressure to be too definite in forming the sculpture because there remains the option to change the shape. If using clay, the evidence of what has been done is easily destroyed at the end of the session; it is simply scrunched up.

As well as the inherent flexibility in sculpture, an element of change can be built into the activities planned. At the end of this section we give an illustration of a warm-up activity where group members were asked to make an animal. They were given a few minutes to do this and were then asked to stand up and move on to continue the work of the person sitting next to them, a process that was repeated a number of times. In this activity a state of change was part of the activity and that change was effected by more than just the original creator, shifting the responsibility to a more collective base. In another group we worked with a moving sculpture constructed with the intention that it would alter. The sculpture was based on the four elements of earth, air, water and fire, which provided a natural link to creation. The quality of change was quite poignant – the sculpture remained on the veranda outside the creative therapies room for some time, while the group continued to meet over a number of sessions. It was as if a tangible form of change mirrored the change that was taking place within ourselves and within the group.

As with all the other media, when using clay and sculpture the emphasis is on the process that occurs rather than the creation of an end product. Clay, in particular, is a very tactile medium and an easy way of encouraging individuals away from a preoccupation with the end product is to ask them to work with the clay with their eyes closed (Rogers, 1993). This can be useful in a warm-up activity to set the tone for the session or as a shared group exercise.

The use of sculpture lends itself very well to the incorporation of other media. We use the 'Owl and the Pussycat' example to illustrate a variety of ways in which this might be achieved.

- Paper and paint was used to add to the sculpture. It decorated the boat, made the sails and constructed the seagull flying overhead. As a warm-up to the activity of constructing the boat we could have also used paper and paint to draw plans of the project. As an extension to the activity, perhaps in a later session, we could use paper and paint to represent our individual fantasies for the destination of the boat.
- Sound and rhythm provide an additional medium, through choosing appropriate construction, sailing or rowing music to play in the background. Alternatively, music could help us determine the final destination of the boat as a piece could be played and the group asked to suggest what sort of a location it made them think of. This real or imaginary location might have been where we set sail to.
- The use of body and movement was inherent in the overall activity. In constructing something large like the boat, there was a great deal of moving about and working around one another. This was a very physical, tactile and expansive process which also involved a good degree of physical contact. This was generally non-threatening because it had a functional purpose. We could have chosen to use body and movement in a more primary way; for example,

we might have acted out a story in the boat, perhaps a shipwreck or, less dramatically, a day out fishing together.
- Text and verse can be incorporated into the activity. We might have written about our individual fantasies for the destination of the boat and discussed these while on board.

Having considered the qualities of clay and sculpture we will now go on to review some of the considerations relating to the process of using this medium in creative therapies.

Process

In reviewing the process of using sculpture it is useful to start by thinking about the structure that sessions might take. A creative therapy session usually follows the format of a warm up, a main part and a closing part. There are some specific considerations relating to the use of clay and sculpture within this structure. The group can get very involved in the construction of the sculpture, which can be time consuming, perhaps more than with any other medium, and it is therefore important to set ground rules relating to practical issues at the beginning of the session. The group needs to agree how much time is available for the construction and how much for other aspects of the session. If this is not made explicit and agreed it is easy to get carried away with the activity and perhaps avoid addressing the psychodynamic work of the session. The therapist needs to offer reminders to the group near to the end of that time limit to help them work within it. With 'The Owl and the Pussycat' activity there was a real risk of this – the life of the group while engaged in this activity was so strong – but the leaders prompted us and we were able to move on.

With use of all creative media it is important to consider what will happen to the end product at the close of the session, but there are specific issues when using clay and sculpture. If the sculptures are large they create storage problems. When working on a group project the whole group needs to reach a consensus about what will happen to the end product. These issues highlight the very important need for the group to set ground rules regarding the end product at the beginning of the activity. The closing activity might be used to dismantle the sculpture in a way that is acceptable to the group. Using clay and sculpture can be very messy and consideration needs to be given to clearing up: this takes time, which needs to be set aside. Again, clearing up could form part of the closing activity.

Using clay and sculpture lends itself well to grading. Clay and sculpture activities can be quick to execute or can be very time consuming, they can be small-scale individual projects or large-scale group projects. Sculptures can also effectively be used over a number of weeks, firstly through the process of creating them and then through using them to explore psychodynamic issues. For example in the 'Owl and the Pussycat' we described how it was made and used but also offered other ways of developing it, such as using a text and verse exercise to determine the destination of the boat or body and movement to act out a scene. All of this could gradually be developed over a period of weeks. In this way the actual sculpture will hold less of a primary focus and will fall into the background over time as other creative media are used to push the psychodynamic process forward. Rogers (1993) calls this linking and use of creative media 'The Creative Connection'.

Masks and puppets

These are two ways of using clay and sculpture in creative therapies which we think deserve special mention.

Masks

Masks have a long history and are evident in most cultures, where they largely play a part in rituals. Even in Western society, which we might not associate with the use of masks, they are present in the uniforms of soldiers, the wigs of judges and the caps and gowns of professors (Bihalji-Merin, 1971). They can be used to reveal, for example, when used as a badge of office, or they can be used to conceal, something to hide behind such as a uniform. A lot can be learned about how masks might be useful in creative therapies from writings about the ritualistic and cultural uses of masks.

Mask making was man's first attempt to give shape and meaning to his innermost visualisations and as such it can be used as a form of expression (Sorell, 1973). Creative therapies are about expression of innermost feelings, many of which are difficult to verbalise. Masks may provide a medium for this expression but they can also provide a distance, which might be helpful – the mask is over our face but is not actually our face. Generally masks cover the face or part of the face and head; in doing this they disguise our own expression, offering an alternative one. We can decide what we want this alternative to be and can use it to represent various aspects of our ego. Initially the expression provided by a mask is fixed and lifeless, which may suit our purposes, but it can be animated by movements of the body that might extend the use of the mask or the expressive power of the mask within a session (Sorell, 1973).

We may choose to use ready-made masks, perhaps picking one from a range because its size, shape and expression holds some appeal to us. Alternatively, we may use a mask which we create. In doing this the form and expression of the mask is likely to contain more personal meaning because it has been created from resources within us.

Early humans shaped grotesque masks to represent demonic spirits. It was believed that powers could be transferred to a mask and that these powers could then be transferred to the wearer. The wearers of the grotesque masks truly believed themselves to be in possession of the mask's demonic powers so there was a total sense of identification (Sorell, 1973). From this we can readily consider an application to creative therapies. A mask can be used to give an individual power or qualities that they would normally associate with something or someone else. A whole range of examples could be used for this – it might be a mask of a fictional or mythical figure or of a real life figure, or it might be a mask not attributed to any specific figure but which the individual perceives as having particular qualities. As an example of this a client might choose to make a mask of a cat. They see a cat as having qualities of independence, being guiltlessly self-indulgent and contented and wish to have these qualities for themselves.

The mask we wear and work with in creative therapies may not be a tangible mask in the way that we would normally perceive it. We all put masks on our own faces and those of others, often without being aware of it. We are all mask makers: the woman applying make-up is described as 'putting on her face'; the person in conflict is 'putting on a brave face'. Jung refers to our mask as our persona, the front we display to the outer world or how we would wish to be seen by others. The danger, according to Jung, is when we identify totally with the persona rather than with who we really are (Sorell, 1973; Stevens, 1994). The mask alienates the self and saves the individual from being involved with the full self; it hides, protects and transforms the wearer (Bihalji-Merin, 1971). Many of the people we work with in creative therapies are uncomfortable with their sense of self, and exploration of the 'masks' they use can be useful to the process of integrating the self.

Puppets

Puppetry is gradually developing as a small discipline in its own right among the creative arts therapies, but it is most commonly incorporated as a therapeutic tool by other professional groups such as occupational therapists, speech therapists and psychotherapists. Most skill in the use of puppetry is learnt on the job through experience and working alongside others but very occasionally courses are advertised for therapeutic puppetry training (Aronoff, 1996).

Interest in the therapeutic use of puppetry began in France in the early 1970s. On the Continent there was an emphasis on the use of psychoanalytic theory with puppetry, whereas in Britain puppetry was mainly considered as an educational and social training aid (Campbell, 1979). Obviously it is the use of puppetry with psychoanalytic theory that we are interested in here as it links more closely to our use of this medium in creative therapies.

There are different types of puppets, which range from the very simple to the more complex. These include:

- finger puppets;
- glove puppets;
- rod puppets;
- string puppets; and
- shadow puppets.

As with all media used in creative therapy, the aim is for a simple use so that clients do not get preoccupied with technical skill rather than the desired focus of self-exploration and development. In puppetry, the simplest forms – such as finger, glove and rod puppets – have most to offer as a vehicle for expression and communication for an amateur puppeteer (Campbell, 1979). For great simplicity facial features can be stuck onto common everyday objects to make a puppet – for example a sock, a wooden spoon or a mop (Astell-Burt, 1981).

As with masks, the use of puppets provides opportunities for the individual to identify, project and transfer aspects of the self or ego onto the puppet. Because it is slightly distant from the individual, or once removed, the puppet can be used by the individual to try out free expression and rehearse feelings before actually owning them. Puppets offer an emotional distance (Astell-Burt, 1981) as they facilitate involvement through an impersonal route. A client may be able to use a puppet to portray the rhythm of a music session as a precursor to involving themselves and using their own bodies. They also provide a route for exploring painful personal issues, for example body image or abuse, as they offer a distance which is acceptable to the client.

Like masks, puppets can be purchased in a ready-made form or created by the individual. Bought puppets bring with them acquired features and qualities so are less personally connected to the user. Therefore working with a puppet may be a less demanding option in the first instance. The process of actually creating a puppet invests much more personal meaning as it is the individual who dictates the image.

Forming a puppet makes the individual's ideas concrete (Astell-Burt, 1981). This creative process itself can be very psychodynamic and a vital part of both assessment and treatment (Campbell, 1979). How the individual involves themselves in this creative process and what they create can be very meaningful and may be as far as the process is taken. At this stage, although the puppet contains meaning through its creation, it remains an inanimate object. It is through performance, the human energy of the puppeteer, that the puppet becomes animated; it uses text and movement and it gains meaning through them (Aronoff, 1996). The use of puppets might be developed to incorporate an element of performance from the individual, or the process could start with ready-made puppets to make the performance element the main focus.

When using performance the aim is not to achieve a technically correct play or sketch but to provide a forum for a psychodynamic medium, using it to facilitate self-exploration and self-understanding. In ordinary drama the individual is the actor and is taking on a role, which can be a vulnerable and unprotected position. Developing the use of a puppet in drama allows the client to work through an object and can provide a protective distance (Astell-Burt, 1981). In performing one usually acts out a story and this is no different when using puppets. It might be appropriate for the theme to be the group's own story or that of an individual member but again the proximity of this can be too close for some people to cope with. Instead, it can be useful to begin by acting out a well known story such as a fairy-tale or take on the roles of a television soap opera through the puppets. As long as the group members can relate to it this can be a helpful route for addressing personal issues, which can be explored through the performance.

Illustration

Here we describe and explore a clay and sculpture session run by two second-year undergraduate occupational therapy students with fellow students. The focus of this session was on the use of clay. The session formed part of a series established as learning experiences for the students. For this reason, the psychodynamic processes that might have occurred were secondary to the primary aim of a learning experience: in these sessions the students are not intended to undergo a therapeutic process.

Description

As the group members arrived in the room the two student leaders were already present. The room was arranged with the tables in a large rectangular block surrounded by seats. A large lump of clay and a selection of pottery tools had been placed on the table. Aprons and thin rubber gloves were available should group members require them. Music was playing in the background, a Simply Red tape, which played throughout the session. When everyone had arrived one of the leaders thanked us for attending and said that the content of the session would be experimental and exploratory both for them and the group members as they had not used the activities in this way before. The same leader then went on to remind us of the health and safety issues of using clay and also said that, as we would be moving around in a fairly cramped space, we should ensure that our coats and bags were out of the way.

First warm-up activity

The leaders cut off hand-sized chunks of clay from the large lump and distributed them to each group member. In doing this the leaders were quite jovial in their manner, creating a light atmosphere. We were then asked to make an object from the clay that we might find useful. A group member sought clarification as to whether this was to be 'useful' within the session or 'useful' to us generally. The leaders left the remit open, saying it could be whichever we wanted. Initially there was some discussion about making something which would finish a dissertation (a piece of coursework which all the student members of the group were starting to work on at that time). Following this there was a great deal of concentrated sculpting, with little discussion other than practical requests to have equipment passed on. One of the leaders spontaneously, without any prior announcement, started talking about what he had made, the second leader followed and other group members contributed when they chose.

Second warm-up activity

The group members were asked to look at and consider the person sitting on their right, and then asked to make something with the clay which they thought that person might find useful. Initially there was some laughter and chatter but the group quickly settled down to sculpting. The leaders prompted the start of the discussion part of the activity by directing questions about what they had made for one of the group members. On the whole, group members had made fairly superficial or funny things for their colleagues.

Third warm-up activity

The group members were asked to make an animal with their lump of clay. Members started working on this task, which was accompanied by a lot of conversation about the dissertation. After a few minutes one leader announced that we were to move on. The group complained because they had got quite involved with the activity but hadn't yet had sufficient time to complete it. We were told to stand up and move one place to the right, leaving our clay behind; there was some reluctance and the leader had to be quite firm to move everyone on. Once we had all arrived at our new piece of clay a group member sought clarification as to whether we were to continue with the animal our neighbour had begun. The leader stated that we could do whatever we liked – add things or take things off. We were moved on again and less time was allowed before we were moved on a third time. At this stage some group members were looking back to see what was happening to their original animal. Conversation continued but it had now become more unrelated to the business of the group. It was a social type of conversation about a film currently showing at the cinema. We continued to move on in a similar pattern with the leader prompting the move, allowing varying amounts of time between each move until we had arrived back at where we started with our original animal. There was some laughter with discussion and comment about what the animal had started off as and what it had become.

Main activity

The group was asked to split into three subgroups and to move the tables so each group had a work area. There was some discussion between the leaders about whether or not they would participate in this activity: they decided not to. It took the group some time and a great deal of discussion to work out three subgroups.

We were asked to make a group project from clay, which we could keep if we wanted to. We were not provided with a time frame or a theme. The leaders floated between the groups prompting and encouraging us. When they wanted us to come to the end of our sculpting they checked that we were all ready, and it took a few moments to get each subgroup to stop. All of the group members stayed seated. There was no suggestion from the leaders to bring the subgroups back together to form a whole. We were asked to talk about what we had made. The first subgroup described theirs, followed by little comment from the other groups or the leaders. When the second group went on to describe their sculpture the first group spontaneously got up to circle their table and look at their work. Again there was little comment. The third group described their work and here both the first and second groups circled the table to look. The work of this subgroup elicited some comments as it was something that each of the three groups could relate to – a conceptual sculpture of the author of a well-known occupational therapy textbook.

Closing activity

The leader announced that time was running away, that we would do a closing activity which would take 3–4 minutes. The group remained separated in the three subgroups around different tables. We were asked to make something from the clay which we were looking forward to when we finished that day. After a period of activity we each showed what we had made and explained it. Group members made their contribution when they felt it appropriate.

The leaders thanked us and asked us to fold up the clay. Without prompting the group members helped to tidy the room and put everything away. This took some time and was carried out thoroughly.

Reflection

The presence of the leaders on our arrival and the preparation of the materials and the room gave an initial sense of value as the leaders had taken the trouble for us.

The purpose of having music playing in the background should always be carefully considered. Music has strong associative powers and can also help set the atmosphere and tone of a session. How a tune makes one individual feel may not be the same for all group members. On this occasion, we felt that the music contributed to the light and jovial atmosphere that was created. This atmosphere, along with other factors, prevented this session from operating on a level that would be psychodynamically effective. Our personal feeling is that when using activity at the higher end of the continuum presented in Chapter 1, as we most often do in the practice of creative therapies, the use of background music that is not intended to support the theme of the session is less appropriate.

The leader's acknowledgement that this session was uncharted territory for them also is an interesting point and there are two perspectives to this which should be considered. From one perspective this could be reassuring and inspiring to group members. The leaders, like the group members, were feeling vulnerable in doing something new, generating a sense of all being in the situation together. It might be inspiring to the group because it is new and unexplored with no preconceived ideas about how it will be. The second perspective is that group members might find this admission uncomfortable; if it is new to the leaders then where is the security? We discussed in Chapter 3 how the leader has a key role to play in conveying a sense of security, and this involves being perceived as competent. There is no right or wrong to making such an admission but the therapist should consider how it might be understood. The stage the group has reached and how well it is functioning might inform this.

In this session health and safety issues were a particular consideration, which went beyond relying on a common sense approach. It was professional of the leaders to point out specific considerations and gave us as group members a sense of their responsibility and concern for our well-being.

In the first warm-up activity most people interpreted the instruction as making something which might be generally useful to us. This was interesting because it served to bring an aspect of our outside life into the group. One person made a bicycle pump because they had a flat tyre on their way to the session, another made an alarm clock because they had difficulty in getting in on time. From this we all became a little more aware of one another's lives and the issues we were facing.

The second warm-up activity was an appropriate development of the first. The group had been together for some time, members knew one another well and were aware of many personal and shared issues. Considering this, it seemed strange that most group members sculpted superficial or funny things for their colleagues. On reflection this might have been the first manifestation of the light-hearted atmosphere created by the leaders' style and manner and the lively background music.

The third warm-up activity did not continue the development that could have been achieved in the second activity. It seemed to bring us back down again, moving us away from working effectively on a psychodynamic level. In the first two warm-up activities we had just begun to operate on a personal and interpersonal level and this activity seemed unrelated to them. As an activity in its own right it went on too long – rather than warming us up it served to cool us down. Discussion moved away from interpersonal issues to social conversation. The leaders should have reflected in action. After the second move group members were showing a real interest in what was happening to their original work. It would have been appropriate to return us to our original work after three or four moves; beyond this we had lost interest and no longer had a sense of ownership of it and our involvement with another's clay became superficial, even destructive.

For the main activity the group was given little direction about splitting into three subgroups. This would seem to be a simple task but the group floundered, finding it difficult to agree or to organise themselves. At this stage the leaders could have responded more positively, taking control of the situation and offering more direction. We were given very loose guidance on what was expected. There was no theme, no apparent purpose and no suggestion on how this might build on the previous work. It seemed like just another activity.

At the end of the main activity, when we were asked to show and discuss what we had sculpted, a more conducive atmosphere could have been created if the leader had prompted us to come back together as a whole group. Splitting into subgroups can be fragmenting; the leaders wanted us to re-form to share something but they did not attend to how the physical environment might impede or facilitate it. The leaders then left us in this fragmented arrangement for the final closing activity. At this point it would seem important to regain the cohesion of the group and foster a sense of togetherness before the session closed.

The closing activity was a good choice because it enabled the group members to think beyond the session towards something that would be happening later that day. This became an effective bridge as it linked the work of the group to their life outside. It also encouraged a positive note by asking them to think of something which they were looking forward to.

The group stayed together without prompting and spent some time and effort cleaning the materials and tidying up the room. It might be that this was their response to a feeling of fragmentation. Working together cohesively, even in this practical task, helped inject some of the missing cohesion.

The leaders gave no indication of the time frames we were working to within any of the activities planned in this session. They observed the group and read the situation, choosing when to stop an activity and move on. During this session this was generally an appropriate strategy, except in the third warm-up activity where we were left far too long.

The overall feeling of this session was that it was a series of activities put together rather than a process of activity which gradually developed the group experience working through a warm-up to some serious business and then closing down. The first two warm-up activities had the potential to move the group towards some effective psychodynamic work but this potential was not sustained in the third warm-up activity or in the main activity, when the atmosphere of physical and psychological security was not supported by the leadership style, the background music and the physical set up of the room in the main and closing activities.

Summary

This section has explored the potential use of clay and sculpture in creative therapies. Clay and sculpture are very versatile and flexible and often less bound by previous experience than some of the other creative media we might use. Clay lends itself well to three-dimensional work and the development of large-scale structures; it also offers enormous potential for the inclusion of other media.

We have focused on masks and puppets as two particular ways of using clay and sculpture that provide valuable tools for exploring the self through another object. The section closed with a description and analysis of a creative therapy session involving occupational therapy students. This session focused on the use of clay and served to illustrate a number of points relating to the use of creative media in therapy.

THE USE OF SOUND AND RHYTHM

In this section we consider the use of sound and rhythm in creative therapies. As the title suggests, we want to offer a wide view of this medium and encourage the reader to move beyond the conventional use that is often associated with music. Although we have drawn on some music therapy literature to support this section, music therapy is a separate discipline in its own right. Our intention here is to consider the use of sound and rhythm in creative therapies, an approach used principally by occupational therapists.

We begin this section by introducing the concept of using sound and rhythm in therapy, mainly through providing a historical context. We then will consider the resources required in using this medium within therapy settings, the qualities it has to offer and some other considerations relating to the process of using it in therapy. We close with an illustration of a sound and rhythm session from our work with occupational therapy students.

Alvin (1966) suggests that the magic and significance of music can be traced back to the beginning of time, where it was believed that sound played a major part in the creation of the universe – the big bang! At different times music has been considered to be a gift from God or a tool of Satan. Alvin (1966) goes on to describe the role that music has played in healing over human history. Primitive people believed that illness was caused by magic and music played a vital part in magical healing rites. Although the ancient world considered illness to have a pathological element its occurrence was still considered to be due to supernatural causes. It was seen to be something sent by an angry god, so music was used in purification rites and linked with both physical and spiritual healing. In early Christian times the value of medical treatment was established but saints were still called upon to help with an illness through hymns and music. At this time music became a means of self-expression and man became aware of the power of music over his psychological and spiritual state. The Greeks, who sought to find reason and logic in their world, used music to provide the order and harmony that was seen to be important in overcoming illness, bringing about a cathartic purge of emotions in the mentally ill and thus restoring the individual to harmony. Generally the Greek concept of using music in therapy was through listening to music rather than making it. During the Renaissance the acceptance of pain and disease, for which there was little relief, had to be sublimated and music was used to help. During this time humans gained a more rational view of their bodies and the world. Music was seen as a means of communication and self-expression on a human level and the healing power of music, both physically and psychologically, became increasingly valued and used to assist medical treatment. Today Eastern medicine still makes a great deal of use of singing and chanting to bring about harmony, and in the Western world the use of music in healing is heavily influenced by the past.

Resources

This section considers some of the practical resource issues relevant to using sound and rhythm in the therapy setting. Probably the first thing to consider is the type of instruments required. As Paynter and Aston (1970) suggest, the materials of any art form impose their own limitations, and this applies to the use of sound and rhythm. The types of instruments used for the production of sound and rhythm can be considered within two main categories:

- real musical instruments;
- improvised instruments.

Both of these categories have limitations, advantages and disadvantages which determine their suitability for the type of session planned.

Real musical instruments

These fall into two broad groups.

- More complex instruments which require a reasonable level of skill to play to any effect. Examples include the guitar or the flute.

- Less complex instruments such as percussion instruments like maracas, tambourines, etc. Arguably these also require a level of skill to use but most of us would be able to participate in a session to a satisfactory degree using these instruments.

When using real musical instruments they need to be of good quality (Paynter and Aston, 1970). The ideal is to use the best quality instruments that the service can afford as the quality of the instruments says something about the value placed on the therapy offered and the clients involved. If clients are to use real musical instruments they need to be suitable for the task set. Clients should not be impeded in this task by being expected to use inferior instruments.

As real musical instruments are expensive, the occupational therapy service can build up a selection by gradual purchasing. In the meantime real instruments can be used in combination with improvised ones to provide a wide range of sound sources. It is important to care for the instruments and this should be conveyed in therapy groups, as caring for the equipment serves to engender a sense of value in the therapy process. It is worth finding an old suitcase or investing in a storage box to store and protect the instruments. Today, many therapists work in a number of venues and the portability of the form of storage chosen should be considered.

When selecting instruments to buy or to use in a session the qualities inherent in the instrument should be considered (Jennings, 1975). Some instruments may be more versatile than others and some qualities may be more appropriate for what the therapist is trying to achieve. For example, consider how the instrument can be held – could two people share it and play it together such as the bongo drums? Is it an instrument which provides a range of sounds or which allows the player to be noisy or quiet? Is it a bulky instrument or a small one? Does it require gross or fine motor skills to play? Any of these qualities, and many more, can be used to advantage in a therapy situation.

Improvised instruments

Almost anything is a potential source of sound and, as Paynter and Aston (1970) state, all sound is a potential source of music. Therefore there is a huge and just potential for the use of improvised instruments. In the early years of our school, before we had invested in a good range of percussion instruments, the students had to improvise and in some ways these were among the best sessions. A creative approach to improvisation prevented us from being preoccupied with our individual levels of musical skill. A whole variety of objects was brought in to be used as improvised instruments – from pieces of wood, beads in a jam jar, baking tins, saucepans and spoons to a bicycle pump. Our own bodies can also be used very effectively as improvised musical instruments through patting, clapping, tapping, etc. This can be useful in incorporating an element of physical movement and/or physical contact into a session. The appropriateness of using improvised instruments depends on the clients involved and the aim of intervention. They are at risk of being construed as childish and it might be that their use would be entirely inappropriate, just as the use of real musical instruments might be inappropriate in another situation.

When using sound and rhythm in therapy settings one must pay some attention to the venue available: in itself this may dictate the type of activities used. Consider whether the venue has sufficient space to move around in so that physical movement can be incorporated if you needed. Check what type of seating is available and whether it is appropriate for the instruments likely to be used. Perhaps most importantly, the venue should be in a location where the noise made in a session is unlikely to disturb others. If disturbance is likely warnings might need to be issued or an alternative venue sought. It is important that those overhearing the sound understand what is taking place and the process involved to ensure the approach is not misinterpreted and possibly devalued.

In some sessions access to a tape recorder/player and to both blank and pre-recorded audiotapes might be required. It should be remembered that tape recording any part of a session is dependent on gaining the permission of those involved in advance and that the recorded material is treated as confidential.

A final small, but important, consideration is that antiseptic wipes should be available to clean the mouthpieces of instruments before different players use them.

Qualities

In this section we explore some of the qualities of sound and rhythm as a creative therapy.

The use of this medium in creative therapies may be about creating sounds and rhythms or using those which have already been made, for example through the use of pre-recorded tapes. The way we use sound and rhythm is not principally about teaching the skills of either music appreciation or skills in creating music: as we state throughout this book, the emphasis is on the process that occurs rather than the production of a creative end product or expertise in using the media. This may form part of that process or may be necessary to that process occurring, but it is not the primary aim. In using sound and rhythm in therapy it is important to dispel the elite approach to music that is engendered in most of us through our schooling, where only a particular range of musical ability is considered acceptable. The intention is to create an accepting environment for the creative media to be used as a creative therapy (Boyce-Tillman, 1996). While we may not all be gifted in using sound and rhythm in the traditional sense it can be argued that we all have an innate musicality, we all have some innate sense of rhythm. This is evident in our physiological processes through the regularity of our heartbeat and the way in which we all walk and move with rhythm.

Within creative therapies we can choose to use sound and rhythm at a chaotic, unrefined and purely emotional level or in a very ordered way (Feder and Feder, 1981). To a varying extent this will depend on our level of musical skill and the needs of our clients. This medium can be used effectively in creative therapies by a therapist with very limited musical ability and with clients who have a range of abilities. The therapist needs to recognise their own limitations and those of their clients and work within them. Sound and rhythm does not have to be used in the traditional sense and if the emphasis in a session takes clients away from this traditional view of music then there can be no judgement as to whether the sound is good or bad (Jennings, 1975). The aim of using this approach in therapy is to provide a medium that the client can access, understand and relate to (Gaston, 1968). Using a style of sound and rhythm that holds no meaning for them may have no effect or may even be experienced as offensive. Participation and commitment to the intervention is more likely to be secured, particularly in the early stages, if the individual's preferences regarding sound and rhythm are taken into account. This in turn is likely to lead to more effective intervention (Clair, 1996).

The use of sound and rhythm in creative therapies fosters participation at three levels:

- listening;
- performing;
- composing.

On the **listening** level, by being aware of what influences us and what our mood is at a given time we can use this quality to facilitate our own healing. The listening experience may be organised through a variety of activities. For example, the therapist may play a piece of music and ask those present to allow images to enter their minds freely. Most of those present will describe very different images, which will be flavoured by their own personal heritage. All are acceptable. This activity could then be followed by discussion about these different images and the feelings attributed to them.

Performance could be about singing or playing an instrument. Many people find this difficult because of schoolday experiences, so performance needs to be made acceptable to everyone. Ways of achieving this are through using collective performance, making use of simple chants, clapping or humming and the development of a rhythm.

Composing may seem a little more complicated because few of us feel we have any experience of it. However, it can actually be very simple and most people have been composers at some point – you can probably remember making up a song as you've been driving or beating out a rhythm on the pots in the kitchen! Composing, at a simple level, is about playing with sounds. Poetry or a story can be used to help a group compose (Boyce-Tillman, 1996), and in the illustration at the end of this section we describe how a group of students was set the task of making up a story and telling it through music. They chose the instruments they wished to use, a period of experimentation with sounds followed, and very soon a piece of music was created to tell a story. Another way of simplifying composing is through the use of simple chalked symbols on a board. Crosses might depict a short note and dashes a long one. The conductor then points to the symbols, determining the tempo of the music. The conductor's role could be extended through pointing to different players to call in the range of instruments.

A main quality of sound and rhythm is its character and one needs to be aware of this when using it or making it in therapy. Alvin (1966) suggests that the character of music and the effect it provokes depends on the different elements of sound and their relationship to one another. If you are a practised musician you may already be very aware of these characteristics. If not, an awareness of them may help you to listen to music more actively and consider the effects that a piece of music might have on clients. It could also inform discussion with clients about the emotional resonance of a particular piece of music. We will consider these different characteristics in more detail using the framework provided by Alvin (1966).

1. **Frequency or pitch.** This is produced by the number of vibrations of a sound. Generally rapid vibrations serve as a strong stimulus whereas slow vibrations have a more relaxing effect.
2. **Intensity** depends on the volume and carrying power of the vibrations. The intensity of a sound or piece of music may be nearly inaudible or it may be deafening.
3. **Tone** depends on the harmonies present in a sound. Tone is one of the most suggestive elements of a piece of music and has deep psychological significance because of its associative power. It is this part of a piece of music that reminds us of other events and may induce a strong emotional reaction. In association with frequency and intensity, tone is an inherent part of sound which does not require interpretation by higher functions of the brain. These qualities do not carry intellectual meaning but are vital to the emotional power of the music.
4. **Interval** creates melody and harmony and is based on the distance between two notes. The combination of sounds into a series of intervals can be either pleasant or unpleasant to the ear. The dissonances may be perceived as stimulating, irritating or disturbing.
5. **Duration** is the time element in music, creating sounds of different length. It ensures the rhythm and tempo of a piece of music. Rhythm is the most dynamic and obvious element of music. It is the rhythm of music that allows two or more people to dance together, thus becoming a unifying force. Unity can be difficult for many unwell people but rhythm provides a non-verbal persuasion to act together as it serves to energise or bring order (Gaston, 1968). It may provoke lively behaviour or have a hypnotic effect. A regular rhythm in a piece of music can provide a sense of security, as it is predictable and recurring.

The character of music will, to some extent, determine the response it elicits. Since it is the response to sound and rhythm that interests us most of all in creative therapies we will address this more fully by focusing on four areas:

- its effect on humans;
- its use as a form of communication;
- the associative power of sound and rhythm;
- the effect that previous experience of sound and rhythm might have on an individual's response.

Effect on humans
Sound and rhythm has a profound effect on humans psychologically, physically and behaviourally. Psychologically, it is well accepted that sound and rhythm can alter mood and most of us can think of at least one example of when our mood has been changed by a piece of music or by a persistent or irritating noise. Sometimes this reaction is very powerful or unexpected. Sound and rhythm also affects us physiologically, for example certain types of music have been shown to reduce blood pressure (Alvin, 1966). Sound and rhythm is used in a number of situations to alter our behaviour. Low-tempo, relaxing music may be played in supermarkets to slow us down and calm us so that we take more time to browse the shelves. Fast music may be used in busy throughways, such as a station, to encourage us to walk through quickly thus easing congestion. We can use this response to sound and rhythm in creative therapies to influence the mood or atmosphere within an activity.

A form of communication
Our use of sound and rhythm in creative therapies is often primarily about communication as it provides an alternative form which does not rely on verbal skills. In Western society there is an emphasis on verbal methods of communication (Jennings, 1975) and this is echoed in most of the treatment methods offered. Through sound and rhythm an individual can express themselves in a non-verbal manner and make contact with others and their wider environment, a process which can be experimented with in the security of the therapy setting. Instruments allow the individual to communicate through the sounds made and through the way in which they are played. It is useful to observe the type of instrument the individual selects, as they all have a different quality and the choice may indicate something which the individual wishes to communicate. It is also useful to attend to how the individual is playing as the instrument is an extension of the body and transforms into sound the player's psychomotor impulses. Playing an instrument demands conscious control of movement in time and space (Alvin, 1966). Observation of physical posture, the smoothness or rigidity of movements and facial expression can tell us as much about what the individual is trying to communicate as the sound they are making, and may be used to stimulate discussion about the underlying emotions (Clair, 1996; Jennings, 1975).

Sound and rhythm basically makes use of noise, and we use this in creative therapies to a therapeutic end. For some people permission to make noise can be significant. Using our voices in any way other than in normal conversational tone is discouraged in our culture, which offers few outlets for making uninhibited sounds. Freeing up the use of sound can be a very moving and deeply emotional experience. Being very noisy is quite a bold act; loud sound is frequently associated with violence, anger, attack and trauma and may evoke many feelings (Rogers, 1993). Perhaps someone who is afraid of venting their feelings, or who has perhaps never been one to shout or lose their temper, can try out how this might feel in a slightly distanced way through using sound. They are not actually shouting or losing their temper but they are venting their feelings, thus gaining some insight through this alternative means of communication in a secure environment.

The use of sound and rhythm does not have to be an explicit form of communication in the way that writing might be, so it provides some sense of security for the client. He or she is able to experience the activity, become aware of the emotions it elicits and work with them, yet remain quite private if they wish: there is no requirement to verbalise or to make meanings explicit. Music is often associated with performance and clients can use performance as a way of expressing themselves. Setting up part of a session as a time for performance gives individuals space to express themselves in front of others who are there to listen. This may be a rare experience for someone who feels that they are rarely listened to or heard. It provides a useful outlet and helps them see that they are worthy of airspace and have something of value to express.

Visual skills are also unnecessary in using sound and rhythm, which is unusual among most of the creative therapy media. For this reason it could be used effectively with little remedial adaptation for clients with a visual impairment.

The associative power

We have already alluded to the strong associative power of music, in saying that it has a psychological influence over us and can evoke emotions. This associative power deserves some discussion because it can be important in therapy sessions. Certain types of music do generally produce a similar affect in people: slow melodic music is usually calming, fast music is usually uplifting. However, sometimes people do not experience the expected reaction to a piece of music, and if this becomes evident in a session it is worthy of exploration.

A whole range of factors influence the response to a piece of music and most people have a personal history which relates to this (Clair, 1996). Someone may have been brought up in an environment where classical music is highly appreciated but there is no value placed on popular music, or a certain type of music may have been very popular during the client's teenage years and therefore held with certain affection. An individual may have a very strong reaction to a piece of music because it evokes an association with a real-life experience. We are sure you can think of examples where your own reaction to a piece of music has been affected by its associative power.

There is no way that the therapist can know or predict the associative power that a piece of music may have for an individual. If an unexpected response is observed then this is significant and deserves attention within the session or at an appropriate time. Sometimes students express concern about this, feeling that they must have done or said something wrong if a client becomes upset. While we are not in the business of deliberately upsetting people, therapy is rarely an easy or comfortable process if it is going to effect change. Creative therapies are no exception and it is generally through the uncomfortable times that most progress is made. If an unexpected or emotional reaction occurs then there is obviously significance there for the client which has been released by the medium. There is material to work on and an opportunity to help the individual make some effective progress. Sound and music, like all the creative therapies, can be used in this way to help the individual develop self-knowledge through helping them explore their inner self.

Imagination is one of our most creative faculties (Alvin, 1966) and is something we often draw upon in creative therapies. Partly because of the associative power that sound and rhythm has and partly because it is wordless, this medium is highly evocative and can readily tap into the individual's imagination.

Previous experience

The beneficial effect of sound and rhythm in therapy can often be affected by the client's previous experience of music (Alvin, 1966). If someone has never perceived themselves as very good at music – and perhaps has negative memories from school days – their motivation to use this creative medium may be affected. Conversely, it is not necessarily advisable or desirable for someone who is an accomplished musician to use this medium in therapy: they can be preoccupied with the performance and technical correctness of a musical sound to an extent that using it in this less conventional way can be problematic. The appropriateness of using sound and rhythm will vary from individual to individual and there is no hard and fast rule, but the fundamental point is that it can be effective with people with a whole range of musical talent.

Process

Having considered the qualities of sound and rhythm we will now go on to review some of the considerations related to the process of using this medium in creative therapies.

Most creative therapy sessions follow a pattern of warm-up activities, main activities and closing activities. In the warm-up part of the session the therapist may need to take more time to introduce the medium as participants may be unfamiliar or anxious and need practice in making sounds. The warm up can also serve to set the tone for the session and should be carefully selected to convey the non-traditional use of music. In most creative therapy sessions, a period of verbal discussion about what has occurred and the meaning of the events follow the main activity. This pattern can be used in a sound and rhythm session but returning to a focus on verbal communication may not be desirable. In ending the session consideration should be given to the individual saying 'goodbye' to the medium. The instrument, whether a conventional or improvised instrument, has been used as an extension of the self (Jennings, 1975) and as a tool to express the self. In some way, through a closing activity the individual needs to detach from this.

Just as sound and rhythm can be used to great effect in therapy one must consider its opposite quality – silence. This may have some bearing on how the detail of a session is structured. Silence is very powerful force and is considered in Chapter 3. However, it does deserve a mention here because it provides a strong contrast to the sound (and in some cases noise), which is a feature of using sound and rhythm. Silence provides the backdrop for a sound and rhythm session; it is the 'blank sheet' upon which we work. In providing the contrast to sound it is important. Some clients will enjoy silence, others will find it very uncomfortable and because of its role within each session it must be attended to.

When working in groups using sound and rhythm, the balance between individual and group involvement needs to be considered. It might be appropriate to incorporate activities where individuals alone are making noise as well as those where the whole group is involved. A focus on the individual in this way means that each person has an opportunity to make their contribution, perhaps including an element of performance as discussed earlier. Some individuals will welcome this while others will find it threatening and may need to be prepared through sharing responsibility in group work, working in subgroups, in pairs and finally individually. Alternatively, the focus may be on achieving co-operation in the group, working collectively to create a sound or rhythm. In this case the aim may be to work to encourage increased use of group work.

The duration of sound and rhythm is an important part of the process. Sessions as a whole may be of variable length but within sessions the aim of certain activities may be to create a short piece. The achievement of this requires a time commitment, which cannot be interrupted or it will lose its meaning (Sears, 1968). With most other media a client could do part of an activity, leave it and return a few moments later to add to it but in creating a piece of rhythm this is not possible; one has to commit oneself to it from beginning to end. Obviously this can be made less of a feat by aiming to create only short pieces but this aspect needs to be considered in relation to the client group and the activities should be adjusted accordingly.

Sound and rhythm can be used alone as the sole medium in a session or can be effectively incorporated with other media. On the simplest level, playing music may be used as a background to an art activity, bearing in mind the need to consider the associative power and the distraction of music. Dance or movement tends to be frequently used with sound and rhythm as the two fit so naturally together. The combination can range from moving or swapping chairs for different activities, limited movement such as clapping or swaying, to the incorporation of elements of dance or movements within a song. Again there is no rule about how much or what type of movement should be used in a session. However, a significant lack of movement in any session is generally not ideal. Movement tends to help stimulate and maintain interest and is a natural part of using sound and rhythm in particular.

In creative therapies the end product is rarely the primary issue, although most of the media used do produce an end product which has to be considered as part of the process. Sound and rhythm is different here: through not independently providing an end product it becomes momentary, a spontaneous thing, which happens and is gone. One obvious way of making sound and rhythm less transient, should you wish to, is to record it. Another issue to consider with this medium is that sound is less easy to contain and privacy may be more difficult to ensure, depending on the venue. Outsiders may hear something of what has occurred, which may elicit some comment outside the group and compromise privacy.

Illustration

Here we offer a description and analysis of a sound and rhythm session run by second-year undergraduate occupational therapy students on a group of fellow students. Through these sessions the students are not expected to undergo a therapeutic process. The sessions are established as learning experiences and any psychodynamic processes that occur are secondary to this primary aim.

Description

This was the group's first experience of using sound and rhythm. There were three leaders and seven members. We arrived in the room where comfortable chairs had been arranged in a circle. The leaders were already present and waiting for us. As members gradually arrived we sat down; while not late, two group members were later than everyone else in arriving and there was awkwardness as we waited for them. The group chatted but it was not very involved as we were expecting an interruption at any minute. The latecomers arrived and the informal chat, which was unrelated to the group, continued until the group leaders formally started the session.

First warm-up activity

The group was asked to stand up and the leader introduced the activity, saying that he would begin. The leader was going to start humming and then gradually, as we went round the circle, each group member was to add to the humming until we were all involved. He would then drop a bunch of keys on the floor, at which point we would stop humming and shout out our name as loud as possible. On the first attempt the hum fell to pieces. The leader stopped the activity, reissued the instructions and the activity was completed.

Second warm-up activity

Group members were asked to select a musical instrument from a box and take a few moments to explore it. We were then asked to play our own name with our chosen instrument. In turn, going round the circle we played our name with the instrument and verbalised it in accompaniment. Those with wind instruments played their name first and then verbalised it, mimicking the tune achieved through the instrument. The group was then asked to go round the circle again, playing the tune of our names but this time to continue repeating them with each member gradually joining in until we were all playing our name tunes. This became a real medley of sound, bearing some resemblance to a tune, albeit a chaotic one!

Third warm-up activity

Here the group members were asked to choose an instrument and use it to express the way they were feeling that morning. For this activity we were explicitly advised not to go round the circle in turn but to join in as we felt appropriate.

The leaders participated in the entire warm-up activities.

First main activity
The group was asked to split into two and make up a story using musical instruments. The leaders divided themselves between the two groups and participated. We chose instruments, experimented with them and then separated into our groups. One group was provided with another room to compose and rehearse their story. The two groups were given a clear time frame to work within. At the end of the allocated time the two groups came together to perform their story to the other group. There was a choice of which group would go first. Both groups provided widely differing narratives with instrumental support; both were humorous and received laughter and applause. At the end the leader asked us to discuss how we had found the exercise.

Second main activity
This activity also effectively formed the closing activity for the session. The group was informed that there would be a change of atmosphere and were asked to return our instruments to the box. We were told that in this activity, instead of making music, we would be using music as a stimulus to fuel our imaginations. The leader had taped a variety of obscure musical pieces in the hope that we would not be familiar with them. The leader took a great deal of time in introducing the activity. She asked us to make ourselves comfortable, to relax and to concentrate hard on the music. She suggested that we might find it helpful to close our eyes but acknowledged that some of us might be uncomfortable doing so. She told us that she would play a piece of music, stop it and then provide us with an opportunity to discuss what it made us think of, what pictures or images it had inspired in our imaginations. She suggested that this was an opportunity for free thinking.

In total, six pieces of music were played. The leader started the discussion after the first piece but subsequently invited group members to do so. Discussion always started spontaneously and flowed quite freely. On some occasions the leader used cues to prompt further discussion or to encourage participation. After four pieces of music she asked us if we would like any more: two more pieces were presented, the final one being a long and soothing piece. We were told that after the discussion of this piece the session would end. Following the discussion the leader asked how we felt about the activity and then formally closed the session.

Reflection
Thought had gone into preparing the room – comfortable chairs had been provided, there was a box of musical instruments and the leaders were all present before the group started to meet members as they arrived. This all contributed to

a sense of psychological security and value of the exercise. The leaders had displayed a high level of professionalism; the effort they had made prompted us as group members to do so too.

Standing up for the first warm-up activity immediately physically shifted us and introduced a sense of movement to the group. A degree of physical activity helps to foster psychological activity and it is useful to punctuate a session with this.

While in the first instance the initial warm-up activity was unsuccessful this did not detract from the group experience as the leader effectively dealt with it. He introduced a sense of humour and reissued the instructions differently, with confidence and clarity, leading to a more effective second attempt.

Although the group was already familiar with one another's names the second warm-up activity was useful in restating them but more particularly in introducing the composition of music in a fun and non-traditional way. As a follow-on to the first warm-up activity the group was beginning to get a real sense of the level at which we would use sound and rhythm within this session – it would be a level accessible to all.

In the third warm-up activity, allowing group members to join in when they felt it appropriate enabled us to identify with the mood of others and thus pick our moment to participate. The focus on how we felt that morning helped us all to connect with and acknowledge our feelings.

Dividing the group into two can pose problems. On one level the group has been fragmented, no longer sharing a collective experience. On a practical level it can be problematic to get the two groups back together within the time scale and without one of the groups waiting for the other, thus losing the momentum of the experience. In this instance the splitting worked well; it served a purpose and it was well managed. The individual experiences of the two groups were shared with the whole group to some extent through the 'performance'. Working in a smaller group also increased the cohesion between those members and as this activity formed only one part of the overall session it was not divisive. The leaders gave us a very firm time frame to work within and reinforced it by reminding us of how much time was left as we worked. This was successful. The two groups were able to come back together smoothly and the momentum of the session was duly sustained.

The second main activity worked extremely well. The group really engaged with it, there was a strong sense of togetherness and the exercise served to elicit involvement, humour and disclosure. The preceding activities had done the groundwork in developing the cohesion to enable this activity to be effective. Here there was a real sense of the group working and something happening to us as individuals and as a group. The leader effectively created the atmosphere for this activity. She spent some time setting the scene, explaining to us what would happen, what was expected of us and what she had prepared. Again professionalism and preparation provided a sense of security. The group was offered some choice in how many more pieces they would like to hear, but the leader was decisive from our responses and made it clear at what point the session would come to an end. Throughout we were clear of the boundaries.

Summary

Sound and rhythm has been used throughout history to effect psychological and spiritual healing. In creative therapies the focus is on a non-traditional and boundless use of this medium with the aim of effecting personal change. Sound and rhythm can utilise real and improvised musical instruments, both having their place, and each individual instrument has qualities within it which might make it more suitable for a specific therapeutic end. Sound and rhythm is a transient medium which can be made more permanent through making recordings. It is also difficult to contain. This section closed with a description and analysis of a creative therapy session using sound and rhythm which involved occupational therapy students.

THE USE OF TEXT AND VERSE

When preparing this section we thought there would be a wealth of resources to dip into – we are, after all, surrounded by the written word in a variety of forms. It is the conveyor of information through newspapers and textbooks; it is a leisure pursuit in allowing us to explore and fantasise an alternative world through a novel; it gives us visual prompts throughout our day, locating and informing, so that imparting and absorbing information through the written word becomes continuous. This book itself is a form of creative writing – or is it? It is a text which explores the use of creativity, and the process of completing it is definitely a creative process, but it has a different focus from the psychodynamic one we explore within its words. This text will give information, ideas, and hopefully knowledge, but its very creativity is bounded by the fact that it has to conform. It has to meet an end, an expectation which is on a different level from the therapeutic use of creative writing. It has a creative element within it in that we explore our own ideas and we use the same tools, thoughts and written words. However, this section needs to be about the medium itself, the process of using text and verse as a pathway to self-discovery rather than as a pathway to the product of a textbook, a novel or a poem.

In exploring the role of text and verse within the creative arts we realised there is no specific therapy devoted towards it. We do not have 'word therapists' although we are familiar with art, music and drama therapists. Why, when the written or spoken word is such an everyday part of our existence, is there no speciality surrounding it? The nearest we get are writers-in-residence (Bolton, 1995), who work within the hospice organisation, prisons, hospitals and schools, but these specialists are not using text and verse psychodynamically. Creative writing books focus on the 'how to write' approach, or they consider the use of writing within school life, but few target the therapeutic use of writing. An exception we discovered is Natalie Rogers (1993), who uses writing as one of the themes throughout her book. For her, creative writing has spontaneity, a sound, and a form which enables it to be explored alone or to be linked to other creative media, thus intensifying the experience of self-discovery.

We chose the title of text and verse rather than creative writing for this section because we wanted to extend the scope of the medium. Again this decision came from our work with students, where these sessions tended to follow an expected format. Widening the title enabled their ideas to broaden and taxed our thinking. It has resulted in a richer and more varied approach and one which has provided a more creative forum for the psychodynamic process.

We will make a distinction throughout this section between two aspects of text and verse: we will term these the **original** and the **given**. The **original** will relate to the words which are created by the participants, those who are experiencing the process of using the medium as a therapeutic tool. These are their words, created at the time and owned by each person. The **given** refers to the words which have been provided by someone else, and which we access more formally. Obvious examples are plays, poetry and novels, which may all form the chosen focus of the activity but which rely on the published writing of another to generate the process of exploration within the group. Examples will be taken from our work to illustrate the use of these two different aspects of text and verse.

Resources

Using text and verse in an expressive way requires resources which are perhaps easier to access and use than some of the other media we explore within this book. As always it is important to have a room in which to carry out the activity, one which provides privacy and space. The medium is contemplative; it lends itself to comfortable chairs and carpets rather than to a busy messy environment. The room available may not be equipped with these, but small yet significant changes can be made with a little forward thinking. In preparation for one session the students leading the group had covered the Formica tables with a deep green cloth, arranged a vase of fresh flowers in the centre, and placed a selection of well loved books and pads of paper within easy reach. The effect was warm and welcoming, and immediately drew the group members to the focus of the table and the activity. This had the effect of dispelling any fear and allaying anxieties that had been raised by the title of the session.

In principle all that is required to begin original work is some paper and a tool with which to write. So, does a pad of old paper and a chewed pencil suffice? If we are to respect the medium, and ask our clients to use it as a means of self-expression, then we have a responsibility to provide tools which demonstrate this respect. A range of paper and writing implements enables clients to decide which best suits the work they are undertaking. Some writing materials are easier than others, some are more instant or more permanent, some give an emphasis through colour or texture, but a range within which to dip and explore develops the use of the medium.

It is difficult to write by resting papers on your knee, so some simple clip boards, old magazines or large books could be offered to provide a surface.

Attention to small details makes all the difference within a session, as materials that are thoughtfully prepared enable the work to proceed smoothly, without the irritations that can lead to group members disengaging themselves from the process.

Resources for text and verse tend to be inexpensive, and this is an important aspect to consider when including it within a programme. The materials do not have a shelf life, they are easy to purchase or provide, and they do not normally make a mess. Little special storage is required, and everyday objects can be utilised to suggest a theme or source of expression. Books are a real asset, but they can be borrowed from a local library if necessary. The materials are also quite mobile and can be brought into the environment with ease.

It can be useful to bring in or collect resources about which to write, perhaps using them to develop a theme for the session, so a group of objects can serve as a focus. Photographs, ornaments or items found on a walk are common themes, but one of the most unusual we discovered in our reading for this section was a collection of 'containers' gathered together and suggested by Bolton (1995, p. 215): 'an egg, a sheep's skull, a tom-tit's nest, a policeman's helmet, a Victorian ink bottle'. An imaginative list offering a wide interpretation of the theme of 'containers' and giving the freedom for some imaginative writing!

Texts are a valuable resource, and one which can be used for many different purposes. Texts are the given words, and they can be used on their own or as a theme for a session. A poetry book for example may be passed around the group members to enable each person to select and read a poem. This leads to a discussion about their choice, the meaning of the words for them, and an individual exploration of the emotions and thoughts that surround the words. Alternatively, a single poem can be used as a catalyst to start a process of writing in relation to the given words.

Books contain stories and have a certain familiarity. Many people spend some leisure time reading books, an activity which may have become difficult due to lack of concentration or motivation. Using a given text enables extracts to be prepared which can be explored for personal meaning and identity. This can be particularly effective when familiar stories are used. Some books are illustrated, and the pictures alone may generate conversation and give an opportunity to explore the medium in an alternative way.

Plays provide a different theme for the session. It is possible to purchase or borrow play reading books which have been commercially prepared for a group of people. There is no point in having just one copy for play reading, as all participants need to be able to see the words. Several copies will be needed as they are protected by copyright but they are usually inexpensive. Using play reading in this way gives a structure which extends beyond the text into the use of props, characters and roles to explore and enter into. These play readings can be selected to suit a session in terms of timing, numbers and the scope of the plot, and therefore provide an opportunity for involvement through taking on a character. Within creative therapies the plays are not used for the purpose of producing and performing a 'play': this would be a product focus, where lines are learnt, characters acted and an audience receives and responds to the production. Our use of play reading involves creating the opportunity for self-expression and exploration of the process, perhaps by adopting an unfamiliar role or engaging in the dynamics of a situation. It also provides an opportunity for exploring the process of the activity and the involvement of group members.

Qualities

One of the great qualities of using text and verse is that the medium can be used in so many different ways. Our experience has seen the breadth of the activity, ranging from creating or listening to stories, debating words, using collage to make statements, or reading plays together. Yet the medium remains different; it tends to be more physically static, involving less movement, and it develops the quality of listening in a different way. Work is usually shared and this involves participants listening to each other, listening to the medium in its own right and listening to issues which may be voiced as a result of the reading.

Free writing

For many people writing is a purposeful activity: it presents a message in a visible form. As a means of communication it has been bound by structure and form which ensure that the goal is achieved: for example, the letter has been written, or the report completed. Free writing, however, moves the medium into an expression of creativity, where the message may not be thought through but finds itself expressed on paper, and so becomes a link between the conscious and the unconscious processes. This can be a difficult transition for people to make so both Rogers (1993) and Bolton (1995) use instant timed writing to start the process, where writing simply happens about anything which springs to mind. This free writing is not constrained by grammar, spelling or punctuation, but it begins the process of making words on paper and challenges the blank sheet and the anxiety of 'I don't know what to write'. Rogers (1993) and Bolton (1995) suggest that the only way to overcome the fear of writing is not to talk or think about it, but to get on and do it. Fears about getting started are blocks to using text creatively which prevent the material being expressed either privately or to others. Once the process of writing is under way it can be used individually, in partnership or as a group process.

Working individually

Working individually through text and verse involves having a conversation with oneself. Conversations, even unspoken ones, have a form and rhythm which is never constant. They seem to move around with pauses, phrases, diversions, or reminders. They reflect an aspect of creative thinking described by Abbs (1989, p. 10) as 'stepping sideways out of the track set by logic and downwards into the unconsciousness'. In this way conversations with oneself are freeing, creative affairs, and can be captured and made explicit through the medium of individually writing them down. Writing gives structure to the chaotic internal thoughts, and by capturing these words upon paper they are there for anyone to see and take notice of – even if the only person doing the seeing and noticing is oneself. From a therapeutic perspective creating text provides a way of exploring, and moving towards resolving internal conflict, because the very explicitness of the symbols on the paper makes addressing the problem easier (Jensen and Blair, 1997).

Individual writing can capture an intensity of feeling which may be missed through the use of a spoken word. Consider the following piece of writing by a person who had been admitted to a psychiatric hospital:

Freedom

I fear freedom because
Of the pain of nowhere to live.

This is a very powerful piece of text that gives an insight into so many major issues affecting this person's life: the dilemma between inpatient and outpatient treatment, the issue of care in the community and the reality of those with enduring illness who are difficult to house. It states despair, the lack of normal expectation, the rejection by society. It has a lasting quality and meaning which conveys so much more than the eleven written words. Spoken words may be misunderstood, or not even listened to, but the permanent message of this statement cannot be overlooked. The fact that it is written allows it to be explored and examined because it is a permanent statement.

The above piece of writing brings together various elements. Kennedy (1996) explores how disparate fragments merge to create something which is greater than the sum of its parts, emphasising the power of the 'Freedom' poem. Each person has fragments that are supplied by their characters, their experiences, their emotional lives, and it is these ingredients which develop into a message that can be understood by others. Kennedy discusses personal freedom within a writing journey, seeing it as 'an opportunity to unveil worlds, to explore them as no one else has and then to give them to others' (Kennedy, 1996 p. 5).

The conversation which one has with oneself in preparation for creating text moves the unconscious thoughts to the conscious; it gives permission for exploration and it allows the message to become explicit. Even if words are not shared with others, the act of owning them by committing them to paper has captured their elusiveness, and they have become a tangible statement of the self.

Working in partnership

Working with one other person provides a different arena for text and verse to be explored. It may be a stepping stone between individual and group work, a stepping stone which can be used in either direction depending on its purpose. Sometimes it is easier to write something together, to share work only between two people, building trust and confidence before sharing with a larger group. Examples are where a story is constructed together, or pieces of text are chosen and read to each other in turn. These less threatening situations allow confidence in the medium to develop, and have an important place in the ultimate development of the group.

One activity from our experience which was undertaken in pairs involved the rearrangement of a number of poems which had been cut up and jumbled together. This might be seen as a daunting individual activity, or frustrating for the whole group, but the process of working together was surprisingly successful. There was the need for negotiation, experimenting with the material, communicating to try lines this way or that, which led to a cohesiveness of working. There was also the shared pleasure in achieving the task, and then in reading the verses out to others. Although there was some emphasis on the product in this example in getting the lines into the correct sequence, it was the process of working together which was important within the group.

Working in groups

A quality of text and verse is that it does not need to be a solitary activity, but can lend itself to a collective approach of group work using both original and given words. This may be part of the balance of a session, where different groupings are explored to facilitate a range of experiences. Using the original quality of the activity on a group basis does require some thought and structure to ensure that everyone has an opportunity to contribute their ideas. One example, which worked well, involved each group member writing a list of words describing an imaginary person. These were linked together within the larger group to construct a story around these imaginary people, with each group member ‘speaking’ for their character. This may appear to be a simple activity but in fact is complex as it allows an individual focus to change to a group one, with all the associated issues of negotiation, permission and imagination. The group had to reach a consensus on drawing the story together, which demanded both verbal and non-verbal activity and facilitated interaction. Thus there is a product formed from completion of the task, but there is also the process of working collaboratively to achieve it. This involves all the dynamics of group work through co-operation and communication to achieve the intention.

Word games are often used as an example of a group warm-up activity, each person adding to a word that has gone before to develop the theme, thus encouraging involvement and contribution. Word games should be introduced with care, as although this appears to be an easy task it can create a strong feeling of pressure. When our students have used this activity in sessions they have not anticipated the feelings that have been generated by it. If the word theme follows the circle of members there is a feeling of pressure as it nears you, and a feeling of apprehension as ‘your’ word might be used by another person. It is easy for the mind to go blank at this stage, and for individuals to feel very exposed. If the theme is one which is repeated and built on by each member, then those towards the end of the circle face the task of remembering a complex list, with the attendant fears of getting it wrong. A skilful group leader, observing the anxiety of the last person in the circle, simply drew the whole group in to recall the list of words together, thus creating a strong feeling of group unity from a potentially difficult individual experience.

The given word lends itself to group work through exchanging opinions on texts which have been explored in the session, sharing the roles within a play, or just putting together a group anthology of collected verses. It may provide a less threatening focus, as the emphasis is not so much on individual creativity but on participation. If one purpose of the activity is to encourage working together, then using the given word in these ways will fulfil this aim. Play reading particularly lends itself to group work, as the combined energy of the group project is greater than the contributions of the individuals, making the experience more powerful and satisfying. As the given word provides a clear structure for the group there is less emphasis on originality and imagination. This may be very appropriate for the stage which the group has reached as it provides an opportunity for members to receive, rather than create.

Structure and form

Text and verse have a visual quality to them, as well as a sense of meaning which is made evident through understanding the words which are used. In a written form this meaning is accessed through reading the words to explore their purpose. However, there is the opportunity to arrange words or letters to achieve a greater emphasis, thus developing the medium and extending its use. In this way the shape and positions of words become illustrations in their own right, blurring the distinction between art and writing. Consider the following example, again taken from the work of a person who was in hospital.

Here the writer has enclosed the poem within a circle, symbolising the tunnel, and yet it is not a circle with a hard and defined edge. It is one which is composed of a pattern which leads the eye and the imagination out of the tunnel and into the wider environment of space. The frame is used as a visual message, almost as a picture, to lead the reader to consider more than just the words upon the paper. There is a creative connection (Rogers 1993) between two media, which is used to deepen our understanding. It is important to recognise that the relationship between words and space within a piece of work may be just as meaningful as the actual written word.

Words not only capture meaning by their position but can also give meaning through their formation. Think of a collection of letters which strengthen an image:

S ilently, slowly it falls from the sky
N aming its resting place
O ver the universe
W ordless magic
I nvading
N ature's
G round

Using the first letters strengthens the image of snow, allowing for greater creative expression. Another interpretation was offered by a colleague reading these words: that the longer first line reflected the width of the sky, the snow falling from it in a large mass, gradually diminishing as it fell lower and lower, ending in a short line depicting single flakes upon the ground. It therefore became apparent that words give meanings on different levels which extend our understanding, so a collection of letters symbolises a meaning that may be very personal. If we allow our imagination to move words from one level of understanding to another, we can get in touch with the ways in which they become a creative medium in their own right.

A real quality of writing creatively is the freedom to place words and phrases to enhance meaning. The words do not need to be bound by grammar, spelling or punctuation, but can have a life and a flow of their own. In this way they provide an unbounded medium in which the focus is on expression rather than literary merit. This can be shown by the following example, provided by Galloway (1996, p. 135).

Tray
jug
sweeteners
plates
cups and saucers
another spoon
christ
the biscuits
the biscuits

From Janice Galloway, 'The trick is to keep breathing' in *Mind Readings*, reproduced with permission of Reed International Ltd.

The arrangement here of words explaining the simple task of preparing tea for a guest indicates the thought process of gathering the required materials, and the emphasis on almost forgetting the biscuits cannot be missed. It is an example of the use of literary meaning which does not depend on the structured format of grammar, but which is more powerful because of the freedom of expression both verbally and visually.

Themes

The thought of a blank page and a specific time set aside in which to write can create a frozen feeling which tends to be termed 'writer's block' (in creating this book we have experienced this many times at first hand!) – the frustration of having gained a space of time, and yet the inability to start to use it. Often it is well into the day before the thoughts begin to flow and the creativity of the medium takes over. It would seem that writing cannot be done to order, and space must be allowed for the thought processes to sort themselves out. When we are using text and verse within a therapeutic framework similar difficulties arise, and there can be a need for stimuli to assist people to begin to write. Leary (1994) discusses the use of concrete stimuli, such as a picture, a piece of music or selected objects which form an image from which to begin writing. Peach and Burton (1995) use memories, stimulated by letters, photos, revisiting a location, even smells which evoke particular events. These all provide a beginning, a link which allows the creative process to begin. There is a structure from which to start, but the structure does not impose on self-expression as each act of writing will be personal and unique. Stimuli can provide themes; they are a resource as well as a quality and they can be unpredictable.

Stories

Stories tend to feature in most sessions of text and verse. Occasionally these are stories taken from books, the *given* words, but mainly stories happen as a group process. The group creates them with a freedom and spontaneity which encourages imagination. Their underpinning quality lies in the freedom they allow; there is little need for them to make sense, or to link to reality. Gersie and King (1990) suggest that stories are not bound by reason, giving them permission to roam all over the place.

In reality stories are a part of life which is being reduced to occasional childhood experiences through the influence of instant, accessible entertainment. Yet stories have provided a vital function since time began, a function of communication far removed from logical experience. Myths, legends, fairy tales were all about making sense of a world, and were passed on from generation to generation, providing a verbal history. Each had a beginning, a middle and an end, a structure and form, yet even within this words changed and different meanings were created. Stories became powerful, they were told to chosen people at selected times, and they gathered an importance not just for the teller but for the listener. A story told at the wrong time, based on the wrong information, becomes significant in altering the thoughts of the receiver.

Many people's experience of stories will be with bedtime and the traditional stories which begin with the safety of 'once upon a time'. These were more meaningful than just the words as they portrayed an image surrounded by familiarity and security, which engaged the imagination of the listener. In this way the practical daytime world was being left behind in preparation for sleep. As adults many people read before sleeping, which links to this transition time, where the imagination is allowed to roam freely, fulfilling the same purpose. So a quality of a story is in providing this space for both the teller and the listener.

Using text and verse creatively enables ideas, thoughts, or statements to flow from the originator in an unrehearsed way, allowing images to rise to the surface through the words. These can be unexpected and take time to consider before they are left behind. There is the effect on the listener, the involvement in someone else's story-telling which stimulates a thought process, again capturing images that have meaning and which can provide material for exploration. If the story moves on around the group then each person has an opportunity of extending it, contributing and taking part in the process of its growth. This is an engaging activity, one which encourages participation and contribution, and which often serves to lower anxiety and to allow some fun and creative thinking to emerge.

The use of the given word

The given word brings different qualities to the use of text and verse. These are words which have been deliberately constructed for other people. They are accessed through poems, stories or plays and they remove the part of the process which is about creating the words. The stage of receiving and interpreting these words involves looking at the language and meaning provided, and using them to explore their purpose in a creative way. The first time our students brought play reading to a session made us consider whether it met the intentions of our work – was play reading a creative therapy? Marshall (1974) justifies creativity within a medium if three components are interwoven within the process: the work should contain something within itself, there should be an essential quality within the medium, and it should provide an opportunity for self-expression from those involved with it. Reading aloud portrays the essence of the play, what it is actually about. It allows the group to experience the quality of the play on a number of levels through the words, timing and expression. Finally the play is dependent on the people reading it to convey their own meaning onto it. For us this activity has the potential to satisfy the above criteria and, particularly with the opportunity it provides for self-expression and the projection of personal meaning, we feel happy for it to take a place amongst the other aspects of text and verse.

Play reading gives an opportunity to choose to portray another character. Although the words are set and prompts suggested, the actual portrayal is constructed from the fragments we referred to earlier; those of life experience, personality and imagination. These all contribute to shape the portrayal of a character. The events of the play may stimulate memory through conversation, movements, circumstance, objects and settings and through the portrayal of emotions. This provides an opportunity for self-exploration. There are links between play reading and role play and the same attention should be paid to making sure that people de-role from their parts at the end of the play. Using play reading serves to encourage people to engage in a group process. There is the aspect of active involvement without being responsible for creating the words. There is also the listening role, which is important in its own right – without it there would certainly be chaos! So a seemingly straightforward activity becomes a forum where group interaction and self-exploration take place, although for our use it is the process of using the medium which is the focus, rather than the end product, of simply reading a play aloud.

Other uses of the given word move towards an element of choice and personal selection. Group members may bring text and verse into the session for discussion and sharing. This acknowledges the importance and the accessibility of the written word and moves the process from merely enjoying some writing to exploring the understanding of what that particular piece of writing means for a person. In this way a selected piece may be a trigger for someone, enabling them to consider the meaning in greater depth.

Text and verse can extend to times between sessions, where personal collections are gathered to form an anthology in their own right. These in turn provide material for reflection, as indicators within an individual's life experience. In a similar way keeping a journal or diary will address the need for private exploration of events and feelings, furthering and deepening understanding and self-growth through the use of critical incidents. The process of describing the event is in itself creative, therapeutic and meaningful as using words gives abstract thoughts clarity and meaning.

Listening and hearing

There is a quality in listening to another person's piece of text, whether this be original or given. To begin with there is the auditory aspect, the sound of the words and their rhythm, which convey more than the literal meaning. Receiving the words can be soothing, calming, a gentle activity, or can stimulate, scare or provoke anxiety. There is some safety in being a step removed from owning the narrative: the listener identifies with feelings and moods, but does not own them to the same degree as the writer. Listening can also be an absorbing activity, removing a person from some of the day-to-day distractions which have a habit of filling the mind. With given text, an important aspect is allowing oneself to become lost within the narrative, to fantasise, explore and allow thoughts to grow whilst listening to the words to let it happen.

When a person is reading their own writing perhaps the emphasis of listening is on the understanding, thinking about and relating this work to the writer, using the text as a snapshot into the reader's world at that time. This requires paying attention, showing respect to another and receiving the words in an active way. If another person silently reads a piece of text the experience is changed. It is not such a public sharing of words, the text becomes limited through lack of personal expression, sounds, pauses, silences and so the reading and the imagination has to become more active. Cast your mind back to the example of the tea tray being assembled. At first reading you may have missed the emphasis on remembering the biscuits which were almost forgotten. On rereading this you focus on the words and their position, and it becomes clear – not only through the placing of the text but through the repetition of the words. Try speaking the passage, and there is no way you can miss the emphasis. If one is listening to, or reading, the text created by another the clues within, between and outside the words are significant in their expression. These are the clues to the process that is going on for that person, the way in which the language is being used to creatively explore meaning.

How any of us respond to either original or given words will be an individual experience. Peach and Burton (1995) suggest that our responses are influenced by our own persona, our education, experience of reading, our interests, emotional and physical state, even our vocabulary. There are times when words can exclude as well as include. They may have private meanings, they may be used in complex and convoluted phrases rather than plain speech, they may exclude through dialect, language or culture and misunderstandings can occur. However, the recipient can own his understanding of the words and check it for clarification.

Process

Planning a session around text and verse requires careful consideration of the process which takes place to allow the medium to be the focus. As with any creative activity there is a need for a warm-up part, a main section and a closure that enables the group members to move away from the work of the session.

Warm-up activities introduce the medium for the session. There are endless variations on word games and associations which may be chosen as a group activity, integrating members and beginning to build up group stories. The preparation for the main activity can also be incorporated into a warm up, perhaps collecting materials about which to write or a selection of texts to explore together.

The use of text and verse, especially when using the original rather than the given word, is likely to lead to an end product. Something is created which is written down on paper. Individual work is easy to take away and store as a personal possession, but group work raises issues of joint ownership, and therefore joint issues of disposal. At a session on 'Endings' the students created a group poem to which each person contributed one line. It was a way of leaving their mark upon the process, and they agreed not only to write it together but for each person to have a copy of it. In this way there was a tangible focus to the final session, portraying the strength of group as well as individual feelings.

I feel

I feel glad to have finished, but sad to be leaving
I feel I want to fly off into the future, but I look back to people – colleagues – and I am reluctant to go
I feel like I need to sleep for a week!
I feel full of funny feelings
I feel lucky to have been able to get to know you all, and be a part of OPT
I feel that we are all a very special part of this group
I feel energised
I feel OPTimistic that things can only get better!
I feel I'd like to say a great huge 'thank you', and wish all the best
I feel glad, but sad to say 'goodbye'
I feel full of good lucks and good byes
I feel excited about the future, and will take precious memories with me

For that group of students it was important to own the feelings expressed, to think about them and to make them explicit. It was interesting to realise the conflicts that were made clear, the happy and sad feelings, the excitement yet the anxiety of moving on. There was also an important aspect of making these feelings public, realising that others felt the same way and could identify at first hand.

The explicitness of the written word raises the issue of privacy. In the above example it was agreed at the outset to work together, to share the experience of creating the poem, and therefore to move the words to a more public arena. This was important as it was the final session of the group, and the group had developed a trust and cohesion which made this possible. However, there are times when private writing needs protection, and there should be a space and time for reflection to allow the writer to decide whether or not to share their work. There is tension surrounding this decision, and it is helped by being clear at the start of the session about the expectation of the group. As the focus of the activity is on using the process rather than the product, making work public may bring anxieties regarding the use of grammar, spelling and ideas. It may constrain people to write not what they are thinking but what they think the group will want to hear. The public exposure will then get in the way of the inner voice, and the person may choose not to make explicit in words some of the things that are being explored through the media. To share work involves trust within the group, and this may take time to create. It links to risk taking, and knowing that each person will also share their work in an atmosphere which is non-critical and accepting.

One inpatient group chose to use the end product of their sessions for a different purpose. They collected their pieces of work together into a booklet which they used to publicise the group. The writing was not selected for technical merit, but as a way of gathering material together to encourage others to participate. It gave an example of the group activity, showing its scope and range, the ways in which feelings and emotions were explored and it made explicit the message that the group was for all, not just for skilled writers. In an institution surrounded by the impersonal the group were able to create this book on their thoughts and feelings, and use it to encourage others to join them. It is this booklet which has provided some of the material we have used in this chapter, as the work provides a powerful illustration of people living in a hospital environment.

Illustration

This session using text and verse occurred within an early group, so although the students were very familiar with each other they were not used to working with each other in this way. The sessions were established as learning experiences for the students to help them gain understanding and experience of using creative media in dynamic group work. The intention was not for the students to undergo a therapeutic process, and for this reason any psychodynamic issues that arose were secondary to the primary aim of the learning process.

Description

The two leaders prepared for this group by arranging the chairs in a circle around a multicoloured square rug, which formed the central focus for the group. Members started to arrive, taking seats at random, during which time there was very little conversation. As people settled they took pens and paper from their bags, making the assumption that they would be required for the session.

When everyone was present one leader introduced the group. She welcomed the members and explained that the session was planned around using creative writing as the chosen medium. She reassured the group that they 'would not have to write like Shakespeare', that everyone could write in whatever way they liked, just using odd words or sentences, and that there was no pressure to use correct grammar. The group listened attentively, no one asking for any clarification.

The leader suggested that we should each say our names, which was greeted with quiet amusement, as this group was familiar with each other.

Warm-up activity

The leader introduced the first activity as a 'getting to know you' session. Each member was given a sheet of paper upon which there were six categories. They were asked to fill in their favourite colour, television programme, drink, hobby, animal and pop group. Each person worked independently, filling in the categories, and the anonymous papers were then placed on the floor in the centre of the rug. A group member chose a piece of paper at random and read out the contents, from which the rest of the group guessed who it might belong to, with the owner acknowledging this. The leaders commented that we had guessed most correctly and, although we were asked whether we had anything to discuss, no one else contributed to the conversation.

First main activity

The leaders explained that we were going to write a story, about the length of an A4 sheet of paper. They asked us to go around the circle saying the first word which came into our heads, so we ended up with a collection of nine words: – zip, sky, willow, clock, chimney, sleeping, dances, stick and black pudding. These were used to form the basis for a story. We were then told that we should be prepared to share our writing and each person started their story, incorporating these words. At one point a member got up and left the group, returning some time later when she looked towards the leaders for reassurance, and silently picked up her task where she had left off. After some time the leaders asked if anyone would like to read their story out; there was a silence followed by the leader reading her story to start the process off. Others contributed theirs, some of which were humorous or nonsense tales, causing a little laughter amongst the group. There was a short discussion about the activity, recognising that some words were easier to incorporate than others.

Second main activity

Some prepared words were placed on the rug in the centre of the group. These were statements such as 'Page 3 girls', 'Equal opportunities', 'Cosmetic surgery', 'Zoos' and 'Animal abuse'. Each person was asked to select a topic and write a sentence about their views on it. After some time the leader read her statement out, which related to cosmetic surgery, and there was a short discussion about this topic. Some other group members then followed with their topics and comments. This was a random arrangement, some members contributed and others stayed silent. There was no attempt by the leaders to involve people who were remaining silent.

Closing activity

This was based on 'Consequences' and took the form of a written sentence ending in 'and then', with each sentence being folded to obscure the contents before it was passed to the next member, who added the next sentence. When the paper had passed around the group the leader, who had started the process, unfolded the paper and read out the passage. This was a collection of lines which didn't make any sense so it brought some light relief to the session as people laughed at the end result.

Finally the group leaders thanked the members for participating and the group dispersed. There was no element of clearing up and the chairs were left in the circle rather than rearranged.

Reflection

The most overwhelming aspect of this group was the silence and stillness which accompanied it. Throughout the session each person stayed very still; no one moved from their place except the one member who left the group for a short time. The quietness pervaded the discussion times, where little was contributed, so that the whole process felt unexplored. There was very little verbal interaction between the members, and no physical interaction.

Reflection on the group session enables us to consider the pre-group preparation. Chairs were placed around the rug, rather than around a table, although the activity required the use of writing and it might have been more comfortable for the group to use a table to press on, encouraging shared space. A table can also be used to provide an additional focus for the medium through a pot plant or a colourful container of pencils and pens, making the group feel valued and prepared for. Instead members used odd books to press on, writing on their laps, each person remaining contained within the space of their chair.

It would have been appropriate for the topics in the third activity to be placed on a table, to make them easier to see. The fact that they were placed on the floor meant that they were difficult to read, yet no one stood up or moved around to get a better view. It was as if a pattern of behaviour had been established which was difficult for one person to break.

The activities did not have a clear time scale, and at no time did the leaders mention how long we had to complete a task. This meant that there were times when the group members fidgeted, playing with their hair, tapping feet and generally sending out strong non-verbal messages that their task was complete. The leaders were absorbed in completing the task themselves so they were not aware of the messages, or of the discomfort which accompanied them. If a time scale is made explicit members are able to work within it, achieving an appropriate level of depth for the time allocated. An activity taking a few minutes will give a different outcome from one requiring half an hour.

The ways in which the group did interact were interesting. There were times when some members of the group became more relaxed and contributed to the discussions. This first occurred when we were guessing which things were a person's favourites. It was the choice of a pop group which caused laughter and comment, perhaps because most of the group were young, and were obviously involved with music. This reaction provided an opportunity for the leaders to address the change in communication but they failed to grasp this. There was very little interaction within the stories, where the group showed a polite attention to each other but did not comment on the work. Finally there was some discussion based around the topic areas. These were quite controversial subjects, which could have led to a lively debate, but this did not occur, perhaps because the earlier lack of communication had not been addressed. Two members of the group did not read their stories or discuss their topics disengaging from a large proportion of the session. They were not encouraged into the discussions by the leaders, nor were they asked to contribute their material. Throughout the group they sat very still as they undertook the given tasks but made no independent contribution. This situation often occurs in groups, establishing a pattern for the silent members, eventually making it difficult for them to interact. By using the skills of active observation the leaders have an opportunity to recognise a pattern of behaviour, and to use the group to facilitate change.

The leaders were very clear with their instructions, and at no point did the group ask for any clarification. Perhaps the intentions were clearly heard, or perhaps the atmosphere did not encourage the group to check their understanding. At times members would turn to a neighbour, looking at what they were doing and then carry on themselves without making any verbal comment. Again this raised the issue of how well the group was able to interact, and what was really behind the lack of communication.

Seeking feedback from an activity can be a difficult moment in a group – someone has to start the exercise. In this group the leader took the role each time, reading her own work first. This set a pattern for the group which did not change: they waited for the leader to start and then a few volunteered their work afterwards. Despite the early reassurance of not having to write well, listening to the leader's contribution each time sets some sort of a precedent: the group might think that their work is not as good, not the same. This is a common anxiety and one which can be worked with by stressing the intentions of the session and varying the feedback to encourage it to become an equal role.

This group was planned with an appropriate choice of activities. The 'getting to know you' exercise should achieve some group cohesion and a feeling of membership. It involved everybody and gave them an opportunity to contribute some safe information. A more conducive seating arrangement would encourage this, enabling greater non-verbal communication and interaction between members. The main writing activity was an imaginative one. The initial chosen words could provide a focus for discussion even if the written material is not shared; however, stories provide a valuable route for understanding and acceptance and so are a useful medium within creative therapies.

The final discussion had the potential to involve everybody and to generate ideas and opinions. Placing the topics on a table would make them much more accessible, and would facilitate discussion and sharing, so an altered physical arrangement could encourage the silent members to contribute. At this stage the group leaders should have been aware of the lack of depth of the previous activities, and that they had an opportunity within this period of discussion to push the group forward. The ability to reflect in action results in a chance to make subtle changes within the delivery of the session, using opportunities as they occur to develop the work of the group.

It is important to reflect on the ways the leader demonstrates a sense of value to the group. In this instance having writing materials ready for use, rather than each person finding their own would have enhanced this. A sense of timing provides security within activities, giving a structure which enables the group members to work within it. Finally, acknowledging when a member leaves and returns to the group, even in a subtle non-verbal manner makes each person feel a part of the process, valued for themselves.

Summary

Text and verse considers the use of what we have termed the given and the original word. It reminds us of the vast array of resources that can be explored to facilitate the process of using written words in a creative and psychodynamic way. Rogers (1993) suggests criteria for activities to meet if they are to be used as a basis for psychodynamic work. The criteria include exploring identity and feelings, the unconscious, both energy and insight, problem solving and discovery, all of which are achieved by the medium through the tangible and explicit use of experience and imagination. If inner thoughts are brought into focus, not only through the spoken word but also through the written word, they develop a life, an entity of their own. Whether or not they are kept is less important: they may be deliberately destroyed, thrown away, rejected or secreted carefully in a personal space, but they have taken on a tangible force, accessible not only to the creator but to the receiver. Where speech can be forgotten, but never unsaid, written words can be revisited and changed to explore their meaning more exactly. They can be removed, but their process of creation has brought them into the conscious world of the creator. In this way they do provide a pathway into the unconscious, they expose feelings and make space for these to be actively explored. Through the energy of writing, problems can be sorted and solutions found.

And yet words give the opportunity for release, for imagination of the most personal and creative kind, the fantasy world built around stories where the soul joins the self in journeying far beyond the confines of the body. This journey may begin accompanied by illness and pain, and indeed the links between mental illness and creative writing can be found throughout literature. The medium provides a focus, a venue for enabling the individual not only to use their own creativity in this way but also to receive and grow through the creativity of others.

THE USE OF THE ENVIRONMENT AND NEW IDEAS

In this section we take the opportunity to look at the use of the environment and new ideas in creative therapies. We have done this to encourage you to free your mind to explore your environment and its contents more widely for their potential use in creative therapies. Too often in our work we get set in our practices: we use the same rooms and we tend to stick to things which have been tried and tested, just adapting them slightly to suit the needs of the people we are working with. Here we want to encourage you to be truly creative in your creative therapies!

Our own experiences through teaching have been a revelation in considering using our surroundings more creatively and introducing new ideas into our practice. In our work with undergraduate students we encourage them to consider the creative use of the environment. With second-year students we provide them with just one room for the series of nine sessions which occur in that particular block of teaching. This is a deliberate decision as often therapists are limited in choice of venue and we want to encourage students to consider how they can use the space available to them creatively by the way they prepare the room, arrange the furniture and structure their sessions. In the third year we allow the students more freedom and actively encourage them to consider how they might use the wider environment. By this we mean absolutely anything – the school, the university campus, the city and the county as a whole. Whatever is practicable and can be used meaningfully within a session is considered as a possibility.

In relation to the activities used in the practice of creative therapies we had got stuck in mainly viewing themes associated with art, music, drama, writing and sculpture as the creative media available to us. It was through our work with third-year students that we collectively began to challenge this view. Students came to us with new ideas that they wanted to explore, some of which didn't fit within our view of activities normally suitable for creative therapies. Together we had to consider the essential qualities of an activity to enable it to be appropriate for this way of working. We held on to the students' ideas, kept an open mind and dismissed nothing until we had fully explored its potential. Through this process we were able to see that almost anything can be used in a psychodynamic way and thus be appropriate to the practice of creative therapies.

Over the years we have been inspired by the imaginative ideas of our students, and we have really become convinced that nearly anything goes. The important thing is that the therapist must remain mindful of the principles of psychodynamic practice. They must carefully consider how to present and use an activity and be sufficiently in tune with the individuals and the group to be able to select an activity and adapt it to meet their needs. At this point it is useful to reconsider the activity continuum presented in Chapter 1 and to decide where the suggested activity sits within it.

Resources

The main issue about resources when considering the creative use of the environment and new ideas is that absolutely anything can be a potential resource. It is up to the therapist to open their mind to seeing these opportunities, to consider how they can be adapted to be appropriate, and most of all to be prepared to take the risk of trying something new. New experiences do feel risky but they provide the richness of our working life and are an essential part of working creatively. Being creative inherently involves going beyond the parameters of what is 'normal'. Four main aspects of resources we feel need discussion in relation to the creative use of the environment and new ideas:

- the self;
- the environment;
- the structure and process;
- the medium.

The self

Possibly the greatest resource available in the creative use of the environment and new ideas is oneself as the therapist. The therapist has the opportunity to see things as potential resources, the imagination and skills to adapt an environment or activity to be useful as a creative therapy with a particular client or group, and the willingness to explore these new ideas. To practice creative therapies the therapist needs to be a 'creative therapist' in every sense and we stated in Chapter 1 that there needs to be creativity within the style of the therapist. There are risks to this way of working: such an open approach exposes the self and many of the safety nets associated with familiarity are removed. This is not always a comfortable approach to our work and it doesn't suit everyone. However, it is a very free way to work, a way which is not bound by rights and wrongs and one in which the therapist has to believe in themselves to be able to carry the process through.

The environment

This provides a huge opportunity for creativity and can be viewed on two levels. The first is looking creatively at the environment that is regularly used and the second is looking beyond this to the wider environment and considering whether there are opportunities around which could be explored.

In relation to the environment that is regularly used, it is good practice to give very careful consideration to the way in which the room is set up for each session and how its structure and contents are used. No matter how limited or unsuitable the space available there are almost certainly things to be done to make it more suitable. The environment is a resource to the session and it can facilitate or impede the working process. The chairs and tables to be used need to be considered – perhaps there is a choice available and care needs to be taken in arranging the furniture. An appropriate arrangement of furniture can really facilitate the business of a session. Our room has a series of small tables which are often pushed together to form one large table. On one occasion we were expecting quite a large group and had placed the tables together. It quickly became apparent that this was not appropriate. While the arrangement allowed everyone to have space to sit around the table there was a huge expanse of tabletop between us. This seemed to inhibit the activity and the communication between group members. In theory we were all together, collected around a table, and this should have facilitated the process, but in practice it felt very different. We decided to split the group into two halves and arranged the tables in two smaller collections. From this point the activity flourished: group members were able to engage with it and with one another.

The therapist may wish to make use of props within the environment, to set the scene for an activity or to use spontaneously within the activity itself. This is made easier if a dedicated space is available where items can be kept on display around the room. If such a space is not available, a 'prop box' may be an idea to consider – it might be possible to leave this in or near the room. A large and sturdy container such as a chest is ideal, although if a variety of different venues are used for creative therapies an old suitcase may be more portable. Over time the creative therapy room or the 'prop box' can be gradually filled with a miscellany of items, very few of which need to be bought specifically for the purpose, most being acquired along the way. One item that we have found invaluable, but which was bought specifically, is a rug which is an incredibly versatile prop. It is multicoloured and about two metres square, and is used to create the environment by forming a centre point. We have an uncarpeted room and desk-type chairs available to us, so when we want to create a more comfortable or cosy environment we make the rug our focus, sitting on it or arranging the chairs around it. The rug has also been used as a prop to activities within the session. It can be a base for drama, becoming a magic carpet, an island or anything else we want it to be.

Consider what is available in the wider environment. Sometimes something as simple as running a session outside can make a huge difference. This could be a preplanned or a spontaneous action in response to particularly suitable weather. A garden or grounds may be available nearby or, with some forward thinking, it might be possible to go further afield. We have had some very successful sessions in local woodland, on the beach and in the city centre. Obviously going outside brings with it a whole range of practical implications. It can be necessary to carry equipment out, seating arrangements may be an issue if some members of the group are not sufficiently mobile to sit on the ground, some members might be particularly photosensitive due to medication and the issue of privacy or anonymity is very important. If going further afield the cost and availability of transport also needs to be considered. Most of these issues can be overcome with a little sensitivity and planning. If the purpose and practicalities are well thought through, being outside can be very freeing and open up a whole host of opportunities. Review whether any community resources might be of value to you. Facilities such as museums or art galleries hold huge potential.

We are lucky enough to have the Sainsbury Centre for Visual Arts on our university campus and we were approached by a member of staff there to consider how art galleries might be used in therapy. This was a project we undertook with a group of third-year students. We spent an afternoon in the gallery considering the issue. Our first observation was that being in such an environment surrounded by objects of creativity was in itself inspiring. The art gallery is set up in an informal way, the Sainsbury family especially wanting it to have a 'sitting room feel'. We found this atmosphere conducive to quiet contemplation as well as discussion. In addition to paintings the gallery holds a range of sculptures and artefacts from all over the world, some of which pertain to everyday use such as bowls, hairpins and quilts. This range of media made art feel very accessible – it wasn't so different from some of the things many of us had in our homes. The gallery has a small shop that sells books, posters and inexpensive postcards of a range of the gallery pieces. A tea room is attached to this area, with informal seating areas and seating arranged around tables. We felt that with all these qualities the gallery held a great deal of potential for use in therapy as a whole. In relation to creative therapies specifically the potential seems endless.

Some of the students identified favourite pieces. This process of selection expressed something of them as an individual; they were able to identify with the item in some way so it had personal meaning. Exploring this could provide a route into their sense of self, making the implicit explicit, the unconscious

conscious. Alternatively, the group leader could select a gallery piece to use as the focus for a session. The use of text and verse immediately seems to be a comfortable link here, using it to explore the personal connection with the gallery piece. The availability of postcards also provided the opportunity to bring something of the gallery back to the usual setting of the creative therapy room to be used in later sessions to develop a theme. It was interesting that many of the students had not visited the gallery previously despite being in their final year and having free access to it. This mirrors what often happens in the broader context: many people do not access the resources available to them, sometimes through apathy, lack of interest or feeling that they may be too 'highbrow'. Our experience of the art gallery was that it was a great leveller: it made 'art' accessible to all; the students could see the potential of using it personally as well as professionally in a variety of ways. Each one of them found something within the experience of going to the gallery that was meaningful to them.

The structure and process

It can be useful to look with fresh eyes at the normal process of our groups or the structure we use. It might be that we commonly adopt a set pattern and there may be a good reason to do so: some groups of clients really need the consistency of a regular format. However, it might be that we have just slipped into this without really considering it. Changes to the structure and process can be inspiring – we are sure you can think of examples from your own experiences where sessions have become rather staid yet a small change injects a new interest. Working creatively enables changes to take a variety of forms. The usual style of the warm-up or closing activities may be altered, refreshments might be introduced to the sessions, a completely new medium discovered or a theme used which develops over a series of sessions. We have found that in most cases as soon as a more creative use of environment or a new idea is introduced this involves changes which affect the structure and the process of sessions.

When we involve our students in the new ideas they usually respond very positively. The change inspires them, it shifts the focus and enables things to be viewed differently, it breaks the usual practices and provides opportunities for new ways and roles to be tried. We have said that introducing change can feel risky for the therapist but changes in the structure and process of a session can also feel risky for the participants. These have provided security, a boundary within which to work, there is an element of predictability and within it comes safety. The therapist needs to ensure that a baseline feeling of psychological security is maintained through attention to detail, giving clear explanations of what is expected and reaffirming ground rules. It may be that using a new environment is delayed until the group has had a chance to gain a firm and cohesive identity.

The media

Often we look towards similar creative media to use in sessions. It can be useful to review this and consider why. Sometimes we use a medium because it is what the department has a good supply of, because we feel comfortable using it or because the clients we work with choose to use it. All of these are valid reasons but to get the most out of using creative therapies we cannot always work within these parameters. Again the same issue is at play here, change is often inspiring and inspiration is useful for fostering creativity. It is helpful to ask yourself the following questions:

- How will the department widen its range of resources if I don't create a need?
- How will I feel comfortable using other media if I don't try them?
- How will clients know that it is acceptable to use other media in therapy if I don't introduce them?'

A huge potential for growth is being missed. Look around you and see what is there and available for use. The woods, the town, household bric-a-brac, handicraft stores, builder's skips – in fact anywhere can be a valuable source of potential materials that we are able to explore to access creativity both within ourselves and within the media we use.

In any discussion about resources the issue of cost has to be addressed. We all work within budgets and many of our clients have limited financial resources. Many of the ideas we have suggested can be accessed for free: much is available for salvaging from our surroundings. However, particularly when accessing the wider environment, there can be significant cost implications. Transport may not be readily available or there are entrance fees to pay. In our clinical practice we have often been met with the dilemma of declaring a group as a treatment group in order to obtain free admission. Somehow it doesn't sit comfortably and the disadvantages of this against the advantages of free admission to a venue need to be considered in relation to each situation.

Qualities

The most significant quality about the creative use of the environment and new ideas is that there is always something available regardless of the working environment, the budget available or the therapist's level of skill. Using the environment creatively or incorporating new ideas can occur on a preplanned or a spontaneous basis. To some extent this will depend on the level of skill and experience the therapists perceive themselves to have and on how much spontaneity the clients involved are able to cope with. When using creative therapies one must also accept that the feelings and mood of the therapist, the individuals and the group as a whole on any particular day will affect spontaneity.

In relation to the creative use of the environment there are a range of qualities. Using the environment beyond the clinical setting can be very refreshing. On the simplest level this can be normalising and can help individuals see that achieving a therapeutic effect from the environment can be part of everyday life. To some extent this is something which we, and our clients, can administer to ourselves by providing a chance to see our environment from a fresh angle, an opportunity to enjoy it and use it to energise and refresh. We experienced this in a photography session carried out with students. It was not the main intention of the session but it was certainly the most lasting and valuable aspect of the experience. We found the session energising and it left us with a sense of well-being for two to three days afterwards.

City centre photography

We were experiencing a spell of gloriously hot and sunny weather. The students wanted to explore using photography psychodynamically: they felt the medium lent itself well to being used outside and they wanted to capitalise on the good weather. Sufficient cars were made available to transport us to the city centre quickly and three cameras loaded with film were provided. We divided into three groups, each consisting of three to four members, armed with one camera per group. We were to share the camera between the members of the group and to walk around the city taking pictures of things which caught our eye, whatever we wanted. We were given an hour and a quarter to do this and to deliver the film to a one-hour processing shop. We were then to meet up with the rest of the whole group in a city centre cafe for afternoon tea. The experience of one subgroup was that we amicably agreed about which parts of the city to focus on, each choosing a variety of different things to photograph. Through this activity we became very aware that we were noticing aspects of the city, which we knew very well, in a different way to previous visits – we were really observing the surroundings with fresh eyes rather than simply going about our everyday business. When the photographs were developed we took them to the Castle gardens, found a secluded spot, looked at them, admired one another's and arranged them on the ground in a giant collage. All of us took one or two favourites to keep. The session concluded with a discussion on the experience of using photography in this way.

This is a good example of how an activity may appear to be one thing on the surface, perhaps product focused, yet be operating at a very different level for those participating within it. The experience of seeing familiar surroundings with fresh eyes was a very moving one. It made us question our lifestyle, the pace at which we live and the values we work to in our day-to-day lives. We were all touched in different ways, but gathered over our collage in the Castle grounds this formed the basis of our discussion. We all acknowledged that something in our daily experience of life would change, that each of us could take a personal responsibility for adjusting our outlook, which would in turn affect the quality of our lifestyle. Taking a few favourite photographs to keep served as a reminder and reinforcer of this acknowledgement over the following days and weeks.

The weather forms a huge part of our environment and we encourage its use in creative therapies. Weather has an effect on our mood – a sunny day can lift our mood, damp weather can make us miserable – and this should be acknowledged in sessions where appropriate. Consider the qualities of different types of weather. We often only think about working outside if the weather is exceptionally good but we can make use of other weather conditions. Snow is particularly magical; it has connotations with childhood, it may make us feel playful and as adults extreme weather fosters a sense of pulling together in adversity as we battle to work on dangerous roads or slip our way along icy pavements. Freshly fallen snow also leaves an unusual silence, noises are muffled and there is a sense of tranquillity. When walked upon it creaks and groans underfoot and it can be moulded into sculptures. All of these qualities make snow a useful creative medium. Very windy weather might also provide some opportunities. Wind is powerful and often excites or unsettles us. It could be used as a focus for the activities of a session, perhaps providing a theme for text and verse or drama.

In considering new ideas for use in creative therapies it is important to be clear about the general qualities that are required for a medium or activity to be appropriate for psychodynamic practice. Levens (1986) makes a relevant point in stating that 'It is partly how the occupational therapist develops the use of any particular activity which leads to it being utilised in a more psychodynamic way.' We agree with this. As the examples of this section illustrate, the most unlikely activities can be used psychodynamically if they are developed appropriately by the therapist. The activity needs to have the potential to foster the processes of self-discovery, self-exploration, self-determination and self-help through the action of creativity. Steward (1996) states that for this creative potential to be available any activity which requires specific technical skill, the use of complex machinery or is particularly slow is not ideal for this way of working. While we agree with this in principle our experience has been that many activities which might demand these elements in their traditional use can be adapted to make them more appropriate for psychodynamic practice through creative therapies. When a group of students suggested using cake decorating we were sceptical, on the basis that it required technical skill and was quite a slow and precise activity – however, the students soon showed us how it could be adapted to become highly appropriate.

Psychodynamic cake decorating!

This session was one which a group of students were responsible for planning and running. It fell towards the end of a block of third-year teaching at a time when the students would soon be finishing their course and leaving the school. The students chose to do cake decorating. They came armed with a pre-baked 12-inch square cake already covered in a base icing. They also had a number of packs of moulding icing which had been bought already prepared – some white but other packs were coloured black, green, red, blue etc. They brought some small bottles of food colouring and one or two small paint brushes. The group was asked to make items to go on the cake to decorate it. We were to make these items around the theme of the course and what we had found important for us. The group was given a period of time to do this, placing different pieces on the cake and the board on which it stood. We negotiated with one another where to put our pieces and quite a lot of comment about each other's creations took place. When we had finished the allotted time we were invited to talk about what we had made and how it related to our experience of the course. A great deal of discussion took place, personal meaning about the events on the course and parallels in experience became evident. The sense of looking back over the course inevitably meant that the group had to do some looking forward. This was particularly meaningful at this stage when group members were facing a huge transition from being students to becoming practising occupational therapists. This transition was surrounded by paradoxes – they wanted to leave but they were apprehensive, they wanted to go but they didn't want to separate from the course or their friends. After discussion the cake was eaten with some tea prepared in the room.

This exercise worked well. Coming towards the end of the period of time together it was a good activity to begin the process of closure of the group and closure of the course as a whole. It encouraged members to reflect back over an experience and to look forwards to what lay ahead. Eating the decorated cake also gave a sense of celebration and togetherness in a comfortable activity before we finally separated. The students had successfully managed to enable us to use cake decorating psychodynamically. Because of the way they had prepared the session and presented the activity it required no particular technical skill, nor was it slow to achieve.

Shifting into the unexpected by using the environment more creatively or introducing new ideas for media or activities can be a useful way of working with an issue which is preoccupying the whole group at a certain time. Such issues can dominate, feel very heavy and pervade everything. We were working with a group of students on what was their very last day at the school; they would be having no more teaching sessions together and would only be coming together again for graduation. The sense of leaving was heavy in the air. We, as lecturers, had agreed to plan the session and were very aware that this issue would most likely be uppermost in everyone's mind. We were also aware that each of the group members would have very different feelings about it and that as members of staff we also faced this time with a mixed set of emotions. For this reason we decided to offer some final structure, but wanted the session to evolve and unfold dynamically as the group required. One of our colleagues had a particular flair for creative writing and we asked her to write us some 'gobbledegook' with a flavour of *The Hobbit* by Tolkien (1951). This is what she produced.

In Flubbadub, Ponwy took off his star shaped hat and twiddled the end of his wand down one ear. Such an unruly ending to control, he mused.

What with shifting boundaries, wandering timetables and lecturers that change course midstream, how could one meet assessment deadlines? Half the gnombles were forever turning up in the wrong furtle, the wazzards were disputing boundaries with the izzards and even in the building no-one knew the correct position of the green uniform. Conflicting models of magic confuse the delivery umphs to such an extent that they don't know their places and fall off the end of their cycles.

If only an izzard from each furtle, or a band of gnombles with an umph or two, could simply pool their wasdom and decide what is.

If we knew what was in each furtle and we could put them together then we could make a map ... or a picture ... or a spectoratorumish plan ...OR EVEN A FINALE!!!!!!!!

... send for the izzards bawled Ponwy, screwing his kneecaps back on with a flourish.

Reproduced with the kind permission of Moya Willson.

The students were seated around a large table in our regular meeting room and we simply gave each of them a typed copy of this. They read it in somewhat stunned silence, suggested something had gone wrong with our word processor, asked us what it meant and giggled quite a lot. We offered very little response, encouraging them to read its meaning. The group were uncomfortable for about 20 minutes while they found their direction. In this time they kept looking for guidance from us despite our limited response. We maintained a non-directive role, placing the activity with them as this was the only way it could evolve dynamically to meet *their* needs. They decided to make a wizard's hat and wand and to each cut out five footprints traced around their own feet. Once they had done this, their plan was to go separately around the building and leave one of their own footprints in various places that were significant to them. After this they joined together as a whole group and took a journey around the building collectively. Whenever we came to a footprint, the individual who it belonged to wore the wizard's hat and held the wand and talked about the position of their footprint, their reasons for leaving it in a particular place. It seemed that it was their way of saying goodbye to the building, the people and the course. Wearing the hat and holding the wand provided a slight defence against the emotional depth of the occasion. Group members were sharing some important events and emotions. Using the hat and wand allowed this to happen but also lightened the occasion through humour, helping the individuals to cope with the level of emotion present.

Process

Here we address some specific issues of the process of creative therapy sessions when using the environment and new ideas more creatively. We start by considering some very practical issues. Using the wider environment through taking people outside the clinical setting immediately raises a range of practical concerns. It is necessary to consider how long it will take to get to and from the destination, which will consume some of the time available. It might be possible to incorporate the journey into the session, perhaps making it part of the warm-up activities. On carrying out a session in woodland we have used the walk to the chosen spot in the woods to gather material for the session – fir cones, bracken, fallen branches and so on. The issues of privacy and anonymity are important. Group members need to know where they are going as they may be concerned about meeting someone they know from outside the therapy situation and need to be encouraged to address this as appropriate. Depending on the work setting, some clients may be a risk to themselves or others and a risk assessment might be an issue for taking patients outside the clinical setting.

In this section we have encouraged experimentation with some less conventional ideas. Many of these are activities which take place outside the privacy of a therapy room with a closed door, and as a result there may be an issue around how others perceive them. Here we are not thinking about the clients we are working with, who will have been party to the total experience and will have an awareness of the purpose and benefits. We are thinking about colleagues who may catch only glimpses of a session or soundbites of what has taken place. For us, disappearing into the city for the afternoon or wandering around the building with a wizard's hat on our head did raise some questions from colleagues and also some comments about doing some 'proper teaching'! This issue is discussed further in Chapter 6, but it is timely at this point to consider how our work in creative therapies is perceived by others. Occupational therapy has suffered from the perceptions of others because superficially what we do looks simple and the real experience of therapy is often not observed through glimpses of our practice, so we have to be more outspoken about the meaning of what we are doing. Creative therapies, as a technique used in occupational therapy, is more at risk of this than some of the other techniques we use. It can look so much like just having fun or playing around with activity. Inherent in this is that the psychodynamic processes which occur take some unravelling and are rarely explicit. Where this might be an issue we very strongly encourage you to take the opportunity to explain to colleagues what you are doing before and after sessions. This explanation should not be merely from a structural perspective – 'I've been walking around the building with a wizard's hat on'. It should offer the perspective of what the actual meaning of the event was – 'It was about helping the group prepare for finishing the course and leaving their peers and this is how we did it . . .'. We have a professional responsibility to inform others about our practice. Being explicit in describing our work in this way serves to educate and leads to greater understanding; the benefits of this are clear.

Part of the thrill of writing this book for us has been discovering new things. One particularly exciting discovery has been 'OH cards' and their counterparts 'Saga', 'Ecco', 'Habitat' and 'Persona'. These are a new idea for creative therapy practice and we feel that these have huge potential. For these reasons we have decided to describe them and explore some of their potential in detail.

OH cards and their counterparts

In this section we explore the use of 'OH cards' and their counterparts 'Saga', 'Ecco', 'Habitat' and 'Persona'. These are the cards we are familiar with but more sets are steadily being added to the collection and we know that there are also packs called 'Morena', 'Quisine' and 'Orca', of which we do not have experience. Collectively, these could be termed cards of interaction or association as it is on these levels that they work (Kirschke, 1997). They are basically a game but one of co-operation and sharing rather than competition and achievement. There are no rules to the game; it is not constrained by rights and wrongs or by a defined objective; it is open to the experience of the players, allowing them to find their own course. The only guidance that the cards have is a set of etiquette, which really equates to what we would know as ground rules. This provides a framework within which to work, giving the necessary security for personal disclosure. The etiquette secures confidentiality and suggests that there are no correct interpretations of the cards. It also stresses the importance of ownership of the experience, achieved through using 'I' rather than 'one' or 'you'. It encourages players to work in the present, the experience of now, using the past only in as much as it impacts on the present. Respect should be shown for fellow players, who should not interrupt or offer alternative interpretations. Their role is to listen carefully to what the others have to say.

The cards work to foster interaction and communication between players and within the self. They allow the players to interact with other parts of their psyche, to connect with aspects of their self which may be deeply rooted or hidden. The cards achieve this through their associative powers. They are made up of pictures and symbols which the player cannot help but associate with. If they are open and receptive to this experience, the associations may be acknowledged and their meanings for the individual's life explored. The sets can be used on a variety of levels and this is part of their strength. On one level the players can remain personally detached from the experience, using the cards very much as a game, but on another level the cards can provide a route into the unconscious and the deeper parts of the soul. This is achieved through tapping into the imagination and creativity of the individual. With all of these qualities we see that they fit very comfortably as a tool for the creative therapy approach.

While each set of cards can foster the same processes – those of interaction and association – they each have a unique 'feel' or 'flavour'. Because of this they may lend themselves to a different route for this process. We will try to convey a little of the flavour of each of the sets that we are familiar with. With this we add a disclaimer: these cards are very rich and yet subtle, they go beyond verbal communication and as such trying to describe them through words loses something of their essence. We feel very excited and inspired by these cards and acknowledge that we have only nibbled around the edge of their full potential. We encourage you to explore this resource for yourself and provide some contact details for this in the Appendix.

OH cards

The OH cards contain two packs of cards. The first set comprises 88 word cards, each containing a different word. Some initially appear more emotive than others

– 'cycle', 'home', 'humiliation', 'fear' – yet their association for the individual using them may be very emotionally laden regardless of their first impression. The second pack consists of 88 picture cards. These again are varied, covering a whole range of scenes and images. Examples of cards from these two packs are shown in Figure 5.3. The sets can be used separately or together to access various levels of consciousness. The pictures bypass rational understanding while the words address the intellect (Kirschke, 1997). Used together, by placing the picture inside the word card, our mind takes a moment to adjust to the combination (Kirschke, 1997). The cards are selected blindly, one from each pack, and turned face up on the table for all to see. Initially the word doesn't seem to fit with the picture; it takes a moment and then something happens. When using these cards we have been very aware that sometimes a picture, or a word, or most often the two together, sparks a connection in our mind, something we had previously been unaware of. Our defences have been bypassed – or, as Jung would state, the false mask of the persona is shed. This is a surprising feeling, a sensitive and a moving one.

Another part of the experience of playing is listening to what the other players have to say about the cards they have selected. This experience forms an association on another level, as in some way we can often identify with the feelings that the other person is expressing. This identification may provide the stimulus for communication on a more personal level between the players involved.

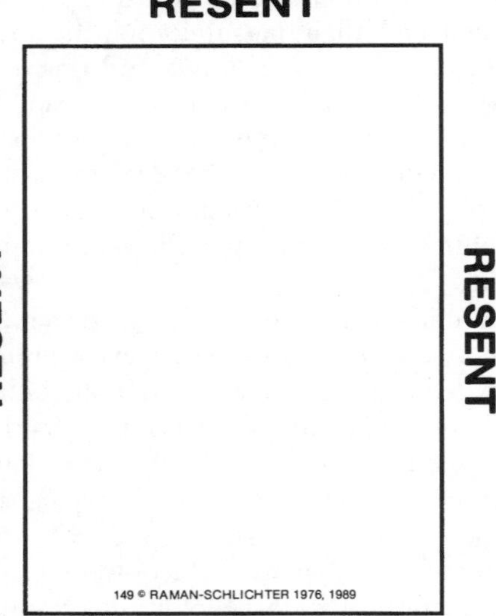

Figure 5.3 OH cards

(OH picture card 17, word card 149 from the set of OH cards by Ely Raman, reproduced with permission of Moritz Egetmeyer, OH Publishing)

Saga

This consists of one set of cards. The pictures relate to mythology, fairytale and legend, which Kirschke (1997) suggests tell something of our personal history as well as our collective history, a link here to Jung's collective unconscious. Used individually we can all connect in some way with the image; for example, a picture of a castle with a drawbridge may associate with feelings of defence, bringing up the drawbridge to protect oneself. The cards can be used through story making. Players may blindly take a card and construct their own myth, fairytale or legend. This may be spoken or written, with the story developed in the first person to keep it personal. If this is a spontaneous act without intellectual filtering, the story developed will in itself say something about the individual.

Ecco

These cards are immediately different from the others as they are exclusively formed of abstract images which are very bright and colourful. Because of their abstract nature they are open to a uniquely personal interpretation. Used with the word cards of the OH set the contrast can be very interesting, the abstract with the literal really challenges the mind.

Habitat

This set contains pictures of man interacting with his environment. The common theme is of the impact man is having on the natural environment and its fragility. Again the cards are open to personal interpretation, which communicates something of the individual's inner world. Like the other cards they can be played in a variety of ways – as an individual narrative, to develop stories between players or in combination with the word cards of the OH set.

Persona

Persona are the final set of cards that we have used and again have a unique flavour. This set is made up of two packs of cards. The first consists of portrait images – male, female, a variety of ages and cultures. The second set are relationship cards, depicted by dots connected by arrows. The number of dots and their sizes, the shape, thickness and solidity of the arrows vary. A format we have used for playing these cards is where players blindly take one relationship card and then select a corresponding number of portrait cards to match the dots on the first card. The player then takes their time to construct a relationship between these portraits, perhaps developing it to consider the arrangement and form of the arrows. This construction forms an association; it has arisen from that player and has personal meaning for them. A development from this, suggested by Kirschke (1997), is that the cards can be used for the players to experiment at being someone else, to try out an alternative role and to explore a different range of relationships. This process may provide insight into the player's current situation and be an early step in a process of change.

All of the above cards are very versatile in their use. They offer another medium and activity to the repertoire of creative therapies. Most of the descriptions above suggest using them as a catalyst to verbal expression but they could effectively be used to spark communication through other creative processes – text and verse, paper and paint, clay and sculpture, sound and rhythm, body and movement. These cards of interaction and association have a clear potential to facilitate psychodynamic processes at a number of levels. Because of this they have a value at all stages of the process of change. They are, however, very powerful, and we urge you to use them with sensitivity and awareness. We have been surprised by the level of emotion they have raised, and suggest that they be introduced when a secure level of working has been reached.

Summary

This final section focuses on the use of the environment and new ideas. It encourages us to be open to new and different opportunities, and to actively seek them out when they are appropriate. We feel that being receptive to new ideas is a very freeing experience, and one which complements our way of working within creative therapies. It challenges preconceived thoughts and boundaries, makes use of the unexpected, and allows us to use our creativity in adapting, exploring and experiencing fresh ways of working. We have considered the resources within the surrounding environment, urging the exploration of galleries, cities, woods and open spaces to add a different dimension to working creatively. We have considered fresh ideas – 'Flubbadub experience', psychodynamic photography, even cake icing. Finally we have considered a new resource, the OH cards and their counterparts, which have opened fresh routes for us to explore.

CONCLUSION

Part 2 has focused on the creative media we use as our tools within creative therapy. This is not an exhaustive list, as we have found that our ideas have changed from time to time, and that we need to be very open minded about our choice of media. We have attempted to move away from preconceived ideas that we will be using art, music, drama, because we have found these terms constraining, preferring to open them up to allow freedom of expression to creep into the titles. Somehow this suits our way of working and the ways in which we think the creative media may be considered.

In each section we have attempted to address the resources required for working in this way, the qualities that might be provided by the media and the process of using them. We have stressed the need to value the experience, using the process of working rather than focusing on completing an end product. There are times when the use of media is daunting, or may bring back childhood memories, so we have recognised the importance of valuing the individual at every stage, facilitating their work within the activity and achieving an awareness of the process of self-discovery, self-exploration, self-determination and self-help.

In our first chapter we stressed the underlying theme of creativity, recognising the place this takes not only within the activities we use but also within ourselves as individuals. This chapter relies on the creativity of the therapist in making media accessible for use, and on the creativity of those who are undertaking the experience, freeing their thoughts and actions to achieve change.

We have tried to be creative in the ways we have presented the media. It is not easy to capture the excitement and pleasure of working in creative therapies, as they are so experiential, so there are times when grasping their essence is difficult to achieve in words. Simply by definition they move beyond the boundaries we are familiar with, allowing us to explore, create, adapt and adjust until we have an opportunity which provides a route for psychodynamic working. Yet they can be easily misunderstood. We have all suffered from a session being perceived on a superficial level as the underneath, where the work is taking place, is invisible and can go unrecognised. For this reason we have to be clear about why we are using a medium within creative therapies, and how we use it to shift what is seen as activity from one end of the continuum presented in Figure 1.1 to the other. In this way we are using our creative activity to turn the creative experience into creative therapy.

Our final section focuses on new ideas, a fitting criterion to explore as using creative media is all about accessing new ideas. Our thoughts are constantly challenged about the ways in which media can provide themes for sessions. Our feeling is that as long as a medium can be used creatively, allowing the key criteria to be found within it, then it provides a suitable route.

We hope that this chapter will inspire you to view creative media with fresh eyes, and that this will be reflected in the ways you incorporate them within your work.

REFERENCES

Abbs, P. (1989) *A is for Aesthetic: Essays on Creative and Aesthetic Education*, Falmer Press, London.

Alvin, J. (1966) *Music Therapy*, Hutchinson, London.

Aronoff, M. (1996). Puppetry as a Therapeutic Medium: An Introduction, *British Journal of Therapy and Rehabilitation*, 3(4), 210–214.

Astell-Burt, C. (1981) *Puppetry for Mentally Handicapped People,* Souvenir Press, London.

Bihalji-Merin, O. (1971) *Masks of the World,* Thames and Hudson, London.

Bolton, G. (1995) 'Taking the Thinking Out of it': Writing – A Therapeutic Space, *Counselling,* 6(3), 215–218.

Boyce-Tillman, J. (1996) Getting Our Acts Together – Conflict Resolution Through Music. In: *Arts Approaches to Conflict* (ed. Liebmann, M.), Jessica Kingsley, London.

Bruce, M. and Borg, B. (1987) *Frames of Reference in Psychosocial Occupational therapy,* Slack, New York.

Cameron, D. (1996) Conflict Resolution through Art with Homeless People. In: *Arts Approaches to Conflict* (ed. Liebmann, M.), Jessica Kingsley, London.

Campbell, C.M. (1979) Puppetry as an Aid in Treatment and Training, *British Journal of*

Occupational Therapy, **12**, 329–330.
Clair, A.A. (1996) *Therapeutic Uses of Music with Older Adults,* Health Professions Press Inc., Pennsylvania.
Feder, E. and Feder, B. (1981) *The Expressive Arts Therapies*, Prentice Hall, New Jersey.
Finlay, L. (1997) *The Practice of Psychosocial Occupational Therapy*, 2nd edn, Stanley Thornes, Cheltenham.
Galloway, J. (1996) The Trick is to Keep Breathing. In: *Mind Readings* (eds Dunn, S., Morrison, B. and Roberts, M.), Reed International, London.
Gaston, E.T. (1968) *Music Therapy,* Macmillan, New York.
Gersie, A. and King, N. (1990) *Storymaking in Education and Therapy*, Jessica Kingsley, London.
Gobey, F. (1996) Conflict, Knowledge and Transformation. In: *Arts Approaches to Conflict* (ed. Liebmann, M.), Jessica Kingsley, London.
Gombrich, E. (1960) *The Story of Art,* Phaidon Press, London.
Hagedorn, R. (1992) *Occupational Therapy: Foundations for Practice*, Churchill Livingstone, Edinburgh.
Jennings, S. (1975) *Creative Therapy*, Pitman, London.
Jennings, S. (1987) *Dramatherapy,* Routledge, London.
Jensen, C. and Blair, S. (1997) Rhyme and Reason: The Relationship between Creative Writing and Mental Wellbeing, *British Journal of Occupational Therapy*, **60**(12), 525–530.
Jones, T. (1972) *Creative Learning in Perspective,* University of London Press, London.
Kennedy, A. (1996) Avoid the Spinning Plates. In: *Mind Readings* (eds Dunn, S., Morrison, B. and Roberts, M.), Reed International, London.
Kirschke, W. (1997) *Strawberries Beyond My Window*, Offset Druckerie Pohland, Augsberg.
Leary, S. (1994) *Activities for Personal Growth,* Maclennan and Petty, London.
Levens, M. (1986) The Psychodynamics of Activity, *British Journal of Occupational Therapy,* **49**(3), 87–89.
Liebmann, M. (1986) *Art Therapy for Groups,* Croom Helm, London.
Liebmann, M. (1996) Giving it Form Exploring Explicit Art. In: *Arts Approaches to Conflict* (ed. Liebmann, M.), Jessica Kingsley, London.
Marshall, S. (1974) *Creative Writing,* Macmillan Education, London.
Patrick, J. and Winship, G. (1994) Creative Therapy and the Question of Disposal: What Happens to Created Pieces following the Session? *British Journal of Occupational Therapy,* **57**(1), 20–22.
Payne, H. (1990) *Creative Movement and Dance in Groupwork,* Winslow Press, Oxford.
Paynter, J. and Aston, P. (1970) *Sound and Silence. Classroom Projects in Creative Music,* Cambridge University Press, London.
Peach, L. and Burton, A. (1995) *English as a Creative Art,* David Fulton, London.
Rogers, N. (1993) *The Creative Connection: Expressive Arts as Healing,* Science and Behaviour Books, Palo Alto.
Schaverien, J. (1987) The Scapegoat and the Talisman: Transference in art therapy. In: *Images of Art Therapy* (eds Dalley, T., Case, C., Schaverian, J., Weir, F., Halliday, D., Nowell Hall, P. and Weller, D.), Tavistock, London.
Sears, W. (1968) Processes in Music Therapy. In: *Music in Therapy* (ed. Gaston, E.T.), Macmillan, New York.
Sorell, W. (1973) *The Other Face. The Mask in the Arts*, The Bobbs-Merrill Company Inc., Indianapolis.

Steward, B. (1996) Creative therapies. In: *Occupational Therapy in Short-term Psychiatry*, 2nd edn (ed. Willson, M.), Churchill Livingstone, London.

Stevens, A. (1994) *Jung,* Oxford University Press, Oxford.

The Attenborough Report (1985) *Arts and Disabled People,* Carnegie UK Trust, London.

Tolkien, J.R.R. (1951) *The Hobbit*, Unwin Paperbacks, London.

Totenbier, S. (1995) A New Way of Working with Body Image in Therapy, Incorporating Dance/Movement Therapy Methodology. In: *Arts Therapies and Clients with Eating Disorders* (ed. Dokter, D.), Jessica Kingsley, London.

Van Ments, M. (1994) *The Effective Use of Role Play,* Kogan Page, London.

Warren, B. (1984) *Using the Creative Arts in Therapy,* Croom Helm, London.

Wethered, A. (1973) *Movement and Drama in Therapy,* Jessica Kingsley, London.

PART THREE

CREATIVE PROGRESS

6 THE CHANGING CLIMATE

INTRODUCTION

We have called the final section of this text 'Creative Progress' as it is the section which moves our thinking on to envisage the remit which creative therapies will have as an intervention within mental health during the next century. To achieve this we need to pay attention to the overarching changes in health and social care, within which we must place our practice. We would suggest that this is never a static picture as these organisations will always be subject to change, evaluation and fresh ideas, which is the concept of progress. The purpose of change is to achieve a better state, through reflection on where we have been, to enable us to develop future practice in the quest for excellence. Therefore we have to be confident in using creative therapies, knowing both where we are coming from and where we are going, and, most importantly, why. We need a sound theory base that provides us with credible practice, and this is addressed in the earlier sections. We then need the tools of delivery, the 'doing' stage which is fully explored through media and professional artistry. Now we need to address the ways which will enable us to be confident that our practice will meet the requirements of the changing health care climate, where clinical excellence will be a key underpinning theme.

To do this we must understand the impact of change within our service. However, change seems to be continuously occurring, making it difficult to capture an accurate picture at a specific moment. This fluid state means that what we write about today may have altered by tomorrow, and indeed much of the thinking which underpins the current political changes has not yet been fully translated into practice. Our responsibility will be to understand the progress that is taking place, to address the changes this brings, and to reflect upon our own practice to ensure that we are achieving its intentions. In this way we will collect evidence that our practice is effective within whatever new health care arena is in place.

This chapter takes a wider view of creative therapies. It considers the changing climate of health and social care and how this impacts upon our current practice of creative therapies. We have called it the changing climate as this title very much reflects the position we find ourselves within at the time of writing. We are on the brink of significant reform, making it difficult to capture the current picture or to speculate about the exact ways in which change will affect the occupational therapy service within mental health. One certainty is the emphasis on quality and accountability, both of which are at the core of the political thinking that underpins the changes.

The current debate focuses on the role of clinical governance as a framework for achieving high-quality care for those with whom we practice. This mechanism encompasses quality assurance, evidence-based practice and life-long learning as the tools by which the ethos of the Health Bill (Department of Health, 1999) will become a reality. In an attempt to ensure excellence of clinical care there are changes to the delivery of services, moving from the era of GP fundholding to reorganisation of primary care. Both of these strands of the legislation will impact on our work within the new century, making it important that we are proactive as therapists to ensure our role within the new arrangements. Change is a permanent state within our professional world and we must learn to accept it and to value the opportunities that are forthcoming. Within creative therapies we consider that the development of a sound theory base, linked with initiatives for collecting evidence to support our practice, will give us scope to be effective agents within change, taking control of opportunities as they occur and grasping the challenges that change can bring.

Within this huge arena of change there are four main aspects which we will explore in relation to creative therapies.

- There has been a gradual and subtle shift in our language from mental illness to mental health, which reflects a change in our thinking and current attitudes.
- The focus of our intervention has shifted to place a greater emphasis on community-based care.
- The move towards ensuring clinical effectiveness through audit, outcome measures and evidence-based practice as key forces behind our practice.
- The changing role of the professional within occupational therapy, with an emphasis on self-regulation and continuing professional development.

CHANGES IN LANGUAGE

Changes have occurred in health-related language, which has shifted almost imperceptibly from 'mental illness' to 'mental health' to reflect modified thinking, attitudes and emphasis in the provision of the services that we offer. Here we consider our potential clients in three groups and explore the relevance of this change in language to the practice of creative therapies in relation to those groups. Our potential clients include:

- those with clinical symptoms of mental ill health;
- those experiencing a heightened response to life events;
- those who are well and for whom the issue is one of health promotion and personal growth.

Many of the clients we work with have clinical symptoms of mental ill health and often come to us with an identified diagnosis. The gradual shift in emphasis towards 'mental health' rather than 'mental illness' represents a wider cultural change in mental health services and this is highly significant in the way that we think about our clients and our work. For many years we have talked about 'mental illness', a phrase which links to the medical model where illness relates to sickness, and therefore to cure, treatment or care. The emphasis within this framework is that there is an intervention by another which will effect a change, so that the responsibility for recovery is taken by someone or something outside of the person themselves (Mitchell, 1987). Illness and care describe a one-way approach of 'doing for' rather than the approach of today which is very much a concept of 'doing with'.

Take a few moments to think about what the terms 'illness' and 'health' mean to you, try writing down the words which you link with them. For us, the words associated with illness include some of the following:

- hospital, doctor, incapacity, sickness, inabilities, a focus on dysfunction, disability, disorder.

Contrast these words with those which we associate with health:

- well-being, ability, quality of life, independence, confidence, self-esteem.

One set of words seems more liberating than the other, with more opportunity to innervate and grow. Is this not what we are trying to engender through creative therapies with our clients?

This shift in emphasis links with the values of the client-centred approach presented in detail in Chapters 1 and 2. As occupational therapists we are familiar with this approach in all aspects of our practice (Canadian Association of Occupational Therapists, 1997) but specifically in relation to creative therapies we can see how two of the key principles:

- that each individual is responsible for themselves and has the potential for their own development, and
- that both the therapist and the client are active within the creative therapy process

are congruent with this shift towards a focus on mental health.

Ewles and Simnett (1992) suggest the notion of health as the foundation for achieving human potential. This recognises not only that each person's potential varies but also that their health needs are different, just as their experiences of health are also different. This view fits very well with our approach within creative therapies. We acknowledge and value the differences within our clients, we recognise potential, but realise that for one person this may be more easily reached than for another. Through creative therapies each of our clients will be working to achieve their specific health potential and individual quality of life, yet each will be different from the next.

Our second group of clients are those who appear not to have clinical symptoms of mental ill health but who are experiencing a heightened response to life events, for example bereavement, redundancy, divorce or childbirth. Their response to these could be either functional or dysfunctional but in both instances people may need some help to adjust. These clients do not have a psychiatric disorder but are on the fringe of requiring mental health services. Early intervention through creative therapies may provide an effective treatment which prevents the development of a psychiatric disorder, thus avoiding the issues of medication, labelling, hospitals and possibly admission.

Alternatively, clients may have a presenting factor which appears to 'sit' within a physical framework. Again, adaptation is the key feature, where the individual needs to adapt to altered physical functioning as well as cope with the psychological shift required. Creative therapies can be a useful intervention in this process. As an example, creative therapies have effectively been used as a technique within palliative care. Heiney (1995) uses the power of stories and collage in her work with terminally ill patients to explore concerns and anxieties and assist in problem solving.

When considering the use of creative therapies with clients whose problems fall within a physical framework we have to recognise that we work within a health climate where there is pressure on beds and resources. This pressure has reduced many occupational therapy interventions to a purely physical focus – mobility, self-care, independence, is the person safe to be discharged? There is little time or space to consider issues beyond this. However, occupational therapy is a holistic profession and it would seem entirely appropriate to consider mental health as an integral part of coping with physical illness. While it may not be realistic to use creative therapies in their fullest sense the occupational therapist can attend to the psychodynamic aspects of interventions with clients. These may provide insight and understanding into the client's behaviour and for the client they can be used to develop an awareness of the need to make changes and provide the confidence to try these out (Levens, 1986; Yaretzky, Levinson and Kimchi, 1996).

Our third potential group of clients are those who are well and for whom the focus is on the issue of health promotion and personal growth. As occupational therapists we have a role, with other professionals, to promote health and this constitutes an important aspect of our work. Ewles and Simnett (1992, p. 19) state, 'health promotion aims to empower people to have more control over aspects of their lives which affect their health.' Much of the activity which occurs through creative therapies is aimed at achieving these principles. The creative therapy approach is client centred and stresses the unique environment within which each individual operates, it emphasises the individual's responsibility for their decisions and personal growth, and it provides a route for the resolution of intrapersonal and interpersonal conflict which is likely to have an effect on health.

As well as working with people with mental health problems, creative therapies have a role in health promotion among the 'well' population in promoting personal growth through encouraging self-exploration and facilitating personal understanding and resolution. In this role creative therapies may be offered privately in the local community, perhaps at evening classes or at a community centre. A series of sessions might be targeted at particular populations within the community, such as people experiencing challenging life events, minority groups, gender groups, or those facing significant change, thus providing a forum to address shared issues. This provision of creative therapies falls outside the statutory provision of services; it is an area which has not been fully accessed by occupational therapists and represents a real opportunity for future practice. Linked with this is the opportunity for using creative therapies in organisations to help members of the organisation work through times of change or periods of conflict. This requires a different angle to be taken but uses many of the concepts and skills of this approach.

In conclusion, the change of emphasis in language from 'illness' to 'health' represents a much wider cultural shift in our view of our clients and our approach to working. Creative therapies fit neatly within that changing emphasis and have something to contribute to that change whether it is in working with clients experiencing symptoms of mental ill-health, with those who are adapting to life events or with those where the emphasis is on health promotion and personal growth.

CHANGES IN THE FOCUS OF CARE

The focus of care in mental health services has undergone, and is indeed still experiencing, significant change. Key in this has been a shift in the location of care from hospital to community. In this section we will explore the political thinking that has underpinned this change, what these changes have entailed and how they affect creative therapies. We will suggest ways in which we can demonstrate that we both understand and are working with the concepts of clinical governance, through ensuring that quality and accountability are explicit within our practice.

To put current and future changes in context we need to reflect on the previous management of mental health care. The history of this is well charted (Baldwin, 1993; Bean and Mounser, 1993; Ramon, 1988; Weller, 1993), providing a level of detail beyond that required in this text. However, it is useful to be reminded of three distinct phases of care within this history. The first was the asylum phase, an approach to care which was motivated by a religious and humanitarian desire to care for and protect the very vulnerable members of society. This led to a custodial phase when sufferers of 'dangerous madness' were locked away, more for the protection of others than for any provision of treatment. Finally there was the remedial phase, which saw greater understanding of mental ill health, the introduction of effective medical treatments and an understanding of psychological theories which influenced the relationship between the body and the mind (Mitchell, 1987).

Significant advances in effective medication coupled with the legislative changes of the 1980s and 1990s (The Griffiths Report, 1983; The National Health Service and Community Care Act, 1990) resulted in the move towards the focus of care being provided within the community. This change was far greater than just the closing of the old institutions, as it signified a whole shift in attitude from the medical model to the social model (Weller, 1993). The change in culture reflected the need for service providers to think in a different way. It shifted the focus onto the person behind the patient, seeing the illness as only one small aspect of the whole person, stressing ability rather than disability and promoting self-determination and autonomy in the patient (Atkinson, 1996; Bowden, 1991 and Finlay, 1997a).

We are now on the verge of another era of change which will impact on our practice in two significant ways. The first is structural change, which relates to the way services are organised and how care is accessed; the second focuses on the drive for quality, the need to make excellence explicit within our practice. Although quality is not a new concept it is now taking on a fresh emphasis through the framework of clinical governance, where it plays a key role towards achieving better standards of care.

One of the main concepts of the Health Bill (Department of Health, 1999), is the change from GP fundholding to Primary Care Groups and, ultimately, to Primary Care Trusts. At the time of writing this bill has not completed the legislative process, but the structural alterations are partly in place, as primary care groups have already taken over from fundholding practices. This organisational change endeavours to modernise the NHS, making excellence of clinical care its main strategy. Primary care groups represent a changed organisational structure which is concerned with identifying the health needs of the community and the development of primary care services. They provide a forum for bringing together a number of important functions, which include addressing the health needs of the community and the development of primary care services. In time they may also be involved in commissioning hospital and community health services (Department of Health, 1998a).

In recognition of the fact that community care within mental health has been problematic we currently have a White Paper, *Modernising Mental Health Services* (Department of Health, 1998b), promising radical reform and large investment. It offers a vision of providing a safe, sound and supportive system and stresses that care will be individual, recognising that each person has different needs and preferences. It also stresses that services should be available when and where people need them, acknowledging that partnerships will be required to cross traditional organisational boundaries. The Mental Health Act (1983) is no longer the most effective legislation in view of the developments which have occurred within this area of health care.

The renewed drive for quality is evident within The Health Bill (1999) as this places a statutory duty of quality on both NHS Trusts and Primary Care Trusts. Clinical governance will provide 'the framework through which NHS organisations are accountable for continuously improving the quality of their services and safeguarding high standards of care, thus creating an environment through which excellence in clinical care will flourish' (Department of Health, 1998c). The mechanisms that will achieve this include clinical audit, quality assurance and professional development, all of which are addressed later in this chapter. These are the tools which will provide evidence of good practice, enabling us to achieve both quality and accountability, ensuring that our practice fits within the ethos of future health care. Clinical governance is perhaps the main 'buzzword' at the time of writing, influencing our practice through making all professionals responsible and accountable for the effectiveness of their practice. This personal responsibility demands evidence from each of us that we can justify the effectiveness of our interventions and that our practice reflects life-long learning.

It is apparent that change is not limited to how we deliver a service, what we actually do in creative therapies, or even where that intervention is taking place. It is clear that the changing climate of today's mental health care involves justifying our interventions, providing outcome measures which ensure that we are 'value for money' and providing evidence of the effectiveness of our interventions. Mental health care reflects a complex range of interventions which are provided by a diverse workforce. As occupational therapists we need to be able to justify our position and prove that our practice works. Therefore we have to be able to provide evidence of both quality and effectiveness as part of the overall drive towards continuous improvement within the health service.

QUALITY ISSUES

Quality is a cyclical process to which there is arguably no finite end point; quality issues gradually build upon one another with the ultimate aim of achieving the highest level of attainment possible. This process is reflected in the evolution of quality issues in health care. From a basis of very little formal evaluation we are gradually becoming more and more sophisticated in evaluating quality from a range of perspectives.

There has always been a desire to provide a service of high quality within health care but until relatively recently this was based on professional good intention. Before the 1980s some quality mechanisms were in place, yet little was done to monitor them. The situation changed when the issue of quality was first formally addressed in the Griffiths Report and the White Papers which preceded and informed The National Health Service and Community Care Act (1990). This Act was the driving force behind the widespread use and application of clinical audit. Donabedian (1988) suggests that clinical audit provides a framework for scrutinising the structure, process and outcome of an intervention. In practice we became skilled at auditing the structure and process but the outcomes of many occupational therapy interventions were acknowledged as more difficult to measure (Blom-Cooper, 1989). However, the quality process is advancing and becoming more explicit, so the drive that we face now is to look beyond the quality of the client's experience to the quality of the clinical result, the outcomes of intervention. This drive sits in tandem with the increasing focus on evidence-based practice. While these are two very different processes they are both part of the quality cycle and are at the centre of current health care reform (Department of Health, 1999).

The next sections discuss audit, outcome measurement and evidence-based practice and the place they take within the quest for quality.

Clinical audit

Donabedian (1988) provides a framework for quality based on structure, process and outcome. This can be used as a basis for clinical audit. We go on to apply this framework to creative therapies.

Structure

This relates to the setting in which intervention occurs. This can be broken down into material resources (rooms, equipment, budget), human resources (sufficient staff with the right skills and qualifications) and organisational structure (the management background which supports the service) (Howard, 1996). In addition, Maxwell (1984) highlights the importance of the accessibility of an intervention in terms of the location for it and the waiting times for inclusion. We have considered the importance of the geographical accessibility of creative therapy sessions in Chapter 3 where we address the access issues of public transport, parking and the appropriateness of using sites associated with psychiatric services.

The provision of resources raises the issue of waiting times: as there may be an unequal provision of the service established groups are likely to attract waiting lists. A thorough assessment process will ensure that this consists of clients who are suitable for this therapeutic approach. Resource allocation should be informed by waiting times because there may be a need to provide more groups, so training needs, room costs and materials have to be considered. This type of treatment should be responsive to need, acknowledging that a client's mental health may deteriorate if intervention is delayed.

Process

This involves considering two linked aspects: how creative therapies as a treatment strategy are delivered and the competence of the therapist involved (Howard, 1996). There are a number of activities which need consideration as part of the process of delivery. These will include the provision of

- **good practice** – through support, supervision, further training, co-therapy;
- **time** – ensuring an appropriate number of sessions, pre and post-group time;
- **client selection** – defining appropriate referrals, information about the group, initial assessment procedures;
- **information for clients** – publicity, written and verbal communication, attendance, motivation, commitment;
- **reporting and recording** – procedures for recording intervention, liaison with others;
- **responsiveness to need** – waiting times, assessment, recognition of skills, discharge procedures.

The competence of the therapist raises two issues that are particularly relevant to creative therapies, the first of which is technical performance (Donabedian, 1988). The therapist needs to have the skills and expertise to work in this way, and should be able to ensure that practice is current, informed and (where possible) research based. Through these the intervention offered will be of a high standard, achieving best practice in assessing the client for creative therapies. The process assures quality within an appropriate treatment choice as well as the actual implementation and delivery of creative therapies. The second issue considers quality within the relationship between the therapist and the client

(Donabedian, 1988). This is an essential element of creative therapies as the success of this treatment intervention is highly dependent on achieving a good relationship. We use this relationship, along with the creative media, to gain information about our clients and to explore with them areas of difficulty and dysfunction. Recognising the interpersonal relationship as a quality issue raises the profile of our work as it makes this aspect explicit and measurable.

Assuring quality within an intervention involves setting standards that make each part of the procedure explicit, allowing it to be audited or measured. In order to make the process work standards should be achievable, measurable, observable, understandable and reasonable (Wright and Whittingdon, 1992). To achieve this within creative therapies we need to break the process down into small stages. The examples in Table 6.1 provide one route to defining standards in order to audit the procedure.

Standards can be audited in a number of ways using audit tools, but a system has to be in place to ensure that audit occurs. This may be on an annual basis or may be part of the procedure of evaluation after the group has occurred. The purpose of audit is to improve standards and to ensure quality. This needs to be seen as a continuous process, in which standards will be set, implemented and audited so that the feedback received through this process will be used to inform future practice, the aim being to continually improve performance. It is very

Table 6.1

Standard 1	**The occupational therapy team will ensure that referrals to creative therapies are appropriate**
Outcome measures	1.1 The team will develop guidelines for referral
	1.2 A standard referral form will be produced
	1.3 All potential referrers will receive a copy of the form
	1.4 Inappropriate referrals will be returned to their source
	1.5 All referrers will be contacted on an annual basis to discuss their referrals.
Audit tools	Documentation
	Review of referrals
Standard 2	**There will be a specific budget for creative therapies**
Outcome measures	2.1 Budget allocation will be discussed and agreed with the budget holder
	2.2 The allocation will be defined through a coding system
	2.3 The management of this allocation will be undertaken by the occupational therapist responsible for creative therapies
	2.4 The statements will be sent to this OT on a monthly basis
	2.5 The allocation will be reviewed at the end of the year and the new annual allocation will be agreed.
Audit tools	Budget statements
	Documentation
	Performance review

important that this cycle is completed so that the audit process is actively used to inform practice, leading to changes which are then monitored through a continuation of the cycle (Sealey, 1999).

Outcomes

These are the third part of Donabedian's framework. They relate to the effectiveness of a service in terms of clinical results, the client's satisfaction with the care they receive and its effect on health status. The outcomes of an intervention become the key issue in quality. The first two parts of Donabedian's framework, structure and process, are important precursors because they support the achievement of successful outcomes (Howard, 1996).

Outcome measurement

Outcome measurement is concerned with the effectiveness of an intervention – did it achieve what it set out to achieve? This has been the most difficult part of the quality framework for occupational therapists to grasp. Some of our interventions lend themselves to measurement of outcome, but these tend to be the more quantifiable areas, which can be measured through objective means. In mental health these might be areas of practice concerned with behavioural change or cognitive processes. However, in creative therapies our concerns are often with much more subjective processes. To further complicate the process the desired outcomes of creative therapies may not be evident to either the client or the therapist at the start of intervention. Coupled with the client-centred nature of this area of practice these factors make outcome measurement a difficult task.

Gone are the days of avoiding this challenge because it is difficult. We have external agents demanding evidence of the effectiveness of our practice, and as a professional group the motivation to know that what we do works has always been present. There is a variety of ways in which we can measure the outcomes of creative therapies. The choice of method will be determined by the therapist, taking into account a number of specific factors – the way in which creative therapies is applied, the common features of the client group and the current uses and requirements of outcome measurement within the service.

Evaluating the effectiveness of an intervention should be informed by three main sources: an objective view provided by the use of standardised outcome measurement tools, the view of the client and the view of the therapist. This information can come through a variety of methods – self-rating scales, questionnaires, individualised outcome measures, case documentation, self-assessment and so on. This book is not about outcome measurement so we aim only to introduce the topic, with specific reference to the issues facing creative therapy practice. This area will continue to develop and expand so we advise you to keep abreast of current literature. We will address outcome measurement in creative therapies through three broad routes:

- the use of standardised outcome measurement tools before and after the creative therapy intervention;

- the client's view on whether the intervention has been effective;
- the therapist's view on whether the intervention has been effective.

Standardised outcome measurement tools

Standardised outcome measurement tools are becoming increasingly popular because they are objective and therefore perceived to be more credible (de Clive Lowe, 1996). The ones appropriate to mental health practice tend to measure conventional domains such as symptoms, self-esteem and mood. The use of the tool before the intervention allows the therapist to establish a baseline. Upon completion of the intervention the tool is administered again, measuring the client's progress and the effectiveness of the intervention. It is important that an appropriate outcome measure is selected, but this will depend on factors such as the client group and the clinical setting. Some useful texts, such as that of McDowell and Newell (1996), assist with this selection but another route to selection for evaluating creative therapy practice is to search related psychotherapy research literature and draw upon the outcome measures used. Many of these studies have been conducted by clinical psychologists, who have a much longer history than occupational therapists in using standardised tools.

An example of a standardised outcome measure that has been adopted within our local psychological therapies service, which includes both occupational therapists and creative arts therapists as well as a range of other mental health professionals, is the Clinical Outcomes in Routine Evaluation system (CORE). CORE is gaining in popularity and is becoming widely adopted. It is suitable for a range of service types and client groups under the mental health umbrella as it measures subjective well-being, commonly experienced problems and social functioning. The 34-item tick box questionnaire is easy and quick for the client to complete and can be administered before intervention to establish a baseline and at various stages during and at the end to assess progress. Like all outcome measures it has its limitations, making it difficult to attribute the outcome to one specific intervention. So, if a client attends a service CORE will assess the outcome of the team's involvement but it will not be possible to determine which of the specific interventions have been most helpful in achieving that outcome. We provide contact information for CORE in the Appendix.

Although it is important to use standardised outcome measures because of the objectivity and credibility they provide their use has limitations. Often in clinical practice there can be a sense that the measure has failed to grasp the real essence of what we are doing, the change that has occurred and what is useful for the client. This is where the tools and strategies available to capture the client's and the therapist's view regarding the effectiveness of an intervention can be useful.

The client's view

The client's view on the outcome of an intervention is very important in terms of whether it has achieved what they wanted it to achieve. We have said that creative therapies are a client-centred approach to practice and with this in mind the client's perception of the outcome is especially important.

The client's view can be obtained subjectively by asking them to review their initial aims and consider whether they have been achieved. This might be done in one of the final sessions, perhaps using a creative exercise as a tool, through discussion, writing or the completion of a questionnaire.

One of the problems we face in creative therapy practice is to make highly subjective and often tentative aims measurable. A way of achieving this is to help the client operationalise the aim. This involves making the aim more explicit, exploring how the client would know when the aim had been achieved and what would be different for them (Spreadbury, 1998). For example, a common aim for clients attending creative therapies is to feel better about themselves, to increase their self-esteem. This is a difficult aim to work with, being broad and subjective. We would thus help the client to break it down further by asking how they would know their self-esteem had increased: what would be different? In response they might say they would like to make themselves heard at home. This remains broad so we would continue exploring it with them until it was sufficiently focused to be measurable. So they might eventually arrive at an aim like 'I will have an evening to do my own thing once a week'. In this way the original subjective aim becomes translated into a behaviour that can be observed and therefore measured by either the client or someone else.

Another way of focusing outcome measurement on the client's view is through the use of individualised outcome measures. These will probably prove to be the way forward for outcome measurement in areas of practice such as creative therapies because they overcome many of the problems inherent in more standardised formats. They obtain the client's view and involve the client in the whole process, from setting the aims and directing the course of the intervention to evaluating the outcome (Eames, Ward and Siddons, 1999; Spreadbury, 1998). An example of an individualised outcome measure developed within occupational therapy is the Canadian Occupational Performance Measure (COPM) (Law *et al.*, 1994). The COPM focuses on the three domains of self-care, productivity and leisure, all areas which could be affected when an individual is experiencing the kind of problems we address through creative therapies, and it measures the client's perception of their progress. As the title suggests, the COPM is primarily focused on occupational performance, and so is very firmly grounded within this core concept of occupational therapy.

The therapist's view

The therapist's view on whether the intervention has been successful in achieving what it was intended to achieve is also important. Even within a client-centred approach the therapist's knowledge and experience will be of value in informing the client and helping them to understand their situation in different ways. This may help the client reframe their aims, review their intended outcomes and take a more objective look at their situation.

The therapist's view on the effectiveness of an intervention will be informed by a number of sources, which include both standardised outcome measures and the client's view. In addition to these sources, the therapist will draw upon their documentation, from the initial interview to each subsequent contact with the client. Other involved professionals may also contribute to this understanding, for example the co-therapist or supervisor.

Quality issues such as these must be a transparent part of our practice, as they are integral to an effective service. The recent framework of clinical governance requires NHS organisations to be accountable for continuously improving the quality of the services provided (Department of Health, 1998c), thus standards can be set and audited to provide evidence, which in turn informs policy and service delivery. Outcome measurement is not a straightforward process and has been one which professionals have found challenging. However, to ensure credibility within our practice for our managers, our clients and ourselves we must make the quest for quality explicit, thus creating an environment where excellence in clinical care will flourish. The quality issues discussed so far link into another development of the 1990s: that clinical practice should be based on evidence.

Evidence-based practice

Evidence-based practice uses the evidence available to inform the decisions we make about our involvement with clients (Bury, 1998). These decisions are many and varied; however, if we take creative therapies as our example these decisions may relate to

- **What type of intervention to use.** Would a psychodynamic approach such as creative therapies be more appropriate than using a cognitive–behavioural approach?
- **The timing of the intervention.** Is it effective to use creative therapies at a time when an individual is in acute crisis, or is this more appropriate during a rehabilitation phase?
- **The process of the intervention.** How many sessions are generally needed to reach a satisfactory outcome, and what strategies are used to decide the time frame for creative therapies? Are we able to vary our approach, justifying some 'one-off' interventions, or should we always deliver a series of sessions?
- **The intervention.** Did the intervention achieve an acceptable outcome for a specific client? Are there mechanisms in place to monitor and audit this process?

Evidence-based practice explores custom and practice so that interventions will not take place 'just because they always have' but because they are firmly grounded in evidence.

Bury (1998) suggests that this evidence can be available through:

- research;
- clinical expertise – experience with patients, established practice, experts in the field;
- beliefs of the therapist and patient – based on experience, expectations, social context;

- clinical assessment of the patient;
- patients' preferences.

To make practice more evidence based Rosenburg and Donald (1995) suggest a process which we will follow using a creative therapy example (Table 6.2). It begins by developing a clinical question in relation to your client group.

To date much of our practice in creative therapies has been informed more by clinical expertise, beliefs, assessment and patient opinion than by research. Research evidence is regarded as the best evidence (Bury, 1998) but for an area of practice like creative therapies it is not fully available, either because it has not been conducted or because the standard lacks sophistication. This lack of good-quality research evidence is really a reflection of the stage of development of the profession of occupational therapy. Until recently, research has had a low profile but now, with preregistration degree-level education and therapists undertaking research training to masters and doctoral levels, as well as the service-wide drive for evidence-based practice, this picture is rapidly changing.

A very small amount of research has been conducted on this area of occupa-

Table 6.2

Step 1: Define your clinical question
Are creative therapies an effective treatment for clients experiencing an eating disorder?

Step 2: A literature search
Process: You are looking for evidence which will inform your question. This evidence might not only be research evidence, as it may also include the client's perceptions or clinical opinion. You may start your search with key words, such as creative therapies, eating disorders, but you may need to widen your search to secondary areas, for example occupational therapy, group dynamics, psychodynamics, cognitive–behavioural disorders, self-esteem, interpersonal skills
Tools: CINAHL, Medline, PSYCHLIT, Library catalogues, books, journals

Step 3: Critical appraisal
For research evidence there are useful guidelines, such as those proposed by Bury and Jerosch-Herold (1988), Drummond (1996) and Finlay (1997b). Critically appraising other forms of evidence such as client's perceptions or clinical opinion can be more difficult but a useful forum can be peer discussion with colleagues through journal club-style meetings.

Step 4: Implementing the evidence
Once the evidence has been evaluated the findings can be implemented into your current practice. This process may require significant changes in your approach, or it may be easily integrated depending on the quality and consistency of the findings.

Step 5: Evaluation
The final stage of the process is to evaluate the change which has occurred as a result of the process. If your practice has altered in the light of the evidence you found what has been the outcome of this?
Tools: Reflective practice, diaries, critical incidents, supervision, client satisfaction, peer review.

Step 6: Continuation
The process then becomes continuous, as the evidence gained through looking at one instance informs the next, ensuring up-to-date and well informed practice.

tional therapy practice (Benetton, 1995; Jensen and Blair, 1997). We can also draw on research provided by the creative arts therapists, as much of this offers evidence that can be extrapolated to the approach of creative therapies in occupational therapy. At times, however, even the research that does exist can be difficult to access for practitioners. With the changes in the focus of care already outlined many occupational therapists are working in small teams at community-based facilities. This can make access to library resources difficult. In addition many therapists do not have, or feel confident in, their literature search and critical appraisal skills. Gradually the profession is getting up to speed on this with papers in the professional literature and many short courses and study days being presented locally and nationally to address professional development.

As practitioners in creative therapies, we need to provide the evidence for this approach to our work if we are to be able to use it with confidence. A developed evidence base is important as there is a growing awareness and knowledge amongst our clients, who are taking greater responsibility for decision making and therefore need to be informed about treatment approaches. Additionally those who refer into our speciality require evidence to justify their financial commitment as they have to ensure that their funding is allocated effectively. To promote creative therapies effectively we need to be able to provide clear evidence to support a marketing strategy, ensuring that people reach an informed decision before purchasing the intervention.

Creative therapies provide a highly individual approach for both the client and the therapist involved, and therefore give us an opportunity to reflect this in our research. Methodologies within the qualitative paradigm are of particular value and these include observation, interview and single case design which might incorporate the use of resources such as video and tape recorders, reflective diaries and supervision relationships. While it is not the remit of this text to offer a short course in research skills we hope it will inspire you to consider using methodologies that will add to the research base of this approach to our work.

Finally, although there is an argument that research provides the best evidence, it is important to recognise that many of you will not consider yourselves to be active researchers. This is because you are active clinicians and you may not feel you have the opportunity, skills, interest or resources to undertake a specific research project. For those of you who see yourselves in this way we encourage you to view your clinical work as a research exercise as for every client you work with you follow a quasi-research process. You collect data from multiple sources through your assessment procedures and you pose hypotheses which you test out through your practice. You evaluate practice against some criteria which ascertain whether an intervention has been successful. This in turn informs future practice. By tightening up the stages of this process the standard of clinical practice will be improved, you will be more rigorous in your data collection, the hypotheses you pose will be more explicit and your intervention will be evaluated against defined criteria.

CHANGES WITHIN PROFESSIONALS

The final change which we will explore in this chapter is the change that takes place within us as professionals as part of our continuing professional development. This change is both exciting and challenging. It is exciting because a legislative framework is being developed which addresses the regulation of health care professionals and emphasises life-long learning as a component of clinical governance (Department of Health, 1999). The change is challenging because it requires us to reflect on our clinical practice, to identify our learning needs, to access opportunities to address them and to provide evidence of learning and development.

Continuing professional development is both a personal and a professional responsibility. It is an ongoing and active process which involves accessing resources to facilitate the process through formal training, experiential learning, literature searching, the supervision process and personal reflection on practice. With the legislative framework driving continuing professional development, we need to be able to provide evidence of that development. A route for achieving this is to use portfolios such as the one produced by the College of Occupational Therapists (1996).

We need to explore the issue of continuing professional development in relation to creative therapies. Creative therapies are a highly dynamic way of working and draw heavily on our personal reserves and professional skills. Because of this it is important to stay fresh in our approach and attitude to our practice. It is in meeting this need that continuing professional development has a real role to play. Without this there is a danger that as individuals we will 'burn out', that our practice will become technical and mechanical, and that we will lose touch with the creativity within us which is so essential in this approach to practice.

A fundamental tool of professional development is reflection: it is through reflection that we monitor our practice, identify development needs and adjust our way of working. In creative therapies reflection both in and on our practice is an inherent skill. During sessions we are constantly thinking about our actions, what we say, the activities we use and the effect of all these elements. After sessions we think back over what we did, how we behaved and responded and what occurred. There are processes within creative therapy practice, such as the co-worker relationship and the use of supervision, which have a significant role in facilitating this approach. So, already in our practice of creative therapies we are using some tools to ensure that an ongoing process of professional development occurs. This is a healthy state but we cannot be complacent because of the demanding nature of this approach. In addition to the integral element of reflection it is useful to use a more formalised approach to enable us to collect evidence of continuing professional development.

A series of stages constitute the process of continuing professional development:

- identifying professional learning needs;
- developing a personal development plan;
- putting this plan into action;

- evaluating the outcome;
- providing evidence of the development.

These stages create a cyclical pattern, with evidence informing subsequent learning needs on a continuous basis. They should be familiar to you as they mirror the process of occupational therapy we use with our clients. However, continuing professional development involves the application of these stages with ourselves as the key players.

Let us integrate these stages into an example of a practitioner who wishes to develop skills in creative therapies. Some tools that could aid this approach will be suggested, but should not be seen as finite examples.

Stage 1: Identification of professional learning needs

This stage involves clearly identifying the learning needs. For each practitioner these will be different, and a useful tool for facilitating the process is to undertake a SWOT analysis (Table 6.3). This involves identifying strengths and weaknesses in relation to practising creative therapies and considering the opportunities and threats which surround them (Atkinson, 1998).

Once the SWOT analysis is complete the aim is to build on strengths, turn weaknesses into strengths, make the most of opportunities and plan around threats (NHS Training Directorate, 1991). This is achieved through a personal development plan.

Stage 2: Develop a personal development plan

The personal development plan is likely to be developed in co-operation with the line manager as professional development impacts on running the service and quality assurance. Discussion with the manager will help to refine and prioritise learning needs, which will fall into two categories, those which further the devel-

Table 6.3 Suggested tool: a SWOT analysis

Strengths:	**Weaknesses:**
Lots of ideas for activities	Limited working knowledge of psychological theories
Patients respond well to my approach	Little experience of being group leader
Enjoy working creatively	Not very clear on group dynamics
Flexible	
Some group experience	
Time management	
Opportunities:	**Threats:**
Original group leader going on maternity leave	Previous co-worker will become leader. I have not worked with her before
A group which needs a co-worker	Not used to formal supervision
Good facilities with range of materials	Unsure of my role
Appropriate referrals on waiting list	Aware of waiting list

opment of the individual and those which further the quality of the organisation. The process will be informed through evaluating the individual's previous performance, thus defining future learning needs. The SWOT analysis may provide a starting point for information, so by returning to our example of the practitioner who wishes to develop skills in creative therapy we are able to identify some key discussion areas:

- an enthusiasm and interest to work in this way;
- some useful group experience;
- an identified staffing gap which has to be addressed to enable the group to function;
- a waiting list of clients needing to access this treatment intervention;
- a lack of knowledge of this particular approach, but a willingness to learn.

Suggested tool: A learning contract

Learning contracts enable the therapist to identify their specific learning goals, and the strategies or resources which are required to enable this to happen. They encourage self-direction, as they are responsive to both the pace and the needs of the learner, (Walker, 1999). As they are completed by a process of negotiation with the manager they enable resource implications to be considered as part of the process, and they clarify how and when evidence of individual development will be collated.

The example in Figure 6.1 is based on the needs of our practitioner. This example enables you to see that the goals identified are specific ones, which are achievable by the learner. The resources may involve some extra funding, for example a study day, but many can be accessed within normal resources using departmental books and talking with other colleagues. Evidence of completion of the process can be gained through successful experience, but also by reflecting on the process. This may inform case discussion and records, as well as providing material for future learning.

Stage 3: Implementing the plan

This is the active stage of becoming involved with a creative therapy group. In our example the therapist decides to join the existing group as a co-worker. The learning will be directed to three main sources: the literature which informs practice, the experience of the group itself and personal experience. The process of reflection, which accompanies this stage, enables the therapist to develop skills in self-awareness, to describe and critically analyse a situation, to synthesise ideas and finally to evaluate what has occurred (Spalding, 1998). The learning contract provides a framework for this process, enabling the therapist to see what has been achieved and providing evidence of the learning which has taken place.

Suggested tools: Supervision, reflective diary, critical incidents

Supervision may be provided within the service or from an external source. It is an important process, which facilitates good practice and self-exploration

Name:
Manager:
Date:

Learning goals	**Strategies and resources**	**What is to be assessed**	**Evidence**
To develop greater understanding of the humanist approach	Books, journals Study days Talking to other staff	The ability to discuss this approach with the group leader An understanding of the application within creative therapies	Application of principle to practice
Gain practical psychodynamic experience	A creative therapy group to co-lead Suitable clients Supervision Study day	Ability to run the group Observation of group processes Reflection on the action Use of self Integration of theory and practice	Reflective diary. Client satisfaction Positive feedback Video
Coping with silence in the group	Understanding communication Books, journals Observing behaviour of leader	Ability to tolerate and use silence in a group situation	Reflective diary Video tapes

Figure 6.1

because it enables learning to become explicit through using experience. Supervision provides support for learning, challenging inappropriate ways of working through questioning practice. It protects the interests of clients through developing therapeutic competence.

A reflective diary is a way of recording, evaluating and making sense of experiences as they arise (Alsop, 1995b). The purpose is not to itemise the events of the day, but to provide an opportunity to write about thoughts and reflections on events which are felt to be significant to learning. It is a personal document, a first-hand account involving self-disclosure, honesty and a critical approach which provides a means to reflect on practice and record personal development.

A critical incident is an experience that has made some form of emotional impact on the therapist. An example within a creative therapy group might be when a topic surfaces which arouses uncomfortable memories. The therapist will be disturbed by this, and aware of it happening, but the focus has to remain within the context of the group. Later, during a personal time of reflection the feelings that have occurred may be explored. By making them explicit through documenting them the experience can be learnt from, thus enhancing self-knowledge. This in turn will change practice, informing and developing the therapist's approach.

Stage 4: Evaluating the outcome and providing evidence of development

This is the final stage, where the therapist considers the outcome of the whole experience and supports it through a collection of evidence. The evidence will be used to clarify the development that has occurred, as it will provide the personal details of the learning experience. Again, in discussion with the manager, the therapist will explore ways of taking this learning forwards, ensuring that this becomes a continuous process rather than an end product.

Suggested tool: portfolio

A portfolio is a private collection of evidence which demonstrates the continuing acquisition of skills, knowledge, attitudes, understanding and achievement. It becomes a tool and a framework for recording professional activity, collating evidence that clarifies development (Alsop, 1995a). It can be both a retrospective and a prospective collection of evidence, enabling the therapist to keep a record of personal and professional development through documenting experiences and qualifications. Some of these experiences will be provided through formal routes of learning, attending study days or courses; others will be the more informal learning gained from everyday experience. The portfolio should demonstrate a recognition of experience as a valuable source of learning, encouraging reflection to define the development that has taken place.

One benefit of a portfolio approach is that it collects evidence together which can then be used to inform the next personal development plan, providing a user-friendly source of material with which to demonstrate both personal and professional growth.

It should be stressed that there is no set route to demonstrating continuous professional development, and that the approach we have outlined is only a suggestion. The process should not be seen as a discrete package, as professional development in one area of practice should inform others, increasing clinical expertise and raising the quality of the service (Department of Health, 1998c).

CONCLUSION

Reflecting on this chapter enables us to trace the process of change through language and location, politics and practice. We have looked back over significant changes that have affected health care, changes which have attempted to improve the quality of the service we provide. We have stressed the need to gain evidence of good practice and considered tools that will facilitate this process. In each case we have placed creative therapies at the centre of our discussions, linking our examples to it, whilst finally exploring the tools of professional development as a means of furthering our knowledge and expertise. We have attempted throughout to approach change in a positive manner, seeing it as an exciting challenge but acknowledging its continuous presence. Part of working within continuous change involves understanding where change originates, and what it is attempting to achieve, as it can then be seen as an opportunity rather than a threat. Only in this way will we be empowered to deal with the constant change that professional practice demands.

To allow us to reconnect with our theme of creativity it seems appropriate to end this chapter with a poem, reproduced with the kind permission of Jean Clark (a freelance counsellor and group facilitator in Norwich).

Change is boundaries dissolved
space unlimited reaching stars
Change is being lost in strange
unreadiness to end or to begin
Change is fear of things unknown
approaching
Change is water flowing under bridges
a leaf carried by the flood
to fortune or to oblivion
Change is mourning for things ended
regret for things undone
now never to be known
Change is challenge
to begin ever anew
a letting go, renouncing, moving on
to find an unpredicted life
now shaped.

REFERENCES

Alsop, A. (1995a) The Professional Portfolio – Purpose, Process and Practice, Part 1: Portfolios and Professional Practice, *British Journal of Occupational Therapy*, 58(7), 299–302.

Alsop, A. (1995b) The Professional Portfolio – Purpose, Process and Practice, Part 2: Producing a Portfolio from Experiential Learning, *British Journal of Occupational Therapy*, 58(8), 337–340.

Atkinson, K. (1996) Issues in Community and Primary Care. In: *Occupational Therapy in Short-term Psychiatry*, 3rd edn (ed. Willson, M.), Churchill Livingstone, Edinburgh.

Atkinson, K. (1998) SWOT analysis: a tool for continuing professional development, *British Journal of Therapy and Rehabilitation*, 5(8), 433–435.

Baldwin, S. (1993) *The Myth of Community Care: An Alternative Neighbourhood Model of Care,* Chapman & Hall, London.

Bean, P. and Mounser, P. (1993) *Discharged from Mental Hospitals,* Macmillan Press, Basingstoke.

Benetton, M.J. (1995) A case study applying a psychodynamic approach to occupational therapy, *Occupational Therapy International*, **2**, 220–228.

Blom-Cooper, L. (1989) *Occupational Therapy, an Emerging Profession in Health Care,* Duckworth, London.

Booth, A. and Madge, B. (1998) Finding the Evidence. In: *Evidence-based Healthcare: A Practical Guide for Therapists* (ed. Bury, T. and Mead, J.), Butterworth-Heinemann, Oxford.

Bowden, R. (1991) Power to the User, *British Journal of Occupational Therapy,* **54**(8), 281.

Bury, T. (1998) Evidence-based healthcare explained. In: *Evidence-based Healthcare: A Practical Guide for Therapists* (eds Bury, T. and Mead, J.), Butterworth-Heinemann, Oxford.

Bury, T. and Jerosch-Herold, C. (1998) Reading and critical appraisal of the literature. In: *Evidence-based Healthcare: A Practical Guide for Therapists* (eds Bury, T. and Mead, J.), Butterworth-Heinemann, Oxford.

Canadian Association of Occupational Therapists (1997) *Enabling Occupation: An Occupational Therapy Perspective*, CAOT Publications ACE, Ontario.

College of Occupational Therapists (1996) *Professional Development Programme*, College of Occupational Therapists, London.

de Clive Lowe, S. (1996) Outcome Measurement, Cost-Effectiveness and Clinical Audit: The Importance of Standardised Assessment to Occupational Therapists in Meeting these New Demands, *British Journal of Occupational Therapy*, **59**(8), 357–362.

Department of Health (1998a) Health Service Circular Local Authority Circular, HSC 1998/228: LAC (98) 32. Leeds.

Department of Health (1998b)/0580 *Modernising Mental Health Services*, HMSO, London.

Department of Health (1998c) *A First Class Service: Quality in the NHS*, HMSO, London.

Department of Health (1990) *The National Health Service and Community Care Act*, HMSO, London.

Department of Health (1999) *The Health Bill,* HMSO, London.

DHSS (1983) *NHS Management Inquiry – Griffiths Report*, HMSO, London.

Donabedian, A. (1988) The Quality of Care, *Journal of the American Medical Association*, **260**, 1743–1748.

Drummond, A. (1996) Reviewing a Research Article, *British Journal of Occupational Therapy,* **59**(2), 84–86.

Eames, J., Ward, G. and Siddons, L. (1999) Clinical Audit of the Outcome of Individualised Occupational Therapy Goals, *British Journal of Occupational Therapy*, **62**(6), 257–260.

Ewles, L. and Simnett, I. (1992) *Promoting Health: A Practical Guide,* Scutari Press, London

Finlay, L. (1997a) *The Practice of Psychosocial Occupational Therapy*, 2nd edn, Stanley Thornes, Cheltenham.

Finlay, L. (1997b) Evaluating Research Articles, *British Journal of Occupational Therapy*, **60**(5), 205–208.

Heiney, S. (1995) The Healing Power of Story, *Oncology Nursing Forum*, **22**(6), 899–904.

Howard, L. (1996) Quality of Care. In: *Occupational Therapy in Short-term Psychiatry*, 3rd edn (ed. Willson, M.), Churchill Livingstone, Edinburgh.

Jensen, C.M. and Blair, S.E.E. (1997) Rhyme and Reason: the Relationship between Creative Writing and Mental Wellbeing, *British Journal of Occupational Therapy*, **60**(12), 525–530.

Law, M., Baptiste, S., Carswell, A., McColl, M.A., Polatajko, H. and Pollock, N. (1994) *Canadian Occupational Performance Measure*, 2nd edn, CAOT Publications ACE, Toronto.

Levens, M. (1986) The Psychodynamics of Activity, *British Journal of Occupational Therapy*, **49**(3), 87–89.

Maxwell, R.J. (1984) Quality Assessment in Health, *British Medical Journal*, **288**(1), 470–471.

McDowell, I. and Newell, C. (1996) *Measuring Health – A Guide to Rating Scales and Questionnaires,* Oxford University Press, Oxford.

Mitchell, R. (1987) Dramatherapy in Inpatient Psychiatric Settings. In: *Dramatherapy Theory and Practice for Teachers and Clinicians* (ed. Jennings, S.), Routledge, London.

National Health Service Training Directorate (1991) *Health Pick Up – Marketing Your Services,* Presentation Pack 982170, Intek Europe Ltd, Hove.

Ramon, S. (1988) Community Care in Britain. In: *Community Care in Practice Services for the Continuing Care Client* (eds Lavender, A. and Holloway, F.), John Wiley & Sons, Chichester.

Rosenberg, W. and Donald, A. (1995) Evidence Based Medicine: An Approach to Clinical Problem Solving, *British Medical Journal*, **310**, 1122–1126.

Sealey, C. (1999) Two Common Pitfalls in Clinical Audit: Failing to Complete the Audit Cycle and Confusing Audit with Research, *British Journal of Occupational Therapy*, **62**(6), 238–243.

Spalding, N.J. (1998) Reflection in Professional Development: A Personal Experience, *British Journal of Therapy and Rehabilitation,* **5**(7), 379–382.

Spreadbury, P. (1998). 'You will measure Outcomes'. In: *Occupational Therapy: New Perspectives* (ed. Creek, J.), Whurr Publishers Ltd, London.

Walker, E.M. (1999) Learning Contracts in Practice: Their Role in CPD. *British Journal of Therapy and Rehabilitation*, **6**(2), 91–94.

Weller, M.P.I. (1993) Where We Come From: Recent History of Community Provision. In: *Dimensions of Community Mental Health Care* (eds Weller, M.P.I. and Muijen, M.), Saunders, London.

Wright, C. and Whittingdon, D. (1992) *Quality Assurance. An Introduction for the Health Care Professions*, Churchill Livingstone, Edinburgh.

Yaretzky, A., Levinson, M. and Kimchi, O.L. (1996) Clay as a Therapeutic Tool in Group Processing with the Elderly, *American Journal of Art Therapy,* **34**(2), 75–80.

7 ENDINGS

This chapter brings our journey to a close, and we plan to do this in two ways. First, we will explore the issue of endings in relation to creative therapies as an intervention, a professional perspective which considers the important features of this final stage of development. Secondly, we will look at the whole process of writing this book, bringing this part of our personal journey to an end. These aspects link together. Many of the issues and emotions for one are reflected in the other, and for both the opportunity of an ending gives us a new beginning.

We intend to explore the process of ending, and hope to convey that this too can be a creative experience. We will use illustrations from our work with students, as with them we have been very conscious of the need to define the end, to recognise and celebrate it as the springboard for future learning. In these instances we have used creativity in our thinking as the energy that moves the process forwards, and helps us to reflect back on what has been achieved – the journey we have travelled with them.

Using creative therapies within a clinical environment provides many opportunities to consider the place that an ending holds. It allows us to reflect and evaluate, actively thinking about where are we now, where have we been and where are we going with our clients. It challenges our skills and our emotions, and plays a vital role in justifying our outcomes.

This chapter will begin by looking at the process of ending from three perspectives: the group as a whole, the individual client within the group and the therapist. This enables us to consider the ways we can evaluate the experience which has occurred through the use of creative therapies. We will then explore a final session, creatively considering its content and purpose.

ENDINGS WITHIN A CREATIVE THERAPY GROUP

We have suggested throughout this book that creative therapies tend to be a group experience, although there are times when they are used individually. Here we will focus on the group experience and the issues that are likely to arise from drawing the group to a close.

There are three approaches to terminating contact within creative therapies. One is where the group is limited to a certain numbers of sessions, which is clearly thought through at the planning stage and adhered to (Whitaker, 1985). This forms part of the contract that is discussed within the initial interview, when the purpose of the group is outlined to the potential member. This approach results in a clear structure, enabling the end to be part of the beginning, as the work is planned to be achieved within the stated time frame. The second approach is an open-ended one, where the group meets until it collectively decides it has fulfilled its purpose and has ceased to become a useful intervention. This approach is more difficult to manage, as a consensus is unlikely to occur and there can be a tendency to hold on to the security which the group provides. A variation on this, the third approach to terminating contact, is when individual members leave the group as they achieve their own aims and new members join. This can be a useful strategy as individuals work to their own time scale and benefit from the variety of a steady turnover in group membership. It also means that the issues of initiating and terminating relationships as well as issues of change, adaptability and separation arise regularly within the lifespan of the group (Benson, 1987).

A stated time frame allows for progression to be built into the programme of creative therapy. The group has time to go through the stages of development we described in Chapter 3, reaching the productive phase that precedes the ending. The group should be working cohesively at this stage, with an obvious group identity. There are a number of issues that arise relating to losing this aspect of identity, and at times these make it difficult for the members to disengage and move on. It is important to discuss the place the creative therapy group takes within the member's lives. A regular commitment of time can provide a structure within a week when members know they will have the opportunity to come together and work on issues. There may be the simple fact that the session fills an afternoon in an otherwise bleak and lonely week, and therefore the ending will be viewed as losing an event which filled an empty space.

There is the social loss of the other group members. A group of people who are working to achieve aims of self-discovery and self-awareness will experience a bonding, formed through facing similar difficulties. As creative therapy encourages the exploration of these issues, relying on the active interaction of the members, there will be a strong feeling of cohesion within the group. It then becomes difficult to leave this behind, a process which involves saying farewell to others who will have been influential in facilitating personal growth. This feeling of social loss is an important part of ending intervention, and may be evident in feelings of sadness or occasionally anger. Anger forms part of the denial which accompanies the process of leaving. The group member may feel that they have not reached the point when it would be safe to leave, that there is still work to be done, and will therefore take these feelings out on the therapist or on other members. It is as if by exposing needs in a negative way the ending will be reconsidered and the group will continue.

Some group members may mourn the loss of the media. At first this seems a strange suggestion, but creativity is becoming less of a feature of our lives. Creative therapies use media to enable us to enjoy them as a tool, removing the fear of failure and the persistent inner critic who demands a good product. This is a highly freeing experience, as it enables us to get in touch and connect with ourselves. Rogers (1993, p. 96) explores what she terms the 'expressive arts' as enabling clients to:

Identify and be in touch with their feelings,
Explore unconscious material,
Release energy,
Gain insight,
Solve problems,
Discover intuitive, mythological, and spiritual dimensions of the self.

The media we use for creative therapies achieve these aims, which may not be met within other areas of the client's life. Therefore the experience and opportunity of using these media will be missed when the tools do not appear to be available. If the process of ending is well managed we are able to help clients explore other areas which may provide a similar opportunity, perhaps suggesting joining a class or organisation that encourages self-expression through the use of media.

Often, when a group comes to an end, the members will suggest meeting up together as a means of keeping in touch. At the time this seems an important lifeline, a link that is being established to keep the group identity alive but in reality the group is unlikely to sustain meeting in this way, partly because the purpose of the meetings is different. There are not the same aims to bind members together, and attendance seems to diminish as other life events take over. The group has been used to working within a structure which provided boundaries through ground rules, time, frequency of meetings, and these are lost when it formally disbands. There is also the issue of wanting or being ready to leave the work of the group behind and move on. This is a healthy and desirable state: the intervention has achieved its purpose and members use this opportunity as a springboard for future life events.

If the group is planned to run for a specified number of sessions there can be an increase in activity within the final session. It is as if the group members are trying to fit everything in, to address all the issues, which they have failed to acknowledge in the previous sessions. This behaviour suggests that there is unfinished business, and that the members are pressurising for an extension. This pattern of behaviour may reflect the way the members work within each session, leaving the important issues until the end perhaps in an effort to also increase that time boundary. This pressure should be resisted: the time scale has been in place from the beginning and it is an important framework. At times the experience of participating in a creative therapy group will have brought to the surface some issues which may be hidden to the conscious self; this is a feature of psychodynamic work. If this is the case it might be appropriate to refer these clients to another professional who will work with the specific issue, or a second creative therapy experience may be planned, perhaps on an individual basis or within another group. A break in time between the end of one intervention and the start of another can be useful to allow the client time to consolidate their experience.

There is an aspect of ending which is celebratory, when there is a sense that the aim of the intervention has been met and members are ready to move on. Often in the final session we find ourselves bringing food and drink which we share with the students. This 'nourishment' is both physical and psychological. There is a ritual attached to sharing food, and it forms a part of most celebrations including the 'leaving parties' you will have experienced. Valuing the group in this way acknowledges the work they have undertaken, as the refreshments become a reward and celebration of their achievements. It seems right that this has a place within some of the final sessions.

The theme of giving and receiving may be appropriate within the product of an endings session. We have frequently stressed throughout this book that we are concerned with the process of creative therapies, rather than achieving an end product. The final session is a time when this might be different, as there is a need to capture the identity of the group in a tangible way. The product then signifies a process which has led to this closeness of feeling, the importance of valuing others and recognising the part that they have played in one another's therapeutic process. This need to give and to receive was observed in the following example.

Forget Me Not

The students had planned an activity within the final session which involved planting 'forget me not' seeds. They brought a selection of flowerpots to the session, and each group member chose one which they would decorate for another person within the group. We were asked to paint the name of the recipient on the pot, and then to illustrate it in any way we wished. When this was completed the pots were filled and the seeds were planted. Everyone then had an opportunity to give their pot away to their recipient, explaining the decoration and wishing them well. The choice of the seeds formed a link to the group, not only through their name but also because they would flourish and grow after the group had finished. This was an effective way of making a memory, and creating a way of saying farewell.

This example neatly addressed the issue of disposing of created objects, as these were made specifically for a purpose. However, the final session may also include some discussion of how the group disposes of other pieces that have been created within the sessions. These may represent the external collective work of the group, but will not show the internal journey of the individual, so an object remains which is rather like a husk without the grain (the grain has been internalised as the experience, but the husk stays behind as the vehicle). This analogy is useful as the outer coating seems important at the time of creation, which is why it may not have been disposed of straight away, but becomes less important as time intervenes. The group may have to consider products like joint paintings or shared sculptures which represent work which has taken place. A decision has to be taken about disposing of collective work; this is part of the process of moving on from the experience, taking time to evaluate their significance at this later stage and ensuring that each person's views are respected.

We have discussed endings from an emotional perspective, but there is also a need to acknowledge that endings can be a physical experience. We have found that facilitating a physical farewell assists with the process of moving on, as it pays attention to the important structures which may have played a supporting role throughout the life of the group. In Chapter 5 we referred to the 'Flubbadub' experience, where the students were involved in saying farewell to the building and their important experiences within it. This example demonstrated how the physical structure of the building had become bound with personal meaning, providing a concrete focus for the less tangible experience. Saying goodbye to this eased the process of disengaging with the course, the experiences of it and the colleagues who were important within it.

The following experience also serves to illustrate the poignancy of saying farewell to the physical environment.

Our Norwich

The students were almost at the end of their course and were planning to move away to new areas. Not only was there a sadness of leaving each other but there was also a need for them to acknowledge the part which the city had played over the three years they had lived here. We decided to use a session to address this in a creative way, enabling them to end their connections with the places which had become important to them.

Each person was asked to think about their special place before we met in the city centre. We then shared these locations, and constructed a route which would enable us to visit each place, where we would pause to allow the person to talk to the group about why it had been chosen, and what made it special. As we wandered from place to place we became aware of the feelings that were aroused in each of us in relation to leaving the city behind. We also learned about personal choices, likes and dislikes, finally deciding to capture the journey through an illustrated poem (Figure 7.1). We created this during refreshments in an open-air café. Later we were able to copy the poem, which enabled each person to take away collective memories as well as individual ones.

The journey and the poem were creative interventions as they enabled everyone to contribute a part of themselves to the process and to acknowledge the effect of imposed change as they concluded one part of their lives and moved towards another.

ENDINGS FOR THE INDIVIDUAL

Although many of the issues we have explored will also apply to the individual experience, as the group is created from a collection of individuals, there are some differences which relate to personal issues rather than to the collective whole.

Sally's Place
Pesky pigeons, fish and chips, vantage point,
Fireworks, colourful, continental.
Peace and conflict. Angels with swords.
Terraces, steps to remembering.

Catherine's Place
Original and forgotten,
Bleak, spooky, mysterious and sad.
Shut away. Windowless walls. Prison, ill-gotten gains.

Lucy's Place
Escapism, blue and golds, bright lights,
Modern, sleek and cultured.
Posh and chic. 1970s kitsch,
Happy and celebratory, gathering and dispersing.

Simon's Place
'Whopper', red and orange, smelly
Ugly, quick. Poster pinching.
Shopping break, meeting point.
Convenient blast to hunger.
Veggie burger or bean burger?

Fiona's Place
Waiting, lost relatives, dark wood,
Zebra print scarf, passers-by.
Stable. 'Fags to rags'. Tied to the tie rack.

Andrew's Place
Opportunities, cheap and cheerful, stuffed reindeer.
Plastic flowers. 'Jesus loves you.'
Reminiscent of beach bingo. Resting place.

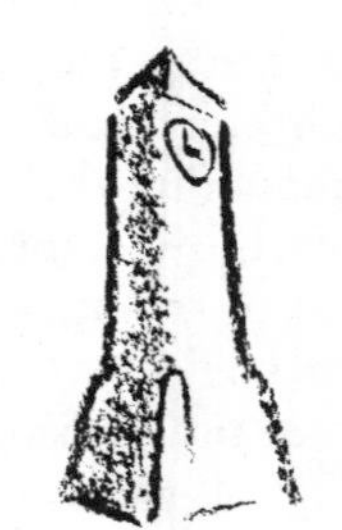

Kim's Place
Coloured tiles, iron lamps and furniture,
Sparkling jewels, art nouveau.
Stopping and looking. Street of interest.
Misplaced, street out of time.

Joanna's Place
Hidden charm, new and old, time bridge.
Suspended but solid. Changing flowers.
Bird's eye view of nature.

Claire's Place
Churches, trees and towers, roofs.
Water tower, ski slope, three-wheeled car.
View, view, view. History erased.
Quiet amid bustle, Norwich's heart.

Emma's Place
Challenging, Gotham City, domination.
Beacon, ugly and supportive.
The clock conflict, Time to stand out.

Mary's Place
Cobbled splendour, cake and coffee, calories,
Tucked away, fairy lights, chilled out.
Cultured and civilised. Baby changing area.
Subtle sculpture and hidden rocks.

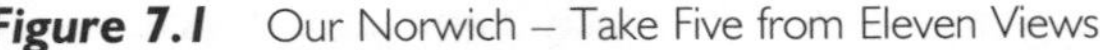

Figure 7.1 Our Norwich – Take Five from Eleven Views

For each person approaching the end of the creative therapy intervention these will be different. There will be a sense of loss (Brandler and Roman, 1991), which will relate to the loss of the intervention as an agent of change, the loss of the individuals involved in the process (including the therapist) and in some cases the loss of the group experience. These feelings are complex and often contradictory. There will be times throughout the process when the individual wants to leave everything associated with the group behind and move on. However, faced with the actual ending this viewpoint may alter, as there will be the need to adapt to a changed situation.

The importance of managing this stage with the individual member cannot be over-emphasised. If it is managed as a process rather than as a sharp closure, there is time and space to work with emotions as they arise (Shulman, 1992). In this way each person is able to verbalise their feelings in relation to the ending stage, and to have them acknowledged and valued. Through this process feelings become explicit and can be explored and resolved.

The aim of moving away from a creative therapy group will be to move towards a more healthy lifestyle. For the individual this will signify leaving behind the therapeutic interventions and moving towards those which are accessed as part of promoting health. This journey may link with some of the activities the member has undertaken within creative therapies, activities which have involved community facilities or new ideas and from which an interest grows through the exposure. This is one of the hidden objectives of using the medium, as it gives confidence and knowledge that facilitates the stage of ending one process and moving on to another which supports the individual but which is outside the therapy context.

Each individual will need to identify an agreed plan which defines the process of terminating their involvement. This will review what has been achieved, the journey the member has travelled, and will look beyond the end of the intervention to the next stages, confirming and consolidating strategies to ensure that these achievements transfer into everyday life. The process enables ending to be a positive and constructive event rather than one in which the member feels abandoned, which could increase the sense of loss and jeopardise the growth that has been achieved.

The following example illustrates one method of reflecting on individual aims, thus reviewing personal change within a creative therapy group.

In the first of a series of creative therapy sessions the students were asked to identify individual aims they wanted to work with over the next six weeks. They defined these aims on a personal basis, and then shared them with the other group members. In the final session the aims were returned to, and the members were asked to consider whether their intentions had been met. They were asked to reflect on the individual sessions, and to try to identify some critical incidents of their creative therapy experience which addressed their specific aims. This enabled individuals to think deeply about the process of the intervention, exploring when changes occurred for them, and what part of the process caused change. They also clarified outstanding aims, which they needed to work with on future occasions.

ENDINGS FOR THE THERAPIST

The process of ending involvement is a complex one for the therapist. There are practical tasks to undertake, there are psychological tasks which relate to managing the process with the clients, and there are personal feelings brought about by ending the involvement.

On a practical level the therapist needs to ensure that the tasks associated with ending an intervention are completed. This may mean cancelling a room booking, transport arrangements or any other external strategy that has been put in place. It will also involve communicating issues which relate to the clients to others through reporting and recording. Discharge mechanisms are activated where appropriate, so that everyone involved with the process is informed of the situation and so knows what has been achieved and what remains unresolved.

Facilitating the process of ending for clients is a skilful task. The therapist should recognise the feelings that will arise during this part of the process, making time and space for them to receive thorough attention. This involves helping the members to let go and move away, which may be a painful process, (Benson 1987). One of the hard issues is to enable members to solidify the gains they have achieved through the process, yet be able to move on and survive the loss (Brandler and Roman, 1991). This can be achieved through a process of evaluation, which ensures that each individual has the opportunity to consider their involvement and progress.

The therapist should be aware of personal emotions which surface as the end of the intervention approaches. These may involve feelings which relate to clients, as the journey has been a joint one and has actively engaged both the therapist and those attending the sessions. As we discussed in Chapter 1, this interaction is one of the key aspects of working in this way, as both the therapist and the client are active within the creative therapy process. We have previously considered the emotional commitment of the therapist, the investment of personality required to enable us to work in this way through our use of the self. Recognising this emotional commitment means recognising that there will be feelings about ceasing to work with the clients who have been part of the experience.

For the therapist there will be the issue of leaving the opportunity of using creative therapy. We firmly believe that the therapist has to enjoy working in this way, and must be comfortable with the media and with the whole elusive and fluid psychodynamic approach. For us there is always an excitement of a new group beginning, and a sadness as it comes to an end. It is important to acknowledge that we enjoy working in this way, as this allows us to be honest about our feelings as the sessions come to an end. As this approach demands such an investment of the self there is a need for the therapist to have a break between one series of sessions and another. This is the time of consolidation, where skills are evaluated and personal strengths are restored, a time of psychological refreshment. Such a space of time ensures that working with challenging interpersonal problems does not become all encompassing. It allows time to regain energy and enthusiasm and if it is not taken and valued as important the creativity and spontaneity required for practising creative therapies will be lost.

We continue by looking at an important part of the process of ending an intervention, which is the issue of evaluation.

EVALUATING THE INTERVENTION

Aspects of evaluating the intervention have been addressed in many places in this book under a variety of guises: effectiveness, outcomes, evidence-based practice. However, evaluation is such an important part of creative therapy intervention, and is so clearly linked to the issue of endings, that it deserves some additional discussion at this point.

Benson (1987, p. 153) outlines the purpose of evaluation, which relates to creative therapy intervention:

- to determine the value of the group for the individual;
- to gauge progress in achieving individual goals;
- to assess whether group objectives were achieved;
- to determine what aspects of the group require modification.

This is a useful summary as it ensures that the therapist considers the outcome, not only in relation to the aims of the individuals involved but also in relation to the process of creative therapy as the approach used. This is the stage where changes may be suggested for the future, so reflection takes place on practice to ensure that involvement with each individual client or group is considered as a separate entity.

The evaluation process offers opportunities for both the therapist and the clients to explore the process in a creative manner. For the therapist the purpose will be to gain evidence of the effectiveness of the intervention. This process will rely on feedback from those who have been involved. Evidence can be collected through written or verbal means, but we have used some creative strategies which seem to complement working in this way. To achieve the first two objectives suggested by Benson (1987) we have used the following activity.

We prepared a very large square of paper, with the core of the group marked as a point at the centre. We drew three circles to surround this point, shown in Figure 7.2. We asked each person to take time to think about the experience of the creative therapy intervention, and then to place a personal object in a space which signified their involvement with this process. Some saw themselves as highly involved, and placed themselves near the centre. Others had found the whole experience difficult, and felt on the periphery; thus they placed themselves

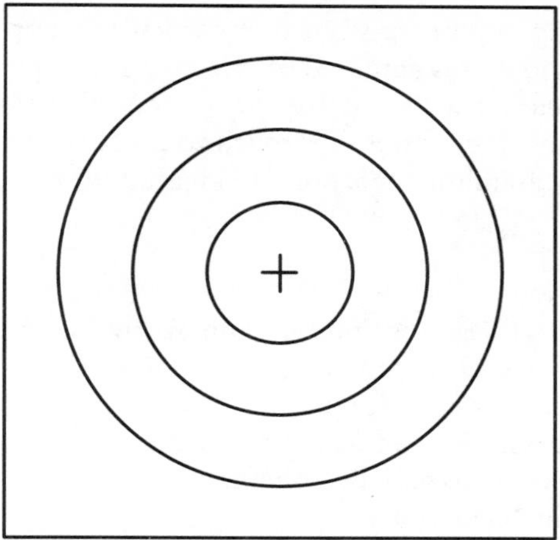

Figure 7.2 The evaluation circles

nearer to the outer boundary. Some placed their objects, but after a few moments of reflection chose to alter the positions. Time was made for discussion.

This is a very useful exercise for both the therapist and the individual members, as it makes the process of defining the experience explicit. It determines the value of the group for each individual, enabling them to consider personal aims that related to their involvement in the process, their engagement, their ability to use the experience and their understanding of the purpose of working in this way.

The therapist may need to evaluate more than the individual journeys, as the creative therapy process itself needs to be considered to see whether changes should be made for the future. This relates to Benson's (1987) fourth purpose of evaluation: to determine whether aspects require modification. Here the reflection is less personal, as it looks at the way the journey has been facilitated, rather than the destination it has reached. We use an 'as if' form of evaluation which asks the members to define certain aspects of the creative therapy process 'as if' they were an object – a tree/kitchen appliance/piece of clothing for example. Therefore we might ask people to 'describe the suitability of the room as if it were an animal'. Individual answers provide clues about the ways this has been perceived. Some may choose a strong, solid animal like a cow, which signifies the security of the room – it was familiar, had a closed door and a 'do not disturb' sign. Others may see it as a flexible, changing environment, choosing a chameleon as their analogy. These examples can then be collated to provide an overall picture which may be more comprehensive than using other means, as the reflection that informs the answer is more carefully considered. Using the distance provided by the activity might make giving less positive feedback easier, for example 'the suitability of the room was like a battery hen, squashed, lacking in light and airless'!

Evaluation is an ongoing process but it is particularly important at the ending stage to ensure that evidence is gathered of effective and appropriate practice. The means by which this can be achieved are various, and there is no correct way. As creativity is at the core of this whole approach to practice, it would seem a missed opportunity to fail to capitalise on its potential within the evaluation process.

THE FINAL SESSION

Throughout the creative therapy intervention we work towards providing our clients with skills that will enable them to be responsible for their own continuing self-development, and so we are preparing to cease intervention from the very beginning of the process. However, despite understanding that working towards ending is part of the whole experience, the final session takes on a specific significance, because it is 'the final session'.

Benson (1987) suggests that a final session should create an ending which celebrates and symbolises for members what the intervention was about. This involves reflecting back to the aims of the individual and of the group but also thinking prospectively, to enable the future to play a part. In this way the final session becomes a mechanism for linking the process together – looking back and looking forward.

Our last example illustrates this aim.

The Island of 1999

For this final session with our students, which took place just before the Christmas break, we prepared the room in a creative way. We removed all the mobile furniture, providing as large a floor space as possible. We placed our rug in one part of the room, and in the other we constructed the rudiments of an island. We outlined the shape with a hosepipe taped to the floor, and filled the enclosure with shredded bark. This gave us two areas of total contrast. The rug was soft, multicoloured and safe, as it had been a constant prop within our sessions. The island was dark and expansive, the bark moved a little as it was walked upon, creating an illusion of mystery and unexplored territory. Strangely this was warm and slightly humid to touch, but quite clean, which added to the atmosphere of this particular medium.

The students greeted the arrangements with surprise. A definite feeling of 'whatever next?' was in the air. They had been asked to bring in any rubbish they had at home: cartons, tubes, papers and any odds and ends which would be useful for a 'creation'. Each arrived with their contributions, which were piled together on one side.

We sat down in a circle on the rug and introduced the activity. We suggested that, as we were approaching the new year, we had created two areas representing 1998 and 1999. The activity was to be a journey which would move from one to the other. How they constructed and interpreted this journey was the business of the group, but the underlying theme would be of leaving the old behind, and exploring the new. This theme was chosen to reflect their position on the course. This was the last time the group would work together before graduating, and we were conscious of one year moving into another, which provided another dimension.

The students spent some time in quiet deliberation, gently formulating ideas and sharing these with each other. They began by focusing on the rug, which symbolised 1998. This rug has a border composed of a series of small rectangles, each with a different colour and pattern. Each student chose a rectangle, and then related this to the issues they were planning to leave behind on this island. Examples were things that were important to them: the confusion of their dissertations, the constant strain of studying, the recurring worry of lack of money. It was interesting to see how the rectangles adapted to this role, as the patterns and colours were used to provide a visual imagery of the quality of their issues.

When everyone had left something behind they were ready to approach the new island, moving forwards into 1999, which symbolised the end of the course as well as many new beginnings.

Some students constructed a bridge to link the two areas together, recognising the threads of knowledge and experience which would transfer from one setting to another and the need to be able to retrieve certain objects which had been left behind. Others created structures on the island. There was a leisure area, with chairs and television in a sunny bay. There was a pot of money which was carefully hidden beneath the bark. One student made a helicopter, providing an opportunity to fly away, to access other opportunities which would arise in her life. Meanwhile the leaders constructed a boat, into which provisions were piled to sustain and nourish the group. When the constructions were in place the group reviewed their creation. This enabled them to reflect on the situation they found themselves within, as it made the time of change explicit and tangible. Creating a focus around the change made it possible to work with the issues that arose, achieving the looking back and the looking forward. The students found this a valuable opportunity, it identified both their fears and their achievements, and enabled them to focus on the future in a positive way.

This final session was successful as it was informed by the key principles for a creative therapy activity that we addressed in Chapter 1. It allowed each person to explore their own route forwards, operating within their individual environment whilst facilitating the aim of the group as a whole. It made explicit links to the outside world through focusing on the future (Brown, 1994). It provided a place for the use of self, through discovery and exploration, and it offered the potential for creativity. There were no rights and wrongs within the activity, and creativity was inherent both in the process of the activity and in the individuals who were carrying this out. It gave space, time and a route to disengage from the group process (Brown, 1994). Through this activity the concept of change became tangible. The students were able to identify the pertinent issues for them and use the group to explore and work towards the resolution of these.

This chapter has explored endings from both a practical and a psychological perspective. They are an inevitable part of any process of intervention, achieving the final stage of group development (Brandler and Roman, 1991). It is important that they receive the degree of attention which their place requires, as a mismanaged ending can undermine many of the positive changes which have been facilitated through the creative use of the media.

AND FINALLY WE REACH THE END . . .

Writing this book has been a journey which reflects in many ways the process of using creative therapy, either with our clients in a clinical setting or with our students. We plan to explore this journey, comparing it stage by stage with the way we facilitate the use of creative therapies.

We started off full of anticipation about the opportunity which writing provides. Our thoughts were those we would have as the first session approaches: excitement but also a feeling of uncertainty. Where would our journey take us, and were we right to start? Would we have the personal resources to complete the task successfully? We had to assess the risks of involvement, much as our clients would when deciding to take part in creative therapy. They too will have ambivalent feelings about undertaking an intervention, on the one hand welcoming the opportunity for change and self-growth, whilst on the other recognising the risks involved in leaving the security of their current position.

Perhaps our first discussions mirrored the initial interview, the selection stage where the aims of the intervention are explored and subsequently clarified. We had similar clinical and educational experience to one another, and were very aware that there was an opportunity to further the concept of creative therapy and to share our thoughts with a wider audience. The initial discussions identified a pathway for our journey, we mapped out the content of the text and took ownership of this. We recognised and discussed the commitment which would be involved, and the support network of using each other. We expect our clients to critically consider the whole issue of involving themselves within creative therapy, to own their part of the process and to decide on their levels of commitment whilst acknowledging the support network available to them. Thus decision making is founded on clear information, which provides an overall aim for their involvement. This part of the process enabled us to clarify our aim, to achieve a textbook that explored the ways we as occupational therapists use creative therapies as a tool for psychodynamic working. We identified our aim, formulating this clearly as our clients do when they first develop their aims.

The writing stage has been similar to the lifespan of a creative therapy group. Early sessions appear tentative and unsure, where there is a testing out of appropriate behaviour and lack of familiarity with the media. This was the case with our early writing. We had not fully formulated our ideas or the roles each of us would take. The 'forming' process of a group seemed familiar as we sought a structure, established our ground rules and began to develop our way forward together.

The process of the work required boundaries as well as freedom. We identify in the first chapter the need for creativity to be present within the style of the therapist, yet this creativity has to be grounded, harnessed to achieve our end product. We sought to establish a baseline, a secure foundation from which to develop. We worked out our theory base, trying it on each other much as we do when exploring new ideas to include within a session. In this way we considered the potential, identified shortfalls, rejected or developed our thoughts using just the same process as we do when faced with planning a series of sessions. We began to use each other creatively. The dynamics that occur within the body of a creative therapy group rely on interpersonal communication to facilitate change, so we shared our ideas and worked through the issues that arose from them. Our clients go through this process as they explore both the conscious and unconscious thoughts which arise through the use of the media, developing their understanding of themselves and using it as a way forward.

Although the sessions of a creative therapy group will be outlined we never know the ways in which they will actually unfold. This was a pattern we became familiar with in our chapters. We had an identified structure, but the actual content explored new paths which could not be predetermined. As the chapters unfolded so creativity pushed our ideas forward; we remained open to fresh thoughts, adapting to opportunities that had not been planned and exploring the routes that presented themselves. Occasionally these routes became dead ends, in a similar way to the creative therapy experience. Others became too free, needing to be captured and brought back through the process of using the other person. At these times we would reflect on our original aims, to ensure that we were still working towards our defined objective.

As every creative therapy session is a unique experience, so there is original thinking within our text. We have attempted to ground our ideas with theory, just as we would when working with our clients. Therefore we have tried to look beyond an idea, to understand where it is coming from and explore the purposes behind it. In the same way we use our theory base to enable our clients to understand their behaviour, taking their thoughts and actions, and making sense of them by applying similar processes.

As with any session there have been hard times and times of excitement and joy. The hard times have brought feelings of quitting, moving away from the experience as one does within a group when the going gets tough. These times have been personally challenging, and we have been affected by the experience. These mirror the 'storming' sessions within a group, where we complain about the constraints, criticise the process and lose our focus. The times of excitement and joy have occurred as we have overcome obstacles and used ourselves creatively to take our journey a little further. To enable this to happen we have used our ideas as we would the media, trying them this way and that, pushing them forwards, rejecting them, changing them and adding the extra dimensions. Like a piece of clay our thoughts were malleable and could be formed and re-formed. We worked though this process until the ideas became clear, representing what we were trying to say. So the medium becomes clear, through much exploration, representing the issues the client wants to address.

The middle stage of the process of writing represents both 'norming and performing'. We had developed a sound basis for working, both with each other and through our use of theory. We knew the boundaries and so were able to apply ourselves more constructively. At this stage we were not phased by challenges, as our tools were effective and we had reached a point of working comfortably. This was a stage of energy and resolution, which occurs with our clients as they settle into the process of using creative therapy.

The theme of creativity became our focus. We could relate this to ourselves, through the ways we approached the activity of creating the book, through our individual styles which balanced and complemented each other, and through recognising the process of change which was occurring as our ideas and thoughts developed. With our clients this stage provides the opportunity for them to explore the focus of creativity. They are able to recognise the part it is playing within themselves, within the activities they are experiencing, and within the therapeutic process of change.

Throughout our writing we reflected both in action and on the action. We reviewed where we were, what was influencing us and where we were going. Reflection in action enables changes to be made as they are needed, perhaps a fresh idea would emerge which needed to be worked into a chapter. Reflecting on the action enabled us to look back to ensure we were working to our original aims, picking up the central threads which link creativity and therapy and reflecting on our own performance. This process enabled us to see each chapter as part of the whole, just as in creative therapies we see each session informing those which follow. Our links mirrored the links we search for with our clients, the threads that inform their story and enable us to develop our understanding. Reflecting gave us the opportunity to implement a better approach, as we needed to ensure effectiveness to achieve our stated goals.

We experienced some major critical incidents, where life events impacted on the process just as they would when working with clients. These caused us to renegotiate with each other, using our skills of client centredness and problem solving to understand the effect of these and to devise fresh routes for our journey. These are the skills we use when clients present us with fresh incidents: we hear and understand their story and use our skill of thinking around an issue to help them to move forwards.

As finishing the text approached we recognised emotions and feelings similar to those occurring as a group process nears its end. We were working to a time frame, just as we do within our groups, so there was a feeling of haste as we tried to complete the work, a process which occurs within a final clinical session. There was a sense of achievement for undertaking the journey, looking at the areas we had visited and glimpsing the final destination. With our clients we review the journey, identifying the times of discovery, evaluating whether their performance has enabled them to achieve their aim. There was a sense of celebration, but also a sense of loss. We needed to consider the part that writing the book was playing in our lives, and to turn our thoughts to the future. We work with our clients to enable them to move on from the creative therapy process, identifying ways forward, and we needed to apply the same strategies to ourselves. This was the time of attending to loose ends, ensuring that nothing significant remained outstanding; a process that occurs as part of the closure of the creative therapy intervention. We ask our clients to reflect on the experience, to work out for themselves whether they have achieved their aims. So we needed to look back over the process of writing, to ensure that we were also working in this way.

However, we have an outcome from our process of writing which differs from the outcome achieved through a creative therapy experience. Our outcome can be recognised as a product, which we hope achieves our initial aims. This makes the process we have undertaken explicit, and defines the journey we have travelled. In creative therapy the product is implicit, achieved through a process of self-discovery, self-exploration, self-determination and self-help. It is evident through the ability of the individual to move away from the intervention towards a more healthy and fulfilled lifestyle. This is the evidence of a successful creative therapy intervention.

The success of our intervention will depend on whether this book has achieved its objective, enabling growth within our reader, encouraging creativity, freeing them to do some thinking of their own. We hope that this process justifies the use of creative therapies, setting it within a context which encourages its use as a therapeutic intervention.

Finally, can the process and product entwine? In our chapter on the art of the therapist we suggested that the product of our intervention is created by the therapist who gathers evidence throughout the process to inform an outcome. At times a product may symbolise this outcome, representing evidence of an individual journey. This thought provides our final illustration, a drawing which was created by a client following a lengthy involvement within creative therapies. She likened her journey to a process of emerging from a chrysalis. As she started creative therapy she was confined within impenetrable boundaries, formed through her experience of life events. As the sessions developed she was able to undertake a process of self-discovery, finding out where she was, what was causing her barriers, and exploring possible routes of escape. As the sessions neared their end she was able to break free, symbolically spreading her wings in the sunshine as she embraced a more healthy lifestyle, leaving the group behind her. She needed to capture this process by creating her product, which she achieved following the final session. She drew her butterfly's wings with a sense of freedom and joy which captures the essence of working in this way.

We hope you have enjoyed your journey, and that you will feel inspired to use creative therapies to reach your destinations. If so, then we have achieved a product from the experience of our process.

Reproduced with permission of the author

Figure 7.3 Butterfly wings

REFERENCES

Benson, J.F. (1987) *Working More Creatively in Groups,* Tavistock Publications, London.
Brandler, S. and Roman, C.P. (1991) *Group Work Skills and Strategies for Effective Interventions*, Haworth Press, New York.
Brown, A. (1994) *Group Work* 3rd edn, Arena, Aldershot.
Rogers, N. (1993) *The Creative Connection Expressive Arts as Healing*, Science and Behaviour Books, Palo Alto.
Shulman, L. (1992) *The Skills of Helping Individuals, Families and Groups* 3rd edn, Peacock Publishers, Illinois.
Whitaker, D.S. (1985) *Using Groups to Help People*, Routledge and Kegan Paul, London.

Appendix

Contact details for OH cards and their counterparts:

OH Publishing
Postfach 1251
D-79196 Kirchzarten
Germany
Tel. +49 (0)7661 - 6362
Fax. +49 (0)7661 - 6312
Email: OH-Publishing@t-online.de

UK distributor:
Stephen Ralston
Scottish Kinesiology Centre
Bogpark Road
off Newhailes Road
Musselburgh
EH21 6RT

CORE system details:

The Psychological Therapies Research Centre
17 Blenheim Terrace
University of Leeds
Leeds
LS2 9JT.

INDEX

Page references in *italic* refer to tables and figures.